SAGE was founded in 1965 by Sara Miller McCune to support the dissemination of usable knowledge by publishing innovative and high-quality research and teaching content. Today, we publish over 900 journals, including those of more than 400 learned societies, more than 800 new books per year, and a growing range of library products including archives, data, case studies, reports, and video. SAGE remains majority-owned by our founder, and after Sara's lifetime will become owned by a charitable trust that secures our continued independence.

Los Angeles | London | New Delhi | Singapore | Washington DC | Melbourne

Advance Praise

This book is an important contribution in the emergent field of 'Indic thought', which is much broader than Vedic Brahmanic tradition. There is a need to retrieve ancient philosophy's relevance and eschew its bygone scriptural diktats. For both, this book should provide a useful reference point.

—**Ajay Gudavarthy,** Associate Professor, Centre for Political Studies,
Jawaharlal Nehru University, New Delhi

The book *Ancient and Medieval Indian Thought: Themes and Traditions* edited by Ankit Tomar and Suratha Kumar Malik is a valuable addition to the existing knowledge on Indian thinkers and their thinking traditions. The analysis beginning with Vedas down to Abul Fazal and keeping the eyes always open to catch the 'Indianess' has been fully comprehensive and successful. This is an address to a very loaded and perhaps normative enquiry about the existence of Indian political thought and traditions. The book will be very useful and helpful to all those who need to study Indian political thinking and also to those who have appetite for knowledge about Indian political theory. A great job!

—**Ashok Kumar Upadhyay,** Professor and Head, Department of Political Science,
Banaras Hindu University, Varanasi

Ancient and Medieval Indian Thought: Themes and Traditions is a welcome edition to the limited body of literature available on the theme. The present work seeks to introduce some important political ideas in a critical perspective with a view to highlight the significant issues of ancient Indian political thought. The book is written in a student-friendly style and can claim to be a comprehensive account of sociopolitical thought of Indian thinkers and traditions. Being an excellent collection of articles meant for undergraduate and postgraduate students, for scholars it can become a useful reference book.

—**Chandrika Basu Majumder,** Professor, Department of Political Science,
Tripura University (Central University), Agartala

This volume provides relevant information for those who care about varied themes and traditions in the vigorous domain of 'ancient and medieval Indian thought'. Prepared while bringing together a number of young perceptive scholars, the book is prefaced with a detailed account of what each chapter contains and equipped with a meticulously prepared index, rich glossary and detailed further references.

—**Ronki Ram,** Fellow and Dean (Faculty of Arts),
Shaheed Bhagat Singh Chair Professor of Political Science, Panjab University, Chandigarh

This is a brilliant volume, good collection of articles and essential reading for the students, teachers and researchers on Indian political thought. It unfolds various dimensions of ancient and medieval Indian society. This book will certainly serve the need of academia as well as interested readers well.

—**R. K. Satapathy,** Professor, Department of Political Science,
North-Eastern Hill University, Shillong; Honorary Director, ICSSR-NERC, Shillong

The editors have done a commendable job by producing this book which is theoretically and analytically rich. It provides a comprehensive account of ancient and medieval Indian thinkers and traditions. A number of complex ideas and issues have been presented in an extremely lucid, straightforward and interesting style. This book will be of immense interest to social scientists in general and political scientists in particular who desire to comprehend different dimensions of Indian sociopolitical thought.

—**Sushma Yadav,** Professor, Vice-Chancellor,
Bhagat Phool Singh Mahila Vishwavidyalaya, Haryana;
Professor of Public Policy and Governance, IIPA, New Delhi;
Member of University Grants Commission, New Delhi;
Member of Press Council of India, New Delhi

Ancient and Medieval Indian Thought

Ancient and Medieval Indian Thought

Themes and Traditions

Edited by

Ankit Tomar

Faculty, Department of Political Science, Kamala Nehru College, University of Delhi, New Delhi

Suratha Kumar Malik

Faculty, Department of Political Science, Vidyasagar University, Midnapore, West Bengal

SAGE | TEXTS

Los Angeles | London | New Delhi
Singapore | Washington DC | Melbourne

First published in 2020 by

SAGE | TEXTS

SAGE Publications India Pvt Ltd
B1/I-1 Mohan Cooperative Industrial Area
Mathura Road, New Delhi 110 044, India
www.sagepub.in

SAGE Publications Inc
2455 Teller Road
Thousand Oaks, California 91320, USA

SAGE Publications Ltd
1 Oliver's Yard, 55 City Road
London EC1Y 1SP, United Kingdom

SAGE Publications Asia-Pacific Pte Ltd
18 Cross Street #10-10/11/12
China Square Central
Singapore 048423

Published by Vivek Mehra for SAGE Publications India Pvt Ltd. Typeset in 10/12.5 pt Minion Pro by AG Infographics, Delhi.

Library of Congress Control Number: 2020933011

ISBN: 978-93-5388-231-0 (PB)

SAGE Team: Amit Kumar, Indrani Dutta, Ankit Verma and Kanika Mathur

This work
is
dedicated to
our teachers

Contents

Foreword by Ranjan Chakrabarti xix
Preface xxiii
Acknowledgements xxv
About the Editors and Contributors xxvii
Introduction by Sibaji Pratim Basu xxxiii

PART I: ANCIENT INDIAN THOUGHT AND TRADITIONS

CHAPTER 1
***Dhārma* in Ancient India: The Moral Law of the Cosmos** **3**
Suratha Kumar Malik

CHAPTER 2
Ancient India: Conception and Forms of Community **21**
Praveen Kumar

CHAPTER 3
Vedās* and the *Brāhmanic* Tradition: The Cradle of *Hinduism **32**
Kanchan Saxena

CHAPTER 4
Manu: A Progenitor of Humanity **52**
Mona Singh

CHAPTER 5
***Yājñavalkya*: A Vedic Sage** **62**
Swasti Alpana

CHAPTER 6
***Cārvāka-Lokāyata* Tradition: A Tradition of Materialist Philosophy** **75**
Balaganapathi Devarakonda and Jayshree Jha

CHAPTER 7
***Śhramanic* Tradition: An Ascetic Reformism** 84
Ankit Tomar

CHAPTER 8
***Śukranīti*: A Political Treatise** 100
Prabira Sethy

CHAPTER 9
Dīgha Nikāya (Aggaññasutta)*: Theory of Kingship and *Aṅguttara Nikāya 116
Ish N. Mishra

CHAPTER 10
Śānti Parva* of *Mahābhārata*: Ideas on the Kingship and *Daṇḍanīti 130
Varun Kumar Tripathi

CHAPTER 11
Kauṭilya: A Pragmatic Thinker 145
Ramakrushna Pradhan

PART II: MEDIEVAL INDIAN THOUGHT AND TRADITIONS

CHAPTER 12
Medieval India: State, Society and Religion 163
Ritu Sharma

CHAPTER 13
Ziyauddin Barani: Ideas on Good *Sultan* and Ideal Polity 175
Santosh Kumar Mallik and Ramesh Chandra Mahanta

CHAPTER 14
Abul Fazl: Views on Governance and Administration 192
Sumit Mukerji

CHAPTER 15
***Islamic* Tradition: A Tradition of Human Affairs and Classical Heritage** 204
Iftekhar Ahemmed

CHAPTER 16
***Sufi* Tradition: A Tradition of Spiritualism and Tolerance** 215
S. M. Azizuddin Husain

CHAPTER 17
Kabir: An Indian Mystic Saint 224
Prabira Sethy

CHAPTER 18
Women in *Bhakti* Tradition: A Critical Reflection **244**
Krishna Menon

CHAPTER 19
Syncretic Tradition: A Tradition of Assimilation **252**
Rajendra Kumar Pandey

Index **I–1**

Detailed Contents

Foreword by Ranjan Chakrabarti xix
Preface xxiii
Acknowledgements xxv
About the Editors and Contributors xxvii
Introduction by Sibaji Pratim Basu xxxiii

PART I: ANCIENT INDIAN THOUGHT AND TRADITIONS

CHAPTER 1: *Dhārma* in Ancient India: The Moral Law of the Cosmos **3**
Suratha Kumar Malik

Reader's Guide 3
Introduction 4
Contextualizing and Understanding the Concept of *Dhārma* 5
Dhārma and *Hindu* World View 6
The *Sanatana Dhārma* 7
Classification of *Dhārma* 9
Rta, Rna and *Dhārma* 10
Dhārma through *Yajña, Dāna* and *Tapas* 11
Dhārma and the Nature of Self (*Sacchidānanda*) 11
Dhārma in *Upaniṣhads* and *Hindu* Epics 12
Dhārma According to *Vatsyayana* and *Patanjali* 15
Conclusion 15
Summary 17

CHAPTER 2: Ancient India: Conception and Forms of Community **21**
Praveen Kumar

Reader's Guide 21
Introduction 22
Historical Evolution of the Concept of Community 23

Forms and Structures of Community in the Prehistoric India 23
The *Vedic* Period and Later: Communities, Their Types and Features 24
Changing Forms of Community: From Class to Caste 26
The Buddhist *Saṅgha* 27
The Trading Community 28
Conclusion 29
Summary 29

CHAPTER 3: *Vedās* and the *Brāhmanic* Tradition: The Cradle of *Hinduism* **32**
Kanchan Saxena

Reader's Guide 32
Introduction 33
Origin and Evolution of the *Brāhmanic* Tradition 34
The Metaphysical Aspects of Society 40
Idea of State and Kingship 41
Varṇa Vyvastha, Āśhrama Life and *Puruṣārthas* 42
Role of Sacred Texts, Mythology and Theism 46
Conclusion 47
Summary 48

CHAPTER 4: Manu: A Progenitor of Humanity **52**
Mona Singh

Reader's Guide 52
Introduction 52
The Life Sketch 53
Theory of Kingship 54
Theory of State 56
Social Order and Classification of Society 58
Dhārma and *Daṇḍanīti* 59
Conclusion 60
Summary 60

CHAPTER 5: *Yājñavalkya*: A Vedic Sage **62**
Swasti Alpana

Reader's Guide 62
Introduction 63
The Life Sketch 66
Dharmaśāstras and *Rājādhārma* 67
Ethical and Social Virtues 68
Karma, Rebirth and Spiritual Liberation 69
Dialogue between *Yājñavalkya* and *Maitreyī* 70

Comparative Study of *Yājñavalkyasmṛiti* and the *Manusmṛiti* 70
Conclusion 72
Summary 73

CHAPTER 6: *Cārvāka-Lokāyata* Tradition: A Tradition of Materialist Philosophy **75**
Balaganapathi Devarakonda and Jayshree Jha

Reader's Guide 75
Introduction 76
Epistemology 77
Metaphysics 78
Ethics 80
Conclusion 81
Summary 82

CHAPTER 7: *Śhramanic* Tradition: An Ascetic Reformism **84**
Ankit Tomar

Reader's Guide 84
Introduction 85
Origin and Evolution of the *Śhramanic* Tradition 87
The Jaina Philosophy 88
The Buddha Philosophy 92
Conclusion 96
Summary 96

CHAPTER 8: *Śukranīti*: A Political Treatise **100**
Prabira Sethy

Reader's Guide 100
Introduction 101
The Life Sketch 101
Ethics and Kingship 102
Ideal King and His Qualities 104
System of Law and Justice 107
Reforms 109
Conclusion 110
Summary 111

CHAPTER 9: *Dīgha Nikāya (Aggaññasutta)*: Theory of Kingship and *Aṅguttara Nikāya* **116**
Ish N. Mishra

Reader's Guide 116
Introduction 117

Backdrop of the Study 118
Origin of the State 120
Qualities, Functions and the Duties of Ruler 125
Conclusion 126
Summary 127

CHAPTER 10: *Śānti Parva* of *Mahābhārata*: Ideas on the Kingship and *Daṇḍanīti* **130**
Varun Kumar Tripathi

Reader's Guide 130
Introduction 131
The Life Sketch 132
The *Śānti Parva* 133
Origin and Nature of Ancient Indian State 133
Kingship—the *Rājādhārma* 136
Code and Doctrine of Punishment—the *Daṇḍanīti* 138
Conclusion 140
Summary 141

CHAPTER 11: Kauṭilya: A Pragmatic Thinker **145**
Ramakrushna Pradhan

Reader's Guide 145
Introduction 146
The Life Sketch 146
Arthaśāstra: Science of Statecraft 147
Dhārma and *Daṇḍanīti* 148
Saptanga Theory of State 149
Theory of *Mandala* 152
Foreign Policy 153
Ethics and Politics 155
Kauṭilya and Machiavelli 156
Conclusion 157
Summary 157

PART II: MEDIEVAL INDIAN THOUGHT AND TRADITIONS

CHAPTER 12: Medieval India: State, Society and Religion **163**
Ritu Sharma

Reader's Guide 163
Introduction 164
Debates about Classification of Medieval Period 164
Nature of State and Salient Features of Administration 166

Economic and Social Reforms in Medieval Period 167
Religious Traditions in Medieval Period 168
Land Policy and Economic Scenario during Medieval Period 169
Akbar's Contribution 170
Conclusion 172
Summary 173

CHAPTER 13: Ziyauddin Barani: Ideas on Good *Sultan* and Ideal Polity **175**
Santosh Kumar Mallik and Ramesh Chandra Mahanta

Reader's Guide 175
Introduction 176
The Life Sketch 176
Writings of Barani 177
Kingship 180
Ideal Polity 181
Ideal *Sultan* and His Qualities 182
Advices to *Sultan* 184
Conclusion 186
Summary 187

CHAPTER 14: Abul Fazl: Views on Governance and Administration **192**
Sumit Mukerji

Reader's Guide 192
Introduction 193
The Life Sketch 194
Conception of State 195
Kingship, Sovereignty and Ideal Ruler 195
Administration and Governance 198
Religion and Religious Syncretism 199
Conclusion 201
Summary 202

CHAPTER 15: *Islamic* Tradition: A Tradition of Human Affairs and Classical Heritage **204**
Iftekhar Ahemmed

Reader's Guide 204
Introduction 205
Origin and Evolution of the *Islamic* Tradition 205
Delhi *Sultanate* and *Islamic* Tradition 207
Mughal Empire and *Islamic* Tradition 208
Revivalism in *Islamic* Tradition 210
Conclusion 213
Summary 213

CHAPTER 16: *Sufi* Tradition: A Tradition of Spiritualism and Tolerance **215**
S. M. Azizuddin Husain

Reader's Guide 215
Introduction 215
Origin and the Salient Features of *Sufism* 216
Growth of Major *Sufi Silsilahs* and Society 218
Sufism and Society in Medieval India 219
Hindu–Muslim Interaction 222
Summary 222

CHAPTER 17: Kabir: An Indian Mystic Saint **224**
Prabira Sethy

Reader's Guide 224
Introduction 225
The Life Sketch 225
Kabir's Views on Socio-religious Dogmas and Economic Inequalities 227
Syncretism in Kabir's *Bijak* 230
Comparison between Kabir Das and Ravidas 237
Conclusion 238
Summary 238

CHAPTER 18: Women in *Bhakti* Tradition: A Critical Reflection **244**
Krishna Menon

Reader's Guide 244
Introduction: Do Women Have Ideas? 245
Bhakti Tradition in South India 245
Bhakti—An Evaluation from a Gendered Lens 245
Women *Bhakti* Poets of South India—Feminist Pioneers? 246
The Respected Grandmother—Avvaiyar 247
The Ghoul and Her Lord—Karaikal Ammaiyar 247
Celebrating Passion—Andal 248
To Hell with the Body—Akka Mahadevi 248
Conclusion: Beauty, Body and *Bhakti* 248
Summary 249

CHAPTER 19: Syncretic Tradition: A Tradition of Assimilation **252**
Rajendra Kumar Pandey

Reader's Guide 252
Introduction 253
Origin and Evolution of Syncretic Tradition 253

Foreword

Thoughts and traditions are an important and rich source to enlighten or transform the past structures of any society. They not only guide the human behaviour in different social and political milieus but also ensure peace and harmony in the society. In the history of sociopolitical thought, Indian thought represents the East (or non-West), whereas the Western thought represents the Western societies. It is evident that for a very long time, the existence of well-entrenched Indian thought, particularly 'pre-modern Indian thought' has been sidelined, partly because of the popularity of Western (or the 'mainstream') political philosophy and lack of interest in Indian philosophy. Philosophers and scholars have argued that unlike the Western philosophy, which is material and rational in its nature, the Indian philosophy is essentially religious and focuses more on the idea of 'other world' instead of 'this world'. It means that Indian philosophy does not have any secular way of thinking and could not be separated from religion, as an element of mysticism is involved within it. In fact, just a few decades back, serious doubts were cast on the health and vigour of Indian philosophy. It is believed that Indian philosophy does not have a capacity to build or imagine an ideal society.

Moreover, in modern times, it is generally argued that the thought processes which have been produced in the ancient Greek societies are the only marker of a true and scientific philosophical knowledge system as they are based on observation, experimentation, confirmation or regularity, and thus have universal claim of 'superior' knowledge. For them, the Indian knowledge system which is based on various traditions is *not* a part of philosophy!

However, such kinds of arguments reflect only 'eurocentrism' and the hegemony of the West, and also a pathetic lack of knowledge of ancient Indian philosophy and culture. That does not of course mean that we should reject the Western philosophy for upholding the Indian one. Instead of rejecting, we need to accept that Indian intellectual traditions actually represent *different* forms of philosophy which are lesser known in the West than Plato and Aristotle's philosophy. But they have also dealt with the universal issues such as power, justice, ideal social order, forms of government, war and diplomacy.

Thus, despite differences, both the systems of thought, especially political thought, have addressed some of the crucial questions that are relevant even in contemporary times. Here comes the need of a creative, continuous and open dialogue between all the knowledge systems without any sense of hegemony or domination. The present book promises to take a fresh look on these issues.

If the reader looks at the evolution and essential features of the Indian philosophy, then certainly he or she will find that it has a long history of several intellectual traditions and deep engagements among themselves. There is no doubt that Indian philosophy has various trends within it but still we can put all of them under one rubric and call it 'pre-modern Indian thought'. The four main streams of pre-modern Indian thought are (a) *Brāhmanic* tradition, (b) *Śhramanic* tradition, (c) *Islamic* tradition and (d) Syncretic tradition.

The *Brāhmanic* and *Śhramanic* traditions are important and crucial to understand the political thinking and the whole range of ideas which are basically studied and interpreted in ancient Indian political thought. These two traditions are also recognized or interpreted by some scholars as 'orthodox' versus 'heterodox' traditions of ancient India. The *Brāhmanic* tradition (also known as *Hindu* or *Vedic* tradition) has been significantly represented by the *Vedās, Upaniṣhads, Smṛitis, Śhāstras, Purāṇas, Bhagwadgīta, Rāmāyaṇa* and *Mahābhārata.* The reference of ancient Indian thought can also be found in the great epics—the *Mahābhārata* and the *Rāmāyaṇa.* Both the epic texts are important for understanding the politics, political institutions and the issues of governance and administration during ancient times in India. In addition to this, the *Manusmṛiti*, along with other *Smṛitis*, dealt with political institutions and the entire panorama of human life. Another important feature of ancient Indian thought is that it is based on twin concepts—*dhārma* and *daṇḍa*—which ensures order and discipline in the society during that time. Both these concepts form the backbone of ancient Indian political thought. In contrast to *Brāhmanic* tradition, the *Śhramanic* tradition is a more vibrant and powerful discourse of ancient Indian thought, and it is essentially represented by the Buddhist and Jain schools of thought. The *Śhramanic* tradition is famous for its reformist ideas and rebellious tendencies, as it preached the principle of human equality against the fourfold stratification of *varṇa* system. Moreover, it also questions the infallibility of *Vedās* and violence on the name of customary laws and rituals.

The *Islamic* and Syncretic traditions are important sources of medieval Indian thought. Thinkers like Barani and Abul Fazl represent the *Islamic* tradition of India. The unique feature of *Islamic* tradition is that it believes in the universality of laws of the *Qur'an* and *Shari'at.* In addition to this, theocracy and monarchy are the hallmark of *Islamic* tradition. The Syncretic tradition on the other hand is prominently associated with the ideas of Kabir and *Sufis*, and it does not favour to set any new religion; rather, it works to transform or liberalize *Hinduism* and *Islam* for the sake of universal love and egalitarian society.

There is no doubt that Indian philosophy, particularly the pre-modern Indian thought, does not make a distinction between religious and political texts as we can see in the West, but it still gives a detailed advice on the science of statecraft, organization of state, conduct of governmental affairs and so on. Therefore, the study of ancient and medieval Indian thought is a necessary prelude for understanding and exploring the relationship among man, society and polity.

I am immensely delighted to know that while in recent times the teaching of Indian thought has globally acquired a lot of serious professional interest, the present book *Ancient and Medieval Indian Thought: Themes and Traditions* edited by Ankit Tomar and Suratha Kumar Malik is being published. I hope that this volume will be a remarkable addition in this genre. I would like to take this opportunity to congratulate the editors and their entire team.

All the chapters in the volume are well written with in-depth analysis and have very coherently captured the thoughts of all the major Indian thinkers and traditions of ancient and medieval India. The book provides an overview of the evolution of the pre-modern Indian thought and its essential features. Further, not only does it talk about the lives and times of the great Indian thinkers of ancient and medieval India but it also explores the important themes that formed the basis of their political ideologies.

With a comprehensive coverage of both the thoughts and traditions of pre-modern Indian thought, I hope that this book would be useful for the students and researchers of not only political science but also philosophy, history and sociology of different universities across the country, and for the general readers wishing to acquaint themselves with the nuances of ancient and medieval Indian thought.

Professor Ranjan Chakrabarti
Vice-Chancellor
Vidyasagar University, West Bengal

Preface

A 'nation', like a 'person', could not be complete without knowing her own past, culture and the thought of the great intellectuals of the land, their dreams as well as their actions which act as an anchor to the past and a guide for the future. In this continuous attempt to know the past for the sake of building the future, the present volume entitled *Ancient and Medieval Indian Thought: Themes and Traditions* is an industrious endeavour to encapsulate the myriad dimensions of ancient and medieval Indian thought. Moreover, the study of sociopolitical thought of various thinkers and traditions of the Indian subcontinent has become one of the most significant components of undergraduate and postgraduate curricula of political science and other allied disciplines in almost all the universities and colleges of India. Thus, this book is a noble attempt to provide a road map that can orient the students to the main themes and traditions of ancient and medieval India. In fact, the prime aim of the book is to acquaint the reader with India's glorious past, rich composite cultures, mosaic civilizations, different ideas regarding society, state, kingship and so on. It is necessary for our generation to be familiarized with the diverse but unique Indian thought and traditions that have evolved with the tide of times. The unity in the diversities of thought have made Indian thought and traditions unique in the world which represents the existence of all ideas, religions, cultures, philosophies, traditions and faith where the present volume is wishful in this noble effort.

The present volume is a lucid and comprehensive account of the sociopolitical thought of major Indian thinkers and traditions. It is the outcome of a sustained conversation, continuous dialogue and untiring discussion between its editors regarding the pedagogy of Indian thought. The idea of producing this kind of textbook originated in October 2016, when we were discussing about the scarcity of reading materials on the revised syllabus of Indian political thought introduced for undergraduate students under the University Grants Commission's Choice Based Credit System (CBCS) and various similar courses offered in most Indian universities and colleges. Indian thought and tradition constitute significant elements of the syllabus of major Indian universities and colleges across the discipline including the syllabi of political science, sociology, history and philosophy. Keeping the diversity of its implications and interdisciplinary nature in mind, the topics are contributed by faculties across the country from different fields and disciplines as per their specialization and subject expertise.

The discerning feature of this volume is that it departs from the idea of conventional texts in the field and incorporates the contribution of great Indian thinkers and traditions such as *Yājñavalkya*, Kabir, the *Brāhmanic*, *Islamic* and Syncretic traditions. At the same time, it does not ignore the ideas of other thinkers such as Kauṭilya, Manu, Barani and Fazl. This multi-authored volume has contributions from professionals and experts of the subject from different premier universities of India, and it will help students to understand the basic concepts and notions of political thought and develop a critical understanding of the thinkers on the important themes and issues, such as community, state, kingship, culture and religion more competently, with the addition of unique and wide perspectives.

Divided into 19 core chapters under 2 parts (ancient and medieval) in addition to an introductory chapter, and a foreword from a distinguished academician, the text lucidly explains with clarity of information and concepts. It has a rich content which gives a panoramic view of Indian thought and traditions.

The book begins with a detailed discussion on the development and articulation of political thought and traditions that evolved in India, focusing on the nature and perspectives of the ancient and medieval Indian thought and traditions. It gives a comprehensive coverage analysis of different Indian traditions and ideas of various ancient and medieval thinkers of India. The chapters on different thinkers not only talk about their lives and times but also discuss and examine their contribution to the contemporary period.

The volume basically targets the syllabuses of major Indian universities and colleges, especially the undergraduate (including the CBCS syllabus), postgraduate students of political science and the aspirants of different competitive examinations such as UGC-NET and civil services examinations. It is a text-cum-reference book which will be immensely helpful not only for the students but also for the research scholars, teachers and other general readers who are interested in the in-depth study of Indian thought and traditions, that is, political ideas, state, administration, society, culture, philosophy and religions.

The unique feature of this volume is that it includes not only some model questions which are important from the universities/colleges' examination point of view but also some thought-provoking analytical questions for the purpose of critical reflection on the topic. It includes a detailed glossary for understanding the concepts, difficult words and abstract ideas. The book covers updated references and further readings other than the thematic sections, conclusion and chapter summary. Each chapter starts with a chapter outline and reader's guide which will familiarize the readers about the chapter and its learning objectives. The volume is a unique endeavour and an earnest attempt by the editors (though young but promising) which will fulfil the needs of the time.

Acknowledgements

We are indebted to a number of people who have, directly and indirectly, helped us in the preparation of the book. First and foremost, we would like to express our deepest gratitude and profound intellectual debt to all our teachers who honed our academic skills as well as provided a lively intellectual setting that helped us to pursue our individual teaching and research interests. We are also extremely grateful to all the contributors for having readily consented to be a part of the project and patiently revising the chapters to incorporate all the suggestions put forward from time to time to improve the quality of the work. We hope that the volume at least partially vindicates their steadfast belief in our academic project and the long wait for its completion.

We are highly honoured to be associated with SAGE. Our special thanks to SAGE and their representatives for responding so promptly and positively to our proposal and agreeing to publish the book for wider attention. In fact, it would not have been possible without the personal care and interest of Ms Indrani Dutta, Senior Development Editor and her competent team members. The constant feedback and untiring efforts from the editorial and production team kept us on our toes and allowed our understanding and vision to be transformed into this volume within stipulated deadlines. We extend our thanks and acknowledgements to the anonymous reviewers at SAGE for accelerating the progress of this project and enabling its journey from conception to completion. We would like to take this opportunity to record our heartfelt gratitude to Professor Ranjan Chakrabarti, honourable Vice-Chancellor of Vidyasagar University, West Bengal, for writing the foreword of the book. We express our special thanks to Professor Sibaji Pratim Basu of Vidyasagar University for kindly agreeing to write the introduction of the volume. We also express our profound indebtedness to our students, whose critical queries in the classroom compelled us to produce a quality work on the pedagogy of ancient and medieval Indian thought. If they find the book useful and intellectually stimulating, we will achieve what we aimed for.

Last but not least, we fondly acknowledge the unflinching support and contribution of our families who have always been wonderful, ever trusting and supportive during the process of writing this book. This project would not have been possible without their constant support, love and encouragement.

About the Editors and Contributors

Editors

Ankit Tomar teaches political science at Kamala Nehru College, University of Delhi. He holds an MA in political science from the University of Delhi and an MPhil in international politics from the School of International Studies, Jawaharlal Nehru University (JNU). He is currently on the verge of submitting his PhD to the Centre for International Politics, Organization and Disarmament (CIPOD), JNU. He has contributed various chapters and articles to several reputed institutions of India including Institute of Life Long Learning, University of Delhi. He has also participated in different seminars, conferences, workshops and training programmes at national and international levels. His areas of interest include Indian and Western political philosophy, theories of international relations and public administration.

Suratha Kumar Malik is an Assistant Professor in the Department of Political Science, Vidyasagar University, West Bengal, since 2012. He has completed his master's degree and master of philosophy degree from the Centre for Political Studies, JNU, New Delhi, and received his Doctor of Philosophy from Vidyasagar University, West Bengal. He was awarded Dr Harekrushna Mahatab Award, UGC NET, Junior Research Fellowship (JRF) and Nirman Foundation Fellowship (Lord Bhikhu Parekh endowment). His research interests and specialization include Indian political thought and philosophy, Dalit and tribal issues and politics, social–political movements, marginalization and identity politics. He has three books and more than a dozen of research articles and chapters in different edited books and journals of national and international reputation to his credit, which include SAGE, Springer and so on. He has also presented papers in more than 30 international and national seminars/conferences across the country and abroad, including Imperial College London, Dubai and Malaysia. As the Principal Investigator (PI), he has recently completed the University Grants Commission (New Delhi)-sponsored Major Research Project. Twelve MPhil students have been awarded degree under his supervision. He is the life member and editorial member of different bodies and organizations. Recently, he was awarded with 'Vivekananda Excellence Award' for his academic and research contribution (in the category of literature) by Seva Youth Guild, Kolkata (affiliated to the Ministry of Youth Affairs and Sports, NYKS, Government of India).

Contributors

Balaganapathi Devarakonda is a Professor and the Head of the Department of Philosophy, University of Delhi. He holds a PhD in philosophy from the University of Hyderabad. He was formerly an associate professor at the Department of CDL and Philosophy, Dravidian University, Kuppam. His publications include *Social and Political Philosophers of Modern Andhra* (2006) and *Globalization, Multiculturalism and the International Order* (edited with Penchalaiah S. and Sam Christopher C., 2009). His research articles have appeared in various journals, including *Journal of Philosophy, Culture and Traditions, Jadavpur Journal of Philosophy, Calicut University Research Journal, Suvidya Journal of Philosophy and Religion* and *Journal of the Inter-University Centre for Humanities and Social Science.* His areas of interest include social and political philosophy, historiography of Indian philosophy, philosophy of religion and human rights.

Iftekhar Ahemmed is a Professor in the Department of Political Science, Aligarh *Muslim* University (AMU), Aligarh, Uttar Pradesh. He has written several research papers and articles in national and international journals. He is associated with the Centre for Distance Education, AMU, and has written self-learning materials (SLMs) for undergraduate and postgraduate courses in the areas of political theory and Western political thought. He has participated in national and international seminars and conferences. His areas of interest include national movement and the constitutional development of India, Western political thought and *Muslim* political thought.

Ish N. Mishra is an Associate Professor in the Department of Political Science at Hindu College, University of Delhi. He did his MA from the Centre for Political Studies, JNU, and MPhil on the 'Politics of Congress Socialist Party' from the Department of Political Science, University of Delhi. He has published many articles in various journals, magazines, web portals newspapers and so on. He has also contributed chapters to edited books. His areas of specialization include Indian political philosophy, Western political philosophy, political economy and Indian politics.

Jayshree Jha is a research scholar at the Department of Philosophy, University of Delhi. She is working as a Research Assistant in UGC Major Research Project on 'A Study of Doctrinal Differences of the Early Buddhist Sects of Andhra'. Her research interests include social and political philosophy and human rights.

Kanchan Saxena is a Professor and the Head of the Department of Philosophy, University of Lucknow, Lucknow. She has done her master's and PhD in philosophy from Lucknow University. Prior to this, she has served in Avadh University and Kurukshetra University as an assistant professor. She has also worked as the Director, Academic, in the Indian Council of Philosophical Research (ICPR), New Delhi. She holds the position of coordinator in the Institute of Women's Studies, University of Lucknow, and has also taught there for several years. She has guided more than 22 students in both philosophy and women's studies. She has authored three books and edited two books in philosophy. She has more than 60 papers and book reviews published in various national and international journals of repute. Her areas of interest include ethics, meta ethics, applied ethics, Indian philosophy, philosophy of religion and women studies.

Krishna Menon is a Professor and Dean at the School of Human Studies, Ambedkar University Delhi. She is a graduate of Lady Shri Ram College, University of Delhi, and obtained her master's and MPhil degrees from the Centre for Political Studies, JNU, and her PhD from the University of Delhi. Her areas of specialization include political theory, Indian government and politics and feminist theory and politics. She has taught postgraduate courses on development politics in India at the University of Delhi and Indian politics at the School of International Studies, JNU. Prior to this, she taught political science for 25 years at Lady Shri Ram College, where she was also the Director of the Aung San Suu Kyi Centre for Peace. She has a long experience of learning and performing Bharatanatyam, Odissi and Mohiniyattam. She is a trained Carnatic musician as well, and has worked as the classical dance critic with *The Indian Express*, New Delhi. Currently she is a regular columnist for *The Deccan Chronicle/The Asian Age*.

Mona Singh is an Assistant Professor in the Department of Political Science at Daulat Ram College, University of Delhi. Previously she has taught in many colleges of University of Delhi, such as Bharti College, Sri Aurobindo College and PGDAV College. She has a number of articles published in reputed journals and also presented papers in various seminars and conferences. Her areas of specialization include international relations and Indian political thought.

Prabira Sethy is an Assistant Professor in the Department of Political Science at Maharaja Agrasen College, University of Delhi. He was a recipient of UGC's JRF and has done his MPhil on '*Islamic* Revivalism in International Politics: A Study of the Taliban Movement' from JNU, New Delhi. He has written a number of articles in various journals and chapters in different edited books. He has worked as a research assistant in many research projects of the institutions such as NCERT, IIPA, GFK Mode and Innovation Project of University of Delhi. He has also presented many papers in national and international seminars and conferences. His areas of interest include international politics, Indian political thought and Indian government and politics.

Praveen Kumar is an Associate Professor at the Centre for Political Studies, School of Social Sciences and Policy, Central University of South Bihar, Gaya. Formerly he was an associate professor at the Department of Geopolitics and International Relations, Manipal University (MU), Manipal, Karnataka. He has a professional experience in teaching, data-driven interdisciplinary research and analysis, project management, institution building and administrative responsibilities of over 14 years with institutions of repute. He completed his higher studies, including PhD, from JNU. His publications include a book (sole author), book chapters and research papers/articles in journals (*Economic & Political Weekly*, *Faultlines*, *Strategic Analysis*, *Asian Affairs*, *World Focus* and *Indian Journal of Society and Politics*) and research portals. He has participated in and organized national/international seminars and conferences, round tables and workshops. He has also been invited as a resource person to deliver lectures in various institutions of repute.

Rajendra Kumar Pandey is an Associate Professor in the Department of Political Science, Chaudhary Charan Singh University, Meerut, Uttar Pradesh. Besides earning his master's, MPhil and doctorate degrees from the University of Delhi, he also holds the prestigious postgraduate diploma (with summa cum laude: excellent grade) in federalism, decentralization and conflict resolution from the Institute of Federalism, University of Fribourg, Switzerland. In the past, he taught graduate students at the Delhi

College of Arts and Commerce (1998–2003), Hindu College (2003–2009) of University of Delhi, and the UGC Centre for Federal Studies, Jamia Hamdard University, New Delhi. Besides publishing research papers in reputed journals, he has co-authored two books—*Indian Government and Politics* (SAGE, 2008) and *Modern Indian Political Thought: Text and Context* (SAGE, 2009). He has also made substantial contribution to develop SLMs for students of open and distance learning in different areas of political science and public administration. The current focus areas of his academic pursuits are public policy and governance with special reference to the issues of disaster management and human rights.

Ramakrushna Pradhan is an Assistant Professor of political science in the Department of Social Science, Fakir Mohan University, Balasore. Dr Pradhan, a PhD from JNU, has also worked in the position of associate editor in *Eurasian Report*—an area study research journal and research associate in Eurasian Foundation, New Delhi, between February 2007 and February 2011. He has authored three books: *Geopolitics of Central Asia: China–US Engagement* (2010), *Geopolitics and Energy Diplomacy* (2016) and *State Politics in Odisha* (2017). He has co-edited *Contemporary Odisha: Realities and Vision* (2011), *Clean Energy Options and Nuclear Safety: An Indian Perspective* (2013), *Women's Rights as Human Rights in India: Problems and Paradoxes* (2013) *Swami Vivekananda: The Man and His Message* (2013), *Emerging Odisha: Problems and Prospects* (2014), *India and the Emerging World Order* (2016) and many more. Besides, he has written several research papers and articles in international and national journals of eminence concerning his area study. He has his expertise on the areas of geopolitics, energy security, strategic studies, Central Asia, India and international relations. He is associated with many research organizations and academic institutions in various capacities.

Ramesh Chandra Mahanta is an Assistant Professor in the Department of History, Utkal University, Odisha. He has completed his master's degree from Utkal University, Odisha, and MPhil from JNU, New Delhi. He has published research papers in *Utkal Historical Research Journal* and *Journal of Orissan History*. He has presented papers in different seminars and conferences. He was awarded the POSCO-Asia Fellowship in the year 2008. His specialization and areas of interest include modern Indian history and world history.

Ritu Sharma is an Assistant Professor in the Department of Political Science at Kalindi College, University of Delhi. She has done her master's from Department of Political Science, University of Delhi. Her doctoral research is in the field of gender studies. Earlier she has also taught in Jamia Millia Islamia. She has written articles and chapters in different books. She has also presented papers in national and international seminars. She is also associated with the One Billion Rising movement with known feminist Kamla Bhasin.

S. M. Azizuddin Husain is a Professor and Head in the Department of History and Culture, Jamia Millia Islamia, New Delhi. He is now the Senior Academic Fellow, Indian Council of Historical Research, Ministry of HRD, Government of India. He was the former head, Department of History, Jamia Millia Islamia. He has almost 37 years of teaching experience and 16 years of administrative experience. He remained as the honorary director of Dr Zakir Husain and His Contemporaries Archives and Portrait Gallery, Jamia Millia Islamia, New Delhi, w.e.f. 27 January 2004 to 11 December 2006. He was the director of Jamia's Premchand Archives and Literary Centre, Jamia Millia Islamia, New Delhi, from 12 December 2006 to 30 April 2008 and from 8 November 2010 to 2 April 2012. He was the honorary director of Child Development Centre, Jamia Millia Islamia, New Delhi, from 20 May 2009 to 30 July 2010. He remained as the dean, Faculty of Humanities and Languages, Jamia Millia Islamia, New Delhi, from 14 June 2009 to 2 April 2012. He officiated as the Vice-Chancellor of Jamia Millia Islamia, New Delhi, in the absence of the Vice-Chancellor from 10 August 2015 to 30 April 2016. He has published 27 books and 118 research papers. He has published 9 book reviews and 14 newspaper publications. Nineteen PhD scholars (Indian and foreign scholars) have been awarded their degrees under his supervision. He has organized 20 international and national seminars/conferences. In his credit, he has completed 196 research projects and other academic assignments. Presently he is working on a research project—'Biographies of *Sufis* of India' assigned by the Indian Council of Historical Research, Ministry of HRD, Government of India.

Santosh Kumar Mallik is an Assistant Professor in the Department of History, Gangadhar Meher University, Sambalpur, Odisha. He has received his education in history, art history, archaeology, Odia literature and tourism management from prestigious B. J. B. Autonomous College and Utkal University in Odisha and completed his doctoral studies in art history from School of Arts and Aesthetics, JNU, New Delhi. He has also qualified UGC NET JRF in archaeology and a regular contributor to regional, national and international research journals, as well as various vernacular newspapers and periodicals. He is a professional photographer, theatre actor, orator, counsellor, and has a work experience of director and co-director in various dramas and stage programmes. He has also kept his position in the various social works for downtrodden mass as NSS active member, and as a Red Cross volunteer. His areas of interest include ancient Indian historiography, social and cultural history, archaeology, iconography, inscriptional studies, manuscriptology, tourism and heritage management.

Sibaji Pratim Basu is a Professor at the Department of Political Science and Dean, Faculty of Arts and Commerce, Vidyasagar University, Midnapore. He is a well-known political scientist and political commentator from West Bengal. He graduated from Presidency College (1981) and postgraduated from University of Calcutta (1983). He obtained his PhD also from the University of Calcutta, on the thesis 'The Concepts of Nationalism and Internationalism: Tagore and Gandhi'. With a teaching and research career spanning more than three decades, he has taught, written books and articles, conducted and guided research in areas such as modern Indian political thought and politics; socialist thought; forced migration in South Asia; popular movements; and people's 'sustainable rights' in India. He has also contributed articles to several edited volumes. He is a member of the editorial board of *Vidyasagar Rachanasamagra* (The Complete Writings of Pandit Iswar Chandra Vidyasagar) published by Vidyasagar University. He is a board member and presently the Secretary of Mahanirban Calcutta Research Group and also holds membership of the Institute for Development Studies Kolkata (IDSK—as a nominated member) and West Bengal State Book Board (Member, Political Science), besides being the life member of West Bengal Political Science Association. He had widely published in SAGE, Routledge, Oxford, Frontline and so on.

Sumit Mukerji is a Professor in the Department of Political Science and former Dean, Faculty of Arts and Commerce, University of Kalyani, West Bengal. He is also the director of Centre for Studies on Bengali Diaspora in the same university. He is also a recipient of Fulbright Nehru Award. He has more than 33 years of experiences of teaching to undergraduate and postgraduate students. He has published 5 books and more than 100 research articles in various national and international journals. He has also participated in different seminars, conferences, workshops and training programmes at state, national and international levels. His areas of interest include studies on Netaji and Indian freedom movement, conflict resolution and peace studies, diaspora studies and political thought.

Swasti Alpana is an Assistant Professor in the Department of History at Satyawati College, University of Delhi. Presently she is on deputation duty of Deputy Proctor at University of Delhi. She has written articles and chapters in different books. She has also presented papers in national and international seminars/conferences. Her areas of interest include ancient Indian history, gender and cultural studies.

Varun Kumar Tripathi is an Associate Professor and the Head in the Department of Philosophy and Culture at Shri Mata Vaishno Devi University, Katra, Jammu and Kashmir. He did his graduation from St Andrew's College, Gorakhpur, in 1997, master's in Philosophy from DDU Gorakhpur University in 1999 and PhD in non-dualistic *Vedānta* philosophy from Banaras Hindu University, Varanasi, in 2003. He was a Junior Research Fellow (2001–2003) and General Fellow (2004–2005) of ICPR, New Delhi. He is a member of the Academic Council of Shri Mata Vaishno Devi University. He was also awarded Associate Fellowship of Inter-University Centre of UGC at Indian Institute of Advanced Study (IIAS) Shimla in 2011. He has published research papers, designed courses in the areas of Indian ethics, Indian logic and religion. He has also been a content writer of numerous course modules under the E-PG Pathshala Programme of UGC. He has organized numerous national and international conferences and seminars in philosophy. He has also been invited for special lecture series at institutions such as Amrita Vishva Vidyapeetham, Banaras Hindu University and University of Jammu. He specializes in Indian philosophy in general and non-dualistic *Vedānta* philosophy in particular. His areas of deep interest are Indian ethics, Pāli Buddhism, Indian psychology and history of civilizations. His deep interest in Indian literary theories and Indian philosophy of language has enabled him for greater appreciation of Indian philosophy, which he has included in numerous courses also. He has been giving lectures on themes such as Indian theories of meaning, the problem of centrality of meaning in *Nyāya* philosophy and *Śābdabodha* in *Nyāya* philosophy. He has also developed his interest as a value educator and has been part of the team of designing a course titled 'Discourse on Human Virtues' and has also delivered related lectures at other institutions too.

Introduction

Sibaji Pratim Basu

> The ancient civilisation of India differs from those of Egypt, Mesopotamia and Greece, in that its traditions have been preserved without a break down to the present day. Until the advent of the archaeologist, the peasant of Egypt or Iraq had no knowledge of the culture of his forefathers, and it is doubtful whether his Greek counterpart had any but the vaguest ideas about the glory of Periclean Athens. In each case there had been an almost complete break with the past. On the other hand, the earliest Europeans to visit India found a culture fully conscious of its own antiquity—a culture which indeed exaggerated that antiquity, and claimed not to have fundamentally changed for many thousands of years. India and China have, in fact, the oldest continuous cultural traditions in the world.
>
> —Basham (1959)

One might not completely agree with the above narrative of 'continuous cultural traditions' as found in A. L. Basham's classic book on ancient India, but deep in their minds, even the sceptics would acknowledge that the story (or stories) of India can neither be fully understood through the specs of 'discontinuous history'.[1] Rather it should be seen as a complex of continuities and changes. It also stands true for any discussion on Indian political thought.

The beauty of the Indian political thought is that the flow of continuity always assimilated new *changes* and evolved into a syncretic flow in which, notwithstanding the coming of new systems and institutions, some of the basic values and understandings flowing from the *past* have been retained. This is true in the case of the first *change/break* during the medieval period: despite new influences of *Islamic* political thought and institutions, we find the instances of the syncretic *bhakti* movement along with the syncretic and secular political philosophy of Akbar, the emperor. It remained so even during the British colonial times. Although with the advent of the colonial regime, a host of 'new'/*modern* political ideas and institutions influenced the minds of the Indians as never before, the basic spirit of the modern Indian political thought was still *never* fully 'derivative'.[2] Rather, it tried to claim supremacy in the realms of 'spirituality' and 'culture' over the notion of the *power* of the West.

Nature and Significance of Ancient Indian Discourse

Ancient India: Basic Elements of Political Thought

Dhārma

Ancient Indian political thought is part and parcel of the ancient Indian philosophy in which the central principle is the concept of *dhārma*. Here, we need to understand that the word *dhārma* has many connotations. It is not simply equal to what we call 'religion' in the Western sense of the term, which means the codes/ways and institutions of worship. Etymologically, it originates from the Sanskrit root word *dhri* which literally means 'to hold, maintain or keep'. It also stands for the eternal and inherent *nature* of reality, *justice*, *right behaviour* and *social order*.

The rules and regulations of *dhārma* are contained in different *Dharmaśāstras*. According to these texts, *dhārma* means the right duty of a person. It means a virtuous path. It stands for the 'higher truth'. It is also the moral law or natural law and the natural order of things. It is the cosmic order. It is also the social order. It controls one's ethical behaviour. It also means service to the community and self-expression.

People, according to *Dharmaśāstras*, must live according to *dhārma*. It must govern the life of the individual and the society. It means that each human being has a purpose of life. Each person has a duty in life. He/she must perform his/her duties. This is the only method of purification of his/her soul. By this way, he/she will get '*nirvana*' or *mokṣa*, that is, the final emancipation of the soul. Here, also note that besides *Hinduism*, *Buddhism* and *Jainism* also believed in the concept of *dhārma*.

Dhārmas are of several types. Going through several *Dharmaśāstras* and *Dharmasūtras*, some of them can be identified as follows:

1. *Vyakti dhārma* (the *dhārma* of an individual)
2. *Parivarika dhārma* (family *dhārma*) (also called *kutumba dhārma*)
3. *Samaja dhārma* (*dhārma* of society)
4. *Rāja dhārma* (duties of king/ruler)
5. *Manava dhārma* (the *dhārma* of mankind)
6. *Varṇa dhārma* (professional *dhārma* or *dhārma* of each caste)
7. *Āpad dhārma* (special *dhārma* for exceptional/abnormal situations)
8. *Yuga dhārma* (*dhārma* for an age)
9. *Āśhrama dhārma* (*dhārma* for different stages of life)

Daṇḍa

In this regard, let us remember that *dhārma* stood above the king, and the king's failure to preserve the sacred tradition would lead to disastrous consequences. It was the function of the power of sanction and coercion (*daṇḍa*) to ensure compliance with *dhārma*, and the *rājadhārma*—the *dhārma* of the king—thus existed as guarantor of the whole social order with its hierarchy of privileges and duties. Behind this doctrine, lay the belief that it was only the fear of punishment that used to make men righteous in their conduct. In Kauṭilya's *Arthaśāstra* (Shamasastry, 1915), we find a detail of the principles of *daṇḍa* or *daṇḍanīti*.

The term *daṇḍa* is derived from the words *dam and dand*, which refer to tame, subdue, to conquer or to restrain. This term also means a stick. *Daṇḍa*, in fact, is one of the main elements of a state. The main reason for the institution of *daṇḍa* is to bring about discipline in the lives of human beings who by nature are evil and corrupt. According to Manu, it is only the king who can protect the entire mankind and for this protection, the king uses *daṇḍa* as a means or as an instrument.

In the ancient Indian political system, it was the responsibility of the king to maintain *dhārma* by means of *daṇḍa*. It was widely believed that mankind could be made more disciplined only through fear of punishment. It is this punishment that kept a check on their actions consciously or subconsciously.

However, this punishment should be inflicted only when necessary after much consideration. Otherwise, the concept of *daṇḍa* is lost. Further, ancient Indian thinkers were of the opinion that *daṇḍa* should not be used as per the whims and fancies of the rulers, but it should only be used when there is the presence of any antisocial elements in the society.

They further stated that *daṇḍa* is a code given to the humanity by God to follow a righteous life. This code should bind *daṇḍa* against his subjects for their wrongdoings. Even the people can collectively take action against the king if he does any wrong.

Idea of Social Contract

Social contract theory is one of the ancient theories of the origin of state as it explains the consensual basis of the origin of state as against the divine. Although this theory was expounded in both Greek and Indian traditions, the Indians were the first to expound it. It was Gautam Buddha, the greatest philosopher India has produced, who advocated it. There are the following three traditions of social contract theory in India:

1. Buddhist theory of social contract
2. Kauṭilya on social contract
3. The *Mahābhārata* on social contract

The Buddhist theory of social contract is based on the following principles:

1. The state is an artificial institution created by men to perform certain functions.
2. The basis of the state is social contract based on a mutual agreement between the people.
3. The state arose to establish order in society by enforcing first decrees in the society.
4. In return of protection, the people agreed to pay a portion of their agricultural produce to the state in the form of taxes.
5. The king was called *Mahāsammata*—one who was elected by the people or the great elect.

This contract theory was followed by social contract theory expounded by Kauṭilya in his *Arthaśāstra*. In this theory, Kauṭilya puts forward the following principles:

1. In the absence of the king, there would prevail the logic of fishes (*matsyanyaya*) in society, and to overcome the logic of fishes, the establishment of kingship was felt necessary.
2. The people agreed to make *Vaivasvat Manu* as their king to overcome the logic of fishes.

3. The people decided to give one-sixth of their produce to the king to provide him with his *Yogakshema* or means of livelihood.
4. The king agreed to provide protection to the people and Kauṭilya argued that the people who did not pay taxes and the king who did not provide protection deserved censure.

Kauṭilya's ideas on social contract were further developed by *Bhīṣma* in *Mahābhārata*, in the *Śānti Parva*. In Chapter 68 of the great epic, the traditional social contract theory, as expounded in the *Arthaśāstra*, is elaborated. The only addition is that Manu is sent by God *Brahmā* as the king.

In the *Arthaśāstra*, the divine origin of kingship was not mentioned. But *Bhīṣma*, a very important character of the Indian epic *Mahābhārata*, lays down the contractual basis of kingship and held that the king was a servant of the people and taxes were his wage. The theory occurs in *Śānti Parva*,[3] which begins with a long discussion on the importance of *daṇḍa* and *daṇḍanīti*.

It is stated that *Viṣṇu* created a son—*Viraja*—born out of his mind to undertake the responsibility of administration, but he and several of his descendants renounced the world, which ultimately led to the tyrannical rule of *Vena*. The sages put an end to the life of this ruler, and created *Prithu* out of his right thigh, who was the eighth in descent from *Viṣṇu*. By means of a contract, the sages clearly laid down the conditions on which *Prithu* would hold the throne. The sages asked him to swear that he would rule according to the principles of *daṇḍanīti*, that he would consider the *Brāhmaṇs* above punishment and that he would save the world from the intermixture of castes.

Varṇa as Social Order

Varṇa is a Sanskrit term that appears in the *Ṛigveda*, where it means 'colour, outward appearance, exterior, form, figure or shape'. The word means 'colour, tint, dye or pigment' in the *Mahābhārata*. *Varṇa* contextually means 'colour, race, tribe, species, kind, sort, nature, character, quality, property' of an object or people in some *Vedic* and medieval texts. *Varṇa* refers to four social classes in the *Manusmṛiti*.

The earliest application to the formal division into four social classes (without using the term *varṇa*) appears in the late *Ṛigvedic Purusha Sukta* (*RV* 10.90.11–12), which has the *Brāhmaṇa*, *Rajanya* (instead of *Kṣatriya*), *Vaiśya* and *Śūdra* classes forming the mouth, arms, thighs and feet at the sacrifice of the primordial *Purusha*, respectively.

Although there is much controversy as to whether the *varṇa* division based on the *guna* (virtues) and *karma* (deeds) had transformed itself into hereditary *jāti* (caste) system or not, ideally speaking, it insisted that the law of social life should not be cold and cruel competition, but harmony and co-operation. Society should not be a field of rivalry among individuals. The ancient Indian religious as well as social/political texts emphasized the importance of maintaining social order by maintaining the *Varṇa* system. This also formed one of the essential duties of a ruler.

Classification of Different Elements of the State

The authors of *Arthaśāstra* tradition (even before Kauṭilya) tried to classify different elements (*angas*) of the body of the state (Chousalkar, 2018). Kauṭilya famously classified it into seven (*sapta*) elements in his *Arthaśāstra*, which is known as his *saptanga* (*sapta* + *anga*, i.e., seven elements) theory of the state.

These seven *angas*/elements are: *Swami* (master/ruler), *Amātya* (ministers and bureaucrats), *Jānapada* (territory with people living in it), *Durga* (different kinds of forts), *Kośa* (treasury), *Daṇḍa* (sanction/coercion) and *Mitra* (friendly kingdom/state of a given state).

The Government: Not Sovereign

From its very nature of existence, the government in ancient India could not be regarded as sovereign in the Austinian sense of the term. It did not impart validity to the orders; rather, it shared in its validity. On the contrary, the government had no independent existence of its own. The sustenance of the social order was merely its function. Sovereignty was, in fact, ultimately sourced in the divine will. On the part of the individual, there was no unified allegiance, no single loyalty except to society as a whole. Only the pluralistic theory of sovereignty can grasp the Indian phenomenon.

No Clear Distinction between the State and Society

The governmental organization and politics were looked at as a part of the larger whole called society. In other words, society was at once religious, political, economical and military. It was generally viewed in a comprehensive manner. The habit of looking at society from a political angle was not cultivated. As a result, there was no clear conception of either the State or the government. Both were interchangeable.

The Medieval Indian Thought

The Medieval Age in India

Medieval India presents us with a unique and baffling spectacle. It is an age characterized by decay and break in the old edifice, addition and amalgamation of the new forces and upsurge of ideas and institution of a very complex character. With the establishment of *Muslim* rule in India in the 13th century, a new set of political ideas and institutions was put in place, though the old one still held sway in many parts of the country. The *Sultanate* period from the 13th to 16th centuries was marked by the rise and fall of many *Turko–Afghan* dynasties, that is, slave, Khalji, Tughluq and Lodhi. It was during these centuries that the *Hindu* kingdom of Vijay Nagar in the South attained great heights—both politically and culturally. Besides this, kingdoms of Orrisa, Mewar and Kamrupe (Assam) exercised great power and influence. Thus, we find that India in those medieval centuries witnessed two different political systems—large parts of India, under the Delhi *Sultanate*, were being governed on the basis of *Turko–Afghan* ideas and institutions, whereas some parts of India, particularly the South and West, were being governed on the basis of indigenous ideas and institutions.

The following are the salient features of the *Turko–Afghan* government, the predominant political system of the Middle age:

1. *Muslim* polity like its Indian counterpart had a theological basis. The injunctions contained in *Qur'an*, *Hadis* and *Shari'at* were the guiding principles of the successive *Sultans*. The *Sultan* was considered to be Caesar and Pope combined in one. The office of *Caliph* always commanded respect of the *Muslim* rulers. Most of the *Sultans* kept up the pretence of regarding the *Caliph* as the legal sovereign, although they themselves were his representative or vice-regent.
2. The real source of *Sultan's* authority was his military. As the supreme head of the executive, the *Sultan* transacted the business of state with the help of ministers and advisers of his choice. The state being essentially military in character, the *Sultan* was the chief commander of forces. He was also the chief law-giver and final court of appeal.

3. The *Sultans* of Delhi devised the administrative machinery with a regular hierarchy of offices in change of various departments who did not, however in any way, check his authority but rather carried out their respective duties according to *Sultan*'s orders.
4. The fiscal policy of the Turkish *Sultans* of India was modelled on the theory of finance of the Hanafi School of *Muslim* jurisprudence. The principal sources of revenue were *Kharaj* or land tax from *Hindu* Chiefs and landlords, *Khams* or one-fifth of the spoils of war, land-revenue obtained from crown lands. The revenue policy of the state and the working of the revenue department depended on the personality of the *Sultan*.
5. The standing army of the *Sultans* consisted of the royal bodyguards and the troops of the capital which were reinforced by the levies sent by provincial viceroys. The main branches of army were infantry, cavalry and the elephants. There was nothing like artillery which was used in later times.
6. The whole kingdom was divided into a number of provinces which varied from 20 to 25; each province was placed in the charge of viceroys who were called *Naib Sultans*. A province was subdivided into smaller portions. The village communities continued unaffected by the establishment of a new government in the country.

The *Turko–Afghan* machinery of administration, according to Professor R. C. Majumdar,[4] lacked the force of habit, derived from tradition, and of will, derived from the national support, both of which are necessary for the security and permanence of a government. The State grew on military strength. Its rulers, in most cases, were concerned with measures calculated to strengthen their own authority and aristocracy, and without any consistent policy, they pursued selfish interests. The 16th century saw the *Mughal–Afghan* contest for supremacy in India, in which the *Mughals* led by Babar emerged victorious. The foundations were laid for the *Mughal* Empire which remained in existence till 1857 when the British Government took over the reins of administration in its hands.

The *Mughal* Empire was a combination of Indian and extra-Indian elements. Historians describe it as the Perso-Arabic System in an Indian Setting. It was based on ideas and principles different from those of the *Sultans* of Delhi.

Its features are summarized as follows:

1. It was a centralized autocracy and the king's power was unlimited. His word was law and none could dispute his will. He was the head of the State, commander of the State forces, the chief legislator and the fountain of justice. He was the *Caliph* of God required to obey the scriptures and *Islamic* traditions, but a strong king could ignore the sacred law if he so desired.
2. There was nothing like a cabinet of ministers in the modern sense. The ministers were not always or necessarily consulted. It depended upon the pleasure of the emperor to consult them. The personality of the emperor and his ministers mattered much. Although the *Mughal* emperors appointed a number of officers in different departments, the chief departments of state were: (a) the imperial household under the *Khan-e-Saman,* (b) the exchequer under the *Diwan,* (c) the military pay and accounts office under *Bakshi,* (d) the judicial department under *Qazi* and (e) the religious endowments under chief *Sadr*. The *Diwan* or *Wazir* was usually the highest officer of the State.
3. The *Mughal* nobility, a heterogeneous body composed of *Turks, Tartars, Persians* and *Hindus,* could not organize itself as a powerful baronial class. A noble had only a life interest in his *jagir* which reverted to crown on his death. The nobles led an extravagant life and squandered their

money in unproductive luxury. This prevented them from acting as a check on royal autocracy and safeguarding public liberty.

4. The *Mughals* tried to streamline the revenue system in order to strengthen the foundation of the State. In this connection, the contribution of Akbar is notable who, with the help of Muzzaffar Khan Turbati and *Rājā* Todar Mal, introduced a number of reforms. The major sources of central revenue were land revenue, customs, mint, inheritance, presents and the poll tax.
5. Nothing like modern legislation or a written code of laws existed in the *Mughal* period. The only notable exceptions to this were the 12 ordinances of Jahangir and a digest of *Muslim* law prepared under Aurangzeb's supervision. The judges chiefly followed scriptural injunctions; they also took into account the customary law and observed principles of equity. The *Mughal* emperors regarded the speedy administration of justice as one of their important duties and did not support any special protection for officers of the empire. Akbar is said to have remarked, 'If I were guilty of an unjust act, I would rise in judgment against myself'. The love of justice of emperors such as Jahangir and Shahjahan has been attested to by contemporary European travellers. *Mughal* emperors such as Akbar and Jahangir granted to their subjects the right of direct petitioning, something which was won in England after a hard fight.
6. In 1580, Akbar divided his empire into 12 provinces and by the time of Aurangzeb this number had risen to 21. The governor or *Sipah Salar* was the head of the civil and military administration of the province. He was assisted by a number of subordinate officers such as Diwan, Bakshi and Faujdar.
7. To maintain the military strength of the *Mughal* Empire, it was necessary for the *Mughal* emperors to employ a large number of foreign adventurers. But Akbar inaugurated the policy of 'India for Indians' and threw open the official careers to the *Hindus* as well. Every officer of the State had *mansab* or official appointment of rank and profit, and as such was bound theoretically to supply a number of troops for the military service of the State. Thus, the *mansabdars* formed the official nobility of the country and this system was, in the words of a historian, 'army, the peerage and the civil administration all rolled into one'. Akbar classified the office-holders into 33 grades ranging from the 'commanders of 10' to the 'commanders of 10,000'.

Mughal Era: Emergence of Syncretic Culture

A syncretic culture also emerged during the *Mughal* era in India. In this regard, we may refer first to the contributions of the *Sufi* mystics (*Islamic* mystics), who found a resemblance between the ontological monism of Ibn al-'Arabi and that of *Vedānta*. The Shattari order among the Indian *Sufis* practised *Yogic* austerities and even physical postures. Various minor syncretistic religious sects attempted to harmonize *Hindu* and *Muslim* religious traditions at different levels and with varying degrees of success. Of these, the most famous are Ramananda, Kabir and Guru Nanak. Kabir harmonized the two religions in such a manner that to an enquiry about whether he was a *Hindu* or a *Muslim*, the answer given by a contemporary was, 'It is a secret difficult to comprehend. One should try to understand'. Guru Nanak rejected the authority of both *Hindu* and *Muslim* scriptures alike and founded his religion Sikhism on a rigorously moralistic, monotheistic basis.

Among the great *Mughals*, Akbar attempted in 1581 to promulgate a new religion *Dīn-e Ilāhī* which was to be based on reason and ethical teachings common to all religions and which was to be free from priestcraft. This effort, however, was short-lived, and a reaction of *Muslim* orthodoxy was led by Shaykh Aḥmed Sirhindī, who rejected ontological monism in favour of orthodox unitarianism and sought to channel mystical enthusiasm along *Qur'ānic* lines. By the middle of the 17th century, the tragic figure of *Dārā Shikōh*, the *Mughal* emperor Shāh Jahān's son and disciple of the *Qādirī Sufis*, translated *Hindu* scriptures, such as the *Bhagwadgīta* and the *Upaniṣhads*, into Persian. In his translation of the latter, he closely followed Shankara's commentaries. In his *Majma'al-baḥrayn*, he worked out correlations between *Sufi* and *Upaniṣhadic* cosmologies, beliefs and practices. During this time, the *Muslim* elite of India virtually identified *Vedānta* with *Sufism*. Later, *Shāh Walī Allāh*'s son, *Shāh 'Abd-ul-'Azīz*, regarded Krishna among the *awliyā'* (saints).

Ancient Indian and Western Political Thought: A Brief Comparison

There are many meeting points between the ancient Indian and the Western political thoughts. The similarities are found mostly in comparison to the ancient Greek political thought. For example, *first*, both in ancient Indian texts and Plato's *Republic*, we find the distinctions between different types/classes of the people on the basis of different virtues. Plato classified them as the Guardians (erudite ruling elite), Auxiliaries (warriors) and the Artisans (workers). These *types* to a great extent resemble with the *varṇa* divisions in Indian society based on the virtues of *Brāhmaṇa*, *Kṣatriya*, *Vaiśya* and *Śūdra*.

Second, Plato thought that it is the supreme duty of the rulers to *maintain harmony* among these classes of people, and thereby establishing 'Justice' in the society. In ancient India too, it was the main duty of a king/ruler to maintain the social order by maintaining the *varṇa* order and maintain *dhārma*, which is another name for 'Justice'.

Third, ancient Greece, as we know from Aristotle's *Politics*, had various kinds of rules in their city-states or polities such as monarchies, aristocracies and democracies. In India too there existed kingdoms, republics and aristocracies.

Fourth, like ancient Greece, Indian political thought was 'teleological' in nature, which means that it had some *a priori* desired ethical goals. In ancient Greece, the emphasis was on how the people could attain higher ethical selves by joining the *polis* (city-states). In India, the main goal of all the good states was to follow dictates of *dhārma*, which would lead to the attainment of the ultimate goal *mokṣa*, following the lower steps—*ārtha* (money/material) and *kāma* (objects of desire).

However, there are also points of divergence. Some of the points have already been discussed above. First, in the West, 'power' has always been the constitutive element of politics. Thus, drive for power often led to struggle for power, whereas in ancient India, the concept of *dhārma* in its myriad meanings and forms stood above the power of the ruler/king.

Second, since, unlike the West, there was hardly any clear-cut distinction between the society and the State, it was very difficult (except for *Arthaśāstras*) to develop an independent theory of the State.

Third, even when such distinction was attempted, the position of society seemed higher than the State/kingdoms in the eyes of the people.

Fourth, unlike the Western politics, Indian politics had hardly witnessed any major clash with the institutions of religion like the church. There was no monolithic institution like the Roman Church in India, even in the medieval period, which tended to subordinate different rulers in India.

Fifth, as mentioned earlier, the governments were *not* 'sovereign' in the Western sense of the term.

Reasons for Limited Influence of Ancient and Medieval Indian Thought

Question may arise as to why despite rich tradition in political and social philosophy, the Indian political thought of the ancient and medieval times could not come to prominence, like its Western counterpart. We can identify some reasons behind this. First, there were some basic differences between the ancient and medieval political systems in India and the Western ones during the same times. We have discussed above about some of the differences between the two systems. These differences had led to different directions of political thought in the two places.

Second, the differences in political systems were based on different world views of the notions such as 'power', 'state', 'religious institution' and 'society'. For example, the notions of *power* (of the state/church) occupied the centre-space of the ancient and medieval Western political thought, whereas in India, society was more important. Thus, maintaining social order was the most important function of the ruler. And since the constitutive principle of both the society and State was *dhārma*, the State could never claim absolute allegiance of its subjects. These differences were pointed out even by the modern thinkers. For instance, Rabindranath Tagore, Nobel laureate and India's national poet, talked at length about the differences between the 'society'-based Indian civilization and the power-centric Western nations in his book *Nationalism* (Tagore, 1985). Moreover, like the medieval Europe, India did not have a centralized monolithic church/religious institution.

Third, and most importantly, the Western ideas, economy and statecraft became universal only after colonizing of the world by the Western powers. It is mainly through colonialism that non-Western/oriental world came to know about the Western political thought, and since the time of colonial expansion (18th and 19th centuries) coincided with the time of industrial revolution and enlightenment of the 18th century, the Western political thought became compulsorily universal in the colonies.

Fourth, the Western ideas became universal only during the Enlightenment-driven modern times. Thus, through the modern/Western education, the Western political thought influenced the minds of the native elite in India than their own tradition of political thought of ancient and medieval times. However, in their quest for nationalism or autonomy in the realm of thought, the modern Indian political thought did not blindly copy the West. All the thinkers such as Ram Mohan Roy, Bankimchandra Chattopadhyay, Rabindranath Tagore, Swami Vivekananda, Swami Dayānanda Saraswati, Bal Gangadhar Tilak, Aurobindo Ghosh, Mahatma Gandhi and others had to face this problem. And what we found was a synthesis between the Western and Indian political thoughts.

Sources for the Study

We have already mentioned about some of the sources for the study of ancient and medieval Indian political thoughts. Let us recall those again. For the ancient Indian thought, the primary sources are: (a) the *Vedās*; (b) *Dharmaśāstras* and *Dharmasūtras*; (c) the *Mahābhārata*; (d) the *Arthaśāstras*; (e) *Manusmṛiti*; (f) political texts like *Nītisāra* and *Nītivākyāmrta* (of Gupta age); (g) inscriptions and edicts and (h) accounts of foreign travellers. For the medieval period (the demarcation of which is controversial), especially for the *Islamic* period, we have to depend on various laws—both religious and secular—important official documents and greatly on the accounts of different persons, such as Barani, Fazl and even an autobiography of a ruler like Babur (*Baburnama*) or a philosopher like *Shahzada* (prince) *Dārā Shikōh*.

Based on these primary sources, there are some important books on the subject. Works of the pioneering modern writers such as Rajendralal Mitra, R. C. Dutt, R. G. Bhandarkar, H. C. Raychaudhuri, U. N. Ghoshal, R. C. Majumdar and others can be mentioned. The Marxist School beginning with D. D. Kosambi and historians such as Romila Thapar, Ram Sharan Sharma, D. N. Jha and others also made important contributions to the study of the subject.

About the Present Volume

The present volume, *Ancient and Medieval Indian Thought: Themes and Traditions*, is an exhaustive one dealing with almost all the aspects of Indian political thoughts during the ancient and medieval times. Two young editors—Ankit Tomar of Kamala Nehru College, University of Delhi, and Suratha Kumar Malik of Vidyasagar University, West Bengal—have tried hard and their best to accommodate the myriad themes and traditions within the two covers of the present volume. Contributors comprise a number of nationally well-known political scientists along with some young bright scholars. Most of them are with political science backgrounds. Others belong to philosophy, history and Sanskrit.

The volume is divided into two parts. Part I, *Ancient Indian Thought and Tradition*, has 11 chapters. Chapter 1 containing '*Dhārma* in Ancient India: The Moral Law of the Cosmos' has been nicely elaborated by Suratha Kumar Malik of Vidyasagar University, West Bengal. Chapter 2 deals with 'Ancient India: Conception and Forms of Community'. It is elegantly penned by Praveen Kumar of Central University of Bihar. Kanchan Saxena of Lucknow University has discussed at length on '*Vedās* and the *Brāhmanic* Tradition: The Cradle of *Hinduism*' in Chapter 3. The next chapter (Chapter 4) deals with 'Manu: The Progenitor of Humanity'. Mona Singh of Daulat Ram College, Delhi University (hereafter DU) is the author of the chapter. Chapter 5, dealing with '*Yājñavalkya*: A *Vedic* Sage' has been analysed by Swasti Alpana of Satyawati College, Delhi University. Chapter 6 on '*Cārvāka-Lokāyata* Tradition: A Tradition of Materialist Philosophy' has been dealt by Professor Balaganapathi Devarakonda of DU and Jayashree Jha, Research Scholar, DU. Chapter 7 discusses '*Śhramanic* Tradition: An Ascetic Reformism'. The writer is Ankit Tomar of Kamala Nehru College, DU. Chapter 8, containing '*Śukranīti*: A Political Treatise' has been elaborated by Prabira Sethy, Maharaja Agrasen College, DU. Ish N. Mishra, Associate Professor, *Hindu* College, DU, wrote on '*Dīgha Nikāya (Aggaññasutta)*: Theory of Kingship and *Aṅuguttara Nikāya*' in Chapter 9. '*Śānti Parva* of *Mahābhārata*: Ideas on the Kingship and *Daṇḍanīti*' is written by Varun Kumar Tripathi in Chapter 10. The last chapter of Part I (Chapter 11) deals with 'Kauṭilya: A Pragmatic Thinker'. The author is Ramakrushna Pradhan, Assistant Professor at PG Dept of Social Science, Fakir Mohan University, Odisha.

Part II, *Medieval Indian Thought and Traditions*, has eight chapters. In Chapter 12, written by Ritu Sharma, Kalindi College, DU, we find a long discussion on 'Medieval India: State, Society and Religion'. Chapter 13 deals with the political ideas of the 14th century thinker, Barani as 'Ziyauddin Barani: Ideas on Good *Sultan* and Ideal Polity'. It is jointly written by Ramesh Chandra Mahanta of Utkal University and Santosh Kumar Mallik of Gangadhar Meher University, Sambalpur, Odisha. Chapter 14, written by a well-known political scientist, Sumit Mukerji of Kalyani University, West Bengal, brilliantly deals with 'Abul Fazl: Views on Governance and Administration'. In Chapter 15 on '*Islamic* Tradition: A Tradition of

Human Affairs and Classical Heritage', we find an important analysis by Iftekar Ahemmad of Aligarh *Muslim* University. S. M. Azizuddin Husain of Jamia Milia Islamia, New Delhi, elaborated with details on '*Sufi* Tradition: A Tradition of Spiritualism and Tolerance' in Chapter 16. Prabira Sethy of Maharaja Agrasen College, DU, wrote on the great Indian saint and a representative of the syncretic culture as 'Kabir: An Indian Mystic Saint' in Chapter 17. The next chapter (Chapter 18) offers a critical reading of the role of women in *Bhakti* movement with the title 'Women in Bhakti Tradition: A Critical Reflection'. The author, Krishna Menon, Professor, Ambedkar University, Delhi, is well known for research in this area. The last chapter (Chapter 19) elaborates the discussion on 'Syncretic Tradition: A Tradition of Assimilation', which is written by Rajendra Kumar Pandey of Chaudhuri Charan Singh University, Meerut, Uttar Pradesh.

Even a cursory look on the above list will surely convince the reader that the present volume is an authoritative and exhaustive work on the Indian political thought of the ancient and medieval eras. If the students at the undergraduate and postgraduate levels in particular and the readers in general, who bear some curiosity and interest in Indian political thought, find the volume useful and thought-provoking, the diligence and hard work of the present editors would not go in vain.

Endnotes

1. For a detailed and 'discursive' discussion on 'discontinuity' in history, see, Foucault (1972, 1989).
2. For a detailed argument, see, Chatterjee (1986).
3. There are a host of books that deal with ancient Indian political thought. See, for example, Ghoshal (1959), Saletore (1963), Sharma (1996), Varma (2010).
4. For a detailed account, see, Majumdar (1967, 1974).

References

Basham, A. L. 1959. *The Wonder that was India*. New York: Macmillan.

Chatterjee, Partha. 1986. *Nationalist Thought and the Colonial World: A Derivative Discourse?* London: Zed Books.

Chousalkar, Ashok S. 2018. *Revisiting the Political Thought of Ancient India: Pre-Kautilyan Arthashastra Tradition*. New Delhi: SAGE Publications.

Foucault, Michel. 1972. *The Archaeology of Knowledge and the Discourse of Language*. New York: Pantheon Books.

Foucault, Michel. 1989. *The Order of Things: An Archaeology of the Human Sciences*. London/New York: Routledge.

Ghoshal, U. N. 1959. *A History of Indian Political Ideas: The Ancient Period and the Period of Transition to the Middle Ages*. Bombay, London, etc.: Oxford University Press.

Majumdar, R. C. 1967. *The History and Culture of the Indian People: The Delhi Sultanate*, Vol. 8. Bombay: Bharatiya Vidya Bhavan.

Majumdar, R. C. 1974. *The History and Culture of the Indian People: The Mughul Empire*, Vol. 7. Bombay: Bharatiya Vidya Bhavan.

Saletore, Bhasker Anand. 1963. *Ancient Indian Political Thought and Institutions*. New Delhi: Asia Publishing House.

Shamasastry, R. ed. 1915. *Kauṭilya's Arthaśāstra*. Bangalore: Government Press.

Sharma, Urmila, and S. K. Sharma. 1996. *Indian Political Thought*. New Delhi: Atlantic Publishers.

Varma, V. P. 2010. *Ancient & Medieval Indian Political Thought*. Delhi: Lakshmi Narayan Agarwal.

Tagore. 1985. *Nationalism*. Madras, Bombay: Macmillan India Ltd.

PART I

Ancient Indian Thought and Traditions

Chapter 6
Cārvāka-Lokāyata *Tradition: A Tradition of Materialist Philosophy*
Balaganapathi Devarakonda and Jayshree Jha

Chapter 7
Śhramanic *Tradition: An Ascetic Reformism*
Ankit Tomar

Chapter 8
Śukranīti: *A Political Treatise*
Prabira Sethy

Chapter 9
Dīgha Nikāya (Aggaññasutta): *Theory of Kingship and* Aṅguttara Nikāya
Ish N. Mishra

Chapter 10
Śānti Parva *of* Mahābhārata*: Ideas on the Kingship and* Daṇḍanīti
Varun Kumar Tripathi

Chapter 11
Kauṭilya: A Pragmatic Thinker
Ramakrushna Pradhan

1
CHAPTER

Dhārma in Ancient India: The Moral Law of the Cosmos

Suratha Kumar Malik

CHAPTER OUTLINE

- Introduction
- Contextualizing and Understanding the Concept of *Dhārma*
- *Dhārma* and *Hindu* World View
- The *Sanatana Dhārma*
- Classification of *Dhārma*
- *Rta, Rna* and *Dhārma*
- *Dhārma* through *Yajña, Dana* and *Tapas*
- *Dhārma* and the Nature of Self (*Sacchidānanda*)
- *Dhārma* in *Upaniṣhads* and *Hindu* epics
- *Dhārma* According to *Vatsyayana* and *Patanjali*
- Conclusion
- Summary
- Points for Discussion

असतो मा सद्गमय
तमसो मा ज्योतिर्गमय
मृत्योर्मामृतं गमयेति
Lead me from falsehood to truth,
lead me from darkness to light,
lead me from death to immortality.

—Bṛhadāraṇkya Upaniṣhad (1.3.28)

Reader's Guide

The aim of this chapter is to familiarize the readers with the idea of *dhārma* in Ancient India, which is universal and much broader than the contemporary idea of religion and exists since the time immemorial (*sanatana*). It encompasses the concepts like *Rta*, *Rna*, *Dāna* and *Tapas* and wholly represents a natural equilibrium in the universe in both humans and non-humans. After reading this chapter, the reader will be able to analyse the meaning of *dhārma*, its components, sources of *dhārma* in *Hindu Śhāstras* and literature including *Vedās*, *Upaniṣhads* and *Purāṇaṣ*. Additionally, the reader will be able to understand the greatness of *Hindu dhārma* which is the 'right order', maintains equilibrium of the universe and considers the world as a family. The concept of *dhārma* in ancient India was the 'moral law of the cosmos'. It is the natural principle which governs the universe and the ethical base, the right order, the selfless action and existed beyond time and space. It is the process and natural order of the creation that connects the particles with the matter, the humans with the God, the souls with the supreme soul, the creature with the creation and the finite with the infinite.

Introduction

The classical Sanskrit noun *dhārma* is a derivation from the root *dhṛ*, meaning 'to uphold', 'to support', 'to sustain', 'to maintain' or 'keep', and takes a meaning of what is established or firm. Thus, another interpretation of the word in English would be 'the collection of natural and universal laws that uphold, sustain or uplift, that is, law of being, law of nature; individual nature, prescribed duty; social and personal duties; moral code; civil law, code of conduct; morality; way of life, practice, observance; justice; righteousness, religion, religiosity and harmony'. The famous verse from *Mahābhārata*:

धारणात् धर्म इत्याहुः धर्मों धारयति प्रजाः।
यः स्यात् धारणसंयुक्तः स धर्म इति निश्चयः।।

(*Mahābhārata*, *Śānti Parva*, 109-9-11)

Dhārma that upholds people, also upholds the universe, supports it and sustains it, without which the universe just falls apart. *Dhārma* sustains and maintains the social, moral, political and economic order.

In the *Ṛigvedā*, the word appears to be used in the sense of upholder, supporter or sustainer (*Ṛigvedā*, X. 92. 2). It is derived from an older *Vedic* Sanskrit *n*-stem *dhārman*, with a literal meaning of 'bearer' or 'supporter', and in a religious sense, it conceived as an aspect of *Rta* (Sharma 2003, 71). *Rita* (in *Sanskrit*, *Rta*) manifests itself in physical universe as the ground of determination of various phenomena. In fact, the entire universe is founded on *Rita* and moves within its parameters (ibid.). When looked at from the conceptual standpoint, the word *dhārma* simply refers to the word 'law' and in the *Vedic* tradition it is called *Rita*, which is the forerunner of the concept of *dhārma*.

Dhārma is the higher metaphysical truth (*Satyam*). The absolute is viewed as self (*Purusa*) which in its nature and function is conceived as an objective and impersonal law. It is the ground of rationale of all that happens in the moral and physical aspects of cosmos. As essentially spiritual in nature, it imparts two realms: 'order' as well as 'harmony'. It is semantically similar to the Greek *Themis*, which means fixed decree, statute or law. In classical Sanskrit, and in the *Vedic* Sanskrit of the *Atharvavedā*, the stem is thematic: *dhārma*. In Pāli, it is rendered as *Dhamma*. In some contemporary Indian languages and dialects, it alternatively occurs as *dharm*.

The evolving literature of *Hinduism* linked *dhārma* to two other important concepts: *Rita* and *Maya*. *Dhārma* is generally accepted to have been derived and superseded from the *Vedic* concept of *Rita*, which literally meant, 'the straight line'. *Rita* in *Vedās* is the truth and cosmic principle which regulates and coordinates the operation of the universe and everything within it. *Rita* refers to the 'law of nature'; it signifies moral laws based on righteousness. When something is *Rita*, it simply meant that thing is true, right and nothing more. *Dhārma* evolved side-by-side of *Rita* but eventually took over it, as the old concept of *Rita* was not able to cope and solve the issue emerging with increasing social complexities (Rathore 2015, 4).

Maya in *Ṛigvedā* and later literature means illusion, magic, fraud and deception that misleads and creates disorder, thus is contrary to reality, laws and rules that establish order, predictability and harmony. Paul Horsch suggests, *Ṛita* and *Dhārma* are parallel concepts; the former being a cosmic principle, the latter being of moral social sphere. *Maya* and *dhārma* are also analogous concepts, the former being that which corrupts law and moral life, the latter being that which strengthens law and moral life (cited in Kovacs 2012, 33).

Contextualizing and Understanding the Concept of *Dhārma*

There are three sources and means to discover *dhārma* in *Hindu* philosophy. These, according to Paul Hacker, are: first, learning historical knowledge, such as *Vedās*, *Upaniṣhads*, the epics and other Sanskrit literature with the help of a teacher. Second, observing the behaviour and example of good people. The third source applies when neither one's education nor exemplary conduct is known. In this case, *atmatusti* is the source of *dhārma* in *Hindu* philosophy, that is, the good person reflects and follows what satisfies his heart, his own inner feeling.

The concept *dhārma* is associated with Indian culture since time immemorial. Most Indian languages have this word as is or at least have the concept. *Dhārma* is the universal principle that sustains and supports everything. It is the mechanism of nature. It is a universal virtue. It is truth in action and the sustainable growth. Depending on the context, *dhārma* can mean one of the following: 'sustainability', 'support', 'law', 'justice', 'rule', 'principle', 'duty', 'value system', 'virtue', 'way of life' or 'state'.

The idea of *dhārma* is an affirmation that there are no absolute truths in the human world. There are only transient, relative truths. And since they are relative, they have to be understood in the context of a bigger canvas. *Dhārma* does not impose anything on us. All it requires us to do is to ask ourselves a simple question: 'Is this action of mine sustainable?' By using the word 'sustainable', we automatically include the world at large. After all, I, as an individual, can sustain only as long as the world around me is sustained. If my family is unwell, how can I be healthy? If my friends are depressed, how can I be happy? If my workplace is filthy, how can I be clean? Therefore, we ask ourselves if our present action will be sustainable in the long run, not just for us but for everyone concerned. When we put our actions through this filter, we automatically tend to become more natural—we become more honest, compassionate, clean and gentle. After all, nature is the best example for sustainability. If humans do not interfere, nature expresses itself so beautifully, for it is a self-sustaining organism. Violating *dhārma* is like chopping off the branch of a tree on which we are sitting. It is like poisoning a well from which we drink water. One way to understand *dhārma* is to observe what we expect from others. Do we expect others to be honest? Or would we rather have people tell us lies? Do we expect people to be friendly? Or would we rather have them be hostile? Ideally, we should behave with others in a way that we would expect them to behave.

Dhārma in contradiction to general opinion does not mean religion nor it supports any, but it is a whole body of rules and believes including in itself the religious rights, rules of conduct and duties. Here, when we talk about religious rights or duties, it does not prefer anyone over the other but describes it for all religions. *Dhārma* is founded on the revelation which is conducive to the welfare of the society, ordained by the great *Vedās*. *Dhārma* is primarily based on the *Vedās*, has many indices, such as *Sruti*, *Smṛiti* and moral laws (sadachar), and governed the lives of people in the ancient time. *Dhārma* was a duty-based legal system, that is, every individual owed a duty towards other members of the society, as Duguit says:

> The only right which any man can possess is the right to do his duty and his theory of Social Solidarity states that even the sovereign or the state does not stand in any special position or privilege and its existence is justified only so long as it fulfils its duty. (Cited in Rathore 2015, 6)

The elaborate and duty-bound *dhārma* therefore is in direct contrast to the present-day legal system which specifies rights rather than the duties. According to the authoritative book, *History of Dharmaśāstra*, in the hymns of the *Ṛigvedā*, the word *dhārma* appears many times. *Dhārma*, in the ancient texts, also takes a ritual meaning. The ritual is connected to the cosmic, and *dharmani* is equated to ceremonial devotion to the principles that used to create order from disorder, the world from chaos. The ritual and cosmic sense of *dhārma* that link the current world to mythical universe, the concept extends to ethical-social sense that links human beings to each other and to other life forms. It is here that *dhārma* as a concept of law emerges in ancient *Hindu Śāstras* (Kovacs 2012, 30). However, the ideas overlapping to *dhārma* are also found in other ancient cultures, such as Chinese *Tao*, Egyptian *Maat* and Sumerian *Me* (Kovacs 2012, 32).

Dhārma and *Hindu* World View

Dhārma in ancient India was an organizing principle that applies to human beings in solitude, in their interaction with other human beings and nature as well as between inanimate objects, to all of cosmos and its parts. It refers to the order and customs which make life and universe possible, and includes behaviours, rituals, rules that govern society and ethics. *Hindu dhārma* includes the religious duties, moral rights and duties of each individual as well as behaviours that enable social order, right conduct and those that are virtuous. According to Van Buitenen,

> *Dhārma* is that which all existing beings must accept and respect to sustain harmony and order in the world. It is neither the act nor the result, but the natural laws that guide the act and create the result to prevent chaos in the world. It is innate characteristic that makes the being what it is. It is, the pursuit and execution of one's nature and true calling, thus playing one's role in cosmic concert. (Van Buitenen 1957, 36)

In *Hindu* philosophy, it is the *dhārma* of the bee to make honey, of cow to give milk, of sun to radiate sunshine, of river to flow and so on. In terms of humanity, *dhārma* is the need for, the effect of and essence of service and inter-connectedness of all life (Shivananda 1997, 2).

The notion of *dhārma* as duty or propriety is found in India's ancient legal and religious texts. In *Hindu* philosophy, justice, social harmony and happiness require that people live per *dhārma*. The

Dharmaśāstra is a record of these guidelines and rules. The available evidence suggest that ancient India once had a large collection of *dhārma*-related literature (*Sūtras, Śāstras*); four of the *Sūtras* still survive and these are now referred to as *Dharmasūtras.* Along with laws of Manu in *Dharmasūtras*, exist parallel and different compendium of laws, such as the laws of *Nārada* and other ancient scholars. These *Dharmasūtras* include instructions on education of the young, their rites of passage, customs, religious rites and rituals, marital rights and obligations, death and ancestral rites, laws and administration of justice, crimes, punishments, rules and types of evidence, duties of a king as well as morality.

The *Sanatana Dhārma*

In its original and purest form, *Hindu dhārma* is *sanatana dhārma*, loosely translated as 'eternal truth' or 'timeless religion' or 'eternal way of life' or 'timeless ethic.' It is drawn from nature and thus unrestricted by space-time constraints. However, in the several applications of *sanatana dhārma*, we adopt specific spatio-temporal frames. The word *sanatana* symbolizes eternity. From linguistic and cultural viewpoints, the word *sanatana* is a symbol of an unbiased, non-dogmatic and universal spirit. Its spirit can be loosely communicated in English with words, such as 'global ethic', 'righteousness', 'way of life' and so on. All these words put together signify the sustained implications of *sanatana dhārma*. The term 'Indian culture' is a reasonable approximation to *sanatana dhārma*.

This *Vedic* idea of 'self' constitutes the very foundation of *sanatana dhārma*. The self, which is 'the same and yet not the same as the ego', is the object of ultimate value. Therefore, the self, and not the world, becomes the determinant of all *dhārma*. It is this feature that accounts for the naturalness of *sanatana dhārma* and makes its adherent amusingly independent of all societal constructs in the exercise of his religious choices. This primacy of the 'self' requires and, in fact, engenders a striking societal imperative—liberty. Naturalness expresses itself through liberty and liberty nurtures naturalness. All reformations within *sanatana dhārma* have had this idea for their pivot. In the words of Vivekananda,

> Liberty is our natural right to be allowed to use our own body, intelligence, or wealth according to our will, without doing any harm to others. It is freedom in every way, i.e., advance towards *Mukti* (liberation) is the worthiest gain of man. To advance towards freedom—physical, mental and spiritual—and help others to do so, is the supreme prize of man. Those social rules which stand in the way of the unfoldment of this freedom are injurious, and steps should be taken to destroy them speedily. Those institutions should be encouraged by which men advance in the path of freedom. (Vivekananda 1952, 128)

Other than self and liberty, the other ingredients of *sanatana dhārma* are discussed in the following paragraphs.

Consciousness: Our perception of the world at different levels depends on us; the process of understanding depends on our mental and physical faculties. Thus, our every enquiry in any field of our choice invariably presumes the self-evident existence of ourselves and proceeds from there on.

Can we question our own existence? If so, it stands to reason that even such questions will be the product of our own existence. Therefore, our existence—irrespective of its kind—is eternal as far as we are concerned. None of the differences pertaining to natural or human-made divisions, such as gender, race, age, nationality or economic–social–cultural diversities, are felt in this state. It is a state of complete fulfilment. The *Upanișhads* start their self-enquiry with this analysis.

Purușārthas: In deep sleep, there is no possibility for desires to arise. But in the dream and wakeful states, there is a great play of desires and dissolutions, proposals and disposals, and agreements and disagreements. Desire is the starting point of our individuality, or rather the feeling of our existence and identity. Desires drive us to action, which is essential to fulfil them. Desire stems from insufficiency because it is the incompleteness within us that drives us to obtain something. In chemistry, unsaturated elements in terms of the number of electrons in their outermost orbit become chemically reactive and try hard to become saturated. This is the concept of valence of atoms. Similarly, our desires, according to their valences, trigger action.

According to traditional wisdom, this sequence of incompleteness leading to desire eventually ending in activity is termed as the chain of *avidya* (ignorance), *kāma* (desire) and *karma* (action). Those who do not feel this incompleteness will not get caught in this downwards spiral. In the idiom of economics, desire leading to activity can be understood as demand leading to supply. In the long-run, supply can never catch up with demand because the human mind always harbours desires and demand is not constrained by materialistic limitations. This is not the case with supply.

Typically, our desires get fulfilled in the material world and hence their existence is spatio-temporal in nature. Desire, which is psychological in origin and physical in manifestation, always has an upper hand over the things which try to satisfy it because the agencies which try to meet with the desire are constrained by matter, energy, space and time. There will always be an acute shortage of supply against perpetual demand. We are aware that today we witness the rapid depletion of natural resources at one end and an unlimited, ruthless world of desires constantly escalating at the other end.

In *sanatana dhārma*, the idea of demand and supply is conceived as *kāma* and *ārtha*. *Kāma* refers to desires and *ārtha* refers to the means of satisfying desire. If desire goes on a rampage in a blind quest for gratification, the world will come to a halt in seconds. This does not happen because of the compromise—willing or unwilling—that we have made within and among ourselves. We agree to abide by the rules that we have ourselves set for the smooth functioning of our societies. This compromise evolves naturally because without it, our own existence is threatened. There is no doubt that such a compromise will not be pleasing to everyone; it is always the second-best choice in any situation (the best being what is solely convenient to us). The mode of implementation of this compromise will differ according to the frames of time, space and mind set. If this compromise is enforced from outside, it becomes a rule or an order. When it is realized from within, it becomes responsibility and awareness. *Sanatana dhārma* calls this compromise, which is both a rule and a realization, as *dhārma*.

These three concepts—*kāma*, *ārtha* and *dhārma*—are termed *trivarga* (the group of three) and we may realize them in the physical world. The fourth concept, *mokșa* (loosely translated as 'liberation', 'salvation', 'release', 'bliss', etc.) is termed *apavarga* (the separate group) and is treated separately from the other three since we have to annihilate desires and transcend the physical world in order to realize it. *Mokșa* refers to liberation from the triad of demand, supply and compromise.

The scriptures recommend, first of all, an efficient management of *kāma*/demand by using *ārtha* supply by adhering strictly to *dhārma*/compromise. This leads to a well-rounded life with its share of work and pleasure, neither losing calmness nor becoming stoic. By doing this, we would have prepared the ground for *mokșa*. These four core concepts—*dhārma*, *ārtha*, *kāma*, *mokșa*—are together called the *purușārthas*. In this context, the word *purusha* means 'that which dwells in the body' or 'the self' and *ārtha* refers to 'the means' to understand the self. This wonderful conception of *puruṣārthas* retains relevance across time and place and transcends gender, race, nationality, religion and political ideology or identity.

Classification of *Dhārma*

Dhārma is divided into two groups: *samanyadhārma* (general or universal principles) and *visheshadhārma* (special or particular principles). *Samanyadhārma* includes all basic values which do not change with space and time. They are applicable irrespective of distinctions of gender, race, caste, creed, occupation, nationality and so on. They comprise what we would call human values today—truth, non-violence, non-avariciousness, purity of thought, speech and action, self-control, empathy, forgiveness and so on. The sage-seer 'Manu' defines *dhārma* as having 10 features: courage, forbearance, self-control, abstinence from stealing, cleanliness, control over senses, power of discernment, self-knowledge, integrity and freedom from anger (cited in Jha 1920: *Manusmṛiti* Verse 7.92).

Visheshadhārmas are spatio-temporal in the sense that they are relevant only for a particular time and place. Some of the *visheshadhārmas* are *āśhramadhārma* (the traditional duties of individuals at different stages of life), *varṇadhārma* (the traditional duties of people of different temperaments), *rājādhārma* (duties of rulers) and *āpaddhārma* (duties and exemptions applicable during adverse situations). The specific injunctions of *visheshadhārmas* are only relevant to a particular place and time but the general notions are universally applicable. For example, the rules that were laid down for a king might not be relevant today but the idea that governance needs guidelines will remain forever. The beauty of the Indian tradition is that there has been a constant reinterpretation of these concepts to suit the changing contexts and needs of space and time. This subtle dynamism is what makes *Hindu dhārma* a very robust way of life. In its elaborated form, *dhārma* in *Hindu* philosophy is also categorized according to its nature of practicing *dhārma*. These include:

- सामान्यधर्म/*samanyadhārma* applies to everyone (e.g., being honest or being compassionate).
- राजधर्म/*rājādhārma* applies to kings and rulers (e.g., punishing the wicked and protecting the good, maintaining law and order).
- विशेषधर्म/*visheshadhārma* applies to specific groups (e.g., there are certain rules only applicable to doctors or to miners or to lawyers, and not to the generality of the population).
- आपद्धर्म/*āpaddhārma* applies only to emergencies (e.g., if there is a fire in a building, we should not take the elevator, while it is perfectly normal and safe at other times).
- मोक्षधर्म/*mokṣadhārma* applies to those on the path of liberation (e.g., a *sanyasi* sees no difference between a diamond and a stone; a diamond merchant cannot obviously have such a mindset).

Dhārma can also be classified into many subsets depending on application area and to whom or what is being discussed. For people, the following are examples of *dhārma* that typically apply for day-to-day life:

- *Vyakti dhārma*—the *dhārma* of an individual
- *Parivarika dhārma*—family *dhārma* (also called *kutumba dhārma*)
- *Samaja dhārma*—societal *dhārma*
- *Rashtra dhārma*—national *dhārma*
- *Manava dhārma*—the *dhārma* of mankind

- *Varna dhārma*—professional *dhārma*
- *Āpad dhārma*—exceptional/abnormal situational *dhārma*
- *Yuga dhārma*—*dhārma* applicable for an age
- *Āśhrama dhārma*—*dhārma* for stage of life

Irrespective of the category of *dhārma*, the essential qualification for a true adherent of *dhārma* is the constant accountability—here and now—of thought, word and deed. There is no place for a preacher who does not practice where *dhārma* is concerned. One of the words for teacher in Sanskrit is *acharya*, which means one who himself adheres to the principles that he espouses. The *acharya* is truly aware of what he is teaching. Indeed, the aspects of learning, teaching and practicing merge in one who is a true *acharya*.

In this regard, *sanatana dhārma* upholds the actions of people who are selfless and self-realized with good intentions even if their chosen means is not 'moral' by textbook definition. There is a nice episode in the *Karna Parva* of the *Mahābhārata* where *Arjuna* and *Yudhiṣṭhira* are having a heated argument with regard to maintaining their oaths. *Krishna* pacifies them by giving them an exposition on the nature of truth and declares—"यत् भूतहितमत्यन्तम् तत् सत्यमिति धारणा" (truth is that which is good for all beings, that which is good at the universal level).

Rta, *Rna* and *Dhārma*

The word *Rta* is derived from the root 'ऋ', which means dynamism, vibrancy, seasoning and a sense of belonging. In the *Vedās*, *Rta* is often held supreme and the predecessor to *dhārma* and is the original *Ṛigvedic* concept which refers to the principle of natural order which regulates and coordinates the operation of the universe and everything within it. *Rta* is described as that which is ultimately responsible for the proper functioning of the natural, moral and sacrificial orders. In *Ṛigvedā*, *Rta* appears as many as 390 times. *Rta* has been characterized as 'the one concept which pervades the whole of *Ṛigvedic* thought'. In the early *Ṛigvedic* era, *Rta* was abstract; slowly the universal principle started mingling with the anthropomorphic tendencies of the later *Vedic* period. In due course of time, it became associated with the actions of individual deities.

Eventually *dhārma* overshadowed *Rta* in the later *Vedic* Era. While *Rita* encompassed the ethical principles with a notion of cosmic retribution, *dhārma* was said to be a path to be followed as per the ordinances of *Rta*. Failing to follow this path meant appearance of various forms of calamity and suffering. Committing to the path of *Rta* was *dhārma*, so we can say that *dhārma* was originally conceptualized as a subordinate component of *Rta*. *Dhārma* became a very useful instrument and takes the place of *Rta* in framing religious, moral and social regulations with all discussions of metaphysical and theological ideas.

Once we realize *Rta*, the cosmic order, the value of the whole creation, we become naturally humbled and concerned. For our sustenance, the whole universe is supporting; for our existence the whole creation is toiling. Is this awareness not sufficient to infuse immense indebtedness in our hearts? Such a positive guilt of indebtedness in our sensitive minds is called as ऋण (*Rna*) in the *Vedic* language. Any human being by birth itself will carry this baggage of *Rna*. His or her basic duty is to clear off these debts without which he or she cannot become meaningful. Those who care the least for warding off these debts only breathe and never live. The way of clearing off these debts given by the *Vedās* is *dhārma*. Thus, the awareness of *Rta* leads to the realization of *Rna*, which in turn motivates a person to pursue *dhārma*, the global ethic or the righteous way of life.

Dhārma through *Yajña, Dāna* and *Tapas*

Having realized that adherence to *dhārma* is the ideal way to live, the question arises: How to practice it? The action plan of *dhārma* is given in the pedagogy of *yajña*, *dāna* and *tapas*. *Yajña* is a specific term for the *Vedic* fire ritual. In general, it refers to worship of any form. Metaphorically, *yajña* refers to 'an act of self-dedication', 'service above self' or 'respecting the divine presence'. The word *yajña* comes from the root word *Yaj*, which means 'respect', 'belongingness' and 'sharing'. Respect cannot last without a sense of belonging and this belongingness is not feasible without selfless offering. Helping the world without any expectations and sharing your prosperity with the rest is *yajña*. You will in turn be helped and enriched.

When *yajña* comes into action for the welfare of mankind that is *dāna*, or offering. The literal meaning of the word *dāna* is 'giving', 'charity' or 'offering' but the real import of the word is 'philanthropy'. While engaging in this act of giving, one must not be insecure, or have the feeling that one is losing something. This demands mental and physical preparation. The training that leads to internal and external conditioning for *dāna* and *yajña* is called *tapas*. The term *tapas* translates into 'penance', or 'austerity', but mostly refers to a single-minded focus on work. Thus, the threefold path of *yajña*, *dāna* and *tapas* leads us to *dhārma*.

Dhārma and the Nature of Self (*Sacchidānanda*)

All of us, without exception, want to be happy at all times and at all places. Happiness is our highest goal. All our suffering, struggle and effort invariably point towards the attainment of happiness. Happiness is the one point where all our diverging natures converge. The means by which one attains happiness varies from person to person. What constitutes happiness also varies similarly. In general, the source of happiness is considered to be one or more of the following: health, food, beauty, materials, money, fame, power, social status, art, travel, family, knowledge, love, etc. Needless to say, what brings happiness to one might bring misery to another. But the very nature of happiness, the value, is not divergent. Our own experience reveals that happiness is a state of completeness where no inadequacy is felt. This state of fulfilment, though lasting for a moment, is essentially the same for everyone. Leo Tolstoy starts off his novel Anna Karenina with the words: 'All happy homes are alike. But every unhappy home is unhappy in its own way. Joy has an absolute form while its opposite, sorrow, has many forms—and at a deeper level, they are all illusions' (cited in Shatavadhani 2017, 3).

This absolute state of joy is similar to the blissful experience of sound sleep. During sound sleep, all demands, desires and differences disappear. Even the maladies of the body cease to exist during that time. This suggests that joy is innate, but sorrow is externally thrust upon us. Our over-indulgence in the world brings sorrow. The happiness that we gain externally is short-lived and eventually leads to sorrow because it operates in the material world. But the bliss that we realize internally does not lead to sorrow. It is also interesting to note that sorrow cannot be generated internally, for our true state is bliss and not agony. Light, like happiness, is a positive entity whereas darkness is a negative one. Darkness does not exist as an independent entity but rather, it is the absence of light. Sorrow, like darkness, has no independent existence. It is just the absence of joy. Irrespective of our physical or mental condition, we wish to live on forever, learn everything, have everything and become fulfilled.

This desire for absolute freedom and absolute authority accelerates one's zeal for eternity. This is the quest after perfection.

Sanatana dhārma identifies this desire in a sublime way, considering this to be inbuilt in us as the very nature of our own selves. Absolute existence (*sat*), absolute awareness (*cit*) and absolute bliss (*ananda*) that are independent of external factors constitute the nature of the self (*ātman*). The very nature of *atman* is *sat–cit–ananda* (*Sacchidānanda*) which represents 'existence, consciousness and bliss' or 'truth, consciousness and bliss', is an epithet and description for the subjective experience of the ultimate, unchanging reality in *Hindu dhārma*. The pursuit of attaining *sat–cit–ananda* (*Sacchidānanda*) through materialistic paths leads invariably to corruption and annihilation. Those who seek existence, awareness and bliss from outwardly sources try to establish authority over others. They declare their own freedom at the cost of other's freedom and invariably become tyrants, blemishing humankind. *Sat–cit–ananda* is not something to 'attain' but it is something to 'realize', for it is always within.

Sanatana dhārma clearly distinguishes these two paths in the attainment of self-supremacy. It has always advocated the spiritual path, which is essentially inwardly and has shunned the path of materialism, which is always outwardly. However, we must remember that although *sanatana dhārma* takes such a firm stand, it does not take refuge in a utopia. It recognizes the materialistic and gives it its due but encourages the evolution into the spiritualistic. Materialism is an instrumental value, in that it is only a means and never an end in itself. This is why in the conception of the *puruṣārthas*, the idea is to manage demand (*kāma*) and supply (*ārtha*) by the global compromise (*dhārma*) in order to attain liberation (*mokṣa*). Materialism is inevitable but when pursued for its own sake without adherence to *dhārma* and without the larger goal of *mokṣa*, it leads to destruction of the self and the surroundings. *Mokṣa* is the ultimate value. *Ananda*, which is the very nature of *Mokṣa*, is the fundamental value. All others are secondary and instrumental values.

Hindu dhārma not only crystallized the concept of liberation but also established its instantaneousness. Liberation or salvation is not restricted to a post-death stage but can happen here and now. This brilliant conception is called *jīvanmukti*—being liberated during one's lifetime. The *Upaniṣhadic* conception of salvation is not a post-dated cheque but a demand draft. The *Hindu* idea of *jīvanmukti*, the highest ideal 'liberation' can be attained by anyone, anywhere, anytime. It is within our reach. This is a great teaching. But *Hinduism* never ignores individual accountability and sincerity in practice. It has the two opposite concepts of *papa* (sin) and *punya* (goodness, virtue). Everyone is expected to reduce their *papa* and increase their *punya*. We may explain the material implications of these two concepts using entropy, which is the measure of disorder or chaos in the universe. What recklessly adds to entropy is *papa* and what sincerely avoids entropy is *punya*.

Dhārma in *Upaniṣhads* and *Hindu* Epics

In the *Vedās* and *Upaniṣhads*, the concept of *dhārma* continues as universal principle of law, order, harmony and truth. It acts as the regulatory moral principle of the Universe. It is explained as law of righteousness and equated to *Satya* (truth). Hymn 1.4.14 of *Brihadaranyaka Upaniṣhad*, as follows:

धर्मः तस्माद्धर्मात् परं नास्त्य् अथो अबलीयान् बलीयाँसमाशँसते धर्मेण यथा राज्ञैवम् ।
यो वै स धर्मः सत्यं वै तत् तस्मात्सत्यं वदन्तमाहुर् धर्मं वदतीति धर्मं वा वदन्तँ सत्यं वदतीत्य् एतद्ध्येवैतदुभयं भवति ॥

(*Bṛihadāraṇyaka Upaniṣhad*, 1.4.14)

Nothing is higher than *dhārma*. The weak overcomes the stronger by *dhārma*, as over a king. Truly, *dhārma* is the truth (*Satya*); therefore, when a man speaks the truth, 'he speaks the *dhārma*' and vice versa. For both are one.

In the *Rāmāyaṇa*, *dhārma* is at the centre of all major events in the life of *Rama*, *Sita* and *Lakshman*. In *Rāmāyaṇa*, each episode of *Rāmāyaṇa* presents life situations and ethical questions in symbolic terms. The issue is debated by the characters, and finally the right prevails over wrong, the good over evil. For this reason, in *Hindu* epics, the good, morally upright, law-abiding king is referred to as *Dharmarājā*.

In *Mahābhārata*, the other major Indian epic, similarly, *dhārma* is central, and it is presented with symbolism and metaphors. At the end of the epic, the God *Yama*, referred to as *dhārma* in the text, is portrayed as taking the form of a dog to test the compassion of *Yudhiṣṭhira*, who is told he may not enter paradise with such an animal, but refuses to abandon his companion, for which decision he is then praised by *dhārma*. The appeal of *Mahābhārata*, like *Rāmāyaṇa*, is in its presentation of a series of moral problems and life situations, to which there are usually three answers given: one answer is of *Bhima*, which is the answer of brute force, an individual angle representing materialism, egoism and self; the second answer is of *Yudhiṣṭhira*, which is always an appeal to piety and gods, of social virtue and of tradition; the third answer is of introspective *Arjuna*, which falls between the two extremes, and who symbolically reveals the finest moral qualities of man.

In the *Mahābhārata*, *Yudhiṣṭhira* asks *Bhīṣma* to explain the meaning and scope of *dhārma*. *Bhīṣma* replies:

Tadrisho ayam anuprashno yatra dharmaha sudurlabaha
Dushkamha pralisankhyatum tatkenatra vysvasyathi
Prabhavarthaya bhutanam dharmapravachanam kritam
Yasyat prabhavasamyuktaha sa dharma iti nischayaha.

(*Mahābhārata*, *Śānti Parva*, 109-9-11)

It is most difficult to define *dhārma*. *Dhārma* has been explained to be that which helps the upliftment of living beings. Therefore, that which ensures the welfare of living beings is surely *dhārma*. The learned rishis have declared that which sustains is *dhārma*. In the *Karna Parva*, Lord *Krishna* explains *dhārma* to *Arjuna* in the following words:

Dharanat dhārma mityahu dharmo dhara-yate prajaha
Yat syad dharanasamyuktam sa dhārma iti nischayaha.

(*Mahābhārata*, *Karna Parva*, 69.58)

Dhārma sustains the society. *Dhārma* maintains the social order. *Dhārma* ensures well-being and progress of humanity. *Dhārma* is surely that which fulfils these objectives. Therefore, *dhārma* embraces every type of righteous conduct, covering every aspect of life essential for the sustenance and welfare of the individual and society. Further, it includes those rules which guide and enable those who believe in God and heaven to attain *mokṣa*.

The epics of *Hindu dhārma* are a symbolic treatise about life, virtues, customs, morals, ethics, law and other aspects of *dhārma*. It illustrates various aspects of *dhārma*, by communicating it with metaphors.

The *Śānti Parva* of *Mahābhārata*, is the 12th of the 18 books of the Indian epic *Mahābhārata*, recites the duties of the ruler, *dhārma* and good governance, as counselled by the dying *Bhīṣma*. The *Parva* includes many symbolic tales such as one about 'starving and vegetarian *Vishvamitra* stealing meat during a famine' and fables such as that of 'the fowler and pigeons'. The *Śānti Parva* also provides between a rule of truth versus a rule of rituals, declaring truth to be far superior over rituals. *Śānti Parva* has been widely studied for its treatises on jurisprudence, prosperity and success. *Śānti Parva* has three sub-*Parva* (sub-books or little books) and 366 *adhyayas* or chapters (Bhattacharya 1992, 74). The sub-*Parvas* in this book are:

1. *Rājādhārma Anusasana Parva* (This sub-book describes the duties of kings and leaders, among other things).
2. *Āpaddhārma Anusasana Parva* (This sub-book describes the rules of conduct when one faces adversity).
3. *Mokṣadhārma Parva* (This sub-book describes behaviour and rules to achieve *mokṣa* (emancipation, liberation or freedom).

Śānti Parva begins with sorrowful *Yudhiṣṭhira* lamenting the loss of human lives during the war. He announces his desire to renounce the kingdom, move into a forest as a mendicant and live in silence. He receives counsel from his family and then sages *Nārada* and *Vyāsa*, as well as *Devala*, *Devasthana* and *Kanwa*. The *Parva* includes the story of king *Janaka* and the queen of the *Videhas*, presenting the theory of true mendicant as one who does not crave for material wealth, not one who abandons material wealth for an outward show. *Arjuna* argues it is more virtuous to create and maintain virtuous wealth and do well with it, than to neither create nor have any. *Yudhiṣṭhira* challenges *Arjuna* how would he know. Sage *Vyāsa* then intervenes and offers arguments from *Vedās* that support *Arjuna's* comments, and the story of *Sankha* and *Likhita*. *Krishna* concurs with *Arjuna* and *Vyasa*, and adds his own arguments.

Śānti Parva is a treatise on duties of a king and his government, *dhārma* (laws and rules), proper governance, rights, justice and describes how these create prosperity. *Yudhiṣṭhira* becomes the king of a prosperous and peaceful kingdom, *Bhima* his heir apparent, sage *Vidura* the Prime Minister, *Sanjaya* the finance minister, *Arjuna* the defence and justice minister, and *Dhaumya* is appointed as one responsible to service priests and counsels to the king. This book also includes a treatise on yoga as recited by *Krishna* (Gualtherus and Mess 1986, 36).

The *Parva* dedicates over 100 chapters on duties of a king and rules of proper governance. A prosperous kingdom must be guided by truth and justice. Chapter 58 of *Śānti Parva* suggests the duty of a ruler and his cabinet is to enable people to be happy, pursue truth and act sincerely. Chapter 88 recommends the king to tax without injuring the ability or capacity of those who create wealth, just like bees harvest honey from flower, keepers of cow draw milk without starving the calf or hurting the cow; those who cannot bear the burden of taxes, should not be taxed. Chapter 267 suggests the judicial staff to reflect before sentencing, only sentence punishment that is proportionate to the crime, avoid harsh and capital punishments and never punish the innocent relatives of a criminal for the crime.

Several chapters, such as 15 and 90 of the *Parva*, claim the proper function of a ruler is to rule according to *dhārma*; he should lead a simple life and he should not use his power to enjoy the luxuries of life. *Śānti Parva* defines *dhārma* not in terms of rituals or any religious precepts, but in terms of that which increases *satya* (truth), *ahimsa* (non-violence), *asteya* (non-stealing of property created by another), *shoucham* (purity) and *dāma* (restraint). Chapter 109 of *Śānti Parva* asserts rulers have a *dhārma* (duty, responsibility) to help the upliftment of all living beings. The best law, claims *Śānti Parva*, is one that enhances the welfare of all living beings, without injuring any specific group (Gualtherus and Mess 1986, 36).

Dhārma According to *Vatsyayana* and *Patanjali*

The 4th century *Hindu* scholar *Vātsyāyana* explained *dhārma* by contrasting it with *Adhārma*. *Vātsyāyana* suggested that *dhārma* is not merely in one's actions, but also in words one speaks or writes, and in thought. According to *Vātsyāyana*:

- *Adhārma* of body: *Himsa* (violence), *steya* (steal, theft), *pratisiddhamaithuna* (sexual indulgence with someone other than one's partner).
- *Dhārma* of body: *Dāna* (charity), *paritrana* (succor of the distressed) and *paricarana* (rendering service to others).
- *Adhārma* from words one speaks or writes: *Mithya* (falsehood), *parusa* (caustic talk), *sucana* (calumny) and *asambaddha* (absurd talk).
- *Dhārma* from words one speaks or writes: *Satya* (truth and facts), *hitavacana* (talking with good intention), *priyavacana* (gentle, kind talk) and *svadhyaya* (self-study).
- *Adhārma* of mind: *Paradroha* (ill will to anyone), *paradravyabhipsa* (covetousness) and *nastikya* (denial of the existence of morals and religiosity).
- *Dhārma* of mind: *Daya* (compassion), *asprha* (disinterestedness) and *sraddha* (faith in others).

In the *Yoga* system, the *dhārma* is real. *Dhārma* is part of yoga, suggests *Patanjali*; the elements of *Hindu dhārma* are the attributes, qualities and aspects of *yoga*. *Patanjali* explained *dhārma* in two categories: *yama* (restraints) and *niyama* (observances). The five *yama*, according to *Patanjali*, are: abstain from injury to all living creatures, abstain from falsehood, abstain from unauthorized appropriation of things-of-value from another, abstain from coveting or sexually cheating on your partner and abstain from expecting or accepting gifts from others. The five *yama* apply in action, speech and mind. In explaining *yama*, *Patanjali* clarifies that certain professions and situations may require qualification in conduct. For example, a fisherman must injure a fish, but he must attempt to do this with least trauma to fish and the fisherman must try to injure no other creature during fishing.

The five *niyama* (observances) are cleanliness by eating pure food and removing impure thoughts (such as arrogance or jealousy or pride), contentment in one's means, meditation and silent reflection regardless of circumstances one faces, study and pursuit of historic knowledge and devotion of all actions to the Supreme Teacher to achieve perfection of concentration.

Conclusion

In conclusion, it could be said that it is the *dhārma* of the wind to blow, the *dhārma* of the sun to heat up the world, the *dhārma* of the ice to freeze and melt, the *dhārma* of fire to burn. It is the *dhārma* of the plants to give out oxygen, and the *dhārma* of the animals to give out carbon dioxide. Therefore, behind the delicate workings and interrelations between the various cosmic phenomena, there is an order, an intelligently engineered and organized system, a set of laws that seem to be at work governing the great forces and powers (*Shakti*) at play behind these laws. This is *dhārma* as the cosmic order that includes many dynamic sub-orders, each represented by powers and forces of great intensity and magnitude. Each governed by their own *dhārma* or internal law of being and interacting upon one another, within the boundaries of that law, sustaining, maintaining and upholding all things material and phenomenal in this universe.

Individuals are fallible and prone to fall to the passions of greed, desire, jealousy and anger that may lay hold of the mind and give rise to all forms of social disturbance. To live in peace in accordance to *dhārma*, individuals must learn to gain a free range of expression and experience while at the same time, know not to transgress the freedom and liberty of others. It is the prescriptions and proscriptions that give rise to harmony, workability and stability in any society. Every society has recognized the need for these as seen in religions that have created commandments and injunctions, backed by threats of extraordinary punishments for transgression in the present life and afterlife. *Dhārma* has indeed been given an elevated place in the consciousness, enshrined through numerous stories of *Purāṇas*, epics and tales in order to make it accessible to all, ranging from the uneducated villager to the powerful king, from the *ṛiṣhi* to the merchant, irrespective of their station and role in society. This ensures that *dhārma*, the law of right living and conduct, is enshrined and passed on from father to son, from mother to daughter—from generation to generation.

Dhārma includes all possible values, and not any one specific set of values, defined by any one individual or religious tradition, at a historical point of time. *Dhārma* extends itself into the specific ways of life, our value systems and attitudes. When an individual conforms to a certain universal matrix of behavioural norms, (s)he contributes in the sustenance, maintenance and the upliftment of societal order and thus the society itself. On the other hand, if the universal norms are transgressed, then a chain of actions and reactions takes place, which creates disorder. For example, the abused child becomes an abuser himself, or the hurt individual hurts another.

When the parents perform their duties or discharge their responsibilities towards their children that naturally sustains and uplifts their children. And when children perform their duties towards their parents, their actions sustain and uplift the parents. When there is a break in the discharge of the responsibilities of a parent towards a child, there is set in motion, a great cycle of disharmony and society itself becomes unbalanced in some way. Similarly, when the citizens perform their duties or discharge their responsibilities (i.e., pay their taxes, do not break laws), this sustains the well-being of the society (and the State), and when the state discharges its responsibilities towards its citizens, that upholds, sustains and uplifts its citizens.

Ordinary human endeavours involve the pursuit of *ārtha* and *kāma*—which can be loosely translated as security and pleasure, respectively. In fact, for most people, life is confined to the pursuit of *ārtha* and *kāma*. It is when they awaken to a wider possibility—that of subordinating personal interests in favour of ensuring the well-being of others—whether those others are within the family, neighbourhood, village, city or state, or a specific community or even the country or the world—their lives take on a wider dimension. A commitment to pursue the greater good, clearly sustains, maintains, upholds and uplifts the prevailing social order, especially the community that is the beneficiary. *Dhārma* is therefore inherent to any community service—whether it is the building of a school or running a hospital or an orphanage, or creating a philanthropic foundation or running a shelter for the homeless.

Each human being is endowed with specific qualities and gifts. Ultimately, a human being uplifts himself, sustains and upholds his spirit, when he or she truly fully develops and expresses his or her unique gifts in the service of humanity. When society has created the conditions of harmony and stability, the pre-conditions of progress are created. Such a society flowers naturally and easily, and there is an outburst of human creativity—and all manner of creative expression is found to arise. In short periods of time, such societies have brought forth great advances in art, architecture, science and technology, philosophy and thought, literature and drama, and all other fields of human development.

Indian civilization has always conceived of humanity's progress in spiritual terms, and given it a pre-eminent significance. It is in the context of spiritual progress, that the notion of *dhārma* attains its fullest import. The *Ṛigvedā* was realized and composed on the banks of the *Saraswati* River many millennia ago. It describes the purpose of human life succinctly in the phrase *Atmano mokshartham jagat hitaya cha* which means 'the pursuit of *mokṣa* while keeping in view the welfare of the world' which is the real *dhārma*. From a spiritual context, the ultimate fulfilment of a human life arises in the pursuit and attainment of *dhārma* that is the welfare of the world *or Vasudhaiva Kutumbakam.*

Summary

Dhārma is the cosmic order which sustains the entire universe which includes the physical laws that govern the motion of stars, suns, planets, satellites, asteroids and other physical bodies including human life. *Dhārma* encompasses the moral and social order where it sustains society, maintains the social order and ensures well-being and progress of humanity. It includes the ethical behaviour which preaches the Golden rule 'do unto others as others would do unto you', and therefore the set of all possible values, such as speaking the truth, being kind, speaking pleasant words, being respectful, demonstrating reverence towards the earth and the natural resources etc. includes *dhārma*. *Dhārma* can be said to be expressed in the duties and responsibilities of an individual or a community that ensures the harmony and balance in society as a whole, in terms of its interrelations and its dependencies. So, *dhārma* upholds, sustains and uplifts all the various constituents of this universe, who are woven together in a common interdependent existence. When the society discharges its duties and responsibilities towards the earth and all its inhabitants, that is, plants and animals, then the earth itself is upheld, sustained and uplifted. When humanity consumes the resources of the earth indiscriminately, then that can unsettle the balance and harmony in this world contributing *adhārma* which consequence disaster.

Dhārmic life is a life of self-less service, of sacrifice and contribution. It is the lifestyle that has been held in India from time immemorial as an ideal life, a life worth emulating and a life that one aspires towards. Making a difference in society at large, somehow honours and fulfils the human spirit and brings to life the true possibility and potential of human existence. Every *Purāṇa* thus, extols *dhārma and dhārmic* life. In the *Rāmāyaṇa*, this idea is personified in Lord *Rāma* who is widely called *vigrahavaan dhārma*—the embodiment of *dhārma.*

The meaning of *dhārma* also involves self-expression. Man must grow to his full potential, in conformity with his own inner law of being—his *Svadāhrma*. Such self-actualization is consistent with the complete unfoldment of the specific gifts, talents and qualities that one is blessed with and results in the true fulfilment of one's life's potential as well as bestows these special gifts and talents to those surrounding such a person. This flowering of a human being is also *Dhārma*. It possess developing of an inner potential and possibility to its full height and range of expression, unfolding of human genius consistent with the individual's own inner law of being and action, and this manifestation in physical reality, the power of the human mind, thought, feeling and action.

Dhārma as a means for *mokṣa*, the highest goal of human life according to ancient Indian *Hindu* philosophy. A life that keeps in full view the spiritual end of human life and harmonizes one's everyday life with the progression towards that end. *Dhārma* becomes the means to attain a spiritual end of life. Thus, *dhārma* is that which sustains, upholds and uplifts the spiritual progress of humanity, both individually and as a collective. Without a complete understanding of the essentially spiritual journey that human beings are on, without a recognition of the nature of the inner reality of the individual, and the relationship with the universe, and without establishing a notion of God as the all-pervasive reality of this universe, the word *dhārma* cannot be fully understood.

Points for Discussion

1. Discuss the concept of *dhārma* as the moral law of the cosmos.
2. Examine the nature of *dhārma* as described in ancient Indian *Śhāstras* and epics.
3. How *dhārma* can be achieved through *dāna* and *tapas?*
4. Critically analyse how the concept of *dhārma* is interrelated to the concept of *Rta* and *Rna*.
5. Discuss the concept of *dhārma* as described by *Vatsyayana* and *Patanjali?*
6. What according to you is the ultimate goal of *dhārma* and how can it be achieved?
7. Elaborate the phrase *vasudhaiva kutumbakam*.
8. What do you mean by *Sacchidānanda*? How the concept *dhārma* is related to it?
9. Write an essay on *sanatana dhārma* and '*Hindu* world view'.

Glossary

Ārtha: Wealth, motive and cause. It refers to the material objectives and accomplishments of a person. One of the four *puruṣārthas*.

Āśhrama: The four stages of human life. Human life is divided into *brahmacarya, gṛhasta, vānaprastha* and *sanyāsa*—each stage aims at the development of the individual (*Āśhrama* can also refer to a physical place where a guru imparts spiritual education).

Brahmacharya: Following the path of *Brāhmaṇa*; leading a life of purity and not letting the mind wander around trivial things. One of the four *āśhramas*.

Dāna: Charity and philanthropy.

Dhārma: That which sustains everything; harmony in the universe that sustains greater good. By definition, *dhārma* protects one who protects it. Depending on the context, *dhārma* can mean one or more of: virtue, moral principle, law, righteousness, duty, path, state, etc. One of the four *puruṣārthas*.

Dharmaśāstras: Treatises on *dhārma* include works like *Manusmṛiti, Yājñavalkyasmṛiti, Āpastamba Dhārma Sūtra and Gautama Dhārma Sūtra.*

Jīvanmukti: Attaining *mokṣa* during one's lifetime. To escape the vicious cycle of birth, death and rebirth is one of the ultimate goals of an individual. Typically, one attains *mokṣa* after death but a *jīvanmukta* attains this while alive.

Kāma: Desire, pleasure and passion. It refers to the emotional objectives and accomplishments of a person. One of the four *puruṣārthas*.

Mokṣa: Liberation and salvation. To escape the vicious cycle of birth, death and rebirth. *Mokṣa* is one of the loftiest goals of human life. One of the four *puruṣārthas*.

Purāṇa: Old episodes, stories and legends. There are 18 *purāṇas*.

Puruṣārtha: The four goals or objectives of life: *dhārma* (duty, principle and law), *ārtha* (wealth, motive and cause), *kāma* (desire, pleasure and passion) and *mokṣa* (liberation, salvation and release).

Rta: Cosmic order in the universe, divine law governing the universe and gnostic order inherent in the universe.

Ṛiṣhi: Seer, poet-sage and visionary. The *Vedās* were composed by *ṛiṣhis* (masc.) and *ṛṣikās* (fem.) who were seers as well as poets/singers.

Sanātana Dhārma: Timeless *dhārma*, eternal principle, *Hinduism*, the Indian way of life.

Satya: Truth, integrity, honesty in thought, speech and deed, authenticity, virtue and objectivity.

Tapas: Austerity, penance and single-minded focus on work.

Vedā: Foremost revealed scriptures in *Hinduism*. There are four *Vedās*: *Ṛigvedā, Yajurvedā, Sāmavedā* and *Atharvavedā*. Every *Hindu* ceremony from birth to death and beyond is drawn from the *Vedās*. The word *Vedā* literally means 'to know', so the term can apply to any branch of knowledge.

Yajña: The *Vedic* fire ritual. In general, it refers to worship of any form. Metaphorically, *yajña* can also refer to 'an act of self-dedication', 'service above self' or 'respecting the divine presence'.

Yoga: Form of physical and mental discipline. In a broader sense, *yoga* can mean 'union with the Supreme', 'contemplation', 'oneness of body and mind', 'path' or 'the path of action'. It is one of the six schools of Indian philosophy.

References

Bhattacharya, A. N. 1992. *Dharma, Adharma & morality in Mahabharata*. Delhi: S. S. Publications.

Brihadaranyaka Upanishad (1.3.28) Chapter -1, Brahman-3 Verse -28.

Brihadaranyaka Upanishad (1.4.14) Chapter -1, Brahman-4 Verse -14.

Gualtherus, G., and H. Mess. 1986. *Dharma and Society*. Delhi: Gian Publishing House.

Jha, Ganganatha. 1920. Manusmriti with the Commentary of Medhatithi Verse 7.92, Online Edition. https://www.wisdomlib.org/hinduism/book/manusmriti-with-the-commentary-of-medhatithi/d/doc145595.html

Kovacs, Ivan. 2012. The Concept of Dharma and its Significance in Mahabharata. *The Esoteric Quarterly*, Online Edition. http://www.esotericquarterly.com/issues/EQ08/EQ0801/EQ080112-Kovacs.pdf

Rathore, Shantanu. 2015. Dharma and Law. *Academike*, Online Edition. https://www.lawctopus.com/academike/dharma-and-law/

Sharma, Dharmanand. 2003. '*Dharma* as the Philosophy of India: Some Implications for a New Theory of Morality and Social Life.' *Punjab University Research Journal*, Online Edition. http://purja.puchd.ac.in/articlepdf/dharmanand.pdf

Shatavadhani, R. Ganesh. 2017. *Foundations of Sanatana Dharma*, translated from the original Kannada by K. B. S. Ramachandra, published in The Hinduism Series: Sanatana Dharma from Scratch 2 *Preksa. A Journal of Culture and Philosophy*, Online. https://www.prekshaa.in/hinduism-series-sanatana-dharma-scratch-2

Shivananda, Sri Swami. (1997). *All About Hinduism*. Uttar Pradesh: The Divine Life Society Publishers.

The Mahābhārata. *The Mahabharata of Krishna-DwaipayanaVyasa*, Karna Parva, 69.58. Calcutta: South Asian Books.

Van Buitenen, J. A. B. 1957. 'Dharma and Moksha.' *Philosophy East and West*, Vol. VII (1–2): 33–40.

Vivekananda, Swami. 1952. *The Complete Works of Swami Vivekananda*, Vol. 8, pp. ii. 128. Calcutta. https://www.amazon.in/Complete-Works-Swami-Vivekananda/dp/1296628663/ref=tmm_hrd_title_0?_encoding=UTF8&qid=&sr=.

Further Readings

Sanatana Dharma: An Advanced Text Book of Hindu Religion and Ethics. Varanasi: Central Hindu College, Benaras. https://www.amazon.in/Sanatana-Dharma-Advanced-Religion Ethics/dp/1165864975/ref=sr_1_2?qid=1580642798&refinements=p_27%3AHindu+College+Central+Hindu+College&s=books&sr=1-2

Brereton, Joel P. 2004. Dharman in the Ṛigveda. December. *Journal of Indian Philosophy* 32(5–6): 449–89.

Ganguli, Kisari Mohan. 1883. *The Mahabharata of Krishna-DwaipayanaVyasa*, Book 3 (Vana Parva), 600–13. Calcutta: South Asian Books

Horsch, Paul. 2004. Translated by Jarrod Whitaker, 'From Creation Myth to World Law: The Early History of Dharma.' *Journal of Indian Philosophy* 32: 423–48. https://www.hinduwebsite.com/hinduism/essays/dharma.asp

Ingalls Daniel, H. H. 1957. Dharma and Moksa, *Philosophy East and West* 7(1/2): 41–8.
Jain, Vijay K. 2012. *Acharya Amritchandra's Purushartha Siddhyupaya*. Dehradun: Vikalp Printers.
Koller, J. M. 1972. Dharma: An Expression of Universal Order. *Philosophy East and West* 22(2): 136–42.
Manusmṛti. http://www.hinduonline.co/vedicreserve/smriti/14Manu_Smriti.pdf
Murthy, K. Krishna. 1966. 'Dharma—Its Etymology.' *The Tibet Journal* XXI(1): 84–7.
Olivelle, Patrick. 2009. *Dharma: Studies in Its Semantic, Cultural and Religious History*. Delhi: MLBD.
Radhakrishna, S. 1995. *The Principal Upaniṣads*. London: George Allen & Unwin.

2
CHAPTER

Ancient India: Conception and Forms of Community

Praveen Kumar

CHAPTER OUTLINE

- Introduction
- Historical Evolution of the Concept of Community
- Forms and Structures of Community in the Prehistoric India
- The *Vedic* Period and Later: Communities, Their Types and Features
- Changing Forms of Community: From Class to Caste
- The Buddhist *Saṅgha*
- The Trading Community
- Conclusion
- Summary
- Points for Discussion

THEN was not non-existent nor existent: there was no realm of air, no sky beyond it. What covered in, and where? and what gave shelter? Was water there, unfathomed depth of water? Death was not then, nor was there aught immortal: no sign was there, the day's and night's divider. That One Thing, breathless, breathed by its own nature: apart from it was nothing whatsoever.

—*Ṛigvedā (Book 10. Hymn CXXIX. Tr. by T. H. Griffith)*

Reader's Guide

'Community' is a term that we come across quite often. In academic literature and in every day-to-day conversation, the term is used and heard frequently. We are familiar with terms like religious community, primitive community, students' community, farmers' community, teachers' community, the village community, the urban community, the community of foreigners, national community, linguistic community, Indian community and international community among others. While we may use the word 'community' to refer to an aggregation which may have a distinct identity of its own in terms of its origin, habits and practices, the term is also required to be understood with respect to the context in which it is being used and also with reference to its evolutionary process. To understand the meaning of the term in terms of its origin is important because it gives us some reference point to understand the people, their practices and even sometimes their behaviour. The term cannot be understood in isolation and detached from history. In this light it is important to understand how this term could be related to certain periods in history. This chapter is an endeavour to explain some of the forms and meanings of the term in ancient Indian history.

Introduction

The term community in ancient India can be understood with reference to the group of people, who primarily shared a 'common pursuit'. In the later phase of its evolution, this meaning is required to be understood with reference to *Hinduism*. This is applicable to most of the period of ancient India for which we have literary and other source materials. Although this may fall short of giving a precise description, it is the closest we can come in order to make a sense of community among the ancient Indian people. Applicable to the earliest forms that we can characterize as community, there are specific features that could be identified to make out the underlying structures of the community of people in ancient India. These features may vary when we endeavour to understand a community of hunter-gatherers, for instance, to the understanding of community during the *Vedic* period. However, at the larger level, one common culture could be identified to make sense of the Indian community. A stage-wise development in some chronological order is difficult to make out when we try to understand the structure of community among the ancient Indian people. This is because some of the community features may be found to be common in two different phases of the history in ancient India. On the other hand, this would also be seen that certain features may exist in parallel in two communities, completely different in other aspects.

The purpose of this chapter is to bring out the way in which community(ies) might have been constituted in ancient India. In its initial phase of evolution, the understanding of community may defy the sociological definition that a community may refer to a 'particularly constituted set of social relationships based on something that the participants have in common usually a common sense of identity' (Marshall 1998, 97). This is because of the dynamism that we can attach to the formation of communities and possibly the horizontal and vertical arrangements that can be identified in the ways communities constituted themselves in ancient India. Also, the process of community construction was closely associated with the evolution of a common culture that provided a unifying bond at the larger geographical level, what could be understood as something that culturally constituted India. Religion during the *Vedic* period and onwards, of course, was the dominant feature in this respect. Thus, when it comes to making sense of community based on some form of common consciousness that made Indian community distinct from the outside world, the reference point was *Hinduism*. It is the latter that becomes the rallying point of community structures within and to make sense of the larger Indian community different from and distinct to the outside world.

Historical Evolution of the Concept of Community

The existence of human beings is unthinkable independent of the community, which he or she may belong to. In its earliest form, community could have found its expression in the form of kinship groups. With the settled life and adoption of agriculture the kinship groups gave way to larger clans and they became reference points for the identification and differentiation of community, one from the other. Sociologists believe that religion might have existed in the form of ancestral worship in its earliest form. This also might have helped people to identify themselves as a community different from others. As clans expanded, and different tribes came to stay together, nature worship became the predominant mode of religious life. In Indian context, with the coming of the *Vedic* age, *Hinduism* became the defining feature of community life, where social structures came to be influenced by religious values. This also brought in certain form of stratification in the society, as the size of community expanded. However, religion remained the predominant feature of the larger community, within which smaller and stratified community existed, as per the predominant religious values in the society. The German philosopher Otto von Gierke was apt to highlight that 'man owes what he is to union with his fellow men' (Gierke 2002, 2).[1]

Understanding of community in its evolutionary form becomes relevant in the present context as some sociologists have understood that 'community is currently under transition as a result of important social, cultural and political development'.[2] Among the Western literature one finds the impression that the term has gained prevalence in present times due to the insecure conditions of modernity. Appreciation for the concept is also to be located in the context of rise of the 'global world'.

> Traditionally, communities have been based on ethnicity, religion, class or politics; they may be large or small; 'thick' or 'thin' attachments may underlie them; they may be locally based and globally organized; affirmative or subversive in relation to the established order; they may be traditional, modern and even postmodern; reactionary or progressive. (Delanty 2003, 2)

However, in the case of India, the nation has been hospitable to the cultures, which might not have been Indian in origin, to begin with, but the Indian culture has, through the centuries maintained its integrity. This aspect has a significant influence on the evolution of the forms and concepts of community in the Indian case.

Forms and Structures of Community in the Prehistoric India

To develop an understanding of community in ancient India, one has to rely on historical evidences. These have been collected from the literature and works on ancient Indian history. Thus, a study of ancient Indian history would reveal that in the earliest phase, a small band of people, constituted primarily of a few families, were grouped together. In such groups, there was no attachment to status; rather, people were linked through kinship. The group depended on natural resources, primarily resources of forests. Such groups existed independent of similar groups existing elsewhere. Such groups could at best be called as the *communities of hunter-gatherers* (Thapar 2002, 55). If one has to understand the characteristics of such communities, at this stage, the consciousness of being constituted into a community would be non-existent. A sense of common culture or language would not have developed at this stage. Also, such groups would be mobile and would not be tied to a particular geographical location. Thus, a sense of being attached to geography (territory) would also be missing in such communities. They, however, could be understood as communities in a sense that they were unified by some sense of solidarity. This solidarity was an outcome of the common purpose or objective, which was survival and security for the group. Thus, again in a sociological sense, such groups could not be characterized by what Ferdinand Tonnies called as *gemeinschaftlich* relationship (Tonnies 1957). However, they did constitute a community in a sense that has been described in the preceding sentences. Such communities may, possibly, belong to the Palaeolithic phase of history, where the communities did not have a settled life and they also did not have an idea of agriculture, nor did they know about fire (Majumdar, Raychaudhury, and Datta 1970, 10–1).

Another group of people who could be understood to have formed into some form of community would be constituted of *pastoralists*. Such communities would be both, nomadic and semi-sedentary. Other characteristics of communities at this stage would include practice of minimal agriculture (Thapar 2002, 57). Thus, some form of differentiation of work can be seen to be developing in these forms of communities and the linkage may be formed through some 'system of exchange' between the 'cultivators' and 'pastoralists'. However, such communities would also be characterized by migration and movement, and family would form the 'core' of the community. Thus, these groups, probably, would be the Neolithic men, who depended solely on the stone implements. They lived in caves and also domesticated animals like ox and goats. The use of fire and pottery making was known to them (Majumdar, Raychaudhury, and Datta 1970, 11).

If one has to make sense of the structures of community in prehistoric India, then first traces of settled village communities one could find in 'Baluchistan and lower Sind, perhaps dating from the end of the 4th millennium' (Basham 2004, 11). The inhabitants could be distinguished from each other primarily by the different types of painted pottery. The settlements were small, spread over a few acres. The dwellings were made of 'mud brick with lower courses of stone, and (they) made good pottery' (ibid., 13).

In addition to the village communities, city dwellers also formed a distinct community in the areas of what is known as Harappan culture in the early part of the third millennium. The civilization was theocratic and conservative in nature. Basham writes:

> Each city had a well-fortified citadel, which seems to have been used for both religious and governmental purposes. The regular planning of streets, and the strict uniformity throughout the area of Harappan culture in such features as weight and measures, the size of bricks, and even the layout of the great cities, suggest rather a single centralized state than a number of free communities. (ibid., 16)

The Indus Valley Civilization, may, thus, have been characterized by agricultural economy and some form of cosmopolitanism that included Mediterraneans, proto-Australoids, Alpines and Mongoloids. While a variety of religious practices might have existed, worship of lord Shiva was prominent (Lal 1975, 17–8). Thus, if we have to make sense of community in the case of prehistoric India, certain features and structures underlying the way in which community(ies) were constituted need to be paid attention.

The *Vedic* Period and Later: Communities, Their Types and Features

Before going into the details of the types of communities and some of their features, some broad categorization and general observations should be in place. By the time one comes to the *Vedic* period, the communities are characterized, mostly, by patrilineal descent, often traced from common ancestor.

Identity is kinship-based and tribal identity could be identified where the 'membership of a tribe generally included those claiming common grazing grounds and descent from a common ancestor, with a common language and customs as well as rituals' (Thapar 2002, 58). The tribes still could be pastoralists, however, the important elements, as mentioned in the preceding sentences could be identified as regards to the dominant characteristics of a tribal community. These include some reference to 'territory', 'common language' and 'customs and rituals'. The development of community at this stage was also influenced by interventions, from time to time, by the pastoralists from Central Asia (ibid., 58).

If looked at the macro level, then the categorization may include the community of peasants, trading community and townsmen, distinct from the village/tribal community. Peasants were the producers of food, and also provider of revenue. The land use was intensive over a small area. The peasants were sedentary and were the permanent occupants of land. They were more frequently identified by caste, as distinct from clans. They were not, generally, kin-related and did not own resources in common (ibid., 60). Identification of a community with respect to the townsmen, on the other hand, depended on the nature of functions that happened in the town. A town may have had its importance as a centre of administration, or centres of crafts production or pilgrimage, or centres of trade and exchange.

Understanding of the community in a modern sociological sense, possibly, takes its full meaning with respect to the *Aryans*. It is likely that, along with a sense of being part of the community, they were also conscious of their identity as a community. This would be reflected in the form of, among others, common language, common religion and their geographical location. This identity was also shaped in the presence of and in relationship with the 'other' community. With respect to the *Aryans*, Burrow (1975) has noted that,

> a series of related tribes, settled mainly in Punjab and adjacent regions, speaking a common language, sharing a common religion and designating themselves by the name Arya are represented as being in a state of permanent conflict with a hostile group of peoples known variously as Dasas or Dasyu. (ibid., 28)

History records the appearance of *Aryan* culture in India somewhere around 1,500 BC and their further migration to North India, and eventually to the South of India about 800 BC (Thapar 1966, 29, 33). In the initial phase of their history, *Aryans* were cattle breeding people, who later settled in small village communities and gradually took to agriculture. The main literary sources are the *Vedās*, which provides a great deal of information on the *Aryan* communities. *Ṛigvedā* describes various tribes and inter-tribal conflicts 'such as the battle of Ten Kings' (ibid., 33). Cattle stealing and land disputes were possibly the main causes of conflicts. *Sudas* was the king of Bharat Tribe and *Vishvamitra* was his chief priest and advisor (*Ṛigvedā*, Hymn LIII).

During the *Vedic* period, we also see the formation of the image of the other, when it comes to the identity of the self as a community. *Aryans*, for instance, were in constant conflict with the non-*Aryans* in the North India, described as *Dasas* or *Panis* in the *Vedic* literature and the latter were held to be inferior because of their dark colour and flat features. In contrast, the *Aryans* had fair skins and clear-cut features.

In initial periods, *Aryans* owned land in common with the whole village. However, gradually tribal units declined and the land was divided between the families in the village. This possibly could have been the beginning of private property among the *Aryans*. At this stage, when agriculture became an important occupation, this led to a number of allied activities and hence wide range of occupations came into existence. The rise of occupation-based communities can be taken to be an important characteristic of the form of community that the *Aryan* culture gave rise to at this stage of history. Thus, one can see that there is rise of 'metal workers, potter, tanner and the weaver' which could be identified as occupation-based communities, who formed the larger village community (ibid., 35). Among the occupation-based communities, 'the carpenter remained a highly honoured member of the community'. Agriculture led to trade and settlements arose along the banks of the rivers, which served as highways of trade. The community of traders possibly arose from among the wealthy agriculturalists, who could afford to employ others to cultivate their lands (ibid).

Emergence of political organizations also gave rise to the political and ruling community. The tribes were organized along patriarchal lines, and with the passage of time and requirement of more protection, the most capable protector was elected as chief. However, there were also two tribal assemblies, known respectively as *Sabha* and *Samiti*, which could be considered as distinct political communities. The former was constituted of council of tribal elders, and hence more exclusive, and the latter the general assembly of the entire tribe. Thapar (1966) writes that 'the tribes, which did not have an elected monarch, *sabha* and *samite*, exercised the functions of government and authority'. Political units, however, were small (ibid., 36). In the religious sphere, the priest occupied the supreme position, and it can be believed that a community of priests, too, existed. As regards the larger political community, literature suggests that the concept of *rashtra* (kingdom state) was known to the *Vedic* age people, which contained 'tribes (*jana*), tribal units (*vish*) and villages (*grama*)' (ibid., 37).

Changing Forms of Community: From Class to Caste

In the initial phase of evolution of the *Aryan* culture in India, the *Aryan* community appears to have been divided into 'three social classes, the warriors or aristocracy, the priests and the common people', and caste consciousness appears to be missing from the community (ibid). Also, professions were, possibly, not hereditary, and the *Aryans*– were not an endogamous community. Caste appears to have acquired significance in terms of defining the community identity, with respect to the distinctions between the *Aryans* and non-*Aryans*. Thus, the *Aryans*, to preserve their distinct identity, kept the *Dasas* (the local non-*Aryan* people in the North) beyond the social pale. The distinction might have to do with the skin colour of the *Aryans* and non-*Aryans*. The *Dasas* were darker in colour and were alien to the *Aryan* culture. Thus, the community identity of the *Aryans* was defined with respect to what the non-*Aryans* were not. Two distinct communities, *Aryans* and non-*Aryans* come to the scene of Indian history at this juncture, and one can see the advent of caste identity taking shape. The *Aryans* were the *dvija* (twice born castes), and consisted of *Brāhmaṇs* (priests), *Kṣatriyas* (warriors) and *Vaiśyas* (cultivators). The fourth caste consisted of *Śūdras*, who were the *Dasas*.

By the end of the *Ṛigvedic* period the fourfold division of the society was 'regarded as fundamental, primeval, and divinely ordained' (Basham 2004, 138). The Indian society at this stage had also developed the concept of *dhārma*, which was different for the different stages in the life of an individual, and was also different for different communities, even though there may have been a 'common *dhārma*' for all. Basham (2004) refers to Manu to illustrate that the communities were bound, among others, by their prime duties, and were also identified as such. Thus, *Brāhmaṇa* would study and teach, *Kṣatriya* must protect the people and the *Vaiśya* must engage in the production activities, including trade and commerce. *Śūdras*, on the other hand were meant to serve the other three *varṇas*. However, it is significant to note that various professions could have been arranged within the larger framework of this kind of organization of the sections of people. Also, caste status of an occupation could change. Thapar (1966) writes that the *Aryan Vaiśyas* became traders and landowners, and *Śūdras* could become cultivators, even though they were excluded from the *dvija* status.

A careful study of this kind of arrangement would reveal that the *Vedic* period had given rise to a particular system of community arrangements. In this kind of system, different intra-community groups could have been arranged in a way that the relationship emerged as a kind of mutual interdependence. The communities (*varṇas* and later castes) within the community (*Hinduism*) were like the parts of the whole and were interlinked and interdependent and, as a whole, the system was dependent on the proper functioning of the parts. Thus, the arrangement could be understood as the existence of the larger community identified and sanctioned by its larger religious identity, which had intra-community arrangement for its proper functioning. The system was, of course, seen as evolutionary and providential, both. The division gradually took the shape of vertical stratification. Thapar (1966) writes that the King was the dominant power, and hence *Kṣatriyas* were of the first rank in the caste, followed by *Brāhmaṇas* and *Vaiśyas*. *Śūdras* came the last in this kind of arrangement. However, there also existed intra-community flexibility, which facilitated the incorporation of new ethnic groups within the *Hindu*-fold, even though the three upper castes would, gradually, appear to be closed groups. Burrow (1975) writes, 'during the *Brāhmaṇa* period, the *Aryans* maintained in essentials their ethnic identity and *Vedic* culture' (ibid., 28). All *Aryans* had an identity as a member of one of the communities. Children, ascetics and widows were outside the system. This kind of arrangement uniformly existed throughout India, even though the Southern part of India might have experienced it little late.

The system gradually became hereditary and was gradually guided by caste laws that included non-commensality and endogamy. This also depended on the vast network of sub-castes which was connected with occupation. Thapar (1966) writes that eventually sub-caste (*Jāti*) came to have more relevance for the routine working of the *Hindu* community (ibid., 40). This also prevented mobility of one caste member (primarily from the lower stratum) to another caste. Thapar, however, writes that 'vertical mobility was possible to the sub-caste as a whole and depended upon the entire group acting as one and changing both, its location and its work' (ibid.).

Still there was a section below the *Śūdras*, within the larger *Hindu*-fold, which can be considered as the 'early representatives of the people who were later called untouchables, outcastes, depressed classes or scheduled castes' (Basham 2004, 146). This group of people was serving other members of the community in very menial and dirty tasks. Reference to *Chandals* can be made in this regard whose main task was the carrying and cremation of corpses. They also served as executioners of criminals.

While the discussions in the preceding sentences would be helpful, in their own way, to the understanding of the concept of community with respect to ancient India, there could be other classifications that could be used to make sense of community in the ancient Indian history. This could be, for instance, with reference to the system of professions, which was emerging with the evolution of the social system in India. Important in this respect was the rise of trading community. Another was the understanding of community linked to and developing by the side of the *Hindu*-fold, Buddhist *Saṅghas*, for instance. These would be discussed in the following paragraphs.

The Buddhist *Saṅgha*

The definition of community pertaining to Buddhist *Saṅgha* is to be understood with respect to a 'sense of fellowship'. Meaning, the sense of 'community' was dependent on the understanding of belongingness to the same order. This would be understood as community in a slightly different sense. On the one hand, this could be in contrast to the understanding of community that the chapter has endeavoured to trace with respect to *Hinduism* and *Aryan* culture in ancient India. Also, this would be, in a sense, similar in some respect as it involves some common pursuit and shaping of identity with respect to *Hinduism*.

To begin with, this can be referred to as 'new community' in ancient India. Buddha brought together first five ascetic followers, who joined him as the core of the community that grew over a period. Sixty more, after the original five, joined later and with more followers joining the *Saṅgha*, the size of the *Saṅgha* kept on growing (Lownstein 2012, 32). In one significant aspect, *Saṅgha* was different at this stage in terms of meeting the sociological definition of the community. The body of monks, who became part of the *Saṅgha* would accompany Buddha and would take up the missions of preaching Buddhism and conversion. Thus, *Saṅgha*, would consist of a mobile group, which was cohesive and had an identity, but was not yet tied to a particular location, meaning geography. The members could speak a distinct language, *Prakrit* or Sanskrit, were constituted together into a single group and had some common pursuit. However, members of the community or *Saṅgha*, or the latter itself did not have any possession of their own. They depended on donations of every kind, including food items. Only during the three rainy months in a year the *Saṅgha* would settle down to a place, and that too in the parks, which would be donated to them by the wealthy followers. The primitive huts where Buddha and his *Saṅgha* dwelled were later developed into Buddhist monasteries (*viharas*) (ibid.). The *Saṅgha*, too, however formed a community, as they had constituted themselves into a cohesive group, had unique identity, spoke some common language and had common pursuit or objective, which was adhering to the order of Buddhism and spread of Buddhism. They, however, still constituted a part of the whole, which was the larger Indian identity and *Hindu* culture. Their identity and existence both depended on the larger *Hindu* culture that existed around them, at that point of time in Indian history.

The Trading Community

The agricultural economy during the *Vedic* period needed clearing of forests, and related activities that would require, among others, a system of supply and exchange of other goods, which would be necessary for a sedentary living of the *Aryans*. This led to the emergence of trading community. With the rise of empire and kingdoms in India, the trading community continued to develop and prosper. Intra-country trade was supplemented by trade with the countries overseas. India had trade relations with the Greeks and Romans, and the regions of the Mediterranean, Western and Central Asia and China. India had developed a very systematic way of carrying out trade from India to the outside world. The trading community had developed a system that would facilitate trade within and also with the countries overseas. Important feature related to the trade activities and the community of merchants was the formation of guilds that, of course, had existed since the Mauryan period.

The guilds were important feature of urban life in ancient India. The guilds played an important role in organizing production and also in 'shaping public opinion' (Thapar 1966, 109). The guilds were important for social status and a sense of security for the members of the trading community. The guilds had developed as an important entity for the people belonging to the mercantile community is supported by the fact that the guilds had to be registered in the locality where they functioned. Thus, locational identity served as an important factor for the functioning of the guilds, in addition to their unique identity as being composed of the people engaged in a specific trade. Change of location for a guild would require the permission of the authorities, again. Leading guilds were those of potters, metal workers and carpenters. The guilds played an important role in deciding the rules of work, and price and quality control. The guild was guided by *shrenidhārma*, which had the force of the law and the guilds had their own court to keep control over the behaviour of its members, including their private life (ibid., 110). Thus, in addition to the profession that decided the mercantile identity of a particular trading community, the respective mercantile communities were also unique in terms of their cohesiveness and were uniformly guided by the rules of the guild. Moreover, to the caste identity that an individual from the trading community might have, he also had an identity as being a member of a particular guild. Thus, guilds or people belonging to a specific trade could be considered as forming a community of their own.

Conclusion

There could be various reference points to understand the term community in ancient India. As has been seen in the preceding sentences, the underlying structures and the way community was constituted could be helpful in this regard. Constitution and evolution of a community or the communities may depend on a given religious and cultural identity, or profession or still a common objective or pursuit. However, for the major part of ancient Indian history for which literary and other sources are available, the dominant feature that shaped the understanding of community was primarily *Hinduism*. In addition, the term community may be understood at micro and macro levels. For instance, within the larger Indian or *Hindu*-fold, there could be constituent communities that may be based on caste or professional identity. However, as has been shown in the chapter, the construction of community with reference to ancient India has to be understood as an organic whole, where with the larger identity, smaller constituent communities existed.

Summary

The ideas and forms of community in ancient India, thus, can be understood with reference to the sociocultural processes that were at work at different phases of the evolution of the *Hindu* society. What is required to be understood is that common living and common purposes might have bound the people together in the form of exclusive groups with a distinct kinship, clan or tribal identity, however, the strong foundations of community structures were laid during the early *Vedic* period, which grew stronger later. For early Indians, thus, community living and religious living were not two different things.

Points for Discussion

1. Evaluate the historical evidences of the structure and forms of community in India in prehistoric period.
2. Critically analyse the evolution and nature of community in ancient India, especially in the *Vedic* and post-*Vedic* period.
3. Did the changing forms of community in India ensue the concept of class to caste? Give your opinion.

4. Are the values that we have in ourselves and the culture that we enjoy due largely to the community living? Explain.
5. How far the formation of community in ancient India can be seen as closely related to *Hinduism*?

Endnotes

1. In view of von Gierke, associations increase power of those alive at a time and (more importantly) the existence of associations outspan that of the individual personality. They unite past generations with those to come and give the humans possibility of evolution and history. Von Gierke, however, was in favour of giving community autonomy with respect to the state (see Gierke, 2002, 2).
2. The classical understanding of community has faced challenge by 'developments relating to postmodernism, globalisation, the internet and the third-style politics' (see Delanty, 2003, 1).

Glossary

Caste: An ascribed social category to which a person belongs by birth. The caste group is an endogamous community, and is marked by group division with hierarchy in its classical or traditional form.

Community: The collective unit in which an individual finds his true worth through a set of interactions that have meaning and expectations between its members, and the interactions are based on shared expectations, values and beliefs.

***Dhārma*:** It means rightful duty or righteous conduct that sustains the individual, community or the society.

***Hinduism*:** It is about religious beliefs, practices and cultural and philosophical tradition that is common to India, which has developed from the *Vedic* religion.

Kingship: The condition of being king (rule by single male).

Nomadic: It means not living a settled life or wandering around in community.

Pastoralist: It stands for the social organization based on cattle rearing and farming.

***Saṅghas*:** It is a Buddhist monastic order or community of Buddhist monks or nuns.

References

Basham, A. L. 2004. *The Wonder that Was India*. Basingstoke and Oxford: Pan Macmillan.

Burrow, T. 1975. 'The Early Aryans.' In *A Cultural History of India*, edited by A. L. Basham, 20–9. New Delhi: Oxford University Press.

Delanty, Gerard. 2003. *Community: Key Ideas*. London: Routledge.

Gierke, Otto von. 2002. *Community in Historical Perspective*, edited by Antony Black. Cambridge: Cambridge University Press.

Lal, B. B. 1975. 'The Indus Civilization.' In *A Cultural History of India*, edited by A. L. Basham, 11–9. New Delhi: Oxford University Press.

Lowenstein, Tom. 2012. *The Illustrated History of the Ancient World: The Civilization of Ancient India and Southeast Asia*. New York: Rosen Publishing Group.

Majumdar, R. C., H. C. Raychaudhury, and Kalikinkar Datta. 1970. *An Advanced History of India*. London and Basingstoke: Macmillan and Company Ltd.
Marshall, Gordon. 1998. *Oxford Dictionary of Sociology*. Oxford: Oxford University Press.
Rig Veda, trans. by R. T. Griffith. www.hinduonline.co/DigitalLibrary/SmallBooks/FourVedasEng.pdf.
Thapar, Romila. 1966. *A History of India*. Harmondsworth, Middlesex: Penguin Books.
Thapar, Romila. 2002. *The Penguin History of Early India: From the Origins to AD 1300*. New Delhi: Penguin Books.
Tonnies, Ferdinand. 1957. *Community and Society: Gemeinschaft und Gesselschaft*. Trans. and Ed., Charles P. Loomis. East Lansing: The Michigan State University Press.

Further Readings

Altekar, A. S. 2002. *State and Government in Ancient India*. Reprint, Delhi: Motilal Banarsidass.
Bell, Colin, and Howard Newby. 1974. *The Sociology of Community: A Selected Reading*. Oxon: Frank Caas and Co. Ltd.
Drekmeier, Charles. 1962. *Kingship and Community in Early India*. Stanford: Stanford University Press.
Jha, Vivekanand. 1991. 'Social Stratification in Ancient India: Some Reflections.' *Social Scientist* 19(3/4): 19–40.
Mazumdar, R. C. 2003. *Ancient India*. Reprint, Delhi: Motilal Banarsidass.
Srinivas, M. N. 1980. *India: Social Structure*. Delhi: Hindustan Publishing Corporation.
Srinivas, M. N. 1980. *The Remembered Village*. Berkeley and Los Angeles: University of California Press.

3

CHAPTER

Vedās and the *Brāhmanic* Tradition: The Cradle of *Hinduism*

Kanchan Saxena

CHAPTER OUTLINE

- Introduction
- Origin and Evolution of the *Brāhmanic* Tradition
- The Metaphysical Aspects of Society
- Idea of State and Kingship
- *Varṇa Vyvastha, Āśhrama* Life and *Puruṣārthas*
- Role of Sacred Texts, Mythology and Theism
- Conclusion
- Summary
- Points for Discussion

Ekam sat vipra vahudha vadanti

—*Ṛigvedā* (164, 46)

Reader's Guide

The chapter highlights the philosophical origin and evolution of *Vedic* and *Brāhmanic* tradition. The chief objective of this chapter is to explain the basic features of the *Brāhmanic* tradition and to explore the metaphysical, religious and ethical views prevalent in ancient Indian culture, especially in the *Vedās* and *Brāhmanic* systems of thought. In doing so, it also elaborates the social and political trends of both the systems. One of the important learning objectives of this chapter is to present a clear picture of the *Brāhmanic* views related to the various aspects of human life. It also provides an understanding of philosophical and religious views of the system of ancient India. The customs and the duties of a person according to his/her social status are also the points of reader's attraction in this chapter.

Introduction

Spiritual life is the true genius of India. Those who make the greatest appeal to the Indian mind are not the military conquerors, not the rich merchants or the great diplomats, but the holy sages, 'the *riṣhis*' and the *Brāhmaṇs* who embody spirituality at its finest and purest. By their lives, they teach us that pride and power; wealth and glory are nothing in comparison with the power of spirituality. India's cultural heritage is the most ancient, but it is also one of the most extensive and varied. The cultural heritage of India is to be found primarily in her philosophy and religion. India has stood like a 'Rock of Ages' weathering many a fierce storm, because her foundations are the eternal values of philosophy and religion, which lies in the tradition of *Vedās* and *Brāhmaṇas*.

The present chapter digs deep into the past and reveals to our view the prehistoric glimmerings of Indian culture. It gives us glimpses of the *Vedic* civilization when the grand spiritual foundations of Indian *culture* were laid. The *Ṛigvedā* was regarded as the fountainhead of everything Indian, the repository of the essence of Indian culture; the source of philosophical ideas and religious beliefs, of cultural life, of code of conduct and of all the sciences was traced to the *Ṛigvedā*. According to Sri Aurobindo,

> the *Vedā* is a mystic and symbolic poetry. The *Vedā* is not full of silly and childish conceptions, nor is it a barbarous and unintelligible Hymnary, tedious and commonplace, representing human nature on a low level of selfishness, which amounts to putting our own conceptions into the words or *Ṛiṣhis*. The *Vedā* symbolises the passions of the soul and its striving after higher spiritual planes. (Cultural Heritage of India 1937, 163)

The religion of *Vedic Aryans*, who dominated the Indian scene after the decline and collapse of Indus valley civilization, is known from their literature. In general, Sanskrit literature may be classified under two broad categories: *Vedic* and non-*Vedic* or rather *Vedic* and post-*Vedic*. The *Samhitas*, *Brāhmanas*, *Aranyakas* and *Upaniṣhads* are included in the *Vedic* literature, while the *Sutras*, *Smṛitis*, *epics*, classical literature, philosophical works, commentaries and manuals, all these come under post-*Vedic* literature.

The *Vedās* and *Brāhmanic* tradition laid the very foundation of Indian philosophy, religion and culture. It has certain specific features, such as *Varṇaāśhrama* tradition, law of *karma*, transmigration of soul, concept of *Puruṣārtha*, *Chaturvarna* and *Mokṣa*. A striking trait of the *Vedic* religion (including the religion of the *Ṛigvedā* and of the later *Samhitas* and *Brāhmaṇas*) is its practical and *utilitarian* character. The *Suktas*, though highly poetic in nature, are at the same time meant to be recited or sung by the *Purohitas* on occasions of sacrifice. The *Vedic* religion is *Pravṛitti-māργi* or this worldly. It assures the worshippers or householders not immortality or heaven, but a long life of full 100 years, prosperity, warlike offspring, in short, all the pleasures of this world. Conquest of enemies, freedom from diseases, abundance of food and drinks seem to be the most desirable objects for the *Vedic Aryans*. It is only immortality (*Amarattva*) or dwelling with Gods in heaven (*Swarga*) that is referred to.

Another important thing to be noted is that '*Vedic* religion is essentially a religion of priests' (Dutta and Chatterjee 2007, 96). The priests enjoy a very important position in the ritual. They are the mediators between princes and Gods. Further, it is to be noted that the *Vedic* religion was the religion of the upper castes. It was definitely different from the popular religion or the religion of the poor masses with its humble rites and reliance upon magic and medicine man, the description of which is found in the Atharvavedā and *Grhya Sutras*.

The *Ṛigvedic* poets were deeply impressed by the apparently mysteries working of the powerful forces of nature, the unexplained mysteries of whose working invests them with almost a 'supernatural' or divine character. They looked upon these various natural forces as divinities and natural events as sections of personified beings. The religion of the *Ṛigvedic Ṛiṣhis* was thus in the beginning essentially a polytheistic one in which natural forces were defied and worshipped as Gods.

As regards moral ideas, the central ethical teaching of the *Brāhmaṇas* is that life is a duty and a responsibility. Man is born with certain debts (*Rnas*) which he must pay in his life. He has a debt to pay to the Gods (*Deva Rna*) to the *riṣhis* (*Riṣhi Rna*) and to the parents (*Pitra Rna*). He can discharge them if he worships the Gods, studies the *Veda* and gives birth to children.

The advance of the *Upaniṣhads* on the *Samhitas* and the *Brāhmaṇas* consisted in 'an increased emphasis on the monistic suggestions of the *Vedic* hymns, a shifting of the centre from outer to the inner world, a protest against the externalism of the *Vedic* practices and an indifferences, to the sacredness of the *Vedās*'. The monotheistic idea of the *Upaniṣhads* arose from the very nature of the early *Vedic* Gods.

Having the above-mentioned background, the chapter begins with the origin and evolution of the *Brāhmanic* tradition. It also discusses the salient features of the *Brāhmanic* tradition, such as *varṇaāśhrama vyvastha*, law of *karma* and rebirth, theory of incarnation, *saṁskāra*, sacrifice, life-after death, *Bramhan* and *ātman*, *jiva* and *jagat*, self-realization and its means. Further, it throws lights on the metaphysical aspects of the society, that is, human, nature (world) and God. The idea of state and kingship has also been given due space in this chapter. In the next section, a detailed version of *varṇaāśhrama vyvastha* and the notion of *puruṣārthas* have been discussed. Theism and its various forms found in the *Brāhmanic* tradition have also been discussed in the chapter along with the roles of sacred texts and mythology. In the last section of the chapter, an analysis of the *Brāhmanic* tradition and the findings of the chapter have been given.

Origin and Evolution of the *Brāhmanic* Tradition

The *Vedās*, the sacred books of India, are generally believed to be the earliest literary record of the Indo-European race. It is indeed a difficult task to say when the earliest portions of these compositions came into existence. Many shrewd guesses have been offered, but none of them can be proved to be incontestably true. 'The *Vedās* are the earliest available records of Indian literature and subsequent Indian thought, especially philosophical speculation, is greatly influenced by the *Vedās*, either positively or negatively' (Murti 1960, 10–35). Further, it seems that when the *Vedās* were composed, there was probably no system of writing prevalent in India. But such was the scrupulous zeal of the *Brāhmaṇs*, who got the whole *Vedic* literature by heart by hearing it from their preceptors, that it has been transmitted most faithfully to us through the course of the last 3,000 years or more with little or no interpolations.

The word *Vedā* literally means knowledge and supreme knowledge too. But secondarily, it is applied to the *Vedic* literature, comprising of *Samhitas*, *Brāhmaṇas*, *Aranyakas* and *Upanishads*, books which are considered to be direct revelations from God, embodying the supreme truth that could not be gained by any effort of the human minds. So they are regarded as *apauruseya*, that is, not of the human origin. *Vedās* are sometimes known as '*Śruti*' which means oral tradition based on hearings. 'The *Vedās* are called *Śruti* either because they were directly heard from God or because the traditional method of studying and getting them by heart is by hearing then recited by the preceptor' (Cultural Heritage of India 1937, 182). The *Vedās* were handed down orally from a period of unknown antiquity, and the *Hindus* generally believed that they are *Apaureseya*, meaning that they were never composed by men. It was therefore generally supposed that either they were taught by God to sages, or that they were of themselves revealed to the sages who were the 'Seers of the hymns'. Thus, we find that

> when some time had elapsed after the composition of the *Vedās*, people had come to look upon them not only as very old, but so old that they were believed to have been revealed at some unknown, remote period at the beginning of each creation (Das Gupta 1932, 10). There is also the belief that the texts that constitute the '*Śruti*' have not been composed by any human, divine or transcendental being. They exist since the beginning of the universe from eternity. (Tola and Dragonettt 1980, 12–4)

Vedās in its wider sense is not the name of any particular book, but of the literature of a particular epoch extending over a long period say 3,000 years or so. As the *Vedic* literature represents the total achievements of the Indian people in different directions for such a long period of time and therefore it must be of a diversified character. If we roughly classify this huge literature from the points of view of age, language and subject matter, we can point out four different types, namely the *Samhita* or collection of verses. *Brāhmaṇas*, *Aranyakas* and the *Upaniṣhads*. All these literature, both prose and verse, were looked upon as so holy that in early times it was thought almost a sacrilege to write them; they were therefore learnt by heart by the *Brāhmaṇs* from the mouth of their preceptors and were hence called *Śruti*.

The *Vedic* literature consists of the four *Vedās* and several auxiliary works. The four *Vedās* are *Ṛigvedā*, *Samavedā*, *Yajurvedā* and *Atharvavedā*. The first three constitute the 'triad' (a set of three similar things) which are the original *Vedās*, and which enjoy highest authority. The *Atharvavedā* is a later edition. Each *Vedā* has three divisions, that is, the *Samihitas*, the *Brāhmaṇas* and the *Aranyakas*. The *Samihitas* are mostly verses. The *Brāhmaṇas* are commentaries in prose. The *Aranyakas* are forest treatises and the *Upaniṣhads* are mostly parts of the *Aranyakas*. The *Samavedā* contains the hymns of the *Ṛigvedā*, which are to be chanted in sacrifices. The *Yajurvedā* contains large portions of the *Ṛigvedā*, which is the earliest. The *Ṛigvedā* was hitherto regarded as the fountain head of everything. The great repository of the Indian culture, the source of philosophical ideas and religious beliefs, code of conduct of all sciences was traced to the *Ṛigvedā* (Cultural Heritage of India 1937, XIVI). Thus, we have a religious line—*Vedism*, *Brahmanism* and *Hinduism*—with more or less 35 centuries of existence, and presents of course, the changes and transformations of any social phenomenon, maintaining, notwithstanding a fundamental unity and identity through all of them.

Brahmanism had its supreme foundation in the *Vedās*, which designates as sacred knowledge orally transmitted by the *Brāhmaṇs* from generation to generation. At the beginning of *Vedism*, there is a text (*Vedā*), a book of a mysterious nature which fixes the limits of human knowledge and restrains it within its boundaries. The respect to that text, the adhesion to it and the submission to its authority determined one's own belonging to *Brahmanism* (Omvedt, 47).

Essential Features of the *Brāhmanic* Tradition

Brahmanism is a dominant tradition of Indian philosophy and culture. It is essential to have a clear and transparent view regarding *Brahmanism.* In order to explain certain basic features of *Brahmanism*, the following essential characteristics are analysed in detail.

1. ***Varṇa* and *Āśhrama Vyvastha***
   Brāhmaṇs laid the claim to *Vedic* Aryan origin, took the *Vedās* as their sacred texts and continued the priestly ritualistic orientation. While claiming high status for themselves as a social group, they began to interpret the various other classes of society with their broad framework of varying social function. The beginning of the process was the proclamation of the divine creation of the *Varṇas* in the *Purushukta* considered a later interpolation in *Ṛigvedā*. It is said in the *Ṛigvedā* that the four *Varṇas* were created from the body of eternal *purusha* (supreme deity). *Brāhmaṇs* originated from his mouth, *kṣatriya* from his arms, *vaiśyas* from his two thighs and *śūdras* from his two feet.
   Indian ethics comprises two kinds of *dhārmas* (duties), respectively, called *varṇaāśhrama dhārmas* (duties pertaining to one's social class and one's specific stage in life) and *sadharana dharmas* (common duties, the duties which are equally binding on all the members of the community). The *varṇas* recognized by Indian sociology are four in number, namely, the *Brāhmaṇs*, *Kṣatriyas*, the *Vaiśyas* and lastly, the *Śūdra*. Like the concept of *varṇa*, the concept of *Āśhramas* was also incorporated in the day-to-day life of man. *Āśhramas vyavastha* was meant for the regulation of the social life of man. *Āśhramas* were also four in number, namely *Brahmacharya*, *Grhastha*, *Varnaprastha* and *Sanyasa*.
2. **The doctrine of *karma* (action) and *punarjanma* (rebirth)**
   The doctrine of *karma* and *punarjanma* is another essential feature of *Brāhmanic* tradition. Anticipations of the *karma* doctrine are to be found in the *Vedic* concept of *Rta*, which meant not only the ordered course of things but the moral order as well. The principle of *karma* is the counterpart. In the moral realm of the physical law of causality, every action has its consequence either in the present life or life ahead. But, what is noteworthy here is that the philosophy of *Upaniṣhads* postulates the possibility of the soul's release from the cycle of *karma*.
   Karma theory is the law of conservation of moral energy. According to this principle of *karma*, there is nothing uncertain or capricious in the moral world. We reap what we sow. The good seeds bring a good harvest, the evil brings evil. The concept of *karma* is related with *punya* (virtue) and *papa* (sin) and was well known in the age of *Upaniṣhads*. In this connection it is stated that 'as one does so one becomes. A good doer becomes a saint and an evil doer becomes a sinner. Merit is attained by good deeds whereas sin is attained by sinful deeds'.[1] Dr S. Radhakrishnan has also written;

   > the attempt to overleap the law of *Karma* is as futile as the attempt to leap over one's shadow. It is the psychological principle that our life carries within it a record that time cannot blur or death can't erase. Not through sacrifices but through good deeds a man becomes good. A man becomes good by good deeds and bad by bad deeds. Again man is a creature of will. Accordingly as he believes in this world, so well he be when he is departed. So, we are asked to will the good and do the good. (Radhakrishnan, 2009, Vol. 1, 245)

   Law of *karma* states that every action (*karma*) has a definite effect (consequence) which takes shape according to the nature of *Karma*. In other words, law of *Karma* is based on *Karma-Phala* (fruit of the action). No one can escape from the results of his/her *karmas*. For this, we have to accept the immorality and eternity of soul, because in absence of this, there may be a situation in which one will get the consequence (reward or punishment) of an action, which he or she has performed. Likewise, we are also bound to accept the notion of *punarjanma*, because it is not possible to reap all the consequences for action, performed in one life. So, many births are required to reap the consequences of one's actions. In the words of Dr S. Radhakrishnan;

> The law of *karma* tells us that millions of lives are consumed before one perfect life is produced. For thought to reach the highest plane, we must plan, toil and agonize a lot. For our heart to pulse with joy, countless hearts must be crushed by suffering. Many strivings and sacrifices are needed to generate a holy character. Most men climb up the ladder to the spiritual heights only rung by rung. Few can fly from the bottom to the top at one bound. The *Varṇaāśhrama dhārma* or the discipline of the classes and stages of life is the Hindu's device for the gradual improvement of human nature. (Radhakrishnan, 2009, Vol. 1, 78)

All the Indian systems agree in believing that whatever action is done by an individual leaves behind it some sort of potency which has the power to obtain for him joy or sorrow in the future birth according to the nature of *karma*—good or bad. When the fruits of the actions are such that they cannot be enjoyed in the present life or in a human life, the individual has to take another birth as a man or any other being in order to suffer them.

3. ***Avataravad* (theory of incarnation)**
Theory of incarnation is a profound characteristic of *Brāhmanic* tradition. The concept of Trinitarian God (*Brahmā*, *Viṣṇu* and *Mahesh*) was popular in the later *Vedic* period. It was believed that the God (ultimate reality) takes birth in the human body (*Avatara*) to rescue the people from evil powers. Its evidences may be traced in the most famous holy text of *Brāhmanic* tradition—*Srimad Bhagwadgīta*—where Lord *Krishna* advised to *Arjuna* that 'whenever righteousness (*dhārma*) is on the decline, and unrighteousness (*adhārma*) is in the ascendant, then I myself took birth in the human form for the protection of the virtues, for the extirpation of evil doers, and for establishing *dhārma* (righteousness) on a firm footing and I am born from age to age'.[2] *Krishna's* major promise in the *Gīta* is that he takes shapes as an *avatar* (incarnation) again and again to prevent chaos, to save *dhārma* and to protect the good persons and the world against the bad. *Viṣṇu*, the second of the *Brāhmanic* Trinity of Gods, was said to have many *avatars* or incarnations of whom the most appealing was *Krishna*. Many legends surrounded *Krishna*, a ruler of the *Yadavas* and an ally of the *Pandavas* in the epic *Mahābhārata*.
4. ***Sanskara* (observance or ordination)**
Brāhmanic tradition is based on *Vedic* philosophy, religion and culture; therefore, it is inevitable to avoid *Vedic* rituals. In the history of *Dharmaśāstra*, there are mentions of several *sanskaras*, which are to be performed in the daily life of a person. The most popular *sanskaras* are *Garbhadhan Sanskar*, *Mundana Sanskar*, *Upnayan Sanskar*, *Vidyarambh Sanskar* and *Vivah Sanskar*. *Brāhmanic* tradition also has faith in all these *sanskaras* and follow them rigorously.
5. **Tyaga (sacrifice)**
The sacrifice was believed to have existed from eternity like the *Vedās* (Das Gupta 1932, 22). The *Vedic* sacrifice is part of an exchange, a nourishing gift proffered to the God by the worshipper with a motive followed by a reward, a perfectly voluntary act of the gladdened deity. The attitude of the sacrificer is not of extreme humility or of deep emotion but of love and determination with full reverence towards the maker of the universe (Cultural Heritage of India 1937, 244). The ritual

of sacrifice invariably produced certain mystic or magical results by virtue of the object desired by the worshipper. The sacrifice is not offered to a God with a view to propitiate him or to obtain from him bliss in heaven. These rewards are directly produced by the sacrifice itself through the correct performance of complicated and interconnected ceremonies which constitute the sacrifice, although in each sacrifice certain Gods were invoked and received the offerings. Sometimes through sacrifice the worshipper may attend a higher divine place above the God. It means to say that sacrifice was superior to Gods also. These Gods attained supreme rank through sacrifices. Sacrifice was regarded as almost the only kind of duty, and it was also called *Karma* or *Kriya* (action) and the unalterable law was that these mystical ceremonies for good or for bad, moral or immoral were destined to produce their effects. Thus, we find the simple faith and devotion on the *Vedic* hymns on one hand being supplanted by the growth of a complex system of sacrificial rites and on the other hand, a monotheistic or philosophic knowledge of the ultimate reality of the universe.

6. ***Punarjanma* (life after death)**

There is nothing explicitly and definitely said about the future of man, when he enters the other world. According to the Indian philosophy and religion, life in this higher world is ephemeral as in this physical world, for man returns here after enjoying the fruits of his deeds to take up another body.

> This process continues till the final release of soul. This going and coming, this round of births and deaths, is called *Samsara* or transmigration of the soul. In the early *Vedic* literature there is no express mention of this doctrine. We come across it for the first time in the *Upanișhads*. But there is enough evidence even in the *Ṛigvedā* to show that the *Vedic* Aryans knew of this transmigration of the soul.[3]

The *Ṛigvedic Ṛiṣhis* recognized an eternal entity which continued to exist when this physical body expired. This entity goes to another world, where it enjoys the fruits of good deeds. It assumes another body when it enters the higher world after death.

> There is no yearning to get rid of the body and to escape from the shackles of this world. This world was conceived as a place where one can have happiness through the favour of Gods. After death man went to the next world, a place of higher happiness, known as *pitrloka*, where the departed forefathers lived (Sinha, Vol.1, 27)

After the death, the *soul* reached the world of *Yama* (the ruler of the kingdom of the dead). The higher world has a splendid paradise where man recovered his body in good health and without wounds, with which he would enjoy the pleasures he had enjoyed or wished to enjoy in his worldly life; abundant food, intoxicating beverages, hunting, gambling and women without unjust masters, in an inconceivable atmosphere of equality.

7. ***Brahman* and *Ātman* (supreme soul and soul)**

The monism adumbrated in the *Ṛigvedā* is developed into idealistic monism in the *Upanișhads*, which is regarded as *Brahman*, the infinite, eternal, omniscient, omnipresent and pure spirit as the ultimate reality. The temporal, spatial and causality bound world is the manifestation of this infinite and eternal spirit. It is a mere appearance of *Brahman*, which is one, non-dual, undifferentiated and pure consciousness. *Brahman* is non-temporal, non-spatial and non-causal. It is impersonal, transcendental, indefinable incomprehensible and unknowable. It is *nirguna* (no form) and *nirakar* (no size).

Brahmanism also postulated the existence of the *atman*, the spirit or the soul which is the individual consciousness in all its authentic purity, the true consciousness identical with *Brahman* in essence, attributes and mystery. A famous *Upanișhadic* formulation expresses that identity: '*Tat Tvam Asi*', means 'you are That divine'. Because of its notions of *Brahman* and *Ātman*, '*Brahmanism* is a substantial and unitary system of thought' (Murti 1960, 10–35).

8. ***Jiva* and *Jagat* (creature and the universe)**
According to *Brāhmanic* tradition, the individual soul (*ātman*) is different from the body, the *panch-endriya* (five sense organs) *manas* (mind) and *buddhi* (intellect). The body is the chariot, which is guided by the self, which is charioteer. The intellect (*buddhi*) is the driver. The *manas* is the bridle. The sense organs are the horses. The objects apprehended by them are the field. The sense organs are directed by the *manas*. The *manas* is directed by the *buddhi*. The *buddhi* is directed by the self. The *manas* is superior to the sense organs. The *buddhi* is superior to the *manas*. The *ātman* is superior to the *buddhi*. The body is its material vehicle. 'The *ātman* associated with the sense organs and *manas* is the individual self that enjoys the fruits of its actions.'[4]

As far as the concept of *Jagat* is concerned, it is real. It is the expression of the glory of *Brahman*. It springs from him, is sustained by him and absorbed in him. All created beings abide in him, originate in him and are founded in him. *Brahman* is everywhere in the cause of names and forms or determinate objects.

9. **Salvation (*mokṣa*) and its means**
Mokṣa or spiritual freedom, which is the ultimate end of human life, is not a post-mortem experience in a world beyond. It is realizable here and now. *Mokṣa* is the eternal nature of the self, and not a spatio-temporal state. What prevents the soul from realizing it, is its own ignorance or *agyana*. When ignorance is dispelled through wisdom of the nature of self, the soul attains *mokṣa*, even though the physical body may continue to appear for a while. This is known as the doctrine of *Jīvanmukti*, release while being embodied. Emancipation (*mokṣa*) is the natural and only goal of man simply because it represents the true nature and essence of man. It is the realization of our own nature that is called emancipation. Since we are all already and always in our own nature and as such emancipated, the only thing necessary for us is to know that we are so. Self-knowledge is therefore the only desideratum which can wipe of all false knowledge, all illusions of death and rebirth.

According to the *Brāhmanic* tradition, *mokṣa* (self-realization) is freedom from bondage. *Avidya* is bondage, *vidya* is *mokṣa*. *Vidya* is knowledge of *Brahman* or *ātman* in oneself and in all creatures. It is intuitive realization of one infinite, eternal, universal spirit. 'Knowledge of *Brahman* is becoming *Brahman* (Brahman-bhavana)' (Sinha, Vol. 1, 27). It is a state of identity of the individual self with the supreme self. It is free from merits and demerits. It is a state of super moral transcendental purity. It is the state of eternal peace. It is indefinable supreme bliss. It is a sense of perfect fulfilments. It is a state of supreme wisdom, selfless will and ineffable bliss. Like *Brahmanism*, most of the schools of Indian philosophy accept that *mokṣa* is the state of self-realization. Actions (*Karmas*), concentration of mind (*Yoga*), devotion (*Bhakti*) and knowledge (*Gyana*) are the various means to the attainment of salvation. But knowledge (*Gyana*) is the pre-eminent means of self-realization.

10. ***Dharmaśāstra* tradition**
Dharmaśāstra tradition was well accepted by the followers of *Brāhmanic* tradition. The *Manusamhita* is held in great respect among the *Dharmaśāstras*. Max Muller opined that '*Manusamhita* or *Manusmṛiti* is based on an ancient *Dhārma-Sutra*, the code of Manu is mainly

in treatise on ethics and law, but it gives a cosmology and an ontology of the crude type' (ibid., 108). The *Manusamhita* is mainly concerned with duties and virtues, the supreme ends of life and the means to the realization of the highest good. Manu's ethics is a blend of customary morality and personal reflective morality. He tries to formulate the criteria of rightness and wrongness and arrive at a conception of the highest good.

Dhārma is prescribed by the *Vedās*. It is a means to the highest good. *Ṛig*, *Yajur*, *Sama* and *Atharvavedās* and *Smṛitis* all preach that good conduct (*sila*) of persons well-versed in them, and satisfactions of the self are the sources of *dhārma*. *Vedās* prescribed supreme *dhārma* and what is prescribed by a person well-versed in *Vedās* is the *Dhārma*. Perception, reason and the *sastras* are the means of knowing *dhārma*. The *Śruti* is the highest source of *dhārma*. Manu regards the divine law as the moral standard. What is commanded by God is right. What is forbidden by him is wrong. *Dhārma* is done by persons well-versed in the *Vedās*, and always approved by the conscience of virtuous persons. Manu's ethics is more authoritarian than rational and personal. He believes in the social law as the moral standard. He recognizes the customary morality of the society, but it should be in conformity with *Śruti* and *Smṛiti*.

The Metaphysical Aspects of Society

Vedic seers have discussed the fundamentals of metaphysic in quite an elaborative manner. Notions of God (*Brahman*), soul (*Jivatma*) and the world (*Jagat*) have been discussed from both points of view, that is, philosophical and religious.

1. ***Brahman*:** According to *Brāhmanic* tradition, '*Brahman* is the ultimate reality of the universe. The monism adumbrated in the *Ṛigvedā* is developed into idealistic monism in *Upaniṣhads*, which regard *Brahman*, the infinite, eternal, omnipresent, omniscient and pure spirit as the ultimate reality' (ibid., 4–17). It is a mere appearance of *Brahman*, which is one, non-dual, undifferentiated and pure consciousness; *Brahman* is non-temporal, non-spatial and non-causal. It is impersonal, transcendental, indefinable, incomprehensible and unknowable.

   Two forms of *Brahman*: *Brahman* is sometimes conceived as *Saguna* and *Nirguna Brahman*. The *Upaniṣhads* speak of *Para Brahman* and *Apara Brahman*. The former is higher *Brahman*. The latter is lower *Brahman*. The former is indeterminate, unconditional and devoid of attributes (*Nirguna*). The latter is determinate, conditional and endowed with attributes (*saguna*). The former is unqualified and incomprehensible. The latter is qualified and comprehensible. The former is transcendent and non-phenomenal (*Nishprapancha*). The latter is immanent in the phenomenon world (*Saprapancha*). The former is non-spatial, non-temporal and non-causal. The latter is the lord of the spatial and temporal world governed by causality. The former is the transcendental being (*Sat*), consciousness (*Chit*) and bliss (*Ananda*), which constitute its essence. The latter is the infinite, eternal, omnipresent, omniscient and omnipotent creator, preserver and destroyer of the universe, the moral governor and the lord of the law of *Karma*. The higher *Brahman* (*Para Brahman*) is described by the method of negation. The lower *Brahman* (*Apara Brahman*) is described by the method of affirmation.
2. **Soul (*Atman*):** The second metaphysical entity is soul (*ātman*), which is different from body, sense organs, *manas* (mind) and *buddhi* (intellect). As per the philosophy of *Brāhmanic* tradition,

the higher *Brahman* is the Atman, pure universal consciousness, which is the fundamental reality in the individual selves. *Upaniṣhadic* teachings talked about the unity of *Brahman* and *Ātman*, which means the eternal soul is identical with *Brahman*. They accept the non-duality of the ultimate reality, which is *Brahman*. *Brāhmanic* tradition also affirms this and fully accepts this in his metaphysic. '*Atman* is the due, undifferentiated, homogenous, consciousness without inside or outside. It is timeless and also speechless.'[5] 'It is eternal, conscious and many. It is unborn and devoid of infinite knowledge and sovereignty. It is imperishable and immortal. *Ātman* does not perish while the body dies. The *ātman* associated with the sense organs and *manas* is the individual self that enjoys the fruits of its actions.'[6] It transmigrates from one body to another. It is associated with an appropriate body, human, superhuman or subhuman in accordance with its merits and demerits of *karma*.

The individual soul has four conditions. In the working condition, it is called the *Visva* which knows and enjoys gross external objects through the external sense organs. In the conditions of dream, it is called the *Taijas* which knows and enjoys subtle internal objects or cognitions through the *manas*. In the condition of dreamless sleep, it is called *Prajna* which is one homogeneous consciousness and bliss which does not comprehend external objects and internal cognitions. In the ecstatic (*Turiya*) condition, it is called the *Ātman* which knows neither external objects nor internal cognitions. In other words, it is neither consciousness nor unconsciousness, it is universal and super-consciousness and 'this *Ātman* is called *Brahman*'.[7]

3. **World (*Jagat*):** *Brāhmanic* tradition accepts that the world is real. It is the expression of the glory of *Brahman*. It springs from him, is sustained by him and absorbed in him. All created beings abide in him, originate in him and are founded in him. *Brahman* is the cause of names and forms of determinate objects. It existed in concealed condition in *Brahman* before creation. It was manifested by him (*Brahman*). 'The world is pervaded by *Brahman*. The whole spatio-temporal order is *Brahman*. It exists in him. It has its root in *Brahman*, who transcends it. The uniformities of nature are controlled by his will. The world is permeated by the divine spirit.'[8]

   'The origin of the world is traced to creation or emanation. All creatures come out from the *Ātman* or *Brahman*. *Brahman* ejects the world out of himself, and withdraws it into himself, like a spider ejects threads out of its own body and withdraws it. *Brahman* creates the world out of his own nature and absorbs it in himself. He does not create it out of pre-existing material.'[9] Shankaraharya rejects the view that the world is real. He opines that 'the world is real only from practical point of view (*Vyavaharic Satta*). From transcendental point of view the only real existence is of *Brahman*. Physical world is unreal and *Brahman* and *Ātman* are one and inseparable'.[10] This view represents the theory of monism in Indian philosophy.

Idea of State and Kingship

The *Vedic* Indians had just left the nomadic state and were settling down into an agricultural community. 'There are several traces of the nomadic state preserved in the *Vedic* literature. Kings are, for instance, described as the rulers over tribes like the *Kurus*, the *Panchalas*, the *Yadus* and the *Turvasas*. They are not described as rulers over particular regions, nor are the boundaries of their kingdoms defined anywhere. The territorial state, however, was fast coming into existence and the later *Vedic* literature clearly refers to it' (Murti 1960, 10–35). Idea of state and kingship includes the theory of government in ancient India. 'Monarchy was the normal form of the political organization; republics or oligarchies were rare. *Vedic* literature contains some speculations about the origin of kingship.'[11]

'In the early *Vedic* period, when kingship was elective, the power of the king was naturally not extensive. Like the Homeric monarch, the *Vedic* king in the beginning was only the first among his peers, who had assented to this elevation to kingship.' 'It is the *Mahābhārata* which gives the first clear, comprehensive and on the whole, a consistent account of *Hindu* political thought. Government is part of the general social order and scheme of human duties. The *Mahābhārata* repeats the *Vedic* myth of the origin of castes. But it does conceive a state of society when no caste existed' (Prasad, 1974, 23).

At the time of *Mahābhārata*, there is a clear conception of the state of nature which preceded political society. So the state of nature lived for a while but, after some time, the people felt acutely the need of a king. But, gradually the prestige and power of the king began to increase. He probably owned extensive lands and herds of cattle and there was considerable pomp associated with his court. The king was, of course, the leader of a strong military force, and the later *Vedic* literature describes how the king held undisputed sway over his subjects. 'It is, however, interesting to note that, like the Egyptian king, the *Vedic* monarch performed no public religious rituals; they were under the *purohita*. It was held that the *purohita* was indispensable for the success of the king and the prosperity of his kingdom' (Cultural Heritage of India 1937, 23).

Government is instituted by the joint action of human intelligence and divine will on one side and obedience and financial contribution on the other, which are the essential conditions of political organization. 'Herein consists the supreme importance of Government. It is only through fear of the king that people do not eat another. The king alone brings peace on earth.'[12] It follows that within the limits prescribed by the fundamentals of social organization the activity of the government knows no bounds. Its primary duty is to enforce the social order and see that everyone performs his function and adheres to his duty. The government should actively promote righteousness and never allow it to fall into decay.

Varṇa Vyvastha, Āśhrama Life and *Puruṣārthas*

The four *varṇas* and the four *āśhramas* are not social structures, but symbols of a holistic individual and a well-balanced society. When we follow the *Varṇaāśhrama dhārma*, we become whole, we realize the purpose of our human existence (*Puruṣārtha*), we become what we ought to become and we become *satya*.

1. ***Varṇa Vyavastha*:** As it has been mentioned earlier in the essential features of *Brāhmanic* tradition, the *Purusa-sukta*, found in the *Ṛigvedā* (Chapter 10, Hymn 90), inform us that the *Brāhmaṇa* came from the mouth of the *purusa*, the *Kṣatriya* from his hands, the *Vaiśya* from his thighs and the *Śūdra* from his feet. This is the first reference to *varṇa*, the four-fold division of the Aryan society. The four *varṇas* are the four basic needs of the individual and society. These were written into our being by God, who made us humans, and wants us to be full human. They all come from one and the same primordial *Purusa* and hence they are essential for the full growth of every person (*Purusa*).
    a. ***Brāhmaṇa*:** In the traditional setup, the *Brāhmaṇa* imports knowledge to others and officiates at the rituals. He performs the role of a priest. In ancient societies, knowledge was never merely academics. It was intimately linked with life. It enables us to discover the potential

latent within us and thereby makes progress possible. It also provided us the direction that our progress must not take at the cost of others.

b. ***Kṣatriya*:** In the traditional framework, a *Kṣatriya* is expected to provide protection to others. Without a sense of security, neither individuals nor communities can grow to full maturity. There is a story in which Akbar told Birbal that he should feed a goat a very good food for three times a day for a whole month and yet that goat should not gain any weight. Birbal had no options but to agree. Akbar arranged for a goat, and appointed some people to keep a watch on the goat, to make sure it was fed as per his orders. After a month he got the goat weighed and to Akbar's great surprise the goat had not put on any weight, but it had lost some. On being asked to explain, Birbal told him that he had tied the goat near the cage of a ferocious lion. The absence of security not only blocks the growth, but it can also destroy life.

c. ***Vaiśya*:** Trade and agriculture were the specific domain of the *Vaiśya*. Adequate production and equitable distribution take care of our basic needs: food, clothing and housing. In a more advanced context, we expect sufficient health care centres and recreation facilities. 'When a person earns the money he needs and experiences a sense of self-worth *(ārtha)*—the first *Puruṣārtha*. When this does not happen, frustration sets in, which leads of violence, alcohol and drug abuse and other forms of unsocial behaviour.'[13] Every human being has the right to work, and it is the duty of the state to provide employment. Without adequate health and a feeling of well-being, progress is difficult.

d. ***Śūdra*:** This is the fourth category of social division of caste and work. The *Śūdra* was expected to serve the members of the first three *varṇas*. To my mind, the persons/members of society who do not possess any of the three skills mentioned above were supposed to assist the above three *varnas*. It does not mean that they were low caste or of low standard. They were supposed to be a symbol of service. Knowledge, security and prosperity will be really helpful for the authentic growth of individuals and society, if the quest for these is permeated by a spirit of service. Otherwise, we will be faced with exploitative individuals and an unjust society of which we see today. Money has become a major concern. We tend to become its slaves. Priests, educators, judges and police personnel, protectors of law and order, doctors, merchants and farmers are more concerned with how much money they can make. The spirit of service is a rare commodity in a world of cut-throat competition and vulgar consumerism. We should work together for the welfare of humanity without having any superiority or inferiority complex in ourselves. Only when we all become *Śūdras* we will serve the society and can be true *Brahmacharies*, towards universal harmony and peace.

2. ***Āśhrama Vyavastha*:** In *āśhrama vyvastha*, there are four *āśhrama*, that is, *Brahmacharya*, *Grihastha*, *Vanaprashta* and *Sanyasa*.

   a. ***Brahmacharya Āśhram*:** In the *Vedic* framework of the four *āśhramas*, the acquiring of learning was intimately associated with the first *āśhramas—Brahmacharya*. Gradually the *Brahmacharya* came to mean not just the first quarter of the life of a *Dvija*, but a disposition intimately connected with the human quest for wisdom and with our search for *mokṣa*. Hence, the *Yoga Sutra* prescribes it as one of the five *yamas* (*prabritis*) to be followed by a person wanting to practice *yoga* (Yogasutra, Chapter 2, Verse 30).

   The word *Brahman* is derived from the root *brh*, and so we should not be surprised that the substantive is issued both in the masculine and in the neuter with over 20 different meanings, all indicating something or somebody considered great. Eventually 'it comes to denote the greatest of the great, God himself' (Suryakant 1981, 493). The words *carya* and *carin* are derived from the root *car*.[14] Hence, we can redefine *Brahmacharya* as the constant movements towards the great and ultimately towards God, who is the greatest of all. The fact that only human beings can really acquire learning is the traditional function of a *Brahmachari*.

b. ***Grihastha Āśhram***: The second *Āśhrama* is known as *Grihastha Āśhrama* and according to the traditional understanding, after completing his studies, an Aryan man was expected to get married, and become a householder (*Grahastha*). Either a man or woman is incomplete in himself or herself. We become fully human only through communion with opposite sex. To be human is to be necessarily oriented towards other humans. Without entering into deep interpersonal relations, we just cannot grow as healthy persons or will remain fragmented. One important function of a *grahastha* is to offer hospitality to guests, to persons who come into our life unannounced, without a date (*Atithi*). On a deeper level, hospitality does not consist in giving shelter, food and drink, but making place for others in our life, giving them our time, our loving presence.

   Life on earth makes us indebted to many people. This *āśhrama* is the most important among four because only through this *āśhrama* we can obtain the ultimate end of life, that is, salvation. The doctrine of 'three debts' and 'five sacrifices' which every person inherits with his/her birth in this world is related to this *āśhrama*. It is the pious duty of *grhastha* to be free from three debts by performing certain duties. By our very birth, we are indebted to our ancestors (*Pitr*) and so we need to ensure the continuity of the human race. This is known as *Pitr-Rna*. The wisdom of the ancient sages (*Riṣhis*) guides us, and we have to pass on to posterity this wisdom, further enriched by our own experience and insight. This is called *Riṣhi-Rna*. The third Rna is *Deva-Rna* from which a man can be free by performing right actions and the performance of 'five sacrifices'. It is mandatory to get rid from three debts and to perform five sacrifices: *Brahma Yajña*, *Pitra Yajña*, *Deva Yajña*, *Bhoot Yajña* and *Nri Yajña*. The theories of *Pancha-Yajñas* and *Tri-rnas* are the basic duties to household life.

c. ***Vanaprastha Āśhrama***: *Vanyasa* or *Vanprastha Āśhrama* teaches us the way to live with nature in a harmonious relation. In many perennial cultures, nature is seen as feminine, and hence the relation between man and woman is closely linked with the relation of humans with nature. Thus, it is not enough for a person to become *grhastha*. He must also be in communion with nature (*Vanvasa*—the forest is nature in her pristine purity). Nature is not just matter but also our mother. We have a symbiotic relation with her. She is the womb in which we live. She provides us food and drink, fresh air, sunshine, clothes to cover our body and medicinal herbs to keep us healthy. Without these our life would not be possible. Apart from this, 'the stage of *vanvasa* is a preparation for gradual detachment from the material world or *sansar* which prepare us towards *mokṣa* or salvation'.

d. ***Sanyasa Āśhrama***: The fourth and the final stage of life is *Sanyasa āśhrama* which is a life of *Parivrajaka* (wanderer), freely wandering in the society, in the service of the society, for universal well-being. To be a healthy *Brahmacari*, to grow into the full stature of humanity and personhood, we need to be free from fetters that could slow down or even block our progress. A *Parivrajaka* is a person in the fourth *āśhrama* who is symbolic of a pilgrim and free within to journey ahead. The *Parivrajaka* can freely wander wherever he wishes, because nothing stops him, simply because he possesses nothing, not even a roof over his head. He is truly a free person. Inner freedom presupposes that we have a deep awareness of ourselves. The chief objective of this *āśhramas* is the attainment of salvation and obtaining the end of life, through the works for the welfare of humanity.

As symbols, the four *āśhramas* articulate basic human wisdom, and this wisdom is not the preserve of any particular religion. All humans in some way or the other resonate with this doctrine. It is truly universal and therefore authentically secular. In the same fashion, the four *varṇas* are to be understood as belonging to one and the same person and also to society as a whole.

3. **The *puruṣārthas*:** 'The theory of *Puruṣārthas*, a theory of human values, is one of the basic theories of classical Indian philosophy. It is central to classical Indian ethics and even to the whole of classical Indian philosophy of life' (Mohapatra, 5). It pervades in its various pictures, the visions and utopias of human well-being. It has been assumed or appealed to, overtly or covertly, not only in Indian ethical and non-ethical philosophical treatises but also in several literary works.

   The classical Indian term *puruṣārtha* is value which means the object of a man's desire. According to the accepted tradition, the *puruṣārthas* are four in number: *ārtha*, *kāma*, *dhārma* and *mokṣa*. Indological scholars almost unanimously maintain that originally the theory of *puruṣārthas* included only the concepts of *ārtha*, *kāma* and *dhārma*—the *trivarga* and the concept of *mokṣa* was a later addition to the three, as in some early works only the former three are mentioned. The four-membered set (*chaturvarga*) finds mention only in later works. But though whether the original theory consisted of the *trivarga* or the *chaturvarga* may be historically important, it is of no great philosophical significance. The philosophically important question is whether or not the theory resulting out of the addition of *mokṣa* to *trivarga*, that is, the theory comprising the *chaturvarga*, offers a better, more complete, exhaustive or conceptually illuminating classification of *puruṣārthas*. It is generally accepted that it does. *Mokṣa* being admitted to be the highest *puruṣārtha*, the *trivarga* scheme without it is not only inexhaustive but completely misses the point of categorizing the ends of human life. They claim that the *chaturvarga* scheme, on the other hand, presents in point of philosophical theory, a more (or the most) satisfactory classification or categorization.

   a. ***Ārtha*:** *Ārtha* denotes all kinds of material possessions, including everything that one can own, lose or gift etc. *Ārtha* includes all types of material things, irrespective of their potentiality for rightful or wrongful uses. It includes the material means for the performance of religious, social, legal and moral duties, as well as those required for normal living and subsistence.

      Ārtha, which is enumerated as one of the *puruṣārthas*, has been described as having economic value in Indian tradition and it has been taken as an aid to fulfil human wants. It is not correct that our ancient seers were always in favour of denouncing wealth. Moreover, it is admitted that wealth plays a prominent role in the fulfilment of one's desire. All kinds of meritorious works and religious acts may be performed if there is sufficient wealth. 'As per observations of the *Mahābhārata*, poverty is a state of sinfulness.'[15]

   b. ***Kāma*:** *Kāma* means desire but in its occurrence in the theory of *puruṣārthas*, it denotes the satisfaction of desires and, therefore, it may be said to denote pleasure or agreeable feeling. Here, again, there is no definitional restriction that *kāma* can denote only some and not some other desires. In fact, *kāma* can be said to be a categorical representation or hypostatization of man's appetitive life or pursuits.

      The theory seems to highlight the importance of the truth that in the empirical world one's attempt to fulfil a desire derives its significance very greatly from the fact that it involves some interaction, some contact, cooperation or conflict with some other member or members of the society. '*Dhārma* is it's regulator in the sense that any *kāma* can be said to be permissible, or really worthwhile, only if it does not conflict with or go against *dhārma*. *Ārtha* on the other hand, is a necessary condition for the acquisition of *kāma*.' Making *Kāma* subject to the regulation of *dhārma* provides the right direction. It means to say that if *kāma* is not regulated by *dhārma*, then it may have adverse effect on an individual as well as on society.

c. ***Dhārma*:** The concept of *Dhārma* is not only social but also functional in the sense that, though everyone has to follow *dhārma*, the *dhārma* of a person is very much tied to the performance of the functions which have been socially allotted to him. The virtues of a man very much consist in the performance of his functions well. What is presupposed here is a social order which provides for the assignment of clearly identifiable functions to every individual. An individual's functions, in the context of the *puruṣārthas*, are taken to be on account of the nature of the social realities in ancient India, relative to his status in the society. Second, it is also presupposed here that there are more or less clearly indefinable ways of performing various functions one has been required to perform. In this sense, '*Dhārma* can be said to be a higher value than *ārtha* and *kāma*'. This seems to be perfect of *Sita's* saying to *Rama* that '*dhārma* gives everything, wealth and happiness, and is the essence of the world'.[16]

d. ***Mokṣa*:** *Mokṣa*, whenever accepted as a *puruṣārtha*, is regarded as the highest to which *dhārma* is treated as a means. *Mokṣa* also denotes so many things, that is, freedom from the cycle of birth and death, freedom from suffering, freedom from *karmas*, freedom from attachment to the objects of desires, eternal bliss, propinquity with God, identity with God etc. That is why it is often translated as freedom, liberation, salvation and release from bondage. *Mokṣa* is taken to be purely intrinsic value of the highest order. On the other hand, *ārtha* is taken to be only extrinsically, *dhārma* by some as intrinsically while by some others as only extrinsically and *kāma* as intrinsically, valuable. But *kāma* is not generally given at least in later post *Vedic* works (except by the *Cārvākas*, i.e., the materialists) a very elevated status.

Role of Sacred Texts, Mythology and Theism

Role of Sacred Texts

Several sacred texts of Indian philosophy as well as *Hinduism* have played an important role in the development of *Brāhmanic* tradition. *Vedās*, *Upaniṣhads*, *Purāṇas* (especially *Rāmāyaṇa* and *Mahābhārata*), *Bhagwadgīta* and various *Smṛitigranthas*, namely *Manusmṛiti*, *Nāradasmṛiti* and *Yājñavalkyasmṛiti*, etc.) are some of the important texts which reflected the *Brāhmanic* tradition. *Ṛigvedā*, the oldest among the four *Vedās*, has contributed a lot in the framing of *Brahmanism*. The philosophy of *Upaniṣhads* and its fundamental concepts of God, *Brahman*, *Ātman* and *Jagat* have deeply influenced the philosophical thought of *Brahmanism* and were fully incorporated in the literature of *Brahmanism*. The very concept of society, social order and a disciplined way of life was truly reflected by the *Smṛitigranthas*, especially *Manusmṛiti*. The idea of state, position of kings, their rights and duties were well-elaborated in the light of *Vedic* literature. Ideals of *Varṇaāśhrama-dhārmas*, *puruṣārtha*, law of *karma* and rebirth also have influence of *Vedism* and *Hinduism*.

Mythology

The cosmogony of the *Ṛigvedā* may be looked at from two aspects, the mythological and the philosophical. The mythological aspect has in general two currents, as Professor Macdonell says, 'the one regards the universe as the result of mechanical production, the other represents it as the result of natural generation'. Similarly in the *Ṛigvedā*, we find that the poet in one place says, 'what was the wood and what was the tree out of which they built heaven and earth?'[17] A beautiful answer to this question can be seen in *Taittiriya Brahmana*, '*Brahman* is the wood and *Brahman* is the tree from which the heaven and earth were made' (Macdonell, 1995, 11).

During *Vedic* period the Gods are however personalities presiding over the diverse powers of nature or forming their very essence. The powers of nature, such as the storm, the rain, the thunder, are closely associated with one another and the Gods associated with them are also similar in character. The same epithets are attributed to different Gods and it is only in a few specific qualities that they differ from one another. In the later mythological compositions of the *Purāṇas*, the Gods lost their character as hypostatic powers of nature, and thus become actual personalities and characters having their tales of joy and sorrow like the mortals. *Brahmanism* also believed in the similar mythology.

Theism

Brahmanism follows the religio-philosophical trends of the *Vedās* as well as of *Hinduism*. The *Vedic Aryans* worshipped many Gods: *Indra*, *Agni*, *Varuṇa* and so many others. The plurality of the *Vedic* Gods may lead a superficial enquirer to think the faith of the *Vedic* people polytheistic. But an intelligent reader will find here neither polytheistic nor monotheism but a simple primitive stage of belief to which both of these may be said to owe their origin. The Gods here do not preserve their proper places as in a polytheistic faith, but each one of them shrinks into insignificance. The deity who moved the devotion or admiration of their mind was the most supreme for the time. This peculiar trait of the *Vedic* hymns Max Muller has called Henotheism.

This tendency towards extolling a God as the greatest and highest gradually brought forth the conception of a supreme Lord of all beings, not by a process of conscious generalization but as a necessary stage of development of the mind able to imagine a deity as the repository of the highest moral and physical power, though its direct manifestation cannot be perceived. Thus, the epithet *prajapati*, the lord of beings, which was originally an epithet for other deities, came to be recognized as a supreme deity, the highest and the greatest.

Conclusion

We can see that the *Brāhmanic* tradition has its roots in the *Vedās*, *Upanishads* and *Purāṇas*. *Vedic* metaphysics along with its sociopolitical and religious tradition has deeply influenced the tradition of *Brahmanism*. Both *Śruti* and *Smṛiti* traditions have a great impact on the thinking of *Brāhmanic* tradition. The concept of *puruṣārthas varṇaāśhrama vyvastha* not only expresses the spiritual outlook and wisdom of *Vedic* seers but also provides a very well-ordered social framework. Although division of society into four *varṇas* has been severely criticized by the learned scholars and social thinkers, it has been confused with the notion of caste system. Here, it is to be noted that we find clear mentions, both in *Ṛigvedā* and in *Bhagwadgīta* that the basis of the division of society into four classes (*varṇas*) was never the caste. In fact, till the time of *Purāṇas*, the division of society into four *varṇas* had never been decided on the ground of birth. If we have an open view towards this, we will find that this division of the society was made (prevalent) on the basis of an individual's capabilities or qualities, as specifically uttered in the fourth chapter of *Gīta*, later on this *varṇa* system had converted into caste system.

Puruṣārtha is also a very important phenomenon of *Brāhmaṇa* ideology which gives clear directives to the people of that time, how to live in the material world not only with full dignity but also prepare one's life for the attainment of the highest or absolute end of human life. The very concept of *Puruṣārthas* is beautifully designed to proceed for spiritual life while enjoying worldly life and performing one's social duties and responsibilities.

Having a critical perspective, one can say that *Vedic* emphasis on the performance or rituals and sacrificial ceremonies somehow raises a finger towards the rationale of these practices. The motive behind the division of society into four *varṇas* (*Brāhmaṇa*, *Kṣatriya*, *Vaiśya* and *Śūdra*) was no doubt pure and without any prejudices but it was misinterpreted by the later generations and as a result of this *varṇasvyvastha* turn into caste system. The caste system was based on birth, which means a person born in a *Brāhmaṇa* family will be treated as *Brāhmaṇa* whether he or she possess required qualifications for the same or not. This view has given birth to some other social evils, such as gender discrimination, notion of untouchability and caste-based discrimination. All these practices were not only unethical but also inhuman in nature. Even today society is facing so many value crises as a result of previous ill practices, which should be strongly opposed and needed a fair criticism.

Summary

India's cultural heritage is not only one of the most ancient, but it is also one of the most extensive and varied. The *Vedās*, the sacred books of India, are generally believed to be the earliest literary record of the *Aryan* race. It is indeed a difficult task to say when the earliest portions of these compositions came into existence. Many shrewd guesses have been offered, but none of them can be proved to be incontestably true. *Vedās* are sometimes known as *Śruti*, meaning oral tradition based on hearing. When the *Vedās* were composed, there was probably no system of writing prevalent in India. But such was the scrupulous zeal of the *Brāhmaṇs*, who got the whole *Vedic* literature by heart and by hearing it fṛom their preceptors, that it has been transmitted most faithfully to us through the course of the last 3,000 years or more with little or no interpolations at all. *Brahmanism* is the continuation of *Vedic* culture and philosophy. It is also believed that the *Vedic* culture was brought to India by Indo-Europeans or *Aryans* around 1500 BCE.

The chapter has discussed the essential features of *Brāhmanic* tradition, such as *Varṇaāśhrama* system which was determined on capability of the persons, not by birth. The doctrine of *karma* and rebirth is also discussed in detail along with the theory of incarnation (*Avatara*). Concepts of *Brāhman* (the ultimate reality), immortality of soul, reality of world (*Jagat*) and human being (*Jiva*), salvation and way to salvation are also given due space in the chapter. It also throws light on *Dharmaśāstra* tradition. Descriptions regarding the metaphysical concepts of *Brāhmanic* tradition—God, Soul and the world—have also been covered under the heading metaphysical aspects of society. According to the *Brāhmanic* tradition, God (*Brahmā*) is the ultimate reality and soul is inseparable with *Brahmā*. World is real only from a practical point of view. Metaphysical view (*Advaita Vedānta*) does not accept the transcendental reality of the world. They assume that world is unreal.

Idea of state and the kingship is another heading of the chapter which includes the theory of government in ancient India. Concept of *puruṣārtha-chatushtaya*, that is, *dhārma*, *ārtha*, *kāma* and *mokṣa*, has been discussed in detail in the light of *Varṇaāśhrama vyavastha*. There is a controversial point for discussion that whether the basis of class division (*varṇavyavastha*) was caste and determined by birth or the division of class was based on the capability of a person. For example, a person born in a *Brāhmaṇ* family may become *Kṣatriya* or can be *Vaiśyas* and similarly a *Kṣatriya* person can join the *Brāhmaṇ* class due to his/her abilities or qualities. A lot of illustrations have been given in the religious texts of the *Hindus* regarding the same.

As far as the political organization–kingship is concerned, it is to be noted that the *Vedic* Indians had just left the nomadic stage and were settling down into an agricultural community. There are, therefore, several traces of the nomadic stage preserved in the *Vedic* literature. Kings are, for instance, described as the rulers over tribes like the *Kurus*, the *Panchals*, the *Yadus* and the *Turvashas*. They are not described as rulers over particular regions, nor are the boundaries of their kingdoms defined anywhere. The territorial state, however, was fast coming into existence and the later *Vedic* literature clearly refers to it. Role of sacred texts like *Vedās*, *Upaniṣhads*, *Purāṇas*, *Srimad Bhagwadgīta* and various *Smṛitigranthas* have also been discussed in the chapter. Different forms of theism, such as 'Polytheism', 'Henotheism' and 'Monotheism' were also prevalent during *Vedic* period, which has been accepted by various Indian and Western scholars. *Hindu* mythology takes its full-fledged shape during *Brāhmanic* tradition.

Points for Discussion

1. Discuss the origin and evolution of *Brāhmanic* tradition.
2. Write an essay on the essential characteristics of *Brāhmanic* tradition.
3. What was the role of *Dharmaśāstra* tradition?
4. Write an essay on the duties of kings and the rights of citizens.
5. Critically analyse the role of sacred texts, mythology and theism for the contribution of *Brāhmanic* tradition.

Endnotes

1. Brahadarnyakopnishad, IV, 4.3
2. SrimadBhagvadGita IV, 7 and 8
3. Isha Upanishad; Mundakopnishad, ii.1.10, ii.2.5.7
4. Kathopnishad 1-3-4 and i.3.3.9.10
5. Brahadaranyaka Upanishad, IV 5.13.
6. Kathopnishad, i.3.4 and i.3.3.9.10
7. AyamAtma Brahma, Mundkopnishad, 1.2–4,1.2
8. Isha Upanishad, i, Mundakopnishad, i.1.10 and ii.2.5.7
9. Aitereya Upanishad, i.i
10. Brahma Satyam JagatMithya, JivaBrahmaiv Na Para.
11. Kathopnishad 1-3-4 and i.3.3.9.10

12. *Mahabharata*, Shantiparva, LXVIII, 8–9
13. Samvada Series-7 p. 20
14. APTE; The Practical Sanskrit English Dictionary, pp. 429, 437
15. *Mahabharata*, 12.8.16–21
16. Valmiki, Ramayana, Aranyakanda, Canto 9:30, p. 511
17. Rigveda; X-81.4

Glossary

***Āśhramas*:** Four stages of life.

***Avatara*:** Incarnation which means when God takes birth on this earth in human body.

***Brahmacharya*:** Celibacy; control over one's sexual instincts.

Brh: A Sanskrit root word which means to become big or great.

***Chaturvarga*:** Four member set of values, that is, *dhārma*, *ārtha*, *kāma* and *mokṣa*.

***Dhārma*:** The word *dhārma* is used in the sense of virtues as well as in the sense of religious merit; here it means 'duty'.

***Dvija*:** The other name of a *Brāhmaṇa*

Five sacrifices: *Pnacha Mahayajña*, that is, *Brahma-yajna*, *Pitra-yajña*, *Deva-yajna*, *Bhoota-yajña* and *Nra-yajña*.

Five *yamas*: Five vows, that is, truth, non-violence, non-stealing, non-possession and celibacy.

Forest treatises: *Aranyakas*, that is, a part of *Vedās* (*Brāhmaṇas*, *Aranyaka* and *Upaniṣhad*).

***Grahastha*:** Married peoples/couples/householders/people having family. In other words, when a person gets married and lives a family life.

Henotheism: A belief in single God each in turn standing out as the highest.

***Karma-phala-vipaka*:** Fruits or results of *Karma*, results of previous *karmas* performed in the past or present life.

***Mahābhārata*:** A famous Indian epic or a mythological story.

***Parivrajakas*:** *Sanyasin*, a person who has joined ascetic life.

***Papa*:** Demerit, wrong actions producing bad results. The term is opposite to *Punya* and used generally in religious domain.

***Punarjanma*:** Rebirth, when a person takes birth after death.

***Punya*:** Merit or right actions producing good results. The term is especially used in religious field.

***Purohita*:** King's highest religious advisor and performer of various religious ceremonies and rituals.

***Rta*:** Eternal cosmic order, in the *Vedic* age. It is also known as eternal moral order of the universe.

Sacrifices: *Vedic* rituals or religious offerings towards various Gods and Goddesses.

***Sanyasa*:** The ascetic, when a person indulges in the realm of *Sadhana* (spiritual life) and engages himself in the recitation of the name of God.

Three debts: Traya *Rna*, that is, *Deva Rna*, *Pitra Rna* and *Riṣhi Rna*.

Transcendental: Parmarthika, objects beyond the physical world or other worldly.

***Trayi*:** The three *Vedās*, that is, *Ṛigvedā*, *Yajurvedā* and *Atharvavedā*.

Trinity: Three forms of God, that is, *Brahmā*, *Viṣṇu* and *Mahesh* (*Rudra*).

***Trivarga*:** Three set of values, that is, *dhārma*, *ārtha* and *kāma*.

***Vanaprastha*:** The forest-dweller, when a person goes to forest, for spiritual quest and gives up his/her family life.

***Varṇas*:** Four classes of society.

References

Cultural Heritage of India. 1937. Vol. 1. Calcutta: Ramkrishna Institute of Culture.
Das Gupta, S. 1932. *A History of Indian Philosophy*, Vol. I. Cambridge: The University Press.
Dutta, D. and S. Chatterjee. 2007. *An Introduction to Indian Philosophy*. New Delhi: Rupa Publication Pvt. Ltd.
Macdonell, Arthur Anthony. 1995. *Vedic Mythology*. Delhi: Motilal Banarsidass.
Mohapatra, P. K. ed. 1994. *Studies on the Purusarthas*. Bhubaneswar: Utkal University, DSA in Philosophy.
Murti, T. R. V. 1960. *The Centre Philosophy of Buddhism*. London: George Allen & Unwin.
Omvedt, Gail. 2003. *Buddhism in India*. Delhi: SAGE Publications.
Prasad, Beni. 1974. *Theory of Government in Ancient India*. Allahabad: Central Book Depot.
Radhakrishshnan, S. 2009. *Indian Philosophy*, Vol. I. Oxford: Oxford University Press.
Sinha, J. N. 1952. *Indian Philosophy*, Vol. I. Calcutta: Sinha Publishing House Ltd.
Suryakant. 1981. *A Practical Vedic Dictionary*. Delhi: Oxford University Press.
Tola, C. F. F. and C. Dragonettt. 1980. 'Anaditva or Beginninglessness Indian Philosophy.' *Annals of the Bhandarkar Oriental Research Institute* LXI(1–4): 12–4.

Further Readings

Bose, A. C. 1999. *The Call of the Vedas*. Bombay: Bharatiya Vidya Bhavan.
Prasad, Beni. 1974. *Theory of Government in Ancient India*. Allahabad: Central Book Depot.
Radhakrishnan, S. *Indian Philosophy*, Vols. I and II.
Sinha, J. N. *Indian Philosophy*, Vols. I and II.

4

CHAPTER

Manu: A Progenitor of Humanity

Mona Singh

CHAPTER OUTLINE

- Introduction
- The Life Sketch
- Theory of Kingship
- Theory of State
- Social Order and Classification of Society
- *Dhārma* and *Daṇḍanīti*
- Conclusion
- Summary
- Points for Discussion

To the Western world, the code of Manu or Manusamhita is the best known work of its kind…it is the oldest book on Hindu law.

—*D. Mackenzie Brown (1964, 26–27)*

Reader's Guide

The aim or purpose of this chapter is to highlight the contribution of Manu to Indian political thought. The laws of Manu, his political ideas on the origin of state, importance of the state and science of politics, administration of state, duties of the ruler, the *Varṇaāśhrama dhārma*, the issues of caste, diplomacy, politics and morals are discussed at length in this chapter.

Introduction

In ancient India, people believed in having order and regularity of the world as the manifestation of God's will and intent. Hence, the code of laws governing the conduct of individuals, the order and regularity of the *Hindu* society were formulated by many scholars and sages in ancient and early times. Their work is available in the 18 *Dharmaśāstra,* among which the work of Manu (*Manusmṛiti*) is considered as the most important. The laws of Manu in Sanskrit quoted as the *Manusmṛiti* or *Manavdharmaśāstra* is a 'work of encyclopedic scope' (Doniger and Smith 1991, 16). It comprises of 2,685 verses on varied topics interrelated in *Hindu* thought. It contains social obligations and duties of the various castes and of individuals in different stages of life. It further lays down proper guidelines which a king needs to follow to govern. It defines the social relations between men and women of different castes, husbands and wives in the privacy of the home, birth and rebirth, ritual practices, minor details of everyday life. This text is certainly the culmination of the texts of prominent early authors. It is attributed to the legendary figure called Manu—the name of a king, a mythological ancestor of the human race. Manu is considered as the progenitor of human race and the 'Indian Adam' or *Manava.* According to the holy *Purāṇas* and *Ṛigvedā,* he is called as the first law giver and also the father to mankind, the founder of social and moral order, a *Riṣhi* to whom sacred books were revealed. Manu had been an ardent supporter of the 'divine right theory' of the origin of the state. In *Manusmṛiti,* he considered the state to be a creation of God as there was fear and anarchy in the state of nature; therefore, the Lord of the world created the king for the protection of the world. Further, he dealt with the administrative structure of the state, decentralization of the state, dividing the state into units of one village and above it, units of 10, 20, 100 and 1,000 villages (Appadorai 2002, 55).

The Life Sketch

Manu is regarded as the first *Hindu* political philosopher who laid the foundations of India's political traditions in ancient India. Manu was the first progeny of the creator *Brahmā.* The study of Manu has become more relevant with the emergence of *Hindu* revivalism in Modern India. It is impossible to trace the origin of Manu to a particular period. Sir William Jones traces the origin of Manu to 1200 BC, while Bhandarkar talks of the origin of Manu between the middle of the 2nd century AD and the end of 5th century AD. Hopkins in his *Cambridge History of India,* says that Manu lived in the beginning of or even before the Christian era.

According to *Agnipurana,* Manu created himself and exhibited his power of kingship in different periods (*Agnipurana* Ist Part: 60). In the *Manusmṛiti,* it is mentioned that there were seven Manus who existed in different periods. Those were Svayambhuba Manu, Swarochisa Manu, Outtami Manu, Tamasha Manu, Raibata Manu, Chhakshusa Manu and Mahatejasvi Vaivasvata Manu (*Manusmṛiti,* Chapter 1, Hymn 51–62). The *Agnipurana* mentioned about 14 Manus. Besides the above-mentioned seven Manus, the eighth Manu was the son of *Aditya* (the Sun) who created him out of his shadow and his name was *Savarni.* It also talks about its origin to different assumptions. A common strand between all these was that Manu was the creator and first *Hindu* king of ancient India. The essence of the *Vedās* are projected by Manu in his *smṛitis.*

The *Manusmṛiti*

Manusmṛiti is one of the most unique and scholarly works of Manu who had the opportunity of listening to *Brahmā*—the God—and transmitted it to different *Ṛiṣhis* and *Mahariṣhis* like *Bhrigu* and *Marichi*' (*Manusmṛiti,* Chapter I, Hymn 58–59). It is known by various names, such as *Manusamhita, Manudhārma,* etc. The *smṛitis* of Manu occupy an exceptional position and significance. It is considered the most important treatise on society, religion and statecraft. Along with being an important literary source of ancient Indian polity, it is viewed as the major law book for establishing the supreme, sovereign and coercive power of the king for establishing the stringent social hierarchy or the caste system in society and for reaffirming firmly the subordinate role of women in society. *Manusmṛiti* is like the Ganges, having its origin in the *Vedās*. Therefore, it is treated as the most authoritative work. It codified the laws in ancient India. For the first time it created the political theory of a social order, government, *daṇḍa*, law and justice. After the *Vedās*, the *Manusmṛiti* is the most outstanding book on the *Hindu* way of life (Das and Patro 1988, 1).

Chapterization

The *Manusmṛiti* consists of 12 chapters and 2,684 hymns and depicted as an important treatise on society, religion and statecraft. It also describes the nature of government and administration, kingship, the functioning of courts and the division of society into *varṇas*. The various customs which are to be observed during the course of entire life and after death are explained in it. Out of the 12 chapters, the first chapter consisting of 119 hymns deals with the origin of the universe, the second chapter consisting of 249 hymns deals with the different parts and duties of life, such as hereditary occupation, process of purification, *Brahmacharya* (celibacy) and devotion to the *Guru* (the teacher). The third chapter consisting of 286 hymns deals with the householder's life, the system of marriage, rules regarding happy married life, evils of inter-caste marriage. The fourth chapter consisting of 260 hymns deals with the rules of *Grahastha* life and *varṇa* order. The firth chapter consisting of 169 hymns deals with the pure and impure food, ceremonial purification and duties of wife. The sixth chapter has 97 hymns and it is about *vaṇaprastha* and *Sanyasa*. The seventh chapter consists of 226 hymns. The seventh chapter of *Manusmṛiti* deals with various aspects of *rājādhārma* or statecraft, such as who should be a king, what are his duties towards the people and personal, and how the preservation and integration of social order can be achieved. In addition to this, it also explains the court and payment of tax. The eighth chapter includes 420 hymns laying down the civil and criminal law (system of witness). The ninth chapter consists of 336 hymns, deals with divorce, distribution of property and civil law. The tenth chapter consisting of 131 hymns talks about duties of different castes. The eleventh chapter covering 265 hymns deals with system of penance, performances of sacrifice and rules of keeping away from vices. The last and twelth chapter deals with rules of social life, *mokṣa*, self-knowledge, self-examination and duties towards the society and the state (Mohanty 1997, 3).

In these 12 chapters, Manu has depicted the systematized groups of society, religion and polity. It refers to all the aspects of life, administration, kingship and the duties and responsibilities of the king. Moreover, the kind of government, establishments and function of courts are also covered in *Manusmṛiti*.

Theory of Kingship

Brahmā, while in his plan of creation, implanted the human race which started from Manu. Manu was the creator, the philosopher and he is regarded as the first *Hindu* king of ancient India. When creatures were dispersed in various directions out of fear from each other, the Lord created the king for the protection of the society. This king was formed out of the essence of eight deities, that is, *Indra*, *Pawan* (wind), *Yama*, Sun, Fire, *Varuna*, Moon and *Kubera* (lord of wealth) and even in the *Mahābhārata*, we can find the reference of this. Manu is ordained by God, as the ruler of the people, to bring an end to the state of nature. As *Manusmṛiti* says: 'Let no man therefore transgress that law which the king decrees with respect to those in his favour nor his orders which inflict pain on those in disfavour.'

Divine origin of the kingship was given by Manu. The kingship originated as a result of the creation of God. Anarchical conditions faced by the people, their trouble and suffering eventually led to the creation of the king by God on earth. His duties included ensuring peace, prosperity for his people, providing an honest and efficient administration and to meet the needs of the people.

K. P. Jawyaswal holds the view that the theory of divinity of the king was advanced by *Manusmṛiti* to support the *Brāhmaṇa* empire of *Pusyamitra* and also to counter the Buddhist theory of the origin of the state by way of a contract (Singh and Roy 2014, 20). God, being the creator of this cosmic world, was responsible for the welfare and protection of people; therefore, he created the institution of kingship. The king was the representative of God on earth. This has been elaborated in the *Vedās* and *Upaniṣhads*. *Manusmṛiti*, therefore, subscribes to the king as a creation of God on earth.

Qualities of the King

Manu's king was an ideal man, to be well educated, a person of high moral character and intellect. He was to abstain from sexual desires, anger, greed and lust. He too had to be free from corruption, but true to *dhārma*, *ārtha*, *kāma* and *mokṣa*—the four pillars of *Satvik* life. He was also expected to possess qualities like *sāma*, *dāma*, *daṇḍa* and *bheda*. The *daṇḍa* of the king or the coercive authority of the king involved the *daṇḍanīti*, that is, the punishment meted out to be proportional to the severity of the crime committed (punishment of offenders). Manu's king has been an ardent supporter of the divinity principle, the *Matsyasanyaya* and application of *daṇḍa*, that is, the coercive power or authority of the ruler or the power of punishment. As said by Altekar, to Manu, it is the *daṇḍa* which governs the people, protects them and is the custodian of *dhārma*. The whole world is kept in order by the fear of *daṇḍa*. The king who is truthful, wise, virtuous, efficient and impartial is justified to use *daṇḍa*. Since the king was the most important unit of the entire state administration, Manu emphasized on the moral qualifications of the ruler or the king. He was to follow the advice of the *Brāhmaṇs* who were learned in *Vedās*, and in a position to control his senses. On the other hand, a corrupt and inefficient king is destroyed by the same *daṇḍa* which he inflicts. The whole world stands in awe of one who is ready to apply *daṇḍa*.

Certain scriptures like *Manusamhita* explain that the origin of state is from the divine. As in *Manusamhita*, it says, 'the Lord created the king for the protection of his whole creation … even an infant king must not be desposed (from an idea) that he is only a mortal, because he is a great deity in human form'. Manu as a law codifier of ancient India deals with theory of the structure of state, nature and functions of the government (king) and presents a system of law to deal with both the civil and criminal cases that regulates the external human conduct.

Manu's views are a combination of the divine origin theory and the organic theory of state with regard to his views on government. Manu followed the old *Vedic* doctrine of the two powers, such as temporal and spiritual by bestowing ruling authority upon the king. This power was to be exercised by them over the people by divine orientation.[1]

The *Matsyanyaya*—Nature in the *Vedās*—was regarded as a hierarchically ordered set of *mandalas* (circles) and the social world, no less than the natural one, is one of the rulers and the ruled, the consumers and the consumed, the exploiters and the exploited, the strong and the weak. The text says that, those that do not move are the food of those that move. Eating and killing were two sides of the same coin. The *Hindu* metaphor of the Law of Fishes, the *Matsyanyaya*, here the bigger fish eats the smaller one, is the continuation of the *Vedic* assumptions. In other words, this theory proposes that government, rulers and laws are necessary to prevent this natural law of *Matsyanyaya* from operating in human society.

Concept of Divine Theory of Kingship

The king was created by *Brahmā*. Manu gives a theory of the divine right of kingship. When the world was without a king and were trembling with fear, God created the king for the protection of the people. The king was all powerful. He was the fire and wind, the Sun and the Moon, the king of Justice, the *Kubera*, the *Varuṇa* and the great Indra. Though a child, the king is not to be despised as a human being for he is a powerful divinity in man's form (Aurther Coke Burnell, op. at. p. 49).

Manu wanted the divine king to be an embodiment of certain qualities:

1. Worshipper of aged *Brāhmaṇs*, well versed in *Vedās* and threefold sacred science and various trends and professions.
2. Conqueror of his own senses.
3. Immune from 10 vices springing from love of pleasure (*kāma*) and eight vices from wrath (*krodh*).
4. Not to be avaricious.

Theory of State

Manu believed in the organic theory of the state. *Manusmṛiti* says that (a) lord (or king), (b) minister, (c) capital, (d) *rashtra*, (e) treasure, (f) army (or force) and (g) ally are the seven characteristics *(prakratis)* of the state. For this reason, the state is called *Saptanga*—having seven limbs of the state (Sharan 1983, 216). The same view has been expressed by *Yājñavalkya* in the *prakaran* entitled '*rājādhārma*'. According to him, the lord (king), *amatya* (minister), the people *(jana)*, fort (city), treasure, punishment (*daṇḍa*) and ally are fundamentals of the state. That is why the state is called *Saptanga*. In *Manusmṛiti* version of *Saptanga* theory, fort and *jānpada* are replaced by *pura* and *rashtra*, that is, capital and kingdom.

Functions of the King

The functions of the king were many and authority onerous, yet he should not be regarded as absolute or arbitrary. Manu kept the king under the principles of *dhārma* which means that the power of King is subordinate to *dhārma*. According to *Manusmṛiti*, the king performed some executive functions. Among the executive functions, the first one was protection and the second was punishments, that is, the protection of all castes and creed with special reference to the minors and women and safeguarding the weak against the strong. *Daṇḍa* or punishment was considered as the perfection of justice. Manu not only imposed restrictions on the powers of the king but kept him under the grip of the political sovereign and *dhārma*—the law of righteousness. With regard to laws, the king made laws which he could not pass as substantive laws (laws which made him arbitrary). He could pass only regulatory laws. The functions of the king are as follows:

> **Administrative:** It involved making of appointments of officials—appointment making powers, tackling various administrative problems, ending and eradicating corruption and corrupt officials, giving the due punishment if found guilty of corruption. 'Manu made ample provision for the protection of the common people against the dishonesty officials' (Spellman 1964, 133).
> **Legislative:** Since the 18 (Arthashastra B. K., ch. 9-I) titles already existed, the king's major legislative duty was confined to mere application of the regulations already existing. He was to make only regulatory laws and not laws substantive or laws making him arbitrary.
> **Judicial:** The king examined the cases falling under the 18 titles daily in the court.
> **Ecclesiastical:** The king's responsibility included the appointment of the chief priest and also choosing other priests for performing his domestic rites and sacrifices and he was to offer various *Srauta* sacrifices.
> **Revenue:** The regulation of treasury fixation of rates, taxes and duties all were included under the revenue function of the king. However, he realized only the due taxes. In emergencies, such taxes could be enhanced. In the *Manava* code, the king is shown as his own finance minister as he holds the charge of the finance though he is not directly named as such in Manu.
> **Military:** He was to be a *Kṣatriya*, born to be a fighter, who fought courageously and with honour. Appointment of commander-in-chief was one of the functions of the king. Also, other officials, ambassadors appointed by him conducted the war and peace negotiations.
> **Enlightened:** The promotion of culture and learning comprised these functions.

The above enumerate the duties and functions of the king according to *Manusmṛiti*. The enforcement of law governing the social order is part of the protection for which the kingship was constituted.

Other Duties of the King

The king was to punish the wrong doers. If the *Rājā* were not to punish the evil door, the stronger would roast the weaker like fish on a spit, the crow would peck at the consecrated food, the dog would eat the sacred ghee, the rich would be deprived of all their wealth and the twice born would be overcome by the *Śūdra*. 'Not to turn back in battle, to protect the people, to honour the *Brāhmaṇs* are the best means for a king to secure happiness.'

Daily Routine of the King

The daily routine of the monarch for the performance of his heavy duties has been laid down in many works, including Kauṭilya's *Arthaśāstra*, which divides the day and night into 16 equal parts and allocates to each part a particular item of his duties. Manu said that the king should have knowledge of two things, that is, *dhārma* or duty and second, of force or punishment. Without this, he cannot maintain his personality and prestige.

Chapter seven of *Manusmṛiti* deals with the duties of the king. It lists eight types of duties for the king. These include income, expenditure, maintenance of the conduct of the personnel, building of forts (*durg*) and road, and building of ties with allies. Therefore, the king must treat all his subjects equally and not have any apathy towards any section of the people except the guilty. He was to defend the Rajya and to look after the helpless, aged, disabled, pregnant, women, widows, orphans and sick people.

Sachiva

The king has to look into the appointment of ministers and distribution of functions among the ministers according to the efficiency of the person. He pleads for the appointment of high officials or ministers (*Sachiva*) to look after each department of the government separately. The ministers were to be learned, efficient, learned in *Vedās*, loyal to the *Rājān* or king. Important principles underlying the council of ministers include (a) the principle of tradition, (b) the principle of ability, (c) the test of courage, (d) the principle of examination and (e) the principle of fulfilment of objectives. The king was to carry out his duties in consultation with the ministers both individually and collectively, that is, to follow the opinion of the *adhikaris* or ministers with portfolios, the precedents and his subjectives. If the king becomes independent of his council, he might run the risk of ruin.

Importance of Judicial Administration

Under the judicial preview came the duty of the king to examine daily the suits or litigants falling under the 18 titles of law, in accordance with the principles derived from regional usage (*desadrishta*) and from the sacred canon (*sastradrishta*).

Social Order and Classification of Society

According to Manu, the *Brāhmaṇs*, the *Kṣatriyas*, *Vaiśyas* and *Śūdras* sprang, respectively, from the mouth, arms, thigh and feet of the creator. Manu introduced a system of rigidity and made the *Brāhmaṇs* the most privileged caste and even superior even to the kings. The most deprived group was that of the *Śūdras*. Codes of conduct for a *Brāhmaṇa* was that of teaching, reading, sacrifice and sacrificing (as priests) for others. A *Brāhmaṇ* or priest is considered as the lord of the other classes. He is pre-eminent and is best by nature because he maintains the restraints and because of the pre-eminence of his transformative rituals. He exists for the sake of *dhārma* and is for the existence of the *Vedās*. He has said to have described the priest, the ruler and the commoner as the twice born classes, though the fourth, the servant (*Śūdras*), has only one birth. Although considered to be superior, he had to remain poor and ask for alms and abjure political powers. Therefore, Manu demies to the *Brāhmaṇs* the dual powers—economic and political—and suggests rigorous standards of behaviour and discipline.

A *Brāhmaṇa* is a twice born who undergoes the process of sanctifying the body and purifying his life. As Manu has further prohibited *Brāhmaṇs* from marrying in other castes or *varṇas*. A *Brāhmaṇa's* son can be a *Brāhmaṇ* only when he marries a lady of his own caste. A *Brāhmaṇa* needs to undergo austerity and stick to *Vedic* rituals or else he would lose the fruits of a successful *Brāhmaṇa*. The *Brāhmaṇa* is given the exclusive responsibility to guide the king and in turn the king needs to respect him. Another important freedom given to the *Brāhmaṇs* was of occupational mobility, they were allowed to join defence or agriculture.

The *Kṣatriyas* arose from the arms of the creator, *Brahmā*. He was to protect the people, to offer sacrifices and to study the *Vedās* and also abstain himself from sexual pleasures (Buhler 1993).

Manu believed that a society would be considered more secure if there was a harmonious relation between the *Brāhmaṇs* and *Kṣatriyas*. The *Vaiśyas* were to be involved in trade and business, and the *Śūdras* were to be confined to an occupation of serving the above three castes. The *Śūdras* were debarred from all social learning. Manu accorded them a very low profile in the society. This four-hold classification was called the *Chaturvarna* theory. It was designed to maintain harmony in the society.

The *Vaiśyas* emerged from the thighs of the creator and constitutes the third rank in the social hierarchy. Their functions included to tend the cattle, to bestow gifts, to offer sacrifices, to study the *Vedās*, trading, lending money and cultivations of land. Manu gave them the right to study the *Vedās* but cannot teach the *Vedās*. The thread ceremony of *Vaiśyas* would be different from the *Brāhmaṇs* and the *Kṣatriyas*.

The *Śūdras* occupy the lowest position in Manu's code of laws. They are to serve the three other castes and are the most deprived section of society. Just like Plato and Aristotle undermined the importance of the manual labourers, Manu also undermined the importance of the *Śūdras* and said that they can never form a stable society. A kingdom or state having sudras and infested with atheists would be afflicted with disease and famine and soon perish (Prasad and Keith 1968, 72).

Chandalas or *varṇa samskāras* were lower than the *Śūdras*. They were the product of hypergamous unions. Hypergamous union takes place due to either *anuloma* or *pratiloma* marriages.[2] Manu was opposed to *pratiloma* marriages because its progeny becomes a *Chandala* or *varṇa samskāra*.

Dhārma and *Daṇḍanīti*

To Manu, the establishment and preservation of *dhārma* were the most important duties of the king. For the establishment of *dhārma*, the preservation of the family and the prevention of adultery were highly important and necessary. Also, another important duty of the divine king was the preservation of the caste or the *varṇa* system. In fact, this was considered the most important duty of the king. The kingdom prospers only so long as the purity of the castes was maintained otherwise the kingdom perishes. Maintenance of caste is the most important duty of the king, as it is an indispensable element of *dhārma*. *Dhārma*, if violated, would lead to dissolution of the whole society.

The Function of the *Daṇḍa*

The main idea behind the incorporation of *daṇḍa* was to ensure individual security of a person, and property and protection and stability of the social order. *Daṇḍa* was at times identified with *dhārma* or law, indicating that one is the essential means for fulfilling the other. Manu has therefore elaborated the king's unlimited jurisdiction on all the offenders and criminals irrespective of their social status. This stands in similarity with Kauṭilya's *Arthaśāstra* principle of *daṇḍa*. The basic idea behind *daṇḍa* was to punish the wrong-doers, that is, who are actually found guilty, so that they may try to correct themselves and serve as a warning to others. *Daṇḍa* (Rod of authority). Thus, *daṇḍa* was used not only to create the state but also to check mutual struggle amongst the *varṇas*.

Conclusion

Manu's exposition of the concept of kingship, running of the administrative machinery of the state, the role of the king as a protector, the law codes, the *Varṇaāśhrama dhārma*, the theory of *daṇḍa*, all reflect that if economic and political aspects were provided by Kauṭilya then the social laws were given by Manu. In fact, some of the theories as given by Western political thinkers emanated from the minds of ancient Indian political thinkers like Manu.

Summary

Manu was one of the most important figures in the history of ancient Indian political thought. His *Manavdharmaśāstra* or *Manusmṛiti* is the most famous authoritative text of human conduct and Indian polity. In *Manusmṛiti*, Manu has dealt with every aspect of political life and administration. Further, the *Manusmṛiti* laid down the rules to be observed by a righteous person including righteous king.

Points for Discussion

1. Critically analyse the hierarchical social order as propounded in *Manusmṛiti*.
2. Evaluate the structural formulations of Manu on social system.
3. Critically analyse the role of *Manusmṛiti* in the formulations of social laws.
4. Evaluate the political implications of Manu's social laws.

Endnotes

1. The ideas expressed in the *Manusmṛiti* were not original and had already been articulated in the *Vedic* texts. Manu had well defined the existing social practices and prevalent ideas and codified in the texts. These ideas were well preserved in the later Indian thought.
2. *Anuloma* marriage is when there is an inter-caste marriage between the woman of a lower caste with a man of higher caste. *Pratiloma* marriage takes place when a man of lower caste marries a woman of higher caste.

Glossary

Dharmaśāstra: It refers to the science of *dhārma* and a series of text which teach the eternal immutable *dhārma* found in *Vedās*.

Daṇḍanīti: It refers to the laws that are to be followed to punish a person for the crime committed by him or her and also in proper administration of the state affairs.

References

Appadorai, A. 2002. *Political Thoughts in India: 400 BC–1980*. Delhi: Khama Publishers.

Brown, D. Mackenzie. 1964. *The White Umbrella: Indian Political Thought From Manu to Gandhi*, 26–27. Berkeley, CA: University of California Press.

Buhler, G. 1993. *The Laws of Manu*. Delhi: Motilal Banarasidass.

Burnell, Aurther Coke. 1972. *Hindu Polity*. Ludhiana: Kalyani Publishers.

Das, H. H. and P. S. N. Patro. 1988. *Indian Political Traditions*. New Delhi: Sterling Publishers.

Mohanty, Dusmanta Kumar. 1997. *Indian Political Traditions: From Manu to Ambedkar*. New Delhi: Anmol Publications.

Sharan, Parmatma. 1983. *Ancient Indian Political Thought and Institutions*. New Delhi: Meenakshi Prakashan.

Singh, M. P. and Himanshu Roy. 2014. *Indian Political Thought: Themes and Thinkers*. Delhi: Pearson.

Spellman, John W. 1964. *Political Theory of Ancient India: A Study of Kingship from the Earliest Times to Circa A.D. 300*. New York: Oxford University Press.

Further Readings

Doniger, Wendy. 2009. *The Hindus: An Alternative History*. New Delhi: Penguin.

Doniger, Wendy and Brian K. Smith. 1991. *The Laws of Manu*. New Delhi: Penguin Classics.

Ghoshal, U. N. 1966. *A History of Indian Political Ideas*. London: Oxford University Press.

Mehta, V. R. 2014. *Foundations of Indian Political Thought*. New Delhi: Manohar Publishers and Distributors.

Prasad, Beni and A. B. Keith. 1968. *The Theory of Government in Ancient India*. Allahabad: Central Book Depot.

Sengupta, Lopamudra. 2016. *Indian Political Thought and Its Contemporary Relevance*. New Delhi: Atlantic Publishers and Distributors.

5

CHAPTER

Yājñavalkya: A Vedic Sage

Swasti Alpana

CHAPTER OUTLINE

- Introduction
- The Life Sketch
- *Dharmaśāstras* and *Rājādhārma*
- Ethical and Social Virtues
- *Karma*, Rebirth and Spiritual Liberation
- Dialogue between *Yājñavalkya* and *Maitreyī*
- Comparative Study of *Yājñavalkyasmṛiti* and the *Manusmṛiti*
- Conclusion
- Summary
- Points for Discussion

पञ्चधा संभूतः कायो यदि पञ्चत्वमागतः।
कर्मभिः स्वशरीरोत्थैस्त्य का परिदेवताः॥

The body has originated from the five elements of earth, water, fire, air and space, by the fruit of deeds acquired by one's own person and it is dissolved into the five elements, what is there to repent for?

(*Yājñavalkyasmṛiti* II.9)

Reader's Guide

Smṛitis have played a great part not only in determining the features of many a political, social, legal and religious institution and custom of Indian subcontinent but also in shaping *Hinduism* as it is today. This work seeks to analyse the evidence of *Yājñavalkyasmṛiti* on sociopolitical structure and values of *Hindu* India. Although the *smṛiti* texts belong to one particular age and their dicta have particular relevance for the study of thought of that period, their validity and significance are by no means confined to that period alone. The influence of *Smṛitis* like Manu, *Nārada*, *Bṛhaspati*, *Kātyāyana* and *Yājñavalkya* continued to be enormous through centuries after the period of their composition. In fact, this influence can be seen underlying since many of these laws are prevalent even today. An attempt has been made to be as objective as possible in the interpretation of the custom, usage and proclaimed law depicted and enumerated in *Yājñavalkyasmṛiti* for a better understanding of the existing socio-religious and political structure and its relevance.

Introduction

The word *smṛitis* has been used in a wider and narrower sense. In its wider sense, *smṛitis* includes all literature except *Śrutis* or the *Vedās*. The narrower meaning confines its scope to *Dharmaśāstras* (Manu S.II 10). This is often cited for defining the scope of *smṛitis*. Essential elements underlying the prescriptions and prohibitions contained in the *smṛitis* have undoubtedly had a good deal of influence on Indian social structures and values. The sacred literature of the *Hindus* has been broadly classified under two categories *Śrutis* (literally, 'that which has been heard') and *smṛitis* (literally, 'remembered'). According to the belief of the *Hindus*, *Śrutis* and *smṛitis* are direct revelation and so these are regarded as divine in origin. They are thought to embody an eternal, self-existent truth realized by seers in a state of meditation or revealed to them by the gods. In orthodox theory, the origin of the *smṛiti* is attributed to the self-sprung *Brahmā* who communicated it to Manu, who transmitted the knowledge to the 10 patriarchal sages, such as, Marīchi, Atri, Aṅgira, Pulastya, Pulaha, Kratu, Pracetā, Vasiṣṭha, Bhṛigu and *Nārada*. In its wider perspective, the word *Smṛitis* refers to all orthodox non-*vedic* treatises like the grammar of *Pāṇini*, *Manusmṛiti*, *Yājñavalkyasmṛiti*, *Dharmasūtra*, *Gṛhyasūtra*, *Bhagwadgīta*, *Śrautasūtra*, etc. *Vedās*, *Smṛitis* and *Darśanas* constitute the core of Indian sacred philosophical literature, whereas *Vedās* concerns mainly with universe, *Smṛitis* are society oriented and *Darśanas* deals with Individual. Besides laying down rules for the society, *Smṛitis* follows a holistic approach by keeping in tune with the *Vedās* on one hand and *Darśanas* on the other. That is why it is said that *Smṛitis* follow the *Śrutis*. So the vast literature, in the form of *Smṛitis*, occupies a prominent place in the array of the classical literature. Indian tradition believes in the eternity of the *Vedās*. The earliest and one of the sacred religious works of the Hindus, namely, the *Vedā*, belongs to the former. The *Vedic* literature comprises the works like the 4 *Vedās*, the 6 *Vedāṅgas*, the 18 *Purāṇas*, *Nyāya*, *Mīmāṁsā*, *Dharmaśāstra*, etc. (Yāj., I.3). The works related as auxiliary to the *Vedās* and designed to aid in the correct interpretation of the text are *śikṣā* (the science of proper articulation), *Chandas* (prosody), *vyākraṇa* (grammar), *Nirukta* (etymological explanation of words), *Jyotiṣa* (astronomy) and *Kalpa* (ritual) The *Śrutis* and *Smṛitis* are regarded as the source of religious knowledge. The *Smṛitis* are, therefore, a synthesis of all the scriptural writings.

Objectives

There can be no adequate comprehension of the existing socio-cultural system without a proper knowledge of the dynamics of its progress and historical forces that have shaped it. Such knowledge is all the more necessary for a country like India which has maintained noteworthy continuity in its cultural tradition through the thousands of years of its existence. The Indian socio-cultural system and values have undoubtedly undergone great changes with the passage of time, but the continuity has not been lost. *Smṛitis* are one of the main sources of *Hindu dhārma* in its sociocultural and religious aspects. They have played a great role in determining the course of many a religious and sociocultural institution and custom and in moulding the development of modern *Hinduism*. This work seeks to analyse the evidence of *Yājñavalkyasmṛiti* on sociopolitical structure and values of India. Sage *Yājñavalkya* is known as one of the most celebrated authors of a classical treatise known as *Yājñavalkyasmṛiti*. It is a storehouse of information on the social, cultural, religious, ethical, legal, political, educational and geographical life of the period. *Yājñavalkyasmṛiti* as a compendium of ancient Indian wisdom came into existence to systematically epitomize the need of the society for new provisions in matters of *dhārma*, religious and social. The high degree of sophistication in the analysis of the juristic concepts and procedures found in this text is widely recognized.

The Number of *Smṛitis*

The ancient *smṛitis* are considered as a source of *dhārma*. During very ancient times, the number of *smṛitis* were limited. Gautama has referred to Manu only. Āpastamba mentions 10 authors of the *smṛitis*: Eka, Kaṇva, Kāṇva, Kuṇīka, Kutsa, Kautsa, Puṣkarasādi, Vārṣyāyanī, Śvetketu and Hārita. Manu refers to five besides himself. They are Atri, Bhṛigu, Vaśiṣṭha, Vaikhānasa and Śaunaka. *Yājñavalkya* is the first author who has mentioned 20 *smṛitikāras* including himself and regarded Śaṅkha and Likhita as two distinct authors. The *smṛiti*-candrikā gives the following names of smṛitikāras: Manu, Yama, Dakṣa, *Viṣṇu*, Aṅgirasa, Bṛhaspati, Uśanas, Āpastamba, Gautama, Saṁvarta, Ātreya, Hārita, Kātyāyana, Śāṅkha, Likhita, Pārāśara, *Vyāsa*, Śātapa, Prcetas and *Yājñavalkya* (Kane 2006, 303). *Vṛddha Gautamasmṛiti* mentions 57 *Dharmaśāstras*. Despite all these different views, the commonly accepted view is that there are 20 exponents of *Dharmaśāstra*. The founders of these religious codes, as enumerated in *Yājñavalkya*, are said to be the seers like Manu, Atri, *Viṣṇu*, Harita, *Yājñavalkya*, Uśana, Aṅgirā, Yama, Āpastamba, Saṁvartta, Kātyāyana, Bṛhaspati, Parāśara, *Vyāsa*, Śaṅka, Likhita, Dakṣa, Gautama, Śatāpa and Vasiṣṭha (Yāj., I.4–6). Each of them wrote a *smṛiti* namely *Manusmṛiti*, *Yājñavalkyasmṛiti*, *Atrismṛiti*, *Hāritasmṛiti*, *Auśanasasmṛiti*, *Parāśarasmṛiti*, etc.[1] These *Smṛitis* are the products of different and widely separated ages and enumerate the custom and usage of their own time.

The Pre-eminence of *Yājñavalkya*

Among the *Dharmaśāstra* writers Manu and *Yājñavalkya* stand, in fact, pre-eminent as medieval law-writers, renowned philosophers and illustrious *Vedic* sages. The *Yājñavalkyasmṛiti* of sage *Yājñavalkya* occupies an important place among the treatises on criminal and civil laws. One finds the reference of *Yājñavalkya* in the *Bṛhadāraṇyaka Upaniṣhad* as a renowned philosopher teaching the complex doctrines of *Vedānta* to one of his two wives, the philosophically inclined *Maitreyī*. He is credited with having propagated the White *Yajurveda*. It is mentioned in the *Śāntiparva* (Chap. 312) that there was some disagreement between *Vaiśampāyana* and his disciple *Yājñavalkya* and that by worshipping the Sun the latter received the revelation of the White *Yajurveda*, the *Śatpatha*, etc. (Kane 2006, 421). The strained relations between *Yājñavalkya* and his teacher are also mentioned in *Purāṇas* and other religious texts. He delivered his precepts to a number of ancient philosophers assembled in the province of Mithila in Bihar. *Yājñavalkya*'s importance in Indian history lies in the fact that next to Manu it was he who gave the stamp of sanctity to the sociopolitical institution of land, and left to the Indian land a comprehensive code of civil and criminal law.

Date

The date of *Yājñavalkyasmṛiti* is an unresolved matter among the Indologists. There is no doubt about the fact that we can trace strong influence of Kauṭilya's *Arthaśāstra* on the extant treatise. *Arthaśāstra* has been assigned by different writers anywhere in the period ranging from the 4th century BC to 3rd century BC. P. V. Kane is of the opinion that the works of *smṛiti* can be placed between 100 BC and 300 AD. Although there is no unanimous view regarding the date of *Yājñavalkyasmṛiti*, one cannot deny the fact that *Yājñavalkya* is certainly later than Manu. *Manusmṛiti* is supposed to have been composed before the Christian era and *smṛitis* of *Yājñavalkya*, *Parāśara* and *Nārada* were supposed to be composed in the first centuries of Christian era. As the treatise of *Yājñavalkya* is in verse, it appears to be a recast of the old *sūtra* work left by the sage. So it is not unlikely that it was composed during the early period of the Gupta reign which is also regarded as a period of revival of the *Brāhmanical* culture.

The Style and Content of the *Yājñavalkyasmṛiti*

Yājñavalkyasmṛiti is written in the classical *anuṣṭhubh* metre (verse style, a specific form of *śloka*). The author has dealt with almost all subjects that we find in *Manusmṛiti*, but his treatment is more concise and avoids repetition. It is less archaic and more advanced and systematic work than that of Manu, comprising only three instead of 12 chapters, 1,010 for 2,694 verses and comparatively it is more relevant. In this connection we come across different views regarding the number of verses contained in *Yājñavalkyasmṛiti*. For example, the *Yājñavalkyasmṛiti* contains (in the Nirnayasagara ed. of 1892) 1,010 verses, while the Trivandrum edition with the commentary of Viśvarūpa contains 1,003 verses and Aparārka gives 1,006 (Ānandāśrama edition). As stated by P. V. Kane, this difference in the number is mostly due to the fact that Viśvarūpa in the first section on *acāra* (English: code of conduct) omits five verses that occur in the Mitākṣarā (Kane 2006, 423).

Commentaries on the *Yājñavalkyasmṛiti*

Some of the important commentaries on the *Yājñavalkyasmṛiti* are written by Aparārka's, Vijñaneśvara, Devabodha, Śūlapāṇi, Mitramiśra and Viśvarūpa. Aparārka's commentary is regarded as the oldest followed by Mitākṣarā. Mitākṣarā is one of the most celebrated commentaries of Vijñaneśvara and it has received largest share of attention on the part of medieval lawgivers. On account of the paramount importance of the Mitākṣarā in modern *Hindu* law as administered by British courts in Indian subcontinent, the *Yājñavalkyasmṛiti* to some extent has become the guiding work for whole of India and this status it deserves by its clear statement of codes, its breadth of vision and its comparative impartial treatment towards the claim of both sexes and the different *varṇas*. The Bengal school of lawyers holds in highest esteem the commentary on *Yājñavalkyasmṛiti* known as Dīpakalikā authored by Sūlapāṇi, a native of Mithilā.

Brief Description of the Contents of the Three Sections of *Yājñavalkyasmṛiti*

1. **Āchārādhyāyaḥ:** It is devoted to the study of the code of conduct for a person related to the knowledge of *dhārma*. It is divided into 13 *prakaraṇas*. The first *prakaraṇa* clearly mentions the 14 roots of knowledge and religion comprising the *Purāṇa*, *Nyāya*, *Mīmāṁsā*, *Dharmaśastra*,

Vedānga and four *Vedās* (Yaj., I.3). It also lists out the names of the following sages and the authors of the religious codes. Āchārādhyāyaḥ also provides a detail account of rites and rituals or *saṁskāras* from *Garbhādhana* to marriage; *Upanayana*, its time and other details; everyday duties of *bramacārins*, person fit to be taught, period of studenthood; duties of householder and keeping sacred domestic fire, the five great daily *yajña*; honouring a guest, etc. Subjects like acceptable and forbidden food, gifts, oblation for ancestors, peace for planets and administrative rules are also discussed. It prescribes the necessary guidelines for human conduct for a harmonious life.

2. **Vyavahārādhyāyaḥ:** The laws and regulations for the established customs are enumerated in this section. This section also lays down laws relating to the duties of the king and his ministers. As per the prescription of the king, shorn of avarice and anger, should rule according to the codes of law, along with the learned *Brāhmaṇs* who were appointed of *Vedic* knowledge and conversant with the laws of morality. It also contains an exceptional regulation and laws relating to loans to be charged differently from different castes in percentage of the mortgaged property. The text discusses the *Dayabhaga* or division of property among heirs. The laws relating to disputes about boundaries make it clear that the boundary should be determined by elevated lands, charcoal, chaff, huge trees, bridges, ditches and piles of stones. The *smṛiti* prescribes a balanced system of punishment (divine tests) for the persons of each *Varṇa*. The ordeals lay down for proving the innocence of an accused are categorized as *Tulā* (weighing in the balance), *Agnī* (ordeal of fire), *Jala* (ordeal of water), *Viṣa* (poison) and *Koṣa* (treasury). It is stated that these punishments should be applied in cases of serious crimes, when the accused agrees to accept himself the punishment (Yāj., II. 95–96). Laws related to sale and purchase are also mentioned. This chapter dwells on the laws relating to sale of articles by one who is not its legitimate owner. The law clearly mentions that if a person purchases or sells any article secretly or through unfair means, he is to be treated as a thief. One finds that *Yājñavalkyasmṛiti* does not have any room for inconvenience of the affairs of the common people. Rules and regulations for lifting the property and the likes have been carefully framed. One can give away his property, if such gift does not interfere with the maintenance of his kinsmen besides his wife and son. In this context it is worth mentioning that *Yājñavalkyasmṛiti* enumerates laws relating to use of abusive language and defamation. If one maligns another of the same caste, truly or by way of life, he should be severely punished. There are laws relating to breach of control or engagements between master and servant. It is mentioned that one who has been made a slave by force, or one sold by a thief, shall be released; similarly, the slaves who save the lives of their masters.
3. **Prāyaścittādhyāyaḥ:** This section talks about the regulations in different spheres of one's life. It contains 334 verses which are broadly classified into five *prakaraṇas*, namely, *Āśaucadhārma*, *Āpaddhārma*, *Vānaprastha-dhārma*, *Yatidhārma* and *Prāyaścittā*. Purpose of *Prāyaścittā*; names of 21 hells; the five mortal sins and other acts similar to them are discussed in detail. Various categories of *Prāyaścittā* like *Prāyaścittā* for *brāhmaṇa* murder or for killing other persons; *Prāyaścittā* for drinking wine, for other mortal and venial sins and for killing animals of various sorts; greater or lesser expiation according to time, place, age, ability; ostracizing the nonconformist sinner; secret expiations are worth mentioning.

The Life Sketch

The name of *Yājñavalkya* of Mithila is the most historical example of *Vedic* thought. He was also one of the last *Vedic* sages, associated with the later developments of *Vedic* thought and life, as expressed in the elaborate literature of the *Brāhmaṇas* and *Upaniṣhads*. As the chief exponent of the saving knowledge of the *Upaniṣhads, Yājñavalkya* takes his rank as the father of *Hindu* Philosophy. Known for his unsurpassed spiritual wisdom, he is credited to be the revealer of *Brahmajñāna* (Ultimate truth) to King Janaka of Videha and one of his two wives, the philosophically minded *Maitreyī.*

Yājñavalkya was the son of *Devarata*, who was the sister of sage *Vaiśampāyan*. He had studied the *Taittiriya Samhita* from sage *Vaiśampāyan* who was also his preceptor. He was the first reputed author of the White *Yajurveda*. He is regarded as a prominent authority on rituals as mentioned in the Śatapatha *Brāhmaṇa* and on philosophy in *Bṛhadāraṇkya Upaniṣhad*. As for his obtaining White *Yajurveda*, it is believed that once *Yājñavalkya* offended Vaiśampāyan by not adhering to his instruction and persisted to observe some expiatory penance alone. This act of *Yājñavalkya* incurred his preceptor's wrath and so as punishment he was asked to return whatever he had learned from him. Upon the order of his teacher, *Yājñavalkya* vomited out the collection of the Yajus in form of food which is also known as *Krishna* (black) *Yajurveda* on account of it being vomited substance. Afterwards, *Yājñavalkya* determined not to have any human master and propitiated the Sun—God, the master of *Vedās*, for the purpose of acquiring fresh *Vedic* knowledge not known to his preceptor *Vaiśampāyan*. The distinction that he achieved as a student was followed up by better distinction won in his later life. He rapidly grew up to be one of the most distinguished teachers and thinkers of his times. His intellectual and spiritual superiority is challenged, but in vain, by the leading philosophers and intellectuals of the times. His principle of self-realization and the quest of the *Brahman*, mentioned as the 'Ultimate Truth', led him to the crowning deed of his life, the renunciation of the world and adoption of the life of a mendicant. *Yājñavalkya* had two wives, *Maitreyī* and the other *Kātyāyanī*, resolving to leave the house of a householder when *Yājñavalkya* called his wives and announced his intention and tried to make a settlement between his two wives, the philosophically minded *Maitreyī* raised a question, 'does one attain *moksha* with material objects'? *Maitreyī*'s wish for spiritual wisdom pleased *Yājñavalkya* which takes us to the most important philosophical discussion of his life as stated in the *Bṛhadraṇyaka Upaniṣhad*. In this *Upaniṣhad*, *Yājñavalkya* appears as a great philosopher teaching the recondite doctrine of *Brahmā* and immortality to *Maitreyī* and in the same *Upaniṣhad* he is said to have imparted the knowledge of the destiny of the soul after it is released from the bonds of flesh and worldly affections.

Dharmaśāstras and *Rājadhārma*

Dharmaśāstras are one of the major scriptures which clearly enumerates the duties (*dhārmas*) of a king. *Rājādhārma* or the duties of a king became the legitimate part of *Dharmaśāstras* as king being a *Kṣatriya* was second in the line of fourfold division of the society. During ancient period, India was under monarchical form of governance. One finds reference of the glory of monarchs in almost all the *Dharmasūtras, Dharmaśāstras*, epics and other sacred literature of *Hindus*. All these scriptures and texts prescribed very precise guidelines, which were mandatory for a king to follow. The sincerity of following those norms became the benchmark for judging a king.

The codes of Manu and *Yājñavalkya* bring out the codes of governance in a vivid manner. The theories of polity and the conduct of a king as discussed in *Manusmṛiti* served as a model for later literature. According to Manu, *Kṣatriyas* are entitled to rule the state. They are supposed to govern the kingdom in a just manner and to provide protection to their subjects. The same view is held by *Yājñavalkya* also. While discussing *rājādhārma*, the codes also undertake to discuss certain theories of politics, the underlying idea thus being the interrelation between politics and law. In these political norms *Yājñavalkya* adopts a higher standard compared to Manu. Manu's code, for instance, advocates royal absolutism. This was not in accordance with the old tradition of the country and against the old common law. *Manusmṛiti* supported royal absolutism mainly to uphold a political revolution which was also a social revolution—a political revolution by *Brāhmaṇa*. The code obviously finds relief in a new theory. Unlike Manu, *Yājñavalkya*'s approach on this subject is characteristic. He does not count the king among the sources of law, yet he recognizes laws made by kings. *Yājñavalkya*'s has not subscribed to the theory of divine kingship with the right of perfect arbitrariness. Instead, he tells that a king should protect the zealous, grateful, humble, truthful, pure, religious, brave and free from vices. He further tells that any illegal actions on the part of king carry the result of his forfeiture and banishment with his entire family. Condemning any act of oppression towards his subjects *Yājñavalkya* clearly states that acts of oppression to the subject were to entail not only deprivation of majesty and condemnation of dynasty but also infliction of the highest punishment (Yaj., I.340). The accounts of *Yājñavalkya* on the principle of *rājādhārma* thus clearly demonstrate a liberal conservative attitude.

Ethical and Social Virtues

A perusal of the *Yājñavalkyasmṛiti* clearly establishes the fact that an attempt to blend the concept of personal well-being with the social welfare has been accomplished. A definite pattern of life of a man with detailed instructions for his duties in every stage of life has been chalked out. Ethical virtues as enumerated by *Yājñavalkya* are based on the principles of 10 *yamas* (proper conduct) and 10 *niyamas* (positive virtues and observances). As one notices, since Vedic time there has been a mention of various ethical values which were later systematized under the headings *yamas* and *niyamas*. According to *Yājñavalkya*, celibacy, mercy, forgiveness, charity, truthfulness, open-mindedness, abstention from injury, faith, sweetness of temper and restraint of the external senses fall under *yama*. Purity, silence, fasting, celebration of sacrifices, *Vedic* study, service of the preceptor, control of the generative organ, to resist anger and vigilance are called *niyamas*. What is embraced within *yama* and *niyama* is indeed the aggregate of ethical values.

Outlining the various duties of a householder, *Yājñavalkya* prescribes the necessary rules for human conduct for a harmonious life and social well-being. Attempt has been made to harmonize the tendency of renunciation as inculcated in the *Upaniṣhads* with the regular performance of one's social obligations. The code of conduct of *Yājñavalkya* was mainly composed for the proper development of society, to live with mutual respect, in peace and harmony with each other, and promote economic progress, better standard of life and freedom, attaining the fulfilment of *Puruṣārtha-catuṣtaya* (the four human-values of *Dhārma*, *Ārtha*, *Kāma* and *Mokṣa*). These four aims of life correspond to the essential elements of ethics. *Dhārma* stands for social needs; *ārtha* represents man's needs for power and possession; the need for physical satisfaction is represented by *kāma* and *mokṣa* for spiritual value. *Smṛitikāras* (sage) have propounded six kinds of *dhārma*/duties. The six *dhārmas* are *varṇadharma*, *āśhramadhārma*, *guṇadhārma*, *varṇaśhramadhārma*, *nimmittadhārmas* and *sādharaṇadhārma*. *Varṇadhārma* stands for the particular duties of caste, *āśhramadhārma* corresponds to the duties related to the stages of life, *varṇaśhramadhārma* is the duty pertaining to caste and stages of life, *nimmittadhārmas* are the occasional purifying duties and *sādharaṇadhārma* or the universal duties which are to be practised by all irrespective of the castes or orders of life. The six kinds of duties propounded in the *Smṛitis* can be treated as a device for regulating human conduct for a harmonious life. The term '*dhārma*' is popularly held as comprising of two things, such as *abhyudaya* and *niḥśreyasa*. To grow and prosper in material gains and then to have absolute release from the fetters of life is considered as the goal of *dhārma* according to *Smṛitikāras.*

Sage *Yājñavalkya* makes a clear interpretation of class, caste and consciousness and gives us valuable insight into manifold problems relating to the contemporary social structure and the society. *Yājñavalkya*'s account of the caste system is rather an abridged account consisting of eight verses (Yaj., I 90–96) while Manu devotes a chapter of 130 verses for the same. While stating that the *varṇa* system was the keynote of social organization, *Yājñavalkya* differs in many respects from the accounts of the early writers of the legal texts and the *Arthaśāstra* of Kauṭilya. A critical study of *Yājñavalkya*'s account of the caste system shows that his views on the status of *sajāti* (equal castes), enumeration of the mixed castes (*anulomas*, *pratilomas* and miscellaneous castes) and methods bringing change of castes exhibit many new tunes. After stating in verse 10 of Ācārādhyāyaḥ, that the *Brāhmaṇs*, *Kṣatriyas*, *Vaiśyas* and *Śūdras* are the (four) *varṇas* (castes); of these the first three are twice-born (Yāj., I.10) *Yājñavalkya* asserts: 'By men of the same *varṇa* in women of the same *varṇa* are born *sajāti*, that is, sons of equal *varṇa*. Sons (begotten) in unblamable marriages (such as *Brahmā*, etc.) multiply the races' (Yāj., I.90). This definition differs materially from that of writers like Kauṭilya and Baudhāyana. The account of *Yājñavalkya* on class, caste and consciousness shows that like Manu and others he also equated *varṇa* in the framework of *jāti*.[3] Thus, it is interesting to note that both the *varṇa* and *jāti* theories were operating simultaneously in the ancient period, or, in other words the *Smṛitikāras* were trying to convert *varṇa* into *jāti*. On the question of position of women, it has been observed that the *Dhamaśāstra* writers have never entertained the idea of women's liberty, and *Yājñavalkya*, though liberal than Manu and other *smṛitikāras*, also entertains a similar view (Yāj., I.85).[2]

It is interesting to note that on the strength of the above theories and their application, the *smṛitis* have actually overruled some of the specific dicta of *śrutis* that were not in consonance with the spirit of the age, or were coming into direct conflict with it. In principle, *smṛitis* have laid down the norms of behaviour according to different places, times and persons. The dicta contained in *smṛitis* embody ethical judgment, notwithstanding all the juristic sophistication and ritualistic intricacies contained therein.

Karma, Rebirth and Spiritual Liberation

Karma, rebirth and liberation broadly deal with trasmigratory existence and the retribution of actions. While dealing with the doctrine of *karma* and rebirth it may be made clear that the question of life beyond death is mystery. Although the unfolding of the mystery of life and death is a difficult task, still sages and men of vision have tried to solve this phenomenon through the principle of *karma* and rebirth. The word *karman* or *karma* is derived from the root 'kṛ' to do. Thus, etymologically it means work or action, but in a broader sense it includes thoughts as well. The condition of individual in every existence is governed by his own actions or *karmas*. This is a rough description of what is called 'law of *karma*'. Indian sages have formulated the doctrine of *karma* in order to account for the divergences observed in the lives of individuals. The notion of *dhārma* as righteousness, as merit acquired from the right performance of duties or *karma* and release (*mokṣa*) as the main goal of life persists among all the authors of *Dharmaśāstras* including Manu and *Yājñavalkya*. In the *Dharmaśāstras*, the notion of *karma* assumes more markedly its ethical profile. Following the authors of *Dharmaśāstras*, *Yājñavalkya*'s account also maintains that by good deeds good consequences are produced and similarly by bad deeds bad consequences are produced. According to the teaching attributed to *Yājñavalkya*, *dhārma* has a spiritual sense, in the sense of being related to *Brahman* (self). The second section of *Bṛhadāraṇyaka Upaniṣhad* called the *Yājñavalkyakanḍa* deals with concepts like the doctrine of rebirth, the law of *karma* that regulates the rebirth process and the techniques of liberation from the cycle of rebirth. *Bṛhadāraṇyaka Upaniṣhads* emphasizes that everything in this world is mutually helpful towards the sustenance of one another. The notion of *dhārma* and *karma* has been introduced through the creation myth of *Bṛhadāraṇyaka Upaniṣhad*. In this *Upaniṣhad, dhārma* has been given a spiritual and metaphysical position. Here, *dhārma* has been identified as a form of *Brahman*. In order to maintain harmony and to regulate the affairs of the world, the *Brahman* assumes a particular form, which is *dhārma*. Thus, *dhārma* is conceived as righteousness. *Brahman* did not exhibit itself, but he assumed that excellent form of *dhārma*. *Yājñavalkya* thus analyses the nature and process of *karma* and identifies desire as the ultimate cause of all actions and source of continued rebirth. According to *Yājñavalkya Brahman* or true self is distinct from the individual ego and therefore not subject to *karma*; the *ātman* is eternal, unchanging and identified by the monistic principle underlying the universe.[4]

Dialogue between *Yājñavalkya* and *Maitreyī*

Yājñavalkya married two wives. One was *Maitreyī* and the other *Kātyāyanī*. Of the two, *Maitreyī* was a *Brahmavādinī* (conversant with *Brāhmaṇ*). We get the advice on *Ātmatattva* and immortality through the dialogue between *Maitreyī* and *Yājñavalkya*. When *Yājñavalkya* wished to divide his property between the two wives before starting for the fourth *āśhrama* of his life, he wished to give his material property to *Maitreyī*, but she rejected the offer—*Yenāhaṁ nāmṛtā syāṁ kim-ahaṁ tenakuryāṁ*, that is, What shall I do with the property by which I shall not get immortality? *Yājñavalkya* replied that immortality cannot be achieved through wealth. On hearing this, *Maitreyī* requested him to advice on the matter of wealth. Then *Yājñavalkya* elaborately described to her the doctrine of *Ātman*, the way of attaining infinite knowledge and immortality, etc. They may be summed up in the three following propositions:

1. The *Ātman* is the knowing subject within us.
2. The *Ātman*, as the known subject, can never become an object for us, and is therefore itself unknowable.
3. The *Ātman* is the sole reality.

Thus, the central theme of the dialogue between *Yājñavalkya* and *Maitreyī* is the following. All things are dear, not for their sake, but for the sake of the absolute self. This self alone exists everywhere. It cannot be understood or known, for it alone is the knower. Its nature cannot be said to be positively as such. It is realized through endless denials as 'not this, not this'. The self is self-luminous, indestructible and unthinkable.

Comparative Study of *Yājñavalkyasmṛiti* and the *Manusmṛiti*

The sacred legal literature of the *Hindus* can be classified into three categories: the *Dharmasūtras* or the dictum of law of the different schools, the *Dharmaśāstras* or the codes of law attributed generally to names of sages well-known in sacerdotal history, and the commentaries and digests by *Hindu* jurisprudents.

Amongst the treatises the position of the codes of Manu and *Yājñavalkya* is pre-eminent. *Manusmṛiti* is supposed to be the basis of the entire orthodox system of *Hindu* law. Its authority is regarded as supreme by the undisputed verdict of both the lay and legal literature of *Hindu* India. The codes of *Yājñavalkya* is the present-day binding law of the majority of the *Hindus*. It seems that with the object of superseding the orthodox, but unworkable provisions of the earlier code *Yājñavalkya*'s code was promulgated. Unlike the code of Manu it also became the accepted code of law of the Hindus because of its advanced and liberal juridical norms.

It thus becomes imperative to make a comparative study of the two codes with reference to the social, political and economic history of the country as the law codes are not only the idiosyncratic views of *Brāhmaṇs* but also the product of their times. The code of Manu is a product of the early days of the *Brāhmaṇa* Empire, circa 150 BC, and the code of *Yājñavalkya* was compiled about three centuries later. The evolution in law has its full counterpart in the expansion of commerce, sociopolitical institutions and the social wielding of orthodox and Buddhist philosophy. The notion of the *Hindu* nation of the *Brāhmaṇa* Empire is well depicted in the *Manusmṛiti*, and the expression of the prosperous and liberal empire of the Sātvāhanas is recorded in the code of *Yājñavalkya*.

The earliest reference of fourfold division of society is to be found in the *Puruṣa-Sūkta* occurring in the *Ṛigvedā*. In order to give a divine tinge to the concept of four classes of the society, Manu accepted the old theory of creation of four classes as propounded by *Ṛigveda*. The account of *Yājñavalkya* shows that he also followed more or less the same principle of the fourfold division of society, but his attitude was more liberal as compared to Manu. The liberal attitude of *Yājñavalkya* is further illustrated while dealing with the issue of the rise in the status of caste when the original parents are *anulomas* (enumeration of mixed castes). *Yājñavalkya*'s account of the caste system is rather an abridged one consisting of eight verses only, while Manu devotes a chapter of 130 verses for the same. A critical study of these verses shows that he incorporated many new tunes which differ from Manu in many respects. For example, Manu observes that sons, begotten by twice-born men on wives of the next lower caste, they declare to be similar (to their fathers, but) blamed on account of the fault (inherent) on their mothers (Manu X.6). Although some of the later commentators interpret the account to mean that Manu does not accord the status of *sajāti* (equal castes) to such persons, the language shows that the sage is really somewhat vague on the point, while *Yājñavalkya* is very clear. But one also notices that the account of *Yājñavalkya* shows that like Manu and others he had also reduced the *varṇa* in the framework of *jāti*. Thus, we find that both the *varṇa* and *jāti* theories were operating simultaneously.

The code of Manu was centred on the common law which was set in the background of the early *Dharmasūtras*. The *Brāhmaṇs* in the *Manusmṛiti* claims to be the 'lord of all', he claims exemption from capital punishment and many more privileges. In accordance with the old common law, the code of Manu practically overlooks woman. But the code of *Yājñavalkya* treats woman as a full legal persona; *Yājñavalkya* sounds a novel tone when he allows the wife and daughter to inherit property of a sonless deceased. Unlike Manu, *Yājñavalkya* had a very high respect for the womenfolk. Manu holds that by their very nature women are wicked and cast a doubt regarding their sanctity, honesty and character (Manu IX, 17–18). In contrast to Manu's view, *Yājñavalkya* maintains that woman should be treated respectfully, his account are best understood when we realize that to *Yājñavalkya* an ideal woman as an ideal housewife and all her greatness and goodness lie in maintaining happy home. The family laws in the two codes highlight many points of difference. For example, the forms of marriage prohibited by Manu are allowed by *Yājñavalkya*. Woman is brought in the list of heirs by the latter. Different provisions as to maintenance and succession of *Stridhana* or women's property has been made by Manu and *Yājñavalkya*.

One notices these differences which arise from the fact that while Manu regards marriage as a sacrament, *Yājñavalkya* sees it in a contract between the husband and wife. *Yājñavalkya* does not recognize as *stridhana* what is received by a woman as a token of love for this would form part of the contractual marriage. On the other hand, he includes the property or money that would come to her in case of her suppression under the category, for in such case the contract is broken, at least partially and she is to be compensated for it. This does not find a place in Manu's account as he holds a completely different conception of marriage.

Conclusion

An analysis of the text under study along with the works of other *smṛitikāras* clearly reveals the fact that their aim is to standardize life against the background of some fixed values and to adapt law to the changed needs of the times. The course of human life has never been the same. Hence, different *dhārma* writers appeared at different eras to accommodate new elements that had crept in the different sections of the Indian society. New *smṛitis* that were being composed after Manu also provided for an authoritative recognition of new practices or variations in old ones. An important point to be remembered in this context is that the ancient *Smṛitikāras* never tried to reconcile their views of their earlier *Smṛitikāras*. They did make mention of their predecessor's views and where they differed from them they gave their own views fairly in keeping with the spirit of their own times. The *smṛitis* themselves do not support the theory advanced by some that *dhārma* is unchangeable for all times to come. It has also been clearly stated in the *smṛitis* that secular law should be made according to the conventions of religions, territorial and functional associations. They explicitly state that *dhārma* and *ācārya* may change from time to time according to the change in social conditions and practices of the country in their own times (Gajenragadkar 1941, 183).

The rules laid down in the *Yājñavalkyasmṛiti* regarding diverse and important aspects as family, marriage, status of women, social structure, ritual, purity and defilement, inheritance of property, kingship and administration, law and judicial procedure, titles of law, etc., seem to be based on a fairly coherent social philosophy of the *smṛitis* (the social philosophy underlying *smṛitis* is marked as being a nature of sense of practicability, along with the magnificent breadth of vision and pursuit for precision). Undoubtedly, sage *Yājñavalkya*, like other *smṛiti* writers, made full use of his powers of observation and knowledge, but his method of arriving at conclusions was that of thinking on the basis of traditional authority and concepts. What is perhaps more important is that his dicta are essentially normative in nature. *Smṛitis* lay down the norms of behaviour according to different places, times and persons. A perusal of the text reveals that while a good deal of stress is laid on the fulfilment of appropriate duties by members of different *varṇas*, birth is recognized as a decisive factor in determining one's *varṇa*. The norms regarding *varṇa* and caste hierarchy are pervasive that they differentially regulate the observance of rituals; economic matters such as proper rates of interest; inheritance; and fines and punishment to be imposed for various wrongs. *Smṛiti* texts ordain that the punishment for the same offence should vary according to the *varṇa* of the offender. Similarly, the king is charged with the duty not only of safeguarding the interest of his subjects but also ensuring that everyone conforms to the path of his own duty (*svadhārma*). Although the juristic structure and legal procedure laid down in *Yājñavalkyasmṛiti* are elaborate and sophisticated, these are not divorced from the principles of *dhārma*. That is why *smṛiti* continued to have a long hold over the *Hindu* mind.

Summary

The teachings attributed to *Yājñavalkya* represent one of the most important literary products in the history of Indian culture and legal system, both because it played a critical role in the development of legal ideas and because it is an important source for understanding the social, religious, legal and intellectual history of ancient India. The code of *Yājñavalkya* was composed at a time of great social, economic and religious change: it documents the transition from the archaic ritualism of the *Vedā* into new religious ideas and institutions. The teachings of *Yājñavalkya* are distinctive to the new worldview of *Upaniṣhads*. They include the concept of the doctrine of rebirth, the law of *karma* and the techniques of liberation, which contends that the future destiny is determined in accordance with one's past knowledge and action.

Points for Discussion

1. Why both the *varṇa* and *jāti* theories were operating simultaneously during the ancient period?
2. Why the kings were enjoined with the duty of maintenance of the right order?
3. What do you understand by the notion of *Dhārma*?

Endnotes

1. Other *Smṛitis* have been examined for comparative analysis, though less consistently. I have endeavoured to adhere to Sanskrit texts and the following verses from *Yājñavalkyasmṛiti* are quoted specifically in this chapter.
2. Notion of subordination of women was not unique to *dharmasūtra* literature and was widely prevalent in the *Smṛitis* too, indicating permeable boundaries of the two textual traditions.
3. The ideology of the institution of *varṇa* order and the subsequent extensive practice of caste system should be considered essentially a traditional *Hindu* phenomenon that has its origin in the ancient ideology of *varṇavyavasthā* (institution of class order).
4. The doctrine of *Ātman* as the sole reality is no doubt a *Vedic* concept, but *Yājñavalkya* was the first to grasp this conception of the *Ātman* in its complete subjective and scientific precision.

Glossary

***Āśhrama*:** It refers to four stages of life, designed to integrate both household life and renunciation into the social structure: the stages are those of the *bramacārin*, student of *Vedās*; *gṛhastha*, householder; *vanaprastha*, forest dweller and *sannyāsin*, wandering renouncer.

***Brahman*:** It is a neuter word, indicating the abstract quality of the word. It refers to the transcendental energy, the prime source.

Janaka of Videha: Janaka of Videha is a wise and generous king who debates with *Brāhmaṇs* in several episodes of *Brihadāranyaka Upaniṣhad*, and then teaches *Yājñavalkya* about the symbolism of the fire sacrifice.

***Karma*:** It refers to 'work' or 'action'. The earliest uses of the work in its current sense, of any willed activity viewed at bringing appropriate results in future life.

Manu: Manu is the ancestor and lawgiver of human race.

Mokṣa: It means liberation from *saṃsara.*

Yājñavalkya: The sage to whom the principle teaching of *Śatpatha Brāhmaṇa* and *Bṛhadāraṇyaka Upaniṣhad* are attributed.

References

Gajenragadkar, K. B. 1941. 'Some Thoughts on the Interpretation of Smṛiti.' In *A Volume of Studies in Indology*, edited by Sumitra Mangesh Katre and Parshuram Krishna Gode, 183–84. Poona: Oriental Book Agency.

Kane, P. V. 2006. *History of Dharmaśāstra*, Vol. I, 3rd edn. Pune: Bhandarkar Oriental Research Institute.

Further Readings

Acharya, N. R., eds. 1949. *Yājñavalkyasmṛiti*. Bombay: Nirnayasagar Press.

Buhler, G. 1967. *The Laws of Manu: The Sacred Book of the East*, Vol. XXV. 2nd Reprint. Delhi: Motilal Banarsidass.

Buhler, G. 1986. *The Sacred Law of the Aryas: The Sacred Book of the East*, Vol. II. Delhi: Motilal Banarsidass.

Dutt, M. N., ed. 1909. *Manusmṛiti*. Calcutta: H. C. Das.

Dutta, M. N. 1978. *The Dharmaśāstra*. English trans. and Text, Vol. 1. New Delhi: Cosmo Publications.

Ganpati S. T. eds. 1922. *Yājñavalkyasmṛiti, with Viśvarupacāryas Bālakriḍa and Mitākṣarā of Vijñanesvara*. Trivandrum University: Trivandrum Sanskrit Series.

Jayaswal, K. P. 1930. *Manu & Yājñavalkya*. Calcutta: Butterworth.

Jha, G. N. 1924. *The Laws of Manu with the Bhāṣya of Medhātithi*. Calcutta: University of Calcutta.

Jolly, J. 1928. *Hindu Laws and Customs*, trans. B. K. Ghosh. Calcutta: Greater Indian Society.

Katre, S. M. and P. K. Gode, eds. 1941. *A Volume of Studies in Indology*. Poona: Oriental Book Agency.

Olivelle, P. 1998. *The Early Upaniṣads*. Delhi: Munshiram Manoharlal.

Ranganathananda, S. ed. 2005. *The Messages of Bṛhadāraṇyaka Upaniṣad*. Kolkata: Advaita Ashram.

Sharma, Vasudev, eds. 1949. *Manusmṛiti*. Bombay: Nirnayasagar Press.

Srinivasacharya, L. 1914. *Smṛiticandrikā*. Mysore: Govt. Branch Press.

6
CHAPTER

Cārvāka-Lokāyata Tradition: A Tradition of Materialist Philosophy

Balaganapathi Devarakonda and Jayshree Jha

CHAPTER OUTLINE

- **Introduction**
- **Epistemology**
- **Metaphysics**
- **Ethics**
- **Conclusion**
- **Summary**
- **Points for Discussion**

Cārvāka, a very ancient sect in India were rank materialist.

—Swami Vivekananda

Reader's Guide

This chapter aims to provide an in-depth understanding of the essential aspects of one of the ancient materialistic and naturalistic schools of Indian thought to the reader. It also provides a glimpse of one of the critical traditions of Indian thought by discussing how *Vedic* authority, Law of *Karma*, Law of Causation, rebirth, *Mokṣa* and *Dhārma* were contested and questioned. The reader would be able to analyse and comprehend the nurturing of critical debates of essential aspects of Classical Indian thought.

Introduction

Cārvāka darśana, also known as *lokāyata*, is popularly recognized as a materialistic philosophical system of ancient India. This school of materialism does not believe in authority of *Vedās* and is among the oldest heterodox schools. Its references are given quite often in the epics and in the early *Buddhistic* literature. Several imprints show proclaimers of purely materialistic doctrines appeared even in the pre-*Buddhistic* India. In post-*Upaniṣhadic* and pre-*Buddhistic* age, rise of materialism in India was facilitated because of numerous reasons like the idealism of the *Upaniṣhads* did not suit the commoners, the exploitation of the masses by the petty kings, monks and the wealthy class, the lust and greed and petty dissensions in an unstable society. The materialistic way of life, which is popularly summed up as 'eat, drink and be merry' in *Cārvāka* philosophy, is as old as humanity itself and will surely last as long as humanity lasts, yet materialism as metaphysics has never found favour with the Indian philosophers.

According to doxographical works like *Sarvadarśanasaṅgraha* and *Ṣaḍdarśanasamuccaya, Cārvāka* philosophy can be gleaned as Lokāyata is the only *Śhāstra*; perception is the only means of knowledge; consciousness is the product of matter; soul is nothing but the conscious body; pleasure, rather sensuous pleasure, is the only goal of life; death alone is liberation; there is no God, no other world and no life after death.

In many of the polemical works written by various authors of different schools of *Jainism, Buddhism, Nyaya* and *Vedānta, Cārvāka* philosophy is presented in order to refute it. Modern scholars like Radhakrishnan, Hiriyanna and D. P. Chattopadhyaya consider this picture to be an authentic one. They drew implications from it, and criticized or appreciated *Cārvāka* on that basis.

The *Sarvadarśanasaṅgraha* gives the following account of the *Cārvāka* position:

Na svargo nāpavargo vā naivātmā pāralaukikaḥ,
Naiva varṇāśramādīnāṁ kriyāśca phaladāyikah.

There is no heaven, no final liberation, nor any soul in another world,
Nor do the actions of the four castes, orders, etc., produce any real effect.
(Madhavacharya 2002, 17)

Yāvajjīvetsukhaṁ jīvedṛṇaṁ kṛtvā ghṛtaṁ pibet,
Bhasmībhūtasya dehasya punarāgamanaṁ kutaḥ?

While life remains, let a man live happily, let him feed on ghee even though he runs in debt;
When once the body becomes ashes, how can it ever return again?
(Madhavacharya 2002, 19)

Works that might serve as the doctrinal texts for the *Lokāyata* can hardly be found. Even if anything authentic is available, they are incomplete and have suffered through centuries of deterioration. Bare fragments of the *Bṛhaspati Sūtra* which is thought to be written by Bṛhaspati (founder of the system) remains in existence. Due to its obscure nature it provides little insight into the doctrine and practices of ancient Indian materialists. There are few texts which discuss about this school like *Sarvadarśanasaṅgraha by* Madhavacharya and *Ṣaḍdarśanasamuccaya* by Haribhadrasūri. We find another text, *Tattvopaplavosiṁha* of Jayarāsibhatta, which is quite often quoted by modern scholars like D. P. Chattopadhyaya and Ramkrishna Bhattacharya in order to restore *Lokāyata* aphorisms, reinterpret its literature and strengthen it. We can trace varied views attributed to *Cārvākas* through the texts of opponents, presented as refutable views (*pūrvapakṣa*).

Historically, *lokāyata* has been interpreted variedly. In *Sarvadarśanasaṅgraha Lokāyata* was interpreted as 'prevalent among people' (*lokeṣu āyatam*). This interpretation had some limitations since it reduces *Lokāyata* to the pleasure-seeking approach of common people which is not the essence of *Lokāyata* philosophy. So, an alternative derivation of the word was brought forward as *lokena āyatam* 'limited by the approach which disregards other worlds'. *Lokāyata* philosophy in all its versions denies the existence of other worlds which is clearly brought forward in this interpretation of Lokāyata (Gokhale 2015, 11). D. P. Chatopadhyay traces *Lokāyata* to Kauṭilya's *Arthaśāstra*, which regards *Lokāyata* as part of reason-oriented inquiry (*ānvīkṣikī*). *Lokāyata* here probably refers to logic or science of debate and not to the materialist doctrine. *Lokāyata* is also connected to *Vitaṇḍas* (sophists) by *Saddaniti* and *Buddhaghosa* in the 5th century. The term *Lokāyata* was restricted to the school of the materialists only from the 6th century. *Cārvāka* as name was first used in the 7th century by the philosopher Purandara, who referred to his fellow materialists as 'The *Cārvākas*', and it was further used by the 8th century philosophers Kamalaśīla in *Tattvasaṁgrahapañjikā* and Haribhadrasūriin in *Ṣaḍdarśanasamuccaya*. It is approximated that by the 8th century, the terms *Cārvāka/Lokāyata* and *Bṛhaspatya* were used interchangeably to signify materialism.

Epistemology

The entire philosophy of *Cārvāka* is said to be logically dependent on its epistemology. But even within *Cārvākas*, we can find difference in opinion in epistemological positions held. It is usually believed that Madhavacharya's account in *Sarvadarśanasaṅgraha* emphasizes the epistemological basis of the *Cārvāka* position. According to Madhavacharya, *Cārvāka* school propagates that perception is the only means of valid knowledge. All other *pramānas* including inference is to be rejected. Inference here is said to be mere leap in the dark. In inference, one proceeds from known to unknown. Inference is dependent on universal concomitance (*vyāpti*). For inference to be a valid means of knowledge, this relation of universal concomitance should be verified by any other valid *pramāna*. Perception (internal and external) cannot establish such a universal relation, since we never perceive all past particulars and no future ones are ever perceived. Neither can inference establish the universal proposition, since it is obvious that to appeal to inference is to justify inference, and it is to enter into a vicious regress. Since *Vyāpti* cannot be known by means of any of the *pramānas*, therefore inference is not a valid means of knowledge. *Anumāna* and the other *pramānas* are the means to mediate cognition. One cannot be certain about the truth of the cognition that they yield. Testimony (*śabda*) is also rejected as the means of knowledge of the universal proposition, since it ultimately depends on perception or inference. Finally, comparison (*upamāna*) is ruled out too because it can only establish a quite different relation, namely the relation of a name to the object named. These four categories are the four kinds of *pramānas* recognized by the *Nyaya* school and, although the *Vedāntins* recognize two more (*anuplabdhi* and *arthāpatti*), these cover the valid means of knowledge admitted by almost all the schools of Indian Philosophy. One cannot be certain about the truth of the cognition that they yield. Therefore, perception is the only valid *pramāna*. This naïve position of narrow empiricism is attributed to *Cārvākas* in *Sarvadarśanasaṅgraha*.

Jayarāśibhatta in *Tattvopaplavasiṁha* following a sceptical approach, denies even perception as an authoritative means to knowledge. Wherein in *Nyāyamanjari* there were some *Cārvākas* who held a broader form of empiricism. According to them, not only perception but a kind of inference which is testable by perception (*utpanna-pratīti anumāna*) can also be called as a valid means of knowledge. In *Tattvaṁgrahapañjika* by *kamalaśīla*, a *Cārvāka* thinker called Purandara accepts a still wider epistemological framework where common-sensual inference (*lokaprasiddha-anumāna*) is accepted in addition to perception. Those inferences which make our individual and social life in this world intelligible are acceptable in this framework. Such epistemological views of *Cārvākas* possess diversity rather than unity which leads to diversity in axiology and ontology too.

Now, another question which might perturb one's mind is how can these different sets of people who differ in views—one accepting two means of knowledge wherein other accepting one means of knowledge and the third accepting no means of knowledge—belong to same system or trend? This can be answered in two ways. First, there was methodological similarity among *Cārvākas* that they were using arguments constructively or destructively without accepting restrictions based on verbal testimony. With this methodology, they refuted different available systems without propounding their own. Due to this tendency they are known as *vaitaṇḍika*. Not all of them are called so in the strict sense of the term, but some of these can easily be recognized as *vaitaṇḍika*. Second, there was a metaphysical element common to various members of the *Cārvāka* family, although this element was largely negative. All *Cārvākas* accept worldly practices (*loka-vyavahāra*) in a strong or weak way and this was the common positive element, although it was too general and vague. But the negative common elements were too strong and clear. Some of these negative common elements are stated below.

1. There is no soul or self apart from body; consciousness cannot exist independent of body.
2. There is no God, no other world; the doctrine of *karma* is not acceptable.
3. Inference cannot be established as a means to knowledge in the strict sense.
4. No religious scripture is to be accepted as the source of knowledge.
5. Religious obligation (*dhārma*) and disembodied liberation (*mokṣa*) are not acceptable as values.

The epistemological theories given by various *Cārvāka* schools served as ways of supporting this negative element. The non-acceptance of other worldly beliefs was achieved by different *Cārvāka* subschools at different costs. These subschools are at different distances from common sense view of the world, but each of them is making distinct, interesting and illuminating philosophical contributions.

Metaphysics

Cārvāka theory of reality follows from its epistemology. According to the popular epistemological position, perception is the only reliable source of knowledge. Only reality of perceptible objects can be rationally asserted. Concept of God, soul, heaven, life before birth and life after death are all redundant since they are all beyond perception. They establish the theory that 'Matter is the only reality'.

Most of the Indian schools hold that material world is composed of five elements (*pañcabhūtas*), namely earth (*kṣiti*), water (*ap*), fire (*agni*), air (*vāyu*) and ether (*ākāśa*), and these elements correspond to qualities (smell, taste, vision, sound and touch) which further correspond to sense organs (nose, tongue, eye, ear and skin). But *Cārvākas* reject 'ether', because its existence cannot be perceived, it can only be inferred. It was believed that sound was caused in ear due to all pervading ether. But *Cārvāka* school argues that sound is caused due to air touching the ear and not due to ether. Therefore, material world is composed of four perceptible elements. These elements constituted of tiny perceptible particles.

Even the living organisms along with non-living material objects are composed due to combination of these four elements. However, Jayarāśibhatta in Tattvopaplavasiṁha not only denies all means to knowledge, but also *tattvas* (earth, water, fire and air) attributed to *Cārvākas* in *Sarvadarśanasaṅgraha.*

Cārvāka believes that there is no external cause for the four elements coming together and obtaining the qualities of life and consciousness. It is their inherent quality that makes them come together and to acquire those qualities. However, one cannot generalize on this process and establish a law that whenever these four elements come together in certain ratio, life and consciousness will emerge. These elements may alter their nature any time. It will be wrong to apprehend that nature comprises some eternal laws. Each and every event is a probability, and further if it evolves into something, then it develops according to its own anomalous nature.

According to the common understanding of *Cārvāka* school, there is no such thing as *Ātman*. One does not and cannot perceive *Ātman*. Also, one cannot establish its existence with the help of inference, because inference is not a valid source of knowledge. The *Cārvākas* state that consciousness is not due to the *Ātman*. Consciousness is the quality of body as it is perceived to exist in the perceptible living body composed of material elements. When a man dies, his consciousness goes away and one cannot prove that it dissipates and exists somewhere else. *Cārvāka* believed that being conscious is a distinct quality of the living human body. Individual can hold back the consciousness so long as the physical parts are healthy and stay together in a certain form. Consciousness thus is an emergent quality of the physical parts coming together in specific proportions. For example, when yeast is blended with certain juices, they turn into wine which has a totally new property. Therefore, according to *Cārvāka* metaphysics, life also is only a new configuration of matter. Nothing but matter is real.

Therefore, the *Ātman* or self-awareness is nothing but the combination of physical body with a new emerging quality. We often say, 'I have a handsome body, a tall body' and so on. If the 'I' is not different from the body, how can it say: 'I have such and such a body'? To this the *Cārvākas* answer by saying that the use of 'have' in these expressions is only conventional, created by the false impression that the 'I' is different from the body.

Further, one may question that we do not perceive consciousness in any of the material elements. Then how can it be a quality of the body which apparently is the product of a combination of four elements. *Cārvāka* explains it through an example of betel leaf, nuts, and lime; none of these are red originally but a combination of these produces the red colour. So material elements combined together in a particular way may give rise to the conscious living body.

Furthermore, *Cārvāka* metaphysics considers mind (*manas*) or (is) being different from the Ātman. *Cārvākas* apprehend of mind as the consciousness in its knowing function, which is not separate from the body. The body together with its consciousness is the *Ātman* and consciousness in its experiencing function is the mind. Mind comprehends the external world through the senses.

Cārvākas school does not believe in the Law of Causation and its universality. According to *Cārvāka*, the causal relation is not necessary and invariable. It does not explain the diversity of the world. Cause and effect relation is not unconditional. They believe that the inherent nature of things is the cause of the diversity of the world. They deny the fact that a definite effect always arises from a definite cause. Opposed to this they maintain that from a definite cause many effects may arise. The inherent nature or power of things is the ultimate cause of the universe. As it has already been said, the things of the universe originate from the inherent power of the four basic elements (earth, water, fire and air).

To explain the diversity of the world, *Cārvāka* accept naturalism instead of causality. They use the word *Svabhāva* to indicate the inherent energy of things. From this nature, the diversity of the world originates, sustains and destroys. Again, they mentioned that behind the causal relation there is no inherent necessity. According to nature of the things, all events occur on their own. Behind the hotness of fire, coolness of water, sharpness of thorns, there is no agent or cause. These happen according to their nature. Nature has no cause; it is the cause of itself.

No doctrine of creation can be traced in the *Lokāyata*. The principles of *karma* (action) and *niyati* (fate) are rejected because they are deduced from the notion that existence in itself is determined. The fundamental principle of Indian Materialism was *Svabhāva* or nature. This does not suggest that nature itself has no internal laws or continuity. It would be a misinterpretation of Indian Materialism to suppose that it leads to cosmology of chaos. While it postulates no 'creator' or teleology, Indian Materialism projects nature itself as a force that thrives according to its own law. One may conclude that, according to the *Cārvāka* metaphysics, the existence of everything is a chance, and that there are no laws of nature, but every object possesses its own nature.

Cārvākas metaphysics does not believe in the existence of God, since God cannot be perceived. They do not accept God as the creator, sustainer and destroyer of the world. God as an omniscient, omnipotent, omnipresent being is only an imagination. It is not necessary to believe in God as the creator of the world. According to *Cārvākas*, the whole universe, animate as well as inanimate, is composed of the four basic elements. Living beings are born of them and they merge into them after death. The world is not moving towards any definite goal created by God.

Cārvākas believed that some hypocrites and cunning priests had exploited the ignorant and simple-minded common people by introducing the name of God. To satisfy God, the common people perform worships, *yajña*, etc. They offer various valuable things in the name of God by the direction of the priests. According to *Cārvākas* worship, *yajña*, etc., are only for the selfish fulfilment of the wicked priests. Therefore, it is completely meaningless to worship God, because He is non-existent and non-perceptible.

The Law of *Karma* also comprise the concept of rebirth. In *Cārvāka* metaphysics as well as philosophy, there is no place for the doctrine of the Law of *Karma* and rebirth. Since *Cārvāka* philosophy detests the Law of Causation, it rejects the doctrine of the Law of *Karma*. According to the *Cārvākas*, there is no necessary relation between the action and its fruit. Therefore, for them there is no truth in the doctrine of *karma*. There can be no fruit according to its action. It is just an imagination. Happiness, sorrow, pleasure, pain, reward, punishment, etc., are not the results or fruits of one's action. These are not dependent on the actions performed by the people. On the other hand, they depend upon the environment and different conditions, surroundings under which the actions are done. Everything in this world is accidental. From the same action one may get sorrow, unhappiness, but from the same action another person may get happiness or pleasure. As *Cārvākas* philosophy rejects the Law of *Karma*, it unpretentiously does not accept the Doctrine of Rebirth. It holds that man cannot take birth again after his death. There is no soul behind the material body. After death or the destruction of the body nothing is left. So, there can be no question of taking a new birth again. The life after death or rebirth, immortality of soul, etc., are false ideas or mere imaginations. Thus, *Cārvākas* philosophy rejects both the doctrine of *karma* and 'Theory of Rebirth'.

Ethics

In order to discuss the axiology of *Cārvāka* system, one has to get into the discussion about the four human goals, that is, *Puruṣārthas* (*Dhārma*, *Ārtha*, *Kāma* and *Mokṣa*). In Indian tradition, we come across different combinations and configuration of human goals giving rise to different theories. Traditionally, *Cārvākas* are said to have accepted pleasure (*kāma*) and wealth (*ārtha*) as their only goals. *Kāma*, the sensual pleasure, is regarded as the end, while *artha* is realized as the means to the end. *Dhārma* and *mokṣa* were altogether neglected.

One can trace some diversity in ethical perspective of *Cārvāka* too due to its diverse epistemological position. Jayarāśibhatta in *Tattvopaplavasiṁha* denied all means of knowledge and object of knowledge. He does not discuss the problem of values at all. Throughout his writing, he seems to allow some kind of anarchism in the realm of values. In narrow empiricism of the *Cārvākas*, one is in the position to recognize one's own sensuous pleasure as a value. In broad empiricism, *Cārvāka* appreciates *ārtha* (wealth) with *kāma* (pleasure). They uphold a universalistic form of hedonism. The latter position is adhered in most of the texts on *Cārvāka*.

The concept of liberation is one of the most principal issues (provide space) in Indian philosophy. Except *Cārvākas*, all other schools of Indian philosophy believe that liberation or *Mokṣa* is the ultimate destiny of human life. They maintain different ways and views regarding the attainment of liberation. *Cārvākas* maintains that liberation is not the detachment of the soul from the body. Being pure materialist it holds that there is no soul apart from the body. In such a situation, it does not believe in the state of liberation of the soul. After the destruction of the material body, everything is destroyed. The material world is the only world which can be perceived. Human life is full of pleasure, pain, sorrow, happiness, etc. So, there is no state called liberation which is the state of ultimate peace, happiness, etc., where there is no pain, sorrow, grief. Thus, according to the *Cārvāka*, if there is life, then there must be body; where there is body, there must be both pleasure and pain. Human life is a combination of pleasure and pain. Liberation is unreal, because it cannot be perceived.

Conclusion

Even though *Cārvāka* school was highly criticized by other schools, it had a lot to offer. *Cārvāka* school of thought was highly misinterpreted due to absence of original texts giving us knowledge about the original authentic teachings. The small description given by Madhavacharya in *Sarvadarśanasaṅgraha* which is considered to be one of the important texts providing description about *Cārvāka* does not present the real picture since it was written by an *Advaitin*. Since written by opponents, the school was presented in a weaker form. The diverse views attributed to the school were presented in a confused and mixed form without clearly making distinctions between each other. It is quite possible that varied versions of *Cārvākas* philosophy were presented by different thinkers at different periods of time, but opponents did present them as overlapping views. One shall not claim that one trend out of these is genuine and others are mere deviation or distortion. This will lead to dogmatism. All these varied views should be rearranged as belonging to different members rather than *Cārvāka* system in general.

Cārvāka school can be seen as representative of freedom of thought and expression. It was rebellious against other worldly and ritualistic tendencies in Indian philosophies. *Cārvākas* do not buy a religious axiology which attaches value to God, soul or other worlds. Neither did it develop a religion-centric approach to society. But apart from this, a modern *Cārvāka* if he is secular in nature could be open to different social and moral positions. A *Cārvāka* exposed to modern Western Philosophy can be a Marxist or a radical humanist, a phenomenologist or an atheistic existentialist, a positivist or a pragmatist. Similarly, in terms of moral position, he could become a sensualist-hedonist or a utilitarian-liberal or a deontologist. It is intelligible to consider *Cārvāka* philosophy not as a complete and closed system, but as an incomplete and open system.

Summary

Cārvāka, popularly known as *Lokāyata*, is one of the ancient materialistic and naturalistic schools of Indian philosophical thought. The chapter provides an in-depth analysis of the essential aspects of epistemology, metaphysics and ethics of *Cārvāka*. Introduction provides a historical background and availability of textual evidences along with a brief account of the recent works on *Cārvāka*. The first part of the chapter discusses the epistemological aspects such as acceptance of perception (*pratyakśa*) as the only valid means of knowledge and critique of inference (*anumāna*) in detail. Subsequent part presents a comprehensive view about metaphysics of *Cārvāka* where acceptance of earth, water, fire and air as the only elements; rejection of existence of ether, soul and god; identification of mind consciousness with the body; critique of causation, *Karma* and rebirth. The third part of the chapter discusses *Cārvāka*'s conception of hedonistic ethics which lays emphasis on pleasure and enjoyment as the ultimate goals of human life, rather than *puruṣārthas* and liberation. The conclusion sums up the philosophical position of *Cārvāka* by linking it to the modern Western philosophical positions.

Points for Discussion

1. Elaborate the main tenets of the *Cārvāka* school of thought.
2. Critically evaluate the Indian materialistic philosophy of the *Cārvāka*.
3. Critically examine the *Cārvāka* epistemology.
4. Explain the metaphysics of *Cārvāka*. How far *Cārvāka* accept the existence of an eternal soul?
5. Discuss the concept of liberation according to *Cārvāka* philosophy.
6. Do *karma*, rebirth and liberation have any significance in *Cārvāka* philosophy? Justify your answer with suitable examples.

Glossary

***Anumāna*:** *Anumāna* or inference is one of the valid means of knowledge. It is the process of drawing conclusion from the premises.

Axiology: It is the branch of philosophy that deals with the issues related to values.

Epistemology: It is a branch of philosophy that is concerned with various theories of knowledge.

***Karma*:** Action.

Law of Causation: It maintains that every effect must have a cause and causes and the effects are necessarily related. This relation is invariable and it depends upon concomitance. Everything in the world is due to some cause. The things of the world are causally related to one another.

***Lokavyavahāra*:** Worldly practices.

Materialism: It is an ontological view according to which matter is primary and thought or soul is secondary or destructive or derivative.

Metaphysics: Metaphysics is a branch of philosophy exploring the fundamental nature of reality. This branch of philosophy deals with the first principles of things, including abstract concepts, such as being, knowing, identity, time and space.

***Mokṣa*:** Liberation as value of life.

***Niyati*:** Fate.

Ontology: It is a branch of philosophy that deals with the existence of 'being'.

***Pañchabhūtas*:** Five basic elements (earth, water, air, fire and aether) which are the basis of creation.

***Pramāna*:** It is the means of acquiring certain knowledge. There are six *pramānas* usually discussed in Indian philosophy. The acceptance of these *pramāna* differs from school to school in Indian Philosophy.

***Pūrvapakṣa*:** Opponents view presented in order to refute and establish one's own view.

***Tattva*:** Essentially existing thing, important thing, ultimate truth, principle.

***Vaitaṇḍika*:** One who debates with other parties and refutes their position without committing to any position as one's own.

***Vyāpti*:** Universal concomitance.

References

Gokhale, Pradeep P. 2015. *Lokāyata/Cārvāka: A Philosophical Inquiry*. New Delhi: Oxford University Press India.

Madhavacharya. 2002. *Sarvadarśanasaṅgraha,* trans. M. M. Agrawal. Delhi: Chaukhamba Sanskrit Pratisthan.

Further Readings

Bhattacharya, R. 2002. 'Cārvāka Fragments: A New Collection.' *Journal of Indian Philosophy* 30: 597–640.

Bhattacharya, R. 2010. 'Commentators on the Cārvākasūtra: A Critical Survey.' *Journal of Indian Philosophy* 38: 419–30.

Bhattacharya, R. 2011. *Studies on the Cārvāka/Lokayata*. New Delhi: Anthem Press.

Chattopadhyaya, Debiprasad. 1959. *Lokāyata a Study in Ancient Indian Materialism*. New Delhi: People's Publication House.

Haribhadrasuri. 1905. *Ṣaḍdarśanasamuccaya*. Calcutta: Asiatic Society.

7 CHAPTER

Śhramanic Tradition: An Ascetic Reformism

Ankit Tomar

CHAPTER OUTLINE

- **Introduction**
- **Origin and Evolution of the *Śhramanic* Tradition**
- **The Jaina Philosophy**
- **The Buddha Philosophy**
- **Conclusion**
- **Summary**
- **Points for Discussion**

The Buddhists or the Jains do not depend upon God; but the whole force of their religion is directed to the great central truth in every religion, to evolve a God out of man. Thy have not seen the Father, but they have seen the Son. And he that hath seen the Son hath seen the Father also.

—Swami Vivekananda

Reader's Guide

Indian philosophy is a confluence of the *Śhramanic* and *Brāhmanic* streams of thought that coexisted and complementarily influenced each other. The *Śhramanic* tradition or *parampara* is a reformist school within the *Vedic* tradition of Indian philosophy and it is primarily represented by both Jainism and Buddhism. The *Śhramanic* tradition in India emerged as a critical reaction to the ritualistic trends or tendencies of the *Brāhmanical* system. One of the striking points about the *Śhramanic* tradition is that it not only rejects the rationalistic basis of the *Vedās* but is also against the hereditary basis of caste and animal sacrifices. In contrast to the *Brāhmanic* tradition, which has an optimistic worldview about the worldly life, the *Śhramanic* tradition views world as full of sufferings and firmly believed in āhimsa and rigorous ascetic practices. The purpose of this chapter is therefore to trace the origin and evolution of the *Śhramanic* tradition and the critique which it has mounted against the *Brāhmanic* system of thought. In addition to this, the chapter also attempts to outline the common features of the *Śhramana* sects (Jainism and Buddhism).

Introduction

India has rich and diverse philosophical traditions which have been conventionally classified into two broad categories, namely *Brāhmanic* (orthodox) and non-*Brāhmanic* or *Śhramanic* (unorthodox/heterodox) systems. The former being referred as *āstika* and the latter *nāstika*. This classification has been made on the basis of whether or not a system believes in the infallibility of *Vedās*. The schools which directly or indirectly accept the authority of *Vedās* and regard the *Vedās* as an infallible source of knowledge are known as orthodox systems. There are six schools (*darśhanas*) of orthodox (*āstika*) *Hindu* philosophy which include *Nyāya* (the school of logic), *Vaiśeṣika* (the atomist school which devotes itself to the exposition of reality), *Sāṅkhya* (a system that accepts a real matter and a plurality of the individual souls), yoga (discourse on practical discipline), *Purva Mīmāṁsā* or *Mīmāṁsā* (school of interpretation) and *Vedānta* or *Uttara Mīmāṁsā* (the *Upaniṣhadic* tradition, with emphasis on *Vedic* philosophy). Of these, *Mīmāṁsā* and *Vedānta* depend entirely on the *Vedās* and exist in continuation of the *Vedic* tradition. While *Sāṅkhya, Yoga, Nyāya* and *Vaiśeṣika* are not based on the *Vedās*, they accept the authority of the *Vedās*. Besides these, the schools that do not accept that the authority of the *Vedās* are categorized as unorthodox (*nāstika*) systems. The unorthodox systems of Indian philosophy are also known as heterodox systems and it includes three philosophical schools: Jainism, Buddhism and Materialism (*Cārvāka*). According to one interpretation, the Jaina or Bauddha schools cannot be called *nāstika* as they believe in life after death (existence of the future world). In other words, the Jaina and Bauddha schools are in one sense *nāstika*, as they do not believe in the authority of the *Vedās* and in the existence of God but in the second sense they are called *āstika*, as they believe in life after death. Therefore, it will be much more appropriate, if we call them *avaidikas* (non-*Vedic* sects).

Indian Schools of Philosophy

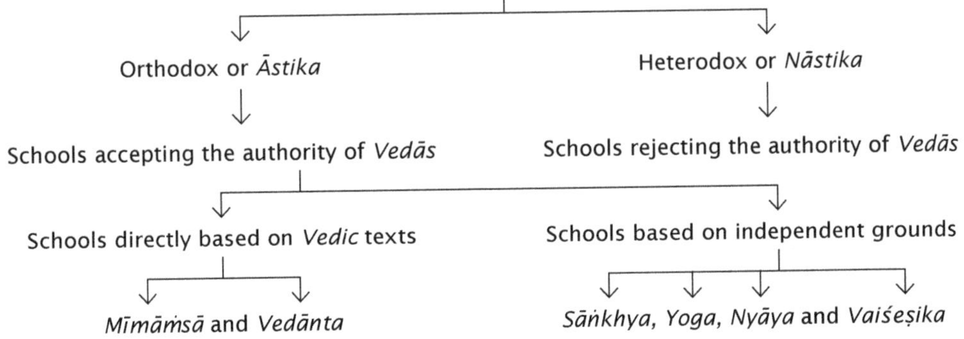

The *Brāhmanic* system or tradition which is also referred as classical or orthodox *Hindu* tradition of Indian political thought was a dominant tradition at one point of time. It has been essentially associated with *Vedic* tradition of Indian philosophy and revolves basically around the three elements, namely continuation of normative and social order, holism (denial of individual autonomy) and hierarchy. It has traced the source of knowledge in the *Vedās* and *Śhāstras*. The *Brāhmaṇs*, therefore, enjoyed considerable power and prestige in the *Brāhmanic-Hindu* tradition. This tradition is basically an inegalitarian and dogmatic tradition of ancient Indian philosophy as it justified the caste-based hierarchical social order and accepts caste-based conception of *dhārma*. According to this tradition, *dhārma* and *daṇḍa* are the two most basic and complementary features of social and political life. *Dhārma*, simply means duties and responsibilities of the individuals and the social groups towards the society. In other words, it is about the moral or natural laws of righteous conduct which holds a society together; violation of it shakes the society to its very foundations and constitutes a mortal threat to its existence (Parekh 1986, 12). The rules and regulations of *dhārma* are contained in the *dharmaśāstras*. The principles and rules of *dharmaśāstras* are not merely analytical and elucidatory but also authoritative and binding in nature. According to *Hindu* political thinkers, an individual's *dhārma* is derived from the caste of his or her birth which is not accidental but a result of his or her *karma* or actions of previous life. In this way, *dhārma* and *karma* of an individual are integrally connected. In contrast to *dharmaśāstra* writers, the authors of *Arthaśāstra* were also aware about the situations when individuals become corrupt and begin to ignore their *dhārma* and this may result in *arajakata* or lawlessness. Hence, the institution of *daṇḍa* becomes necessary to maintain *dhārma* and to rule a territorially organized community. The term *daṇḍa* here refers to the punitive use of coercive power or force. Moreover, although *Hindu* political thinkers were familiar with the republican and other non-monarchical forms of governments, still they concentrated on monarchy and, thus, acknowledged the *Kṣatriya's* right to rule. The duty of *Kṣatriya* king had to maintain or enforce *dhārma* (social order) in society at large (Ibid., 13).

Although it is true that the two approaches of the *Brāhmanic* tradition, namely *dharmaśāstra* and *arthaśāstra* made an attempt to establish *dhārma* in a society, it is also a fact that both the approaches differed primarily in their subject matter. The *dharmaśāstra* approach was more concerned to lay down *dhārma*; therefore, it was moralistic, legalistic and religious in its orientation. In contrast to *dharmaśāstra*, the *arthaśāstra* approach was concerned with analysing the structure and functions of government and institutions. Thus, it was a realistic and secular approach of *Hindu* tradition (ibid., 11).

In the *Brāhmanic* tradition, the acceptance of the authority of the *Vedās* and the alliance or corporate spirit of the *Kṣatriyas* and the *Brāhmaṇas* has played a significant role in perpetuation of the caste-based hierarchy in Indian society. The *Brāhmanic* tradition has also made an attempt for the justification of monarchical system. Its status-quoist and society-centred features led to some reactions and challenges, which ultimately culminated into a very powerful discourse known as heterodox tradition or what is popularly referred as *Śhramanic* tradition. The *Śhramanaic* tradition of Indian philosophy is primarily represented by Jainism and Buddhism. In contrast to *Brahmanism* which is spiritual, the *Śhramana* sects (Jainism and Buddhism) are material in the matter of religion and philosophy. The *Śhramanic* tradition is also sometimes referred to as a reformist school within the *Vedic* tradition because it is not against the *Brahmanism* but against the evils or ritualistic trends of *Brāhmanism*. Both the *Śhramana* sects, Jainism and Buddhism are also believed to continue this reformist and anti-ritualistic trend. The common features of these *Śhramana* sects are as follows:

1. They challenge the authority or validity of the *Vedās*.
2. They criticize *Brāhmanism*, ritualism, casteism and the idea of the existence of God, in the sense of a personal creator or determiner of destiny.

3. They observe a set of ethical principles or laws.
4. They emphasize on self-reliance or the force of *karma* in the quest of salvation.
5. They practise a detached life with a view of liberating themselves from the worldly life.

Origin and Evolution of the *Śhramanic* Tradition

The *Śhramanic* tradition is a non-*Vedic* or non-*Brāhmanical* tradition which arose out of the ritualistic tendencies within a *Brāhmanic* tradition. The modern historians and scholars have different opinions or views about the rise and development of the *Śhramanic* tradition. They tend to attribute the rise of the *Śhramanic* tradition to different sources, which can be broadly classified into three categories: (a) inner dialectics of classical tradition, (b) different ethnic traditions and (c) social change. According to one interpretation, the *Śhramanic* tradition is a reformist school within the *Vedic* tradition which developed by a dialectical interweaving of two types of philosophical outlooks of a single unified *Vedic* tradition, namely *Pravrtti-dhārma* and *Nivrtti-dhārma*. The classical tradition attributes the *Pravrtti-dhārma* to the ritualistic side of *Vedic* religion and the *Nivrtti-dhārma* to the gnostic and ascetic side of the same tradition. Modern scholars like Jacobi and Oldenberg basically attribute the development of the *Śhramanic* tradition to the *Nivrrti-dhārma* of the classical tradition. Some other scholars attribute the rise of the classical-*Brāhmanic* and *Śhramanic* tradition to two different ethnic traditions, *Aryans* and non-*Aryans*. In this respect, the ascetic or the *Śhramanic* tradition was developed by non-*Aryan* ethnic stream. Besides, some scholars attribute the rise of the *Śhramanic* tradition to the social changes implicit in the rise of new classes, such as traders, cultivators, artisans, merchants and skilled labours (Pandey 1978, 4–5). In short, it can be concluded that whatever the source may be responsible for the rise and development of the *Śhramanic* tradition, its main aim is to reform the classical-*Brāhmanic* tradition and, thus, it is critical to *Hindu* social order. However, it must be noted that the *Śhramanic* tradition does not involve a radical and subversive break with the classical tradition as it continued to share some basic ideas or beliefs of *Brāhmanism*, such as the doctrine of *Samsara*, *Karman*, asceticism and monasticism.

Furthermore, there are certain points of belief on which the *Śhramanic* tradition is critical of classical-*Brāhmanic* tradition. The *Śhramanic* tradition antedates the *Vedās* and opposes the *Brahmanism* or *Vedic-Brāhmanic* culture, rejects the idea of God, criticizes sacrifice[1] (*yajña*), the divinely ordained system of *varṇa* (social classes or caste), doctrine of untouchably and customs of *devadasi* and *sati*. In other words, the *Śhramanic* tradition represents an anti-*Vedic* and anti-sacrificial ascetic thought. Thus, it is a mixture of atheistic,[2] anti-ritualistic, ascetic and pluralistic ideologies.

Moreover, it stresses on the non-violence or inoffensiveness (*ahimsā*) and strong sense of egalitarianism (social and legal equality). It also emphasizes on the inexorableness of moral laws and self-reliance for attaining salvation or liberation (*mokṣa* or *nirāvna*) which means that no prayers and worship are of any use against the force of *karma*. According to ascetic *Śhramanic* tradition, the purification of feelings through inward illumination is needed for salvation and this view is quite different from the *Vedic* tradition where illumination comes from outside, either from an eternally revealed world or from the grace of God (ibid., 73). Some of the salient features of the *Śhramanic* tradition are as follows:

1. It denies the authority of the *Vedās* as revealed texts and rejects the hereditary caste system (the theory of *Caturvarṇya*) or social stratification.
2. It questions *Brāhmanical* supremacy and rejects the efficacy of animal sacrifices and rituals for purification.

3. It rejects the material world or life.
4. It represents a sterner variety of religion where the consolation of a personal God is replaced by the guidance of a spiritual teacher.
5. It believes in the individual autonomy and the doctrine of *karma* and rebirth, samsara and transmigration of soul.
6. It opposes the idea of God as creator of the world.
7. It believes in the purification of soul to attain *mokṣa* through āhimsa, renunciation and austerities.
8. It emphasizes on the idea of self-reliance or individual effort/labour (*śrama*) in the quest for salvation.

The Jaina Philosophy

The Jaina system of philosophy arose out of the teachings of 24 teachers (Tīrthaṅkaras or liberated propagators of the faith). The first of these teachers was Ṛṣabhadeva and the last was Vardhamāna (also styled Mahāvīra), a great spiritual hero and a contemporary of Gautama Buddha. Although Mahāvīra cannot be regarded as the founder of Jainism, he gave a new orientation to Jaina faith and teachings. The word 'Jina' etymologically means conqueror; it is the common name applied to the 24 Tīrthaṅkaras who have conquered all passions (*rāga* and *dvesa*), desires and have attained liberation.

There is no doubt that on the basis of some minor details of faith and practice of nudity amongst monks and liberation of women, the followers of Jainism are divided into two sects—Śhvetāmbara (or white-clad) and Digāmbara (sky-clad); however, the differences among these two do not lie so much in the basic philosophical doctrines of Jainism. In other words, the teachings of the Jinas are accepted by both the sects and, thus, the differences between them do not affect the fundamental philosophical doctrines. In Jainism, the Digāmbaras are most rigorous and puritanic, while the Śhvetāmbaras are more accommodating to the common frailties of men. The Digāmbaras hold, for example, that ascetics should give up all possessions, even clothes (or nudity is necessary for liberation), whereas the Śhvetāmbaras hold that the highest monks should wear white robes. In addition to this, the Digāmbaras believe that the perfect saint needs no food, and women cannot obtain liberation but the Śhvetāmbaras do not accept these views.

The Jaina philosophy which is based on the idea of realism, relativism, pluralism and atheism attempts to explain the rationale of being and existence, the nature of the universe and its constituents, the nature of bondage and the means to achieve liberation. The philosophical outlook of Jainism asserts the reality of the external world. Jaina philosophers have used the terms *sat, tattva, dravya, arthapadārtha, tattvārtha* as synonyms for the word reality. According to this school of thought, the objects perceived by us are real and they are many-faced (*anekāntavāda*,[3] i.e., theory of manyness of reality). Jaina philosophy defines reality as possessing origination, decay and permanence or as having qualities and modes. Origination and decay are nothing but the changing modes or forms. Permanence is the same as essential qualities or attributes. Thus, reality is possessed of both change and permanence. Moreover, Jaina philosophy says that permanence is not to be understood as absolute changelessness. Similarly, change is not to be taken as absolute difference. In other words, reality is transitory as well as permanent, different as well as identical. No object can be absolutely destroyed, nothing can be absolutely permanent. In short, reality is a synthesis of opposites—identity and difference, permanence and change.

Along with this, the Jainas reject the existence of God, but for guidance and inspiration, they think that it is necessary to meditate on and worship the liberated, perfect souls (siddhas). According to Jaina philosophy, the liberated souls possess God-like perfections and easily take the place of God. The Jainas adore the Tīrthaṅkaras or the founders of the faith. The Jaina metaphysics is pluralistic and divides all substances into soul (*Jīva*) and non-soul (*ajīva*). The Jaina philosophers believe that every spirit (*Jīva*), that is in bondage now, can follow the example set by the Jainas (omniscient liberated souls) and attain, like them, perfect knowledge, power and joy. In short, the distinguishing features of Jaina philosophy are as follows:

1. Belief on independent existence of soul and matter.
2. Denial of supreme divine creator, preserver and destroyer.
3. Faith in eternal and uncreated universe.
4. A strong emphasis on self-control, potency of *karma*, ahimsa (non-violence), austerities and renunciation.
5. Accent on relativity and multiple facets of truth.
6. Morality or ethics based on liberation of soul.
7. Emphasis on self-reliance and individual efforts for one's liberation (*mokṣa*).

The Jaina philosophy can also be understood in terms of its tattvas or fundamentals which include: *jīva* (soul), *ajīva* (non-living matters), *punya* (results of good deeds), *pap* (results of bad deeds), *āsrava* (influx of *karmas*), *bandh* (bondage of *karmas*), *samvar* (stoppage of *karmas*), *nirjara* (eradication of *karmas*) and *mokṣa* (liberation).

The philosophical outlooks of the Jaina school are as follows:

1. **The Jaina theory of knowledge**: The Jaina theory of knowledge has made a unique contribution to the Indian systems of philosophy by occupying itself with the basic epistemological issues, namely the nature and kinds of knowledge, how knowledge is derived and in what way knowledge can be said to be reliable. It defined knowledge as the essence of soul. Although soul has other characteristics also, the Jaina thinkers always emphasized knowledge to be the chief characteristic possessed by soul. In the Jaina canons there is no difference between the knower and his knowledge and, therefore, in the Jaina theory of knowledge we find an expression that soul is knowledge and knowledge is soul. Moreover, Jainism holds that knowledge is like light. It is self-illuminating as well as other-illuminating.

   The Jainas believe in the validity of perception, inference and testimony as means or sources of valid knowledge. They classify knowledge into two categories, such as perceptual (*pratyakṣa*) and non-perceptual (*parokṣa*). The perceptual knowledge is direct or immediate, whereas the non-perceptual knowledge is indirect or mediate. According to the Jaina philosophy, the knowledge which manifests itself in the soul without the operation of the senses and mind is direct or immediate knowledge, whereas the knowledge which arises with the functioning of the senses or mind is indirect or mediate knowledge. Moreover, immediate knowledge is further divided into three kinds of extraordinary or extrasensory perceptions[4] (*pāramārthikapratyakṣa*) which include clairvoyance (*avadhi*), telepathy (*manaḥparyāya*) and omniscience (*kevala*). *Avadhi* is direct knowledge of things and it functions within a particular area and up to a particular time. It cannot go beyond spatial and temporal limits. *Manahparyāya* is direct knowledge of the thoughts of others. And it is too limited by spatial and temporal conditions. In both *Avadhi* and *Manahparyāya*, the soul has direct knowledge unaided by the senses or the mind. Hence, they are called immediate, though limited. *Kevala* is unlimited and absolute knowledge which can be acquired only by the liberated souls. It is not limited by space and time.

In addition to these, mediate knowledge has two kinds of ordinary knowledge. These are called *Mati* and *Shruta*. By *Mati* we refer to any kind of knowledge which we can obtain through the senses or *manas*, whereas *Shruta* is a knowledge which is obtained from authority. The Jainas point out that perceptual knowledge which is ordinarily regarded as immediate knowledge is only relatively immediate and therefore included in mediate and not in immediate knowledge. It is included under *Mati*. Moreover, it must also be noted that the two kinds of ordinary knowledge, namely *Mati* and *Shruta*, as well as the lowest kind of immediate extraordinary knowledge, namely *avadhi*, are not absolutely free from chances of error. But the two higher kinds of immediate extrasensory knowledge (*manahparyāya* and *kevala*) are never liable to any error.

Besides these five kinds of right knowledge, we have three kinds of wrong knowledge—*Saṁshaya* or doubt, *Viparyaya* or mistake and *Anadhyavasāya* or wrong knowledge. Knowledge may again be divided into two kinds, namely *Pramāṇa* or knowledge of a thing as it is, and *Nyaya*[5] or knowledge of a thing in its relation. Jaina philosophers accepts three *Pramāṇa*—perception (*pratyaksa*), inference (*anumana*) and testimony (*sabda*).

2. **The Jaina theory of judgement**: One of most important contributions of Jainism to Indian school of philosophy is its doctrine of *Anekāntavāda* (or the doctrine of the manyness of reality) which refers to the principles of pluralism and multiplicity of viewpoints about the truth or reality perceived by us. In other words, the Jainas point out that the knowledge which we possess about the objects has innumerable aspects. According to them, an omniscient being can obtain knowledge of an object in all its innumerable aspects but an imperfect being looks at objects from one particular point of view at a time and consequently has the knowledge of one aspect or character of the thing. In other words, reality has infinite aspects which are all relative and we can know only some of these aspects. In this respect, all our judgements, therefore, are necessarily relative, conditional and limited. This epistemological and logical theory of the Jainas is called *Syādvāda* (the theory of relativity of knowledge). As a matter of fact, both *Anekāntavāda* and *Syadvada* are the two aspects of the same teaching which is based on realistic and relativistic pluralism. The story[6] of the six blind men and the elephant illustrates the doctrine of *Anekāntavāda* and *Syādvāda*. In short, the *Anekāntavāda* is a metaphysical side of a reality, whereas the *Syādvāda* which is also known as *Sapta-bhangī-nyaya* is an epistemological and logical side of a same reality.
3. **The Jaina conception of substance**: The Jainas philosophical view of substance is based on the distinction between the characters (*dhārma*) and substance (*dharmi*) which possess the characters. According to Jainas, every substance possesses two kinds of characters—essential and accidental. The essential characters of a substance remain in the substance as long as the substance remains. Consciousness, for example, is an essential character of the soul. In contrast to the essential characters, the accidental characters of a substance come and go. Desires, pleasure and pain are the accidental characters possessed by the soul-substance. It is through such characters (modes) that a substance undergoes change and modification. The Jainas call an essential unchanging character as *guna*, whereas an accidental, changing character is known as *paryāya*. A substance is defined, therefore, as that which possesses qualities (*guṇas*), as well as modes (*paryāyas*). In addition to this, the Jainas believe that substance is real (*sat*) which consists of three factors: permanence, origination and decay.

According to Jaina, the substance can be broadly classified into two categories: extended and non-extended. There is only one substance, namely time (*kāla*), which is devoid of extension. All other substances possess extension and they are generally called *astikāya*. Substances possessing extension are sub-divided into two kinds, namely the living (*jīva*) and the non-living (*ajīva*). The living substances (soul or *jīva*) again can be classified into those that are emancipated or perfect (*mukta*) and those that are in bondage (*baddha*), whereas the non-living substances can be categorized into *dhārma*, *adhārma*, *ākāśa* and *pudgala*.

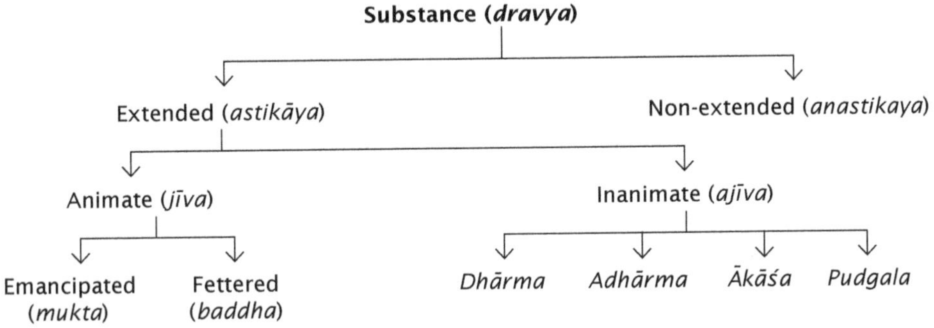

In short, there are six ultimate substances or eternal Reals in Jaina metaphysics: (a) soul (*jīva*), (b) matter (*pudgala*), (c) medium of motion (*dhārma*), (d) medium of rest (*adhārma*), (e) space (*ākāśa*) and (f) time (*kāla*).

4. **The Jaina philosophy of bondage and liberation**: In Jaina philosophy, every soul (*jīva* or a living conscious being) has inherent potentiality of attaining the fourfold perfection (*anantacatussttaya*), namely infinite knowledge, infinite faith, infinite power and infinite bliss or happiness. These qualities are inherent in the very nature of the soul, but they are obstructed by *karmas*, just as the natural light of the sun is obstructed by clouds or fog. *Karma* in this sense is the link which unites the soul to the body. According to Jainas, the *karmas* or the forces of passions (also known as *kasāya* or sticky substances)—anger (*krodha*), vanity (*māna*), infatuation (*māyā*), greed (*lobha*) and desires—attract the flow of karmic matter into the soul and it permeate the soul to attain its natural perfection. In other words, the limitations that we find in any individual soul are due to the *karma* forces and the material body with which the soul has identified itself. In Jaina philosophy, the passions or *karma* forces are the efficient cause of the bondage of a soul and matter (*pudgala*) is said to be its material cause. The flow of such *karma*-matter (*karma-pudgala*) towards the soul to bind it is called, therefore, influx (āsrava)[7] of *karma*. In this way, we have seen that soul in Jaina philosophy becomes bondage[8] due to both *karma* and its association with particles of matter.

   The Jainas, therefore, stress on *mokṣa* or liberation of a soul which can be attained by *stopping the influx* (*samvara* or *stoppage*) of new matter into the soul as well as by *complete elimination* (*nirjarā* or *wearing out of karma in the soul*) of the matter with which the soul has become already mingled. The teachings and lives of the liberated saints (omniscient Tīrthaṅkaras) have also showed a path for liberation. According to them, the three Jewels (*tri-ratna*) or principles of life are necessary for the removal of bondage, such as right or perfect faith (*samyak-darśhana*) in the teachings of the Jaina teachers, right knowledge (*samyak-jñāna*) of the teachings and right conduct (*samyak-cāritra*). Right conduct consists in the practice of abstinence from all injury to life (*ahimsā*), from falsehood (*satyam*), from stealing (*asteyam*), from sensuality (*brahmacaryam*) and from all attachment (*aparigraha*). In short, liberation is the joint effect of these three.

The Buddha Philosophy

The Buddha system of philosophy came into being as a result of the teachings and enlightenment attained by Siddhārtha or Gautama Buddha, well-known as the Light of Asia and the founder of Buddhism. His teachings not only formed the basis for Buddhist philosophy[9] but also aim to help an individual to attain a good life and liberation from suffering. The founder of Buddhist philosophy was born about the middle of the 6th century BC in a royal family of Kapilavastu (on the lower slopes of Himālayas, North India). At his birth there was a prophecy that either he would become a world conqueror, a *Cakravartin*, or he would 'conquer' the world by renouncing it and becoming a Buddha. His father preferred the more tangible kind of conquest and tried to shield Siddhartha from all the evils of life that might tempt him into spiritual reflection. But this strategy backfired; for when, he was at the age of 30 and determined immediately to renounce the world. At this age, he left not only the material luxuries of the Shākya kingdom but also his beloved wife *Yaśodharā* and newborn son *Rāhula* in quest of truth or enlightenment. The immediate cause of his renunciation of the world was the thought or idea of suffering which essentially impressed him when he saw the misery and pain of human life in the form of disease/sickness, old age and death. As an ascetic (*Śramana*), he was restless in search of the real source of sufferings and of the means of complete deliverance. In order to discover the source (origin) and remedy of human suffering, Buddha betook himself at first to severe penance and practised great austerities, but after years of fasting and other ascetic practices, he felt that he had achieved nothing by following these lofty states of extremes asceticism. In fact, he practised severe forms of asceticism, almost to the point of death by starvation, all without gain. Then later on finally he sat down under a tree, *Bodhi* (enlightenment) tree, and began a fresh course of self-discipline and intense meditation characterized by less rigour. In this second endeavour, after years of steady search and meditation, he unravelled the truth about the mystery of world's miseries or suffering and the means of eradicating it. Thus, became the enlightened and the title of 'Buddha'[10] (literally means the awakened or enlightened one) which came to be applied to him afterwards signifies this. The interesting point about the Buddha is that he was a true lover of mankind and, therefore, after getting enlightenment he did not spend the rest of his life in the forest rather he quickly returned to the abodes of men and began to spread the knowledge of truth which had brought him illumination and freedom (Hiriyanna 2000, 133).

The Buddha's philosophical teachings and conversations depend today chiefly on the Pāli Canon called Tripiṭakas or the three baskets, that is, the threefold canon or 'Bible of sacred documents'. The first basket is the Vinaya-Piṭaka which deals with the laws and rules of conduct for the congregation (*Saṅgha*). The second is the Sutta-Piṭaka which is said to be a compilation of the utterances of the Buddha himself and consists of five collections called *Nikāyas—Dīgha, Majjhima, Saṁyutta, Aṅguttara* and *Khuddaka*. The third is called Abhidhamma-Piṭaka which deals with the philosophical discussions. Although Buddha has imparted all his teachings through oral instructions, his three central doctrines have been preserved well. The first of these doctrines is about the doctrine of the four noble truths—(a) there is suffering (*duḥkha*), (b) there is the origination or cause of suffering (*samudaya*), (c) there is the cessation of suffering (*nirodha*) and (d) there is a path to the cessation of suffering (*mārga*). The second doctrine is that of *Pratītyasamutpāda* or doctrine of dependent origination, which is contained in the second and third noble truths. It says that everything in this world arises depending on the cause and is, therefore, impermanent. Buddha believed that suffering, which resulted due to ignorance, led to endless cycles of birth and rebirth. The key to escape from this cycle is said to lie only in realization of true knowledge that can liberate us also. The third doctrine which is contained in the fourth noble truth is called the doctrine of the eightfold noble path and it prescribes the eight steps which leads to knowledge, enlightenment and, consequently, liberation (*nirvāna*). In short, the crux of Buddha's philosophy can be understood when he said to his disciples that 'I teach only two things, O disciples, the nature of suffering and the cessation of suffering'.

Like Jainism, there are some particular points in Buddhist philosophy which are subject of dispute among the followers of Buddhism and therefore they are also divided into two sects—Hīnayāna or Theravada and Mahāyāna. Hīnayāna which first flourished in the south and now in Ceylon, Burma and Siam is claimed to be more orthodox and faithful to the teachings of Buddha. The Theravada tradition strongly emphasizes reading and contemplating the first discourse of the Buddha—'The Discourse That Sets Turning the Wheel of Truth (Dhamma)'[11] as a means to study the four noble (*Aryan*) truths and put them into practice. The Hīnayāna holds that *nirvāna* (salvation) should be sought in order to put an end on one's own misery. In contrast to Hīnayāna, the Mahāyāna flourished mostly in north and its adherents are to be found in Tibet, China and Japan. The practitioners of Mahāyāna tradition are more likely to learn about the four noble truths through studying various Mahāyāna commentaries, and less likely to study the first discourse directly. The Mahāyāna points out that the object of *nirvāna* is not to put an end on one's own misery but to obtain perfect wisdom with which the liberated can work for the salvation of all the suffering beings. The main characteristic features of Buddhism are as follows:

1. Everything is marked by suffering, change and emptiness.
2. There is cause and effect relationship between *karma* and *phala*.
3. A middle way or path between the extremes of dogmatism and scepticism is the best path.
4. Liberation can only be attained by right knowledge and right action.

The Buddha's knowledge and philosophical teaching can also be understood through his contribution in many areas of philosophy, including epistemology, metaphysics and ethics. In epistemology, the Buddha seeks a middle way between the extremes of dogmatism and scepticism,[12] emphasizing personal experience, a pragmatic attitude and the use of critical thinking towards all types of knowledge. In ethics, the Buddha proposes a threefold understanding of action: mental, verbal and bodily. In metaphysics, the Buddha argues that there are no self-caused entities, and that everything dependently arises from or upon something else. The philosophical outlooks of Buddhism are:

1. **The four noble truths (*ārya-satya*)**: The doctrine of four noble truths (*catvāriārya-satyāni*) is regarded as the central doctrine of the Buddhist philosophy. They are said to provide a conceptual framework for all of Buddhist thought. These four truths explain not only the nature of sufferings or misery (*duḥkha*) but also its causes, its cessation and the path leading to the cessation of misery. The first truth is about the existence of misery and it is not simply causal rather it is ordinarily present in all forms of existence and in all kinds of experience. Even the so-called pleasures are

also the real source of pain at bottom. The second truth points out that existence of everything in the world, material or mental, has a cause or condition. There is nothing which is unconditional and self-existent. Everything in this world is conditional, relative and limited. Nothing is therefore permanent in the world. All things are subject to change. Like anything, our sufferings are similarly caused by some conditions. The third truth is about the cessation (nirodha) of misery which means that suffering, like other things, depends on some causes and conditions; therefore, the effect must also cease when these causes and conditions are removed. In other words, one which is born must die. The fourth truth talks about an ethical and spiritual path that leads to the cessation of misery. This path (*mārga*) is known as eightfold noble path (*Aṣṭāṅgika-mārga*) as it consists of eight steps. The eight steps of the Buddhist path are usually divided into three kinds of training, namely (a) training in wisdom/discernment—right views/knowledge (*Samyagdṛṣti*) and right determination/resolve (*Samyagsaṅkalpa*), (b) ethical training—right speech (*Samyagvāka*), right conduct/action (*Samyagkarmānta*), right livelihood (*Samyagājiva*) and (c) training in concentration—right endeavour/effort (*Samayagvyāyāma*), right mindfulness (*Samyagsmṛiti*) and right concentration/meditation (*Samyagsamādhi*). These eight steps remove ignorance and desire, enlighten the mind and bring about perfect equanimity and tranquillity. Thus, misery ceases completely and the chance of rebirth is also stopped. The attainment of this state of perfection is *nirvāṇa*.

2. **The doctrine of dependent origination (*Pratītyasamutpāda*)**: The doctrine of dependent origination or *Pratītyasamutpāda* is the foundational teaching of the Buddha and his all other teachings can be easily deduced from it as corollaries. The coming into being of life which is suffering, as well as its cessation, is explained by the doctrine of *Pratītyasamutpāda*. This doctrine of Buddha is contained in the second noble truth which gives us the cause of suffering, and in the third noble truth which shows the cessation of suffering. It states that events are neither predetermined nor random and they always depend on other things. Moreover, it does not accept the existence of everlasting and absolute entities. According to this doctrine, the existence of everything is relative, conditional and dependent on a cause. In other words, nothing happens fortuitously or by chance. This theory of Buddha's philosophy avoids two extreme views. On the one hand it rejects eternalism or the theory that some reality eternally exists independently of any condition and, on the other hand, it does not believe in nihilism or the theory that something existing can be annihilated or can cease to be. In other words, all phenomenal things hang between reality and nothingness. Buddha claims, therefore to hold the middle view or path (*Madhyamā Pratipat*), namely that everything that we perceive possesses an existence but is dependent on something else, and that thing in turn does not perish without leaving some effect (Chatterjee and Datta 2010, 124).

   Moreover, in Buddha philosophy we find the 12 links of the causal wheel of dependent origination—(a) ignorance (*avidyā*), (b) impressions of karmic forces (*saṁskāra*), (c) initial consciousness of the embryo (*vijñāna*), (d) psycho-physical organism (*nāma-rūpa*), (e) six sense-organs of knowledge, including mind (*ṣaḍāyatana*), (f) sense-object-contact (*sparśha*), (g) sense-experience (*vedanā*), (h) thirst for sense-enjoyment (*tṛṣṇā*), (i) cleaning to this enjoyment (*upādāna*), (j) will to be born (*bhava*), (k) birth or rebirth (*jāti*) and (l) old age and death (*jarā-maraṇa*). Out of these 12 links, the first two are related to past life, the last two to future life and the rest to present life. This is the vicious circle of causation which can be destroyed only when its root cause, that is, ignorance is destroyed.

Twelve Links of Causation

Past life	**Present life**	**Future life**
Ignorance	The initial consciousness of the embryo	Rebirth
Impressions	Psycho-physical organism	Old age and death
	Six sense-organs of knowledge, including mind	
	Sense-object contact	
	Sense-experience	
	Thirst for sense enjoyment	
	Clinging	
	Will to be born	

3. **The theory of *karma***: The theory of *karma* shows that the present and future existence of an individual depends only on the law of *karma*. In Buddha philosophy, it is conceived as an only causation for the explanation of the origin of suffering, birth and rebirth. According to Buddha philosophy, the law of *karma* is a root cause for the continuation and destruction of the vicious circle of birth and rebirth. In short, there is a causal relationship between *karma* (action) and *phala* (result).
4. **The doctrine of universal change and impermanence**: The change and impermanence are the two laws of universe, which show the transitory nature of life and all worldly things. According to Buddha, there is nothing in this universe which is permanent or unchanged. Through his doctrine he tried to explain that everything originates from something and it disappears when the condition ceases to be. In all his teachings, he repeatedly emphasized that everything is subject to change and decay. His doctrine of impermanence is further developed later by his followers into a theory of momentariness (*kṣaṇika-vāda*), which means not only that everything has conditional and, therefore, non-permanent existence but also that things last not even for short periods of time, but exist for one part-less moment only.
5. **The theory of the non-existence of the soul (*Anattā-vāda*)**: The theory of non-self is one of the major and distinctive features of the Buddha's philosophy. The essence of this theory is that it denies the existence of any eternal, essential and absolute substance called a soul, self or atman in living beings. In addition to this, it is one of three characteristics of all existence along with *Duḥkha* (suffering) and *Anicca* (impermanence/nothing lasts). The Buddha held that eternal self is an illusion. The only self that made sense to him was the objective self, which could be identified with a name and form and possessed a physical self. The physical self, according to him, is created by the aggregates of thoughts, memories, desires, expectations, compassion, attachment, illusion and egoism. It is neither eternal nor imperishable and exists as long as the mind and the senses exist. In other words, when the personality is dissolved, the *Anattā*[13] which is dependent on it also dissolves. Therefore, beyond that objective reality of *Anattā*, there is nothing else, such as a permanent, unchanging and eternal self. Moreover, according to the Buddha's philosophy the attachment to the appearance of a permanent self in this world of change is the cause of suffering and the main obstacle to liberation. In a sermon delivered to his first five disciples (*Saṁyutta-Nikāya* 22.59), the Buddha provided a clear reasoning in favour of his no-self argument and advised them to renounce all sense of

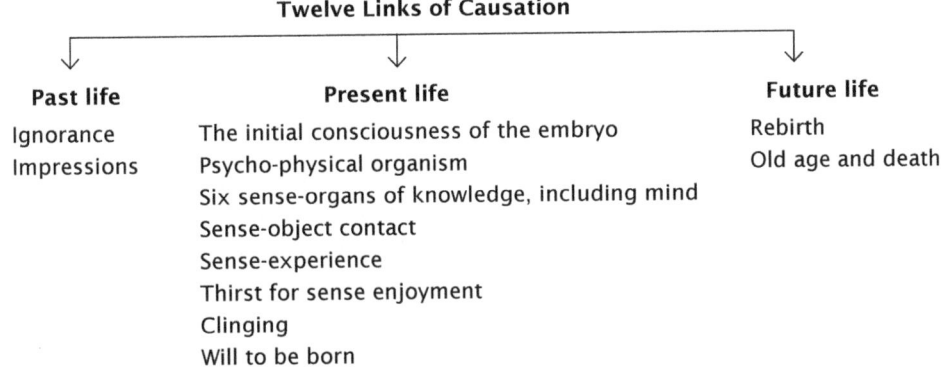

> ownership and possessiveness to end attachment, suffering and the process of becoming. Therefore, he rejects a permanent, a self-existent soul (*ātman*) in favour of *anattā* (non-self) and *anicca* (impermanence).

Furthermore, though Buddha denied the continuity of an identical substance in living beings, he did not deny the continuity of the stream of successive states that compose the life. According to Buddha, life is an unbroken series of states and each of these states depends on the condition just preceding and gives rise to the one just succeeding it. The continuity of the life-series is, therefore, based on a causal connection running through the different states. This continuity can be explained with the example of a river. In Buddhist parlance, life is just like a river, which is ever changing. Since it flows continuously, one may outwardly see the same river, with the same twists and turns. However, it is never the same because its water is continuously replaced by the water flowing from behind. Over a long period, the river itself may change course, or dry up completely, due to the changes in the climate or environment (conditions). In other words, though the water in each flow is different from one another, it is connected causally. Similarly, the end-state of this life may cause the beginning of the next. Rebirth is, therefore, not transmigration, that is, the migration of the same soul into another body. In fact, it is the causation of the next life by the present. In summing up, the conception of an eternal soul in the theory of the non-existence of soul is thus replaced by unbroken streams/series of different states of the life and it depends on its own conditions.

In short, the declared ideal of early Buddhism was the attainment of an utterly tranquil (*upasama*), deathless (*amata*) state of peace (*santi*) and supreme bliss (*parama-sukha*). Destruction of impurities (*āsavakkhayā*), such as desire, ignorance will-to-be, etc.

Conclusion

The *Śhramanic* tradition is largely a product of revolt against the system of animal sacrifice and other ritualistic practices which had crept into the orthodox *Hindu* religion. The *Śhramanic* tradition has not only rejected the existence of *Vedās* but also the authority of the *Brāhmaṇs*, who were considered as the protectors of the sacred learning found in the *Vedās*. In contrast to *Brāhmanic* dogmatism, the *śramanas* believed in free will as well as the efficacy of moral conduct and spiritual practices in order to attain liberation from the cycle of reincarnations. Further, the practitioners of the *Śhramanic* tradition believed in the practice of self-discipline, an ascetic lifestyle and the doctrine of non-violence. Thus in this way, the *Śhramanic* tradition has enriched the philosophical thought of India.

Summary

The origin and evolution of the *Śhramanic* tradition can be traced back to the popularity of *Jainism* and *Buddhism* which have not only criticized the ritualistic practices of *Vedic Brahmanism* but also rejected the authority of *Vedās* and the *Brāhmanic* supremacy based on the caste system. The *Śhramanic* tradition is extremely critical of the *Brāhmanical* system, the hereditary basis of caste, animal sacrifice and other ritualistic practices. It preached the value of moral life in terms of the theory of *karma*. Further, it subscribed to the ideal of liberation by one's own individual effort as transcending the ever-going cycle of birth, death and rebirth.

Points for Discussion

1. Indian political thought is not a single tradition but consists of different traditions of thought. Elucidate.
2. Discuss the distinction made between orthodox and heterodox schools of thought in the Indian philosophy. Explain the common characteristics as well.
3. What are the key elements of the *Śhramanic* tradition? Do you think that it is fundamentally different from the classical tradition? Elaborate and give reasons in support of your answer.
4. Critically examine the *Śhramanic* response to the *Brāhmanic* tradition in ancient Indian political thought.
5. Discuss the *Śhramanic* critique of the *Brāhmanic* tradition.
6. Critically examine the main schools of the *Śhramanic* tradition.

Endnotes

1. It was a hallmark or heart and soul of ancient *Hindu*-tradition and involved violence to living creatures.
2. *Śhramanic* atheism is not a variety of irreligion but of religion.
3. *Anekāntavāda* is a speculative method of looking at a thing from all possible points of views.
4. The extrasensory perception is a perception which is directly derived from the soul.
5. *Nyaya* is a standpoint of a thought from which we make a statement about a thing.
6. In the story of six blind men and the elephant, each one tried to describe the whole animal differently by touching its legs, ears, tail and trunk, respectively. The story indicates that they all came to arrive at different conclusions regarding the real shape of the animal and quarrelled among themselves about their assertion that his description alone is correct. But the one who can see the whole elephant can easily know that each blind man felt only one part of the elephant and this shows that our judgements in the same way represent only one aspect of many-sided reality. Thus, in order to acquire true and complete knowledge one should understand all the aspects of the reality.
7. The state when karmic particles actually begin to flow towards the soul to bind it is called *āsrava*.
8. In bondage, the karmic matter unites with the soul by intimate interpenetration, just as water unites with the milk or fire unites with the red-hot iron ball.
9. The Buddhist philosophy initially developed in South Asia, then later in the rest of Asia.
10. The title of 'Buddha' is conferred to an individual who discovers the path to *nirvana*, the cessation of suffering and propagates that discovery so that other may also achieve *nirvana*.
11. The Buddha gave his first discourse—The discourse of the turning of the wheel of truth to his five former companions at the Deer Park in Isipatana (modern Sarnath) near Benares on the *Āsālha* full-moon day (July), two months after his enlightenment. In it, the Buddha expounded the Middle Path which he discovered and which forms the essence of his teaching.
12. The extreme of dogmatism is represented in Pāli *Nikāyas* by *Brāhmanism* which believed in divine revelation of *Vedās*, caste system and the ritual killing of animals (sacrifice), whereas the extreme of scepticism is

represented in Pāli Nikāyas by some members of the *Śhramanic* movement which consisted of numerous groups of spiritual seekers and wandering philosophers.

13. The soul is only a conventional name for a collection of different constituents, the material body (*kāya*), the immaterial mind (*manas*) and the formless consciousness (*vijñāna*). The existence of soul depends on this collection and it dissolves when the collection breaks up.

Glossary

***Anekāntavāda*:** It is a doctrine of the manyness of reality which means that every object possesses innumerable positive and negative characters.

***Āstika*:** One who believes in God and infallibility or supremacy of *Vedās* is referred as *āstika*.

Epistemology: The nature of knowledge.

Metaphysics: The nature of reality.

***Nāstika*:** One who does not believe in other world and vilify the authority or supremacy of the *Vedās* is known as *nāstika*.

***Nirvāna*:** *Nirvāna* is a state of mind in which all the causes and conditions for rebirth and suffering have been eliminated.

***Śhramanic*:** It essentially refers to a rebellious, reformist and heterodox tradition of Indian philosophy and represented primarily by Jainism and Buddhism.

***Syādvāda*:** *Syādvāda* is the theory of relativity of knowledge. According to this theory, human knowledge about every reality has infinite aspects and this knowledge is necessarily relative and limited.

***Vedās*:** The *Vedās* are the oldest extant literary documents of the human (*Āryan*) mind that we possess.

References

Chatterjee, S. C. and D. M. Datta. 2010. *An Introduction to Indian Philosophy*. Calcutta: University of Calcutta.

Hiriyanna, M. 2000. *Outlines of Indian Philosophy*. Delhi: MLBD Publishers.

Pandey, G. 1978. *Sraman Tradition: Its History and Contribution to Indian Culture*. Ahmedabad: L. D. Institute of Indology.

Parekh, B. 1986. 'Some Reflections on the Hindu Tradition of Political Thought.' In *Political Thought in Modern India*, edited by T. Pantham and K. Deutsch, 17–31. New Delhi: SAGE Publications.

Further Readings

Altekar, A. 1958. *State and Government in Ancient India*, 3rd edition, 75–108. Delhi: Motilal Banarsidass.

Chakravarty, Nilima. 1992. *Indian Philosophy: The Path Finder's and System Builders*. New Delhi: Allied Publishers.

Chatalian, G. 1983. 'Early Indian Buddhism and the Nature of Philosophy: A Philosophical Investigation.' *Journal of Indian Philosophy* 11(2): 167–222.

Dasgupta, S. N. 2004. *A History of Indian Philosophy*, Vol. 1. Delhi: MLBD Publishers.

Dayakrishna. 1996. *Indian Philosophy*. New Delhi: Oxford University Press.

Devaraja, N. K. 1975. ed. *Bhāratīya Darśana (Hindi)*. Hindi Grantha Academy.

Heesterman, J. C. 1988. *The Inner Conflict of Tradition: Essays in Indian Ritual, Kingship and Society*. Chicago, IL: University of Chicago Press.
Hiriyanna, M. 2015. *The Essentials of Indian Philosophy*. Delhi: MLBD Publishers.
Jha, D. N. 1993. *Ancient India: An Introductory Outline*. Delhi: People's Publishing House.
Kosambi, D. D. 1980 *Culture and Civilizations in Ancient India*. Delhi: Vikas.
Lal, B. K. 2017. Contemporary Indian Philosophy. Delhi: Motilal Banarsidass.
Masih, Y. 1971. *Introduction to Religious Philosophy*. Delhi: MLBD Publishers.
Mehta, V. R. 2014. *Foundations of Indian Political Thought*. Delhi: Manohar.
Mehta, V. R. and Thomas Pantham, eds. 2006. *Political Ideas in Modern India: Thematic Explorations*. New Delhi: SAGE Publications.
Mohanty, J. N. 2002a. *Classical Indian Philosophy*. New Delhi: Oxford University Press.
Mohanty, J. N. 2002b. *Essays on Indian Philosophy*, 2nd edition, edited by P. Bilimoria. Delhi: Oxford University Press.
Prevos, P. 2002. *The Self in Indian Philosophy: Hindu, Buddhist and Carvaka Views*. Retrieved from http://prevos.net/humanities/philosophy/self/.
Radhakrishnan, S. 2009. *Indian Philosophy*, Vols. I and II. Delhi: Oxford University Press.
Radhakrishnan, S. and C. A. Moore. 1967. *A Sourcebook in Indian Philosophy*. Princeton, NJ: Princeton University Press.
Raju, P. T. 1985. *Structural Depths of Indian Thought*. Delhi: South Asian Publishers.
Sharma, Arvind. 2000. *Classical Hindu Thought: An Introduction*. New Delhi: Oxford University Press.
Sharma, C. D. 2003. *A Critical Survey of Indian Philosophy*. Delhi: MLBD Publishers.
Sharma, R. S. 1959. *Aspects of Political Ideas and Institutions in Ancient India*. Delhi: MLBD Publishers.
Varma, V. P. 1974. *Studies in Hindu Political Thought and Its Metaphysical Foundations*. Delhi: MLBD Publishers.

8
CHAPTER

Śukranīti: A Political Treatise

Prabira Sethy

CHAPTER OUTLINE

- Introduction
- The Life Sketch
- Ethics and Kingship
- Ideal King and His Qualities
- System of Law and Justice
- Reforms
- Conclusion
- Summary
- Points for Discussion

It is obvious that good actions give good results and evil actions give bad results, so one must always do what is good and right. So, make sure that you do good karma always.

—Sarkar (1975, 67)

Reader's Guide

This chapter tries to identify who was *Śukracharya*, what was written in *Śukranīti* (written by *Śukracharya*) and when it was written down. Second, it has taken up the task of expounding the general rules of ethics or morality laid down in the *Śukranīti* meant to be observed by the king and his subjects. Third, the chapter then goes on to demonstrate about the law which the king has to abide by according to *Sāstras* or social customs while governing the country. Finally, the chapter analyses the social reforms by highlighting a new basis and interpretation to the *Varṇa* system by discarding the generally accepted view that the caste goes by birth.

Introduction

Śukracharya or *Asuracharya* has occupied one of the most important places in the history of ancient Indian political thought. *Śukracharya* wrote a famous book which is known as *Śukranīti* (also called *Śukranītisara*). There are a total of four chapters and 2,200 verses in this text of *Śukranītisara*. The *Śukranīti* is a very valuable book in the field of *Hindu* polity. It is not only a book of theoretical discourse but also a book of practical knowledge and also contains several contemporary ideological trends. It deals with in detail the administrative function of the state, the duties and powers of king, appointment of the council of ministers and other officials, qualification for the appointment of ministers and other high officials, their functions, checks on the functioning of government and the king, keeping of efficient army, judicial system and punishment to be awarded for different crimes. Besides this, it describes the problems of foreign policy and methods of warfare. Thus, fundamentally *Śukranītisara* is a text of *rājādhārma* or political science and its whole subject matter is multidimensional.

Though the scholars admit that the *Śukranīti* was written by *Śukracharya*, there is a diverse opinion among them about who *Śukracharya* was and when this book was written. 'Widely divergent views are held about the written date of *Śukranīti* book. Dr U. N. Ghosal thinks that the book was written between 1200 AD and 1600 AD and the view of R. L. Mehra was also similar to this. The fact is that this work is a composition and was traced down to the fourteenth century, but its later part is to be ascribed to the eleventh or the twelfth century AD.' It is said that *Śukranīti* was not written at a stretch, or written in a period of years, but it was continued to be written for a very long period. It appears that additions in the composition of book of *Śukraniti* were continued to be made as considered necessary, but the bulk of the book must have been written at a time. It was a seat of learning which was occupied by his disciples. This view is corroborated by the fact that *Śukracharya* has been mentioned in *Ṛigvedā* and *Atharvavedā*. It is also mentioned in *Mahābhārata*, so we can safely assume that it was the head of the educational institutions since the age of *Mahābhārata*.

The Life Sketch

Śukracharya is the name of the preceptor of the *Asuras*, who is sometimes identified with the planet *Shukra* (Venus), or is considered its regent. In some *Purāṇas*, he is said to be the strongest of the seven sons born to the *Ṛiṣhi* Bhṛigu and Puloma. He is also known as KāvyaUśanas, who is mentioned in the *Ṛigveda* in association with *Indra*, and is similar to Kava-Ushan of Zoroastrian texts. There are several stories about *Śukracharya* in the epics and *Purāṇas*. According to one passage in the *Mahābhārata*, *Śukra* divided himself into two, and became the *Guru* of the *Devas* and the *Asuras*. The *Viṣṇu Purāṇ* too mentions *Uśanas* as the preceptor of the *Devas* and *Asuras*. However, *Śukracharya* is generally mentioned with the *Asuras*. He lived with the *Asuras* on Mt. Meru. Jewels and jewel mountains belonged to him, of which he gave one-fourth to *Kubera*. The *Mahābhārata* states that he had four sons, who were priests of the *Asuras*. The *Rāmāyaṇa* records that *Śukracharya* made the *Daṇḍakaranya* region barren, after his daughter *Arājā* was violated by king *Daṇḍa* who ruled there. *Śukracharya* was the *Guru* of *Prahlāda* as well as *Mahabali*. Other stories in the *Purāṇas* narrate how he fell in love with an *Apsara* and thus lost his merit and was reborn many times, before he regained his original form (Dalal 2010, 387–8).

Śukra, the Sanskrit meaning is 'clear and pure' or 'brightness and clearness', is the name of the preceptor of the *Asuras*. He is sometimes identified with the planet *Shukra* (Venus), one of the *Navagrahas*. The feminist natured *Śukra* is a *Brāhmaṇical* planet. He presides over *Śukravar* or Friday. He was born on Friday in the year *Parthiva* on *Sraavana Suddha Ashtami* when *Svati Nakshatra* is on the ascent. Hence, Friday is known as *Śukravar* in Indian languages, such as Sanskrit, Telugu, Hindi, Marathi, Gujarati, Oriya, Bengali, Assamese and Kannada. The *Devī-Bhāgavata Purāṇas* refers to his mother as *Kāvyamata*. He went on to study the *Vedās* under the *Ṛṣhi* Aṅgirasa, but he was disturbed by Aṅgirasa's favouritism for his son *Bṛihaspati*. He then went to study under *Ṛiṣhi* Gautama. He later performed penance to Lord *Shiva* and obtained the *Sanjivani mantra*—a formula that revived the dead. *Śukra* married Priyavrata's daughter Urjaswathi and was blessed with four sons—*Chanda, Amarka, Tvastr, Dharaatra* and a daughter by name Devayānī.

During this period, *Bṛihaspati* became the *guru* of *Devas*. *Śukracharya* decided to become the *guru* of *Asuras*. He helped them to achieve victory over the *Devas* and used his knowledge to revive the dead and wounded among them.

In another story, Lord *Viṣṇu* was born as the *Brāhmaṇa* dwarf-sage *Vāmana*. Once upon a time, *Vāmana* came to take alms from the *Asura* king Bali. Lord *Viṣṇu* wanted to deceive the king Bali, who was the grandson of the great king *Prahlāda*, in order to help the *Devas*. The sage *Śukracharya* identified him immediately and warned the king.

The king Bali was, however, a man of his word and offered the gift to *Vāmana*. *Śukracharya* annoyed with the pride of king, shrunk himself with his powers and sat in the spout of the vase from which water had to be poured to seal the promise to the deity in disguise. *Viṣṇu*, in disguise of the dwarf, understood immediately, and picked a straw from the ground and directed it up the spout, poked out the left eye of *Śukracharya*. Since this day on, the *Guru* of the *Asuras* had been known to be half blind.

Being a daughter of *Śukracharya*, Devayānī was rejected by the son of *Bṛihaspati*. She later married Yayāti who belongs to *Kuru* dynasty. In *Mahābhārata* it has been mentioned that *Śukracharya* was one of the mentors of *Pitāmaha Bhīṣma* who taught him political science in his youth.

Ethics and Kingship

Like other ancient thinkers *Śukra* too considered politics is an aspect of ethics. He called it moral science (*Nīti-Śāstra)* (policy science would be more appropriate) because it is the basis of virtue, wealth, enjoyment and salvation. According to *Śukra*, with the help of this science a ruler can conquer a foe and win a friend. While all other sciences deal with their respective spheres of action, it is the supreme science because it deals with all of them. While grammar deals with words, logic with material substances, *Mīmāṃsā* with religious ritual and *Vedānta* with the frailty and destructibility of the material body, the policy science deals with moral philosophy without which no stability can be maintained in human affairs. It plays the same role in human affairs as that played by food in the maintenance and preservation of the human body. In this sense, it is superior to other sciences because it aims at the fulfilment and achievement of the desires and interests of all that man seeks the happiness which is their chief end. *Nīti-Śāstra* tells us to achieve this end. Complete control of oneself and independence from others is the supreme form of happiness for both the individual and king. Great misery comes out of dependence on others. There is no greater happiness than that from self-rule. For the achievement of this, *Śukra* says *Nīti-Śāstra* is indispensable for the king. The two primary functions of the king are protection of subjects and punishment of the guilty and both these functions cannot be adequately performed without *Nīti-Śāstra*. *Śukra* writes 'when the ruler does not follow *Niti*, the kingdom is weakened, the army is handicapped, and the civil service is disorganized and evil prevails everywhere in the state' (Mehta 1992, 64–5).

Unlike the earlier writers, *Śukra* does not insist on a properly appointed ruler. He propagates for constitutional monarchy. It will not be meaningful to presume that checks of the modern type were applicable to ancient Indian monarchies. He was not a mere constitutional head like the President of the Republic of India or even the king of England, but both *de jure* as well as *de facto* sovereign of his state. His ministers were, of course, there and it was expected of a king to consult them individually as well as collectively. In fact, *Hindu* polity has basically agreed on one point, namely that a king without ministers shall not be wise, though relationship between the king and his ministers very much depended on their personality. *Śukra* believes that king is responsible to the public and as such he does not believe in the theory of 'Divine Rights of kings'. Thus, it has become his primary duty to look after the prosperity of his subjects. The people are at liberty to refuse payment of taxes and even leave the land of an unrighteous king. He has gone to the extent of saying that such an unrighteous king be replaced by a righteous king with the help of *Purohita*. A king who fails to promote morality and virtuousness has no moral right to rule over the subjects and the people are justified in disobeying him. The people also expect from a king to preserve and maintain the time-honoured institutions and in case he fails to do so the people can rightly, reasonably and legitimately expect from him the reason therefore.

Śukra has even provided the subjects the right to elect a king and has given an opportunity to them to express their view about the choice of a king either directly or indirectly. At any stage, if a king loses confidence of his subjects he should be removed from the throne. Although *Śukranītiśāstra* discusses the monarchical form of government, but this form of government is bound to bring with it the problem of succession. *Śukracharya*, in principle, does not support the idea of hereditary succession which he believes is not very sound. He has, however, very clearly said that a king with weak moral character or defective or unsound physique should not be allowed to ascend the throne. According to *Śukracharya*, a morally weak king could not set an example before his subjects and thus shall not be in a position to inspire the confidence of the people under him. A nation cannot be expected to have a sound moral character under such a ruler and thus could not be expected to have moral progress and advancement. If otherwise capable and competent, the son of a deceased king should be allowed to succeed his father. *Śukra* supports his argument by saying that the institution of kingship was created for the protection of subjects and not for injuring or harming them. It is mostly with this end in view that *Śukranītisara* provides that a king should always consult his ministers. As far as possible, he should accept their advice. Thus, *Śukra* wanted to put constitutional checks on the authority of the king and did not wish to let him remain unbridled or uncontrolled.

Śukra says that the ruler should rule his subjects in accordance with moral principles. According to him, there can be three kinds of kings, namely *Sāttvika*, *Rājāsika* and *Tāmsika*. *Sāttvika* king is one who is constant in his duties, protects his subjects, performs all sacrifices, conquers his enemies and who is charitable, forbearing and valorous, has no attachment to the things of enjoyment and is dispassionate. *Tāmsika* has the exactly opposite characteristics and such a king goes to hell. A king in whom passion rules, who is attached to the world and its gifts, who is not respectful of morals and who is of an intriguing disposition is a *Tāmsika* king. *Śukra* goes to the extent of saying that the *sāttvika* king enjoys the blessings of the Gods, the *rājsika* those of men, and the *tāmsika* those of mere demons (ibid., 65).

With regard to the qualities of a minister, *Śukra* has said that a good minister should be courteous, energetic, dignified, prompt, loyal, pure, incorruptible and dutiful. It is also expected of a minister that he should supervise the department efficiently so that there is no leakage of information in any way. A minister should also try to give the best of advice to his ruler and realize that his advice was most likely to be accepted and implemented. He should also realize that future of the nation depends upon the success or failure of implementation of his proposal. He should be at his best in the performance of duties where a king is in danger due to either war of succession or external aggression. According to Dr Beni Prasad, 'Dignity and courtesy, energy and promptness, loyalty and devotion, purity and incorruptibility—such are the characteristics of a good Ministers' (Prasad 1974, 78). In ancient India, of course, at later stages, one of the duties of the sovereign was to preserve the caste system. But *Śukranīti* insists on the capacity of a person as the supreme and the most important qualification for holding an office. In this way *Śukracharya* has violated the established principle of caste system.

Ideal King and His Qualities

Śukracharya accepted the traditional notion of the kingdom as an organism with seven limbs, namely the sovereign (head), minister (eye), friend (ear), treasury (mouth), land and population (legs), fort (arms) and army (mind). He assumes that the state is a natural organism and it cannot function properly unless there is a harmony of interests between all the organs of the state. Thus, like Herbert Spencer, *Śukracharya* has supported the idea that the state is an organic whole and has compared each limb of the state with the organism of the human body. For him, since sovereign is the embodiment of all qualities and protector of his subjects, he is like the head of human being. A king sees his subjects as well as comes to know about their grievances and reactions to his activities through his ministers alone. Therefore, the ministers are comparable to the eyes of a human body.

According to *Śukranītisara*, a king should depend upon his *Mitras* or friends insofar as foreign policy is concerned. How other states tolerate him and to what extent they respect his policies and proposals could only be made known to king through his friends. Thus, his *Mitras* were his ears. The army was considered both the defender and protector of the people and also a source of great strength to the king. A capable army could also advise a king about the strategies and as such army was the mind of the state and comparable of human mind.

Like Kauṭilya, *Śukra* has also laid considerable stress on the utility and necessity of forts by describing these as one of the constituent elements of the state. So *Śukra* compares *Durga* with the arms of the human being. Regarding *Kośa* or treasury, *Śukra* agrees with Kauṭilya that national finances must be sound. He also agrees with him that all difficulties arise due to lack of funds and can be abridged only with the help of sound finances. A king can win the sympathy of his people by giving financial assistance and loses that when that is not forthcoming even for executing essential plans. Therefore, he has compared treasury with the mouth, because king speaks on the strength and soundness of his treasury.

However, *Śukra* has given extraordinary importance to *Paura-Jānapada*, that is, land and population by comparing that with the legs of a human being. According to him, as long as legs are sound, the body shall not bow but will stand erect and be unshaky. Therefore, it is comparable to his policy of constitutional sovereignty in which stress was laid on the welfare and prosperity of the people.

Śukra has categorized and graded sovereigns on the basis of their annual revenues. Broadly speaking, these were *Sāmanta*, *Maudalika*, *Rājā*, *Mahārāja*, *Swarat*, *Samrat* and *Virat*. Whereas the annual revenue of a *Sāmanta* did not exceed ₹250,000, that of *Virat* went up to about ₹420 crores. *Śukra* argues that a good and just king not only saves himself but also his subjects, while a bad king goes to hell like the great king *Nahuṣa*. Śukra repudiates the belief that every king is endowed with the power of Gods and declares that 'the prince who is virtuous is a part of the gods. He who is otherwise, is a part of the demons, an enemy of religion and oppressor of subjects' (Mehta 1992, 66–7).

Śukranīti has discussed about the qualities which a king should possess. According to *Śukra*, a king should possess qualities of head and heart. A king should always consider himself as the father of his subjects. He should be the protector of his subjects and like a teacher should guide his people. He should try to nourish his people but never act in a spirit of revenge. He should be religious minded, charitable and valorous. Like a good brother he should claim only a reasonable share from the earnings of his subjects as is permissible under the rules. Hence, a good king combines in himself the attributes of seven persons: father, mother, preceptor, brother, friend, *Kubera* and *Yama* (ibid.).

The king is expected to look after the weak and poor and treat them with kindness. He should not oppress the people. There is no better art for winning over people than the practice of mercy, friendship, charity and sweet words. The king is also enjoined not only to protect the existing wealth but also to take steps to increase it. According to *Śukra*, without earnings even the God of wealth may not continue his own existence for a long time. In exceptional circumstances, the king can levy extra taxes. *Śukra* is convinced that the ruler who extracts his share through cupidity is ruined with his subjects (ibid., 68).

The king should also avoid passion especially for women, gambling and drinking. While the company of a wife is for his happiness and that of other women can be a cause of his ruin, emotions as pleasure should be used for the maintenance of the family and anger against the enemies, respectively. Pleasure with one's own wife is good, with another's wife is not, heroism is good but oppression of one's own subjects is not. Thus, *Śukracharya's* moral code is calculated to create a system which would lead to a harmonious development of our personality.

Thus, along with avoiding the sensuality, the king should also develop art and culture in the kingdom. *Śukra* says that from time to time the king should personally tour the state to get first-hand information about his subjects and that normally a king should depend upon his spies. Above all, he should be responsible to his subjects for his acts of omission and commission. Dr Beni Prasad says that, 'He must follow the rules of polity and must respect old men. He must strive to command the respect of all meritorious people. Let him win the administration of his subjects by great deeds and by generosity its gifts and honours' (Prasad 1974, 74).

According to *Śukracharya*, generosity is one of the main characteristic features of an ideal or perfect state which means that the state should always be respectful to the public opinion. *Śukra* advises the king to be mild and compassionate to the opposition. According to him, the king should never punish the people for holding opinions against him. Nowhere in Indian thought, after the *Rāmāyaṇa* and *Mahābhārata*, is so much stress laid on a king's own discipline and his responsiveness to public opinion than in *Śukranīti*. *Śukra* argues that although it is difficult not to be angry on hearing disparagement of oneself, the king should try to be merciful and affectionate. This is so because if a king is uncharitable or insulting or deceitful or cowardly or passionate, he is liable to be deserted by his own subjects. Only a king who avoids sensuousness, anger, ignorance, cupidity, vanity and passion can hope to rule better and for a long time as kings like *Jāmadagny* and *Ambarīṣa* did. In order to discipline the king, *Śukra*, like all lawgivers, recommends that the king should train himself in material science including logic, the *Vedās*, economics and law (Mehta 1992, 67–8).

Śukra goes into great detail about the construction of the city, the place and the council of chambers and enjoins the king to maintain roads, rest houses, forests and also to provide protection against the misuse of metals, ghee, honey and milk, and to control gambling, drinking, hunting, use of arms, sale and purchase of animals, jewels and ornaments. Thus, it will be realized that the sphere of state activity, according to *Śukra*, should be quite comprehensive (ibid., 69).

According to *Śukracharya*, the first and foremost duty of a king is to provide security to the subjects and punish the wicked and evil doers. It is therefore felt that, the king should use force when absolutely necessary and unavoidable and that too for collective welfare for the community as a whole. However, the use of force should be impartial and a king should not give an impression that force is either being used for achieving his personal ends or that by a particular section of the society is being benefitted. In the words of Dr Beni Prasad, '*Daṇḍanïti* aims at the promotion of general prosperity. It is, of course, particularly useful for rulers. A king who neglects it sinks like a leaky vessel' (Prasad 1974, 66). It is apparent from the above analysis that the main functions of the king are six in number, namely punishment of the wicked, practice of charity, protection of the subjects, performance of the sacrifices, equitable realization of revenues and extraction of wealth from the land. If the princes fail to perform these functions, they are no better than fools (Mehta 1992, 67).

The state administration is to be run on the basis of efficiency. In such matters, no caste or family consideration should be taken care of. In this case, *Śukra* says, only work, character and merit are to be respected. Also, the superiority cannot be asserted on the basis of caste or family. *Śukra* says these considerations are reserved for dinner parties and not for matters of the state. The officers of the state are not to be given to each and every one. The king should select such officers who can advise well, and bear pain, who have virtuous habits and who by the strength of their wisdom can advise a king—men who are pure, and who have no envy, passions, anger, cupidity and sloth (ibid., 69).

Śukra is agreeable that the state should regulate and control the working of the gambling halls, prostitute houses, drinking shops and should issue licences for hunting and bearing arms. The punch of the state authority should be felt by the purchasers as well as sellers of movable and immovable property including that of precious ornaments, jewels as well as animal wealth. Thus, the state should guide and lead the subjects on all important matters and the people should invariably look towards state for redressal of their grievances.

Śukracharya has laid emphasis on sound state finances. Perhaps this was the reason that he has called finances as the mouth of the king. According to him, an overflowing treasury was most essential for national development and prosperity. Whereas tax from productive land should not exceed 50 per cent of the total produce, from barren land such taxation was limited to only about 16 per cent. It was suggested that taxation on commodities for day-to-day use should not exceed 3 per cent. *Śukra* has stated that least amount should be spent on personal comfort of the king and maximum will be utilized for collective welfare including social and religious activities. Thus, there should be judicious expenditure from national treasury. Among other things, he has made it clear that the provision for expenditure on religious affairs should not lead one to the conclusion that *Śukracharya* wanted his king to spend on any particular religion but what he wanted was that such expenditure should be incurred on the promotion of morality and character as well as on all religions.

Śukracharya has also given emphasis on the relationship between the ends and means. While in national affairs, he has given emphasis on the welfare of the subjects, but in international affairs, he has paid scant regard to it. In fact, it appears that the sole aim of it is to prove the king great. In such matters, in order to conquer the enemies, the king can make use of peace, force, punishment and division. If necessary, he is enjoined to make peace with his feudatories. *Śukra* says,

> Property never deserts a man who bows down to the powerful at the proper time, just as rivers never leave the downward course. In warfare, due consideration is paid to time, region and army. War is to be picked with a weak and never with strong one who has powerful army. (ibid., 69–70)

System of Law and Justice

For the well-being and the prosperity of the state, *Śukra* advises the king to look after lawsuits attentively according to the dictates of *Dharmaśāstras* without anger or greed. The king should associate the Chief Justice, *Amātya*, *Brāhmaṇa* and the Priest in deciding the cases. He should neither unilaterally try the cases of the two parties nor hear their statements. Either the wise king or the councillors should never observe secrecy in trials.

Śukra says that where the king cannot personally attend the administration of justice, he should appoint the *Brāhmaṇs*, who are well-versed in the *Vedās*, self-controlled, high-born, impartial, unagitated, calm and active, and devoid of anger. If the *Brāhmaṇs* are not learned enough, the king should appoint a *Kṣatriya* for the purpose or a *Vaiśya* who is versed in *Dharmaśāstras* but reject a *Śūdra*. The judges are required to be conversant with the actions, character and attributes of the people and expected to be impartial to both enemies and friends. Those who are not idle, who are masters over anger, passions and greed and who speak in a gentle manner are to be appointed to offices by the king regardless of their caste considerations (Nagar 1985, 50). The king should, however, appoint officers who are virtuous, well tried and capable of bearing burden of the administration of justice (ibid.).

Thus, in administering justice, *Śukra* is very particular about the injections prescribed by the *Dharmaśāstras* and the consultations with the members of the jury. According to him, the king who through delusion and passion decides the cases against the dictates of the *Śāstras* is soon overpowered by the enemies. Similarly, the arbitrary actions of a king without the advice of the councillors lead to hell and destruction of life and wealth. *Śukra* categorically states that the king who knows the *Śāstras* speaks the voice of God. Even the outsiders who know the law can give their opinions on the cases in dispute. Any man who knows the *dhārma* can speak authoritatively irrespective of his formal position. Anyone who attends the Court should speak the truth. Truth alone blesses the witness and increases the virtue. The man who keeps silence or utters falsehood is a sinner (ibid., 50–1).

Śukra suggests that *Kula*, *Śreṇï* and *Gaṇa* form the threefold hierarchy of bodies of self-adjudication. Whenever these three bodies fail, the king along with officers is entitled to interfere. The cases have to be tried by the king separately with men of various grades of intelligence several times. *Śukra* mentions 10 component requisites of the administration of justice: king, officers, councillors, *Smṛiti*, *Śāstras*, accountant, clerk, gold, fire, water and one's friends (ibid., 51).

The king should enter the court modestly together with the *Brāhmaṇs* and the ministers who know statecraft with the object of investigating the cases. He should proceed with the work after taking the seat of justice. He should put questions to the parties impartially. The king should perform his duty after carefully studying the established customs as mentioned in the *Śāstras* as well as those that are practised by castes, villages, corporation and families (ibid.).

Śukra scrupulously maintains that the king for winning the heart of people should not unnecessarily interfere with the customs and usages of the folk, otherwise they will agitate. *Śukra* prescribes that morning is the best time for adjudicating cases which involve application of the socio-religious regulations laid down in the *Smṛitis*. The day time similarly is good for cases which involve the breach of laws made by the king. However, for cases of murder, thieving, robbery and felonies, no time is fixed. These require immediate disposal (ibid.).

There is a resemblance of modernity in *Śukra's* prescription in case of division of opinion. The king should go by the verdict of the majority, and if there is equality or sameness, he should accept the opinions of the virtuous and always the opinions of those who are well qualified. *Śukra's* views seem modern when he observes that if somebody objects to the judgement as well as the decree of the king on the basis that it conflicts with the canons of *dhārma*, he can have a retrial on the depositing of double the fine. A retrial or appeal may arise in those cases which have been vitiated by the undue pressure of witnesses and officers and by the defects of the king's own actions (ibid., 54).

Whenever an *Amātya* or the president of the judicial assembly would decide a case contrary to law, the king shall re-examine it again but also impose a fine of a 1,000 *paṇas*. Punishment is indispensable in some cases for directing people to the right path. The king should give to the victorious party *Jayapatra* or document of victory after it has been carefully analysed by the officers and accepted by the other party. Otherwise, the king should imprison the plaintiff for many years, and punish him according to the seriousness of the false charges and similarly honour him who is falsely accused (ibid., 54).

Thus, *Śukra* attaches great importance to the judicial functions of the king by emphasizing the fact that the investigation of the cases should be according to the tenets of *dhārma*. He observes that the subjects follow the king as the rivers follow the ocean, who investigates the cases according to *dhārma* by restraining his passions and anger (ibid., 55).

Śukracharya believed, like his predecessors, that justice delayed is justice denied. According to him, a judge should be well-versed in the interpretation of *Vedās* as well as established customs and conventions. He has also suggested that merit should be taken into account only while making appointment of judges. He has also recommended that the king should personally supervise justice and important decisions should be pronounced in the presence of king alone. The king should ensure that justice is impartial. As human life is very precious, therefore, death penalty should be pronounced by king himself.

Śukranīti has emphasized on the need and necessity of quick and cheap justice and impartial judiciary. It discusses about the nature of crimes as well as that of punishment. Among other things he says that the financial motives should not in any way motivate and guide the course of justice. He has prescribed minimum qualifications for judges. He has established a hierarchy in judicial set up. In the words of Dr Beni Prasad,

> in the judicial hierarchy, as a whole, families of *Kulas* came first; next *Śreṇīs* or corporations, next *Gaṇas* or communities, next Royal officers, next the *Adhyakṣa* or Chief Justice, and finally the king who is the director of what should be done and what not. (Prasad 1974, 80)

All trials should be made public and with the help or assistance of the judges. The system was more or less jury system of modern times. The pleaders were allowed to appear but usually it was difficult to get witnesses in criminal cases. In civil cases, pleaders as well as witnesses were encouraged to appear. Women witnesses, however, did not appear unless absolutely necessary.

Reforms

There are indications to suggest that the *Śukranīti* does not believe in the old ideal of the laws in the sacred texts having lasting validity; on the contrary, it speaks of the law undergoing frequent changes and of new enactments overriding the *sastric* injunctions. Thus, it describes the duty of the officer called *Paṇḍita* as being to study the laws obtaining in society in ancient and modern times, those that have been ordained in sacred texts, those now opposed and those which militate against the customs of the people. Later on, it says that owing to the difference in the opinion of new and old authorities, law is undergoing changes every moment. The *Śukranīti* seems to represent the viewpoint of the early British legislators and administrators who recognized the authority of the *Smṛiti* laws without treating them as eternally valid, and transformed them or replaced them by new laws if they went against their own ideas and concepts and the long standing customs and practices of different social groups (Gopal 1962, 547).

In its treatment of the caste system the *Śukranīti* reveals a characteristically modern and realistic approach. It refers to the division of the society into four *Varṇas*, and to there being an infinite number of castes owing to their intermixtures, both *anuloma* and *pratiloma*. But it is not at all concerned with the theory of castes and its corollary explaining the other social, functional and ethnic groups as resulting from the union of particular males and females. The latter claims much space in earlier legal texts, but the *Śukranīti*, with its realistic approach, brushes aside the theoretical explanation of the caste system without giving any detailed consideration to it. It states that in ancient times the castes were divided into four classes by *Brahmā* according to their activities. Thus, though it accepts the fourfold division as divinely ordained it does not repeat any of the justifications or explanations offered in earlier texts. Just after mentioning that the division into four classes was made by *Brahmā* it refers to the infinitude of castes, difficult to explain, resulting from their intermixture.

This suggests that the *Śukranīti* treats thefourfold division as nothing but a myth or philosophical fiction. Probably the author of the *Śukranīti* indulges in sarcasm in adding that only those who regard caste differences as due to birth know the differences in their names and occupations. Elsewhere, he openly discards the generally accepted view that birth is the test of caste and describes the castes in the terms of their virtues and occupations and enumerates the various qualities of each. The *Śukranīti* reflects a general weakening of the rigorous caste system. It says that by qualities and occupations high and low orders are created in course of time and that castes are named after their respective learning and occupation. According to the *Śukranīti*, family and castes are to be considered only in marriage and dinning. Work, character and merit are to be respected and superiority is not established by caste or family (ibid., 547–8).

Śukra was conscious of the importance of wealth. But like all law givers, *Śukra* makes a distinction between wealth earned by right means and that earned by wrong means. He emphasizes that one should try to earn wealth only by good means, for example, by good service, valour, agriculture, storekeeping, arts or begging (Mehta 1992, 70).

The labour laws in the *Śukranīti* are remarkably modern in approach. The text anticipates modern ideas of popular welfare by voicing the need for an equitable rate of wages for labourers. Moderate remuneration is said to be that which supplies the indispensable food and clothing. Good wages are those by which food and clothing are adequately supplied. Low wages are those by which only one person can be maintained. Wages are to be so fixed that the worker may maintain those who are his compulsory charges. It describes workers getting low wages as enemies by nature, auxiliaries to others, always looking for opportunities for trouble and plunderers of treasure and people (Gopal 1962, 544).

The *Śukranīti* mentions many provisions giving benefits to servants. Leave of absence for recreation and on the occasion of festivities is provided for. The servant is given sickness benefit also. No part of the wages is to be deducted if the illness lasts for half a fortnight. A servant who has given 1 year's service is not to be dismissed during sickness, but should be relieved by a substitute. A highly qualified servant is to receive half his regular wages during sickness. After five years' service a servant is entitled to three months earned leave on full pay. The maximum leave with full pay which can be claimed on medical grounds is six months. A servant is to receive a respite of 15 days in a year, which significantly compares with the modern rules about casual leave in the administrative services (ibid., 544–5).

There are also rules about old age pensions. A man who was served for 40 years should have a pension for life at the rate of half his wages. In the case of his death, the pension is to be enjoyed by his minor and incapable son or by his wife and his well-behaved daughters. Like the modern bonus system, a servant is to receive one-eighth of his salary by way of reward every year. If the servant dies on account of his work, his son while still a minor is to enjoy the same salary or remuneration according to his own qualifications. There is provision for a scheme resembling the modern provident fund. The master is to withhold one-sixth or one-fourth of his servant's wages and to pay half of that amount or the whole in two or three years (ibid., 545).

In *Śukra's* scheme of punishment there is no provision for capital punishment. The king should avoid capital punishment as far as possible, but punish the wicked by detention, imprisonment and repression. Greed should not work on the part of the king for imposing financial penalties on the people. *Śukra* gives a long list of offenders, such as the gambler, the thief, the cheat, the taker of the bribe, the poisoner, the addict to the prostitutes, the malicious, the seller of daughters, the murderer, the tamperer of witnesses, the helper of enemies, the abuser of parents, chaste women and friends. To him, such wicked persons should be expelled from the state. They should be bound and transported to island or forts and employed in the work of repairing roads and made to live on insufficient and bad diet. *Śukra* prefers first offenders to be bound in chain, second to be financially penalized in 1,000 *paṇas* for the worst offence. Again he prescribes 500 *paṇas* for the lesser offence, half of *paṇas* for the rest (Nagar 1985, 48–9).

Conclusion

Śukranīti is a treatise which discusses about the nature and character of *Hindu* polity. It has discussed the qualifications of a good sovereign. For that purpose, it has discussed the king's time table and has divided the day into 30 *muhūrtas* (moments) of 48 minutes each. A king should personally attend to finance, prayer, study, charity, distribution of prizes, points raised for consideration by judges and other officers of the state and also attend to the reports of the spies. From time to time he should also tour even the villages of his state. *Śukranīti* also has tried to establish one of the foremost duties of a king to promote welfare of the subjects.

Śukra did not believe in the theory of 'Divine Rights of Kings', but has suggested that a king was responsible to the people for all his activities. The people were at liberty to refuse payment to an unrighteous king. They could also dethrone such a king and replace him by a righteous prince with the help of *Purohita*. The people should also be given a right in the selection of their king. He did not like the idea of unbridled or unchecked sovereign authority. Thus, *Śukranīti* favoured a constitutional rather than absolute monarchy and pleaded for the sovereignty of the people.

Śukracharya believed that the state is an organic whole. He has also discussed the constituent elements of the state. He has compared sovereign with the head of human organism and ministers to the eyes of human body and that his friends are his ears. For him, army was the mind of the state and is comparable to the human mind. Since forts are the arms of the state, he has compared them with the arms of a human body and the treasury is comparable to human mouth. He has given extraordinary importance to *Paura-Jānapada* which has been compared to the legs of human body.

In judicial administration, utmost care was taken to see that justice was quite cheap. It was also seen that the judges were quite well-versed with the *dhārma*. While pronouncing judgement, the old customs and conventions should always be taken into consideration and respected. Not only this, but the judges should not violate *dhārma*. *Śukra* has suggested that the *Brāhmaṇs* should be appointed as judges, but *Vaiśyas* and *Kṣatriyas* should also not be denied these positions, if otherwise found qualified for these positions. He has also suggested that the punishments should be according to crime as well as the nature of the criminals. Fines were allowed to be levied, but it should not be made a source of income.

The king must inform the people of laws in advance. He should hear the petitions of the people and should punish his officers including his spies if they have committed wrong and should be wary of flatterers. In case of conflict between his officers and the subjects, the king is enjoined to side with his subjects. He even suggests that an officer who is accused by 100 men should be dismissed. Indeed, a wise ruler should ever abide by the well-considered decisions of his councillors, office bearers, subjects and other members, attending a meeting and never by his own opinions. *Śukra* is convinced that a monarch who follows his own will bring misery upon himself and his subjects are soon alienated from him. Such actions on the part of the king lead to disasters, poverty, crime, division within the kingdom and ultimately rebellion of the subjects (Mehta 1992, 69).

A good king should also see that the people are most prosperous and that the laws are just. The king was personally responsible to see that law was uniformly being applied and that no section of the society was being oppressed by the operation of state laws. Since human life was always considered very precious and each human being had a right to live, it was therefore considered necessary that death penalty should be pronounced by the king personally or at least in his presence.

Śukranītisara understood the importance of means of transportation and communication for the stability and prosperity of the state. According to *Śukracharya*, the capital city should be well-connected with the roads and so also the villages should be connected with each other by roads. Roads should be annually repaired and convicted labour should be employed for the purpose. *Śukra* even classifies the roads as *Padya*, *Prithi*, *Mārga*, Royal Highway or *Rāja-Mārga*. In between the villages there should be *Sarais* or rest houses.

The work of *Śukranītisara* forges an important intellectual link between tradition and modernity of Indian politics. It is fully demonstrated that the *Śukranīti* is more a political text than a religious scripture. It stands at par with *Kauṭilya's Arthaśāstra* or the *Śāntiparva* of *Veda Vyāsa* when it is judged in terms of its contribution to political theorizing. *Śukranīti* is a profound scripture solely devoted to matters of society and state.

Summary

Śukracharya's thoughts on ethics, laws and reforms can be summarized as follows:

Śukranīti deals with monarchical system of government. *Śukracharya* does not believe in hereditary system of ascending the throne. According to him, he who will succeed to the throne of kingship must have high qualities. If the eldest son of the king is not attached to his subjects or unable to look after them then he must be changed. Here, *Śukracharya* has highlighted on the principle of qualities rather than hereditary as the rule of succession to kingship. Thus, in matters of succession qualities of a succeeding prince should be the primary and in fact, the sole consideration. A king who is devoid of good qualities or overlook people's welfare, in that case the people have the right to change a king. He should also be morally sound because a morally weak king cannot inspire confidence of his subjects. Hence, this emphasis on quality of a king and the right of the people to change their ruler sounds fairly modern in the context of present-day democracy. The king is enjoined to protect the weak and be merciful even to his enemies. According to *Śukracharya*, king was the creation of God to watch and ensure the welfare of the people. He has also laid emphasis on awarding suitable one or punishment to evil doers, law breakers and enemies of the state. A great stress has been laid down on the use of punishment on the evil doers after thorough investigation and proof.

Procedure for appointment of ministers and other officials is laid down in detail. For the first time, the portfolios of different ministers are given in this work and it enables us to have a clear picture of the day-to-day working of ministry with the assistance of the secretaries and under the control of the king. Definite checks have been prescribed over the functioning of king so that he may not become tyrant, unjust and inefficient.

The state as envisaged by *Śukra* was an organization for the welfare of the subjects. It was not only to suppress crime and disorder, but to control gambling and drinking. It was to maintain hospitals and rest houses and encourage learning and scholarship. It was to increase the resources of the country by encouraging trade, developing mines, forests and industries and executing schemes of irrigation (Altekar 1984, 19).

Several ways have been suggested for increasing the resources of government by means of levy of various taxes. *Śukra* has cautioned that the taxes should not be levied beyond the capacity of people. He has also suggested that taxes should be reasonable and revenue should not be lavishly spent on personal comforts. *Śukra* has dealt in detail with the judicial system for different crimes. He has laid down a scientific theory of crime and punishment.

Points for Discussion

1. '*Śukracharya* made a very valuable contribution to the *Hindu* Science of Polity.' Discuss this statement.
2. Examine the main political thoughts described in *Śukranītisara*.
3. Evaluate the contribution of *Śukracharya* as far as politics and administration is concerned.
4. Write a short note on the system of justice as mentioned in *Śukranīti*.
5. Discuss the qualities of an ideal king as per *Śukranīti*.
6. As per *Śukranīti*, justify how ethics and kingship are interrelated.

Glossary

***Amātya*:** The ministers and officials.

***Ambarīṣa*:** A king of *Ayodhyā*, 28th in descent from *Ikṣvāku*.

Aṅgiras: He was one of the seven *Maharṣis* or great *Ṛiṣhis*, and also one of the 10 *Prājāpatis* or progenitors of mankind. He is renowned as a great teacher, ritualist, lawgiver and astronomer, and is identified with the planet Jupiter.

***Anuloma*:** According to *Dharmaśāstra*, a name for a mixed marriage between a man of a higher *Varṇa*, and a woman of a lower one. The term is also applied to any offspring of that marriage.

Asuras: Demon or enemy of the Gods.

Atharvan: A name for the verses of the *Atharvavedā* or the reputed author of the *Atharvavedā*, a famous *Vedic* seer and priest, and who is known as the son of *Brahmā*.

Bali: A good and virtuous *daitya* king. He is also called *Mahabali* and his capital was *Mahabalipura*. He was son of Virocana, son of *Prahlāda*, son of Hiraṇyakaśipu. His wife was *Vindhyāvalī*.

Bhṛigu: A legendary *Vedic* sage from whom the *Bhārgavas* take their name. In the *Śatapatha Brāhmaṇa* and the *Taittirīya Upaniṣhad* he is said to be the son of *Varuṇa* elsewhere the son of *Indra*, *Prājāpati*, *Brahmā* or the first Manu.

***Brahmā*:** The supreme soul of the universe, self-existent, absolute and eternal, from which all things emanate, and to which all return. He is the lord and father of all creatures, and is in the first place of the *Ṛishis* or *Prājāpatis*. He created the gods. He is called the progenitor of all the worlds. The *Viṣṇu Purāṇa* says that the 'divine *Brahmā* called *Nārāyaṇa* created all beings. The *Mahābhārata* represents *Brahmās* springing from the navel of *Viṣṇu* or from a lotus which grew there out. *Brahmā* was the father of *Dakṣa*, who is said to have sprung from his thumb'.

***Brāhmaṇa*:** The first of the four castes, the sacerdotal and learned class, the members of which may be, but are not necessarily priests.

Bṛihaspati: He was a *Ṛiṣhi* and son of the *Ṛiṣhi* Aṅgira. He is also regent of the planet Jupiter. He is called in one place 'the father of the gods'. He is the suppliant, the sacrifice, the priest, who intercedes with gods on behalf of men and protects mankind against the wicked.

***Daṇḍakaranya*:** The forest of *Daṇḍaka* lying between the *Godavari* and *Narmada*.

Devas: Gods or deities.

***Devī-Bhāgavata Purāṇa*:** Traditionally classified as one of the *upa-Purāṇas* (Minor *Purāṇas*), it celebrates *Devī* as the highest independent principle in the universe (*Nirguna Brahmān*), and recounts various myths associated with her. It reinterprets much earlier *Purāṇic* material for the glorification of the Goddess and appears, in part, to be an imitation of the *Bhāgavata Purāṇa*, with *Devī* replacing *Krishna* the object of *Bhakti*.

***Dhārma*:** The precise meaning of it ranges from 'truth' and 'order', to law (both universal and particular), 'teaching', 'duty', 'virtuous behaviour' and 'religion'. The term refers to those actions and laws that maintain the truth as well as inform and order the universe and human society.

Gautama: A name of the sage Śaradvat and a son of Gotama. Traditionally, he is credited with the authorship of the *Nyāya-Sūtra*, and therefore the founder of the Nyāya-Darśana.

***Indra*:** The god of the firmament, the personified atmosphere. In *Vedās*, he is reverenced as the bestower of rain and the cause of fertility and he was feared as the awful ruler of the storm and director of the lightning and thunder.

Jāmadagny: A *Brahmāna* and a descendant of *Bhṛigu*. He was the son of *Ṛcika* and *Satyavatī*, and was the father of five sons, the youngest and most renowned of whom was *Paraśurāma*.

***Kṣatriya*:** The warrior caste.

***Kubera*:** The pan-Indian god of wealth. In the *Purāṇas* and epics, he is said to be the leader of the *Yakṣas* and *Rākṣasas*, and the half-brother of *Rāvaṇa*.

***Mahābhārata*:** 'The great epic about the great war of *Bhārata*' between *Kauravs* and *Pāṇḍavas*.

***Nahuṣa*:** Son of *Āyus* the eldest son of *Purūravas*, and father of Yayāti.

***Navagraha*:** 'Nine Planets'. According to traditional astrology, the nine 'planets' consist of: *Sūrya* (Sun), *Soma* (Moon), *Budha* (Mercury), *Śukra* (Venus), *Maṅgala* (Mars), *Bṛihaspati/Guru* (Jupiter), *Śani* (Saturn) and the ascending (northern) and descending (southern) nodes, *Rāhu* and *Ketu*.

***Paṇas*:** Metallic money

Paṇḍita: Learned advisor.

Prahlāda: A *daitya*, son of *Hiraṇyakaśipu* and father of *Bali*.

Pratiloma: According to *Dharmaśāstra*, a name for a mixed marriage between a man of a lower *varṇa*, and a woman of a higher one. The term is also applied to any offspring of that marriage.

Priyavrata: One of the sons of *Brahmā* and *Śatarūpā*; or according to other statements, a son of Manu Svāyambhuva.

***Purāṇa*:** A huge body of narrative texts, originally mostly in Sanskrit verse, is purporting to deal with an ancient past. The *Purāṇas* celebrate the powers and works of positive gods, and represent a later and more extravagant development of *Hinduism*, of which they are in fact, the scriptures. The *Purāṇas* are all written in verse, and their invariable form is that of a dialogue between an exponent and an inquirer, interspersed with the dialogues and observations of other individuals. The *Purāṇas* are 18 in number, and in addition to these there are 18 *Upa-Purāṇas* or subordinate works. The *Purāṇas* are classified in three categories, according to the prevalence in them of the qualities of purity, gloom and passion.

***Rāmāyaṇa*:** 'The Adventures of *Rāma*.' The oldest of the Sanskrit epic poems written by the sage *Vālmīki*.

***Ṛigvedā*:** It is the original *Vedā* ('Divine knowledge'). (The *Vedas* are the holy books which are the foundation of the *Hindu* religion.) The Ṛigveda is the original *Vedā* from which the *Yajurvedā* and *Sāmavedā* are almost exclusively derived. It consists of 1,017 *Sūktas* or hymns, or with 11 additional hymns called *Vâla-Khilyas* of an apocryphal character.

***Ṛiṣhis*:** Seers—Ancient seer poets, or 'sages' to whom the hymns of the Ṛigvedā were said to have been revealed.

***Śāstra/Sastric*:** It is 'teaching', 'instruction' and 'treatise'. It indicates an authoritative and inclusive Sanskrit treatise on the subject.

Smṛiti: It is a kind of authoritative religious text which is regarded as having been mediated through human authorship. The *Smṛiti* texts constitute a 'tradition' which, although more immediately human in origin, ultimately looks to and derives its authority from parts of *Śruti* (*Veda*).

***Śūdra*:** The fourth or servile caste whose duty is to serve the other three castes.

***Vaiśya*:** The third or trading and agricultural caste.

***Vāmana*:** The dwarf incarnation of *Viṣṇu*.

***Vedānta*:** 'The conclusion, essence, or culmination of the *Vedā*.' It derives its name from its basic dependence on the teachings of the principal *Upaniṣhads* and their attempted synthesis in *Bādarāyaṇa's Brahma Sūtra*.

***Viṣṇu*:** He is the creator and supreme god.

***Yama*:** In the epic poems, *Yama* is the son of the Sun by *Saṁjñā* (conscience), and brother of *Vaivasvata Manu*. He is the god of departed spirits and judge of the dead.

Yayāti: The fifth king of the Lunar race, and son of *Nahuṣa*.

References

Altekar, A. S. 1984. *State and Government in Ancient India*. Delhi: Motilal Banarsidass.

Dalal, R. 2010. *Hinduism: An Alphabetical Guide*. New Delhi: Penguin Books India.

Gopal, L. 1962. The 'Śukranīti'—a Nineteenth-Century Text. *Bulletin of the School of Oriental and African Studies* 25(1/3): 524–56.

Mehta, V. R. 1992. *Foundations of Indian Political Thought: An Interpretation (From Manu to the Present Day)*. New Delhi: Manohar Publications.

Nagar, V. 1985. *Kingship in the Śukranīti*. Delhi: Pushpa Prakashan.

Prasad, B. 1974. *Theory of Government in Ancient India*. Allahabad: Central Book Depot.

Sarkar, Benoy Kumar. 1975. *The Śukranīti*. New Delhi: Oriental Books Reprint Corporation.

Further Readings

Appadorai, A. 1992. *Indian Political Thinking through the Ages*. New Delhi: Khama Publishers.

Biplab. 2015. *Śukranīti may Rajnitika Vichar*. Meerut: Rahul Publishing House.

Chaddha, P. K. 2002. *Pramukha Bharatiya Rajnitika Vicharak*. Jaipur: University Book House (P) Ltd.

Chaturvedi, Madhumukul. 2004. *Pramukha Bharatiya Rajnitika Vicharak*. Jaipur: Raj Publishing House.

Dimmitt, Cornelia, and J. A. B. Van Buitenen, eds. 1998. *Classical Hindu Mythology: A Reader in the Sanskrit Purāṇas*. Delhi: Sri Satguru Publications.

Dowson, John. 1998. *A Classical Dictionary of Hindu Mythology and Religion: Geography, History and Literature*. New Delhi: D. K. Printworld (P) Ltd.

Gopal, Lallanji. 1978. *The Śukranīti: A Nineteenth Century Text*. Varanasi: Bharati Prakashan.

Johnson, W. J. 2009. *A Dictionary of Hinduism*. New York, NY: Oxford University Press.

Kamal, K. L. 2015. *Bharatiya, Rajnitik Chintan*. Jaipur: Rajasthan Hindi Granth Academy.

Mishra, Jagdishchandra. 1996. *Śukranīti*. Varanasi: Choukhamba Soorbharati Prakashan.

Pandey, U. S. 2011. *Indian Political Thought*. New Delhi: D. P. S. Publication.

Pathak, Ram Prabesh. 1999. *Śukranīti may Rajtantra*. Varanasi: Kala Prakashan.

Puntambekar, S. V. 1948. 'Some Aspects of *Śukra's* Political Thought.' *The Indian Journal of Political Science* 9(2/3): 1–12.

Ranjan, Ravi. 2017. *Indian Political Thought*. Delhi: Academic Publication.

Sharma, Yogendra Kumar. 2001. *Bharatiya, Rajnitik Vicharak*, Vol. 1. New Delhi: Kanishak Publishers & Distributors.

Sharma, Ram Sharan. 2005. *Aspects of Political Ideas and Institutions in Ancient India*. Delhi: Motilal Banarsidass Publishers.

Tiwari, Sudarshan. 2006. *Śukranīti may Rajya ka Swarup*. Delhi: Sanjay Prakashan.

Varma, Vishwanath Prasad. 1962. 'Some Aspects of Public Administration in the Śukranīti.' *The Indian Journal of Political Science* 23(1/4): 302–8.

9
CHAPTER

Dīgha Nikāya (Aggaññasutta): Theory of Kingship and *Aṅguttara Nikāya*

Ish N. Mishra

CHAPTER OUTLINE

- **Introduction**
- **Backdrop of the Study**
- **Origin of the State**
- **Qualities, Functions and Duties of the Ruler**
- **Conclusion**
- **Summary**
- **Points for Discussion**

I teach because you and all beings want to have happiness and want to avoid suffering.
I teach the way things are.

—Buddha (The Life of the Buddha)[1]

Reader's Guide

Buddhist theory of the origin of state, as contained in *Dīgha Nikāya* (one of the collections of Buddha's teachings), is a great ancient Indian contribution to the history of political theory. The purpose of this chapter is to explain the need of the state for the maintenance of the social order, arising due to emergence of evils in the society. The origin of state is explained by a social contract under which people gather together and through an agreement choose the best person among them to take upon the responsibility of punishing the wrongdoer and commit to pay him taxes in the form of a portion of their produce.

Introduction

Gautama Buddha epitomizes the motif: 'To rebel is to create'. He rebelled against existing *Brāhmanical* order and the sacrificial religious rituals to create a new order based on the rationally derived principles of righteous life—the *Dhamma*. His alternative, he provides, is quite radical—the egalitarian collectives, modelled on the *Saṅghas* (monasteries) founded by him.[2] The practice of the *Dhamma* would lead to creation of society free from miseries and sufferings, the state of *Mokṣa*.[3] If transported from spiritual to material world, it would get paralleled by the state of human emancipation, the state of the classless society in the Marxist parlance. Buddha (BC 6th–5th century) remains the greatest revolutionary thinker, teacher and activist in the history, like Marx in the 19th century, in terms of the vision of an active campaign for the egalitarian, collective society free from human miseries. Buddha was a philosopher, who not only sought to interpret the world but also to change it. His teachings shall remain valuable till there are miseries and sufferings on the earth. There is no scope or need to digress into the comparison of Buddha with Marx, who too like him, envisaged a world free from miseries—a state of human emancipation free from exploitation of human beings by other human beings. The purpose of reference to Marx is to allude to the similarities in terms of rational comprehension of society; the vision, worldview, conviction and commitment towards a just society in their respective contexts, across the time and space. The alternative is not only for the ethical and social realms but the principles of *Dhamma*, as envisioned by Buddha, are equally desirable in the political realm also. The head of the political community, the state, in the Buddhist teachings, is not a divine or dynastic ruler but a rule of the *Mahāsammata*—the great elect. The history of ancient Indian thought in terms of the theory of state can be traced to the Buddhist texts, *Dīgha Nikāya* and *Aṅuguttara Nikāya*, two of the five Buddhist *Nikyās* (collections).[4] Although these collections contain Buddha's teachings of the *Dhamma*, the principles of the righteous life to the monks, some sections also contain the theory of the state. Thus, Buddhist theory of the origin of the state is the first theory of state in India, though 'the first faint traces' of social contract theory of the origin of state can be found in two '*Brāhmaṇas* which refer to the origin of kingship through election among Gods (*Sura*) on account of compelling necessity of carrying on successful war against the demons (*Asuras*)' (Sharma 1991, 63). Buddha was the first Indian thinker to propound a theory of origin of state by social contract not in the divine but in the real world, as it existed. This chapter shall look into the theory of the origin and the development of the state as mentioned in the *Aggaññasutta* of *Dīgha Nikāya* that traces the source of the validity of its authority to the popular consent of the people—the social contract (ibid., 65).

The history of state is, roughly, as old as the history of civilization itself that evolved with the rise and development of private property and the consequent class division of societies into the classes of the haves and the have-nots. Hence, the state, as an institution of governance is not natural nor universal but historic. It is developed as an instrument of the new status quo, that is, as an instrument of domination over the classes of have-nots in the hands of the classes of haves. Rousseau calls it 'the second fraud played upon people' that transformed the 'theft into legal rights'. Humans began to distinguish themselves from the animal kingdom by producing and reproducing their means of livelihood by exercising labour upon the nature, with hands as the tool to begin with. Henceforth, the human history has been the history of evolutionary and revolutionary development in the production of livelihood and the development of the tools of production. Humans are also called as tool making animals. Humans could develop the techniques and tools of labouring by the development of human species-specific attribute, the ability to think, the mental development. Ever since, labour has been the continuing link of livelihood through all the historical epochs.

In *Vedic* and post-*Vedic* literature, we do not find any theorization about the state, as a law-making and enforcing authority over a fixed domain. They lived in tribal and clan organizations, authorities of which operated on the basis of customs and kinship traditions and bonds, with no fixed geographical territory. As R. S. Sharma informs us, the first implicit divine reference to the process of state formation is found in the *Aitareya Brahmana* (ibid., 64–65).

There was no theory of state, as there was no state. Historically, ideas emanate from the object. State had not yet acquired firm footing; it was still in the process of formation. From the clan and kinship organizations in ancient India emerged advanced political entities in the form of 16 *Mahājanpadas* and the *Saṅghas*, known as the post-*Vedic* republics. The first reference of the contract theory of state is found in *Aitareya Brahmana*. The *Suras* (*Gods*) approached *Indra*, the most efficient war leader among them, for the imminent wars between *Sura* (Gods) and *Asura* (demons)—a euphemism for *Aryan* and non-*Aryan* conflict. By the time of Buddha, the state as a centralized authority of making and enforcing decision in a particular domain had acquired firm footings. The first secular theory of state is found in the Buddhist teachings to his disciples. Although the teachings are meant for the monks of the *Saṅghas* about the *Dhamma*—the principles of the righteous ways of life—they also contain the theory of the origin of the state. It is a social contract theory, anticipating the modern social contract theories of Hobbes, Locke and Rousseau.

Backdrop of the Study

Some people become legends in their own lifetime. Gautama Buddha is one of such ancient legendry figures. Most of the 20th century historians concur that Buddha lived, taught and founded the monastic orders during 6th–5th century BC, during the successive reigns of *Bimbisara* and his son, *Ajatasatru* over Magadha. The most agreed time span of Buddha's life among the 20th century historians is BC 563–BC 483. Plenty of legends and recorded documents about his life and teachings have been transferred to us through generations. He was a committed teacher and an activist philosopher with the life-long mission of imparting knowledge to enlighten people to become their own light.

By the time of Buddha, that is, by the 6th century BC, the state as an institution had clearly evolved and there were numerous, large and small states in the north India. Of these, some were monarchical and some non-monarchical, which could be termed as some kind of republic. Buddha belonged to the *Shakya* republic of *Kapilvastu* in the Himalayan foothills bordering the present-day Nepal. One of the popular legends is that Śuddhodana, meaning 'he who grows pure rice', was the father of Siddhartha Gautama. He was disillusioned with the worldly affairs after seeing a dead body and left home in search of truth and peace of the mind. But his parental place *Kapilvastu* was not a monarchy but one of the post *Vedic* republics. The monarchies were known as *Mahājānpadas* like *Magadh*, *Kashi* and *Koshal* on the south of the Ganga and the post *Vedic* republics, the *Saṅghas* on the north. Kauṭilya also refers them as *Saṅghas* in his *Arthaśāstra*. The monarchies had the standing regular army. In the *Saṅghas* all the men and women had necessary military training. In normal times, they would be pursuing their normal socio-economic occupation and would become warriors in the times of war. Under the leadership of *Vaishali*, 12 republics had formed a confederation for the war times. Siddhartha Gautam's father was the head of the *Shakya* republic of the *Kapilvastu*.

According to one of the legends, he was born on the way to his mother's parental house at Lumbini in the present Nepal. Not much is authentically known about his childhood. The *Shakya* republic had many ruling families who ruled by turn which is sanctioned by some sort of election. The head of the ruling family was known as *Rājā*. At the time of Buddha's birth, it was his father's turn to be the *Rājā*. Siddharth Gautam lost his mother within few days of his birth. At the age of 8 years, he was initiated in education to be taught by learned *Brāhmaṇs* and sages. From them he learned *Vedās* and *Upaniṣhads*. He also learned concentration and meditation. Belonging to warrior class, he was also taught archery and other related traits. At the age of 16, he was married to *Yashodhra* from a noted *Shakya* family. At the age of 20, he was formally admitted as a member of the *Shakya Saṅgha*. He took the same interest in the affairs of the *Saṅgha* as he did in his own life. His conduct as a member of the *Saṅgha* was exemplary, and he had endeared himself to all.

Koliyas, the neighbouring republic of *Shakyas* of *Kapilvastu*, was separated from it by the river *Rohini* and there would be dispute among the two regarding the sharing of the water for irrigational purposes. When Siddharth was 28, there was a major quarrel between the two tribal republics. The army chief (*Senapati*) of *Shakyas* called the assembly of *Shakyas* to decide over declaration of war on *Koliyas*. Siddhartha opposed the resolution of war and proposed the matter to be solved by negotiations between the elected representatives from both the *Saṅghas*. The war resolution was approved by the overwhelming majority. Those siding with Siddharth's resolution, that is, the minority, had the dichotomous choice of submitting to majority or to face action. Siddhartha Gautama openly opposed the war saying that it was inimical to the interest of *Shakyas* and humanity and against the public opinion. With this matter, Siddharth Gautama chose banishment and set on the journey of seeking enlightenment at the age of 28 years. Various collections of teachings attributed to him were passed down by oral tradition.

Over the next six years of wandering, he met many talented meditation teachers and mastered their techniques. Always he found that they showed him mind's potential but not mind itself. He continued his journey, contemplating, discussing and debating the issues concerning happiness of humanity and the existing views and religions He has his first discourse with the learned men at *Sarnath*, near the ancient city of *Varanasi*, where subsequently emperor Ashok constructed stoops and is one of the Buddhist pilgrimages. Finally, at a place called *Bodhgaya*, the future Buddha decided to remain in meditation until he knew mind's true nature and could benefit all beings. After spending six days and nights cutting through mind's most subtle obstacles, he reached enlightenment and became 'Buddha', the enlightened one.[5] *Bodhgaya*, like *Lumbini* (the place of his birth) and *Sarnath* (the place of his first substantial discourse) is also one of Buddhist pilgrimages.

Henceforth, he spent his life wandering mainly in the regions in present Uttar Pradesh and Bihar teaching through discussions, debates and sermons and creating monasteries for *Bhikshus* and *Bhikshunis* (monks and nuns), which functioned on the principles of equality and collectivity. He was invited by many noted and prominent individuals and the monarchs for teachings and debates. At the age of around 80 he died after eating poisonous meat offered by an old woman in *Kushinagar*, another place of Buddhist pilgrimage. His teaching spread in far-off places through monks, particularly after the patronage of the emperor Ashoka of *Magadh* in 3rd century BC. He refuted the *Brāhmanical* principles of divinity and divinely created social order of inequalities. Contrary to the *Brāhmanical* divine theory of origin of state and the kingship, Buddhist theory envisages the origin of the state in popular consent through social contract. It also anticipates, in some way, the 17th century social contract theories of Europe.

As mentioned above, two of the five Buddhist *Nikāyas* (compilations)—*Dīgha* and *Aṅguttara* (400 BC–300 BC)—contain Buddha's teachings regarding the evolution of the society and subsequent formation of the state (Appadorai 1992, 1). These collections contain huge mass of Buddhist canonical literature in *Pali* language consisting of the discourses of Lord Buddha, his sayings, songs and narratives, etc. In *Dīgha*

Nikāya, one comes across the need and the origin of state after the passing away of the golden age of harmony and happiness on the earth due to emergence of greed, selfishness and other evils. The story consists of all the basic factors of the theory of the evolution of the society. It talks of the time when people started building up houses, called *agāra* (huts). The primordial men and women might have lived in the huts. There were two more units of inhabitants called *gāma* (village) and *nigama* (town: indicates some sort of urbanization). *Nigama* might be the place where the products were exchanged, the marketing place. The society, as mentioned in the *sutta*, was an agricultural society. This was the time when self-grown paddy appeared. But after it disappeared, then people started cultivating paddy. It was the time of disintegration of communal property and appearance of private properties and various safeguards of its protection. Persons who stole the paddy were banished. Thus, sense of morality also arose and the decisions were taken in assembly. To institutionalize the system of punishment, arose the need of state. This proves the intimate link between the rise of the private property and the state.

Dīgha Nikāya also throws some light on the duties of the ruler. *Aṅguttara Nikāya* mentions essential qualities of the ruler. The political ideas contained in them can be arranged under the following heads: origin of the state, importance of the state, essential qualities of the ruler and the duties of the ruler.

Origin of the State

In this section, an attempt has been made to find out the counterparts of the Western theories of state in ancient Indian texts, which is a difficult task owing to the uncertainties hanging over many texts regarding their time and the content. For reconstructing the theory about the origin of State on the basis of these texts, it is appropriate to go by the generally accepted chronology: the *Brāhmaṇas;* the Buddhist texts *Dīgha* and *Aṅguttara Nikāyas*; Kauṭilya's *Arthaśāstra* and the *Rājādhārma* section of the *Śānti Parva* of *Mahābhārata* (Sharma 1991, 63). As mentioned above, the contract theory in *Brāhmaṇas* is mythological—a war-oriented contract among the Gods—hence, the Buddhist theory can be considered as the first theory of state formulated in terms of a contractual power. Unlike the Western philosophers of 17th century, Buddha did not depict the individuals in the social contract as essentially egoistic, but he refers to specific historically arisen conditions. Unlike Hobbes, the sovereign emerging out of social contract is not an all-powerful *Leviathan* not accountable to people or the *Brāhmanical* incarnation of God but a *Mahāsammata*, or the 'Great Elect' with the duty of observing and preserving *Dhamma*, the righteous ways of life.

The State of Nature

The origin of the universe and state out of the original state of nature is explained in the *Aggaññasutta*, the 27th *Sutta* of the *Dīgha Nikāya*. It is like other sections of the *Nikāya*, in the dialogue form like Plato's Republic. It is discourse imparted by Buddha to two *Brāhmaṇs, Bharadvaja* and *Vasettha*, who left their family and caste to become monks. Buddha, in his discourse negates the importance of the lineage and emphasizes the moral practices and the *Dhamma*. Anyone from any lineage can become a monk and achieve the state of enlightenment. Then, he explains about the beginning of the Earth and the birth and the rise of the social order. In Buddhist discourse the universe appears *Vivaṭṭa Kappa* (opening up) and disappears, *Samvaṭṭa Kappa* (closing down). In a very long span of time, the society opens up in the particular time and it closes down after millions of periods of that particular time, Buddha said in the *sutta*.

Buddha emphasizes the message of universality in the *Dhamma*. Discussion on the rise of social order, that is the *varṇa* social division, is beyond the scope of this discussion. Buddha rejects the divine origin of hierarchical *Brāhmanical* order, that everyone including *Brāhmaṇs* are born through the biological process from the wombs of the mother and not from different organs of *Brahmā*, as claimed by *Brāhmanical* sources.

According to depiction of the State of nature in *Aggaññasutta* of *Dīgha Nikāya*, there was a time when people were perfect and lived in a state of happiness and tranquillity. This perfect state lasted for ages but at last this pristine purity declined and there set in evils. Distinction of sex and colour manifested themselves and eventually the heavenly life degenerated into earthly one. Now shelter, food and drinks were required. People gradually entered into a series of agreements to set up institutions of family and property. But this gave rise to a new set of problems, for there appeared theft and other forms of unsocial conduct.

> The human beings gathered themselves and said: Evil customs, sins, have appeared among men. For in the past, we were made of mind, we fed on rapture; self-luminous, we traversed the air in abiding loneliness; long-long period we so remained. For us sooner or later after a long while, the savory earth had arisen over the waters. We set to work to make earth into lumps and feast on it. As we did so, our self-luminance vanished; when it was gone, moon and sun, star shapes and constellations, nights and day months and half months, the seasons and years became manifest. We enjoying the savory earth, feeding on it, nourished by it, continued so for a long while. But since evil and immoral customs became prevalent among us, these out growths disappeared. When they had vanished creepers appeared clothed in color, odor and tastes them we turned to enjoy; fed and nourished thereby. We continued so for a long while. But since evils and immoral customs became prevalent among us, creepers also disappeared. When they had ceased, rice appeared ripening in the open spaces.

This description corresponds to the origin of the universe that considers that, in the beginning, there was water all around and in course of time earth appeared.

The reference of creepers (*Vanalata*) and some sort of roots (*Bhumiparpataka*) as the earliest means of subsistence in pre-state societies, in the Buddhist text, corresponds to *the Brāhmanical* and Jain traditions that inform us that earliest means of subsistence was the fruits and the roots of trees. In them 'the description of *Kalpvriksha* as the main source of livelihood of the people is very common affair' (Sharma 1991, 49). Naturally in the earliest states of their lives, humans lived as food gatherers and not as food producers, corresponding with the Rousseau's description of the early state of nature. This is also supported by the modern anthropological studies that point out that the first livelihood was 'natural subsistence upon fruits and roots on a restricted habitat'. Nobody then conceived them as belonging to anyone with any sense of possession or ownership that in distant civilized future developed as a 'commanding force in human mind'.

In the early state of nature, there was no institution like family based on supremacy of man over woman. There is reference of the land of *Kuru* in *Dīgha Nikāya*, where the men live calling no goods their own, nor as their chattels any womankind. Kauṭilya talks about *Vairajya* (stateless society) in *Uttar Kuru* where the concept of family, mine and thine were unknown. There was no division of people into social classes. The absence of social division is also mentioned in *Purāṇạs* (*VayuPuran*). 'In their account of earliest life of humankind, there were no *varṇas*' (Sharma 1991, 50–51). Thus, in the early human societies, without the institutions of family and the property, the state did not exist. Thus, we see that there is a vital connection between the existence of family, private property and the state. This harmonious tenor of the state of nature was destroyed by the discovery of art of cultivation and the idea of ownership of land. Then the idea 'Come now, let us divide off the rice fields and set the boundaries round it' (Appadorai 1992, 2). The fencing of land and the development of the art of cultivation enabled the people to produce more than they could consume leading to the tendency of storing the rice. For the first time, people established their separate houses that made people to claim, 'this is mine and this is thine'. This description finds echo in Rousseau's view. 'The first man who fenced a piece of land and declared it to be belonging to him and found people simple mind to believe him is the founder of the civilisation.'

The repeated mention of rice is the testimony of the fact that during those days the cultivation of rice was the main economic activity. With the emergence of the family and private property and the tendency to store, the evils like theft crept in. 'Now some being, *Vasettha* of greedy disposition, watching over his own plot stole another plot and made use of it' (Appadorai 1992, 3). People thought that to be evil is bad and reminded the person who steal to 'not to do such thing again'. On repetition 'they took him and admonished him'. 'With such a beginning, *Vasettha*, did stealing appear and censure and lying of punishment became known' (ibid., 4).

The state of nature and human nature can be summed up in following stages:

1. In the process of the evolution of the universe, the earliest stage in an indefinite imagined past was divine, where people were 'made up of mind, fed on rapture; ...traversed the air in the abiding loneliness; ....' (ibid., 3).
2. With the passage of stages, the appearance of evils began and the divine stage transited into earthly. The earliest inhabitants of the earth were not food producers but food gatherers. They survived on creepers, fruits and some sort of roots. This view is also supported by *Brāhmanical* and Jain sources and also by anthropological studies about the people of Palaeolithic age. The institutions like family or private property did not exist. The people were not divided into social classes. People lived in egalitarian harmonious communities.
3. With the development of art of cultivation and plantation many stages of division of labour occurred and the institutions of family and property in cattle and land came into existence. People began to produce in surplus to the consumption needs. This was accompanied by a tendency in human beings 'to store rice and appropriate to themselves'. The invention of iron and corn revolutionized the life and ruined the humanity, as stated by Buddha many centuries before Rousseau.
4. With the emergence of individual family and property, evils like greed and theft also appeared. The harmony and peace of the state of nature is disturbed by the appearance of the 'evil customs' like theft of rice and stealing of the agricultural plot by certain errant individuals. This can be compared with John Locke's state of nature, whose state of 'happy freedom' is disturbed by 'certain inconveniences'. These inconveniences transgressed by some individuals into natural rights of life, liberty and property of others in violation of natural laws.

Thus, we see in the fourth stage, the Rousseau kind of state of nature degenerates into Hobbesian state of nature via Lockean state of nature in which people enjoy their natural rights including right to property and right to sell and buy labour. The harmonious state of nature, as described in the *Dīgha Nikāya,* is disturbed owing to the emergence of the institution of property accompanied by the evils like theft of rice or stealing of the rice producing plots of land of others. Thus, the story of creation reminds us of the ideal state of nature of Rousseau followed by the one depicted by Hobbes. The Buddhist description refutes the *Brāhmanical* claim of precedence of the members of one class over the members of the other social classes. There was a time when 'people were perfect and lived in a state of happiness and tranquility that "lasted for ages"' (Sharma 1991, 64). As discussed above this 'pristine purity declined and there set in the rottenness' (ibid.). This rottenness needed to be corrected by punishment to the wrongdoers as deterrent from wrong doing for others. In order to legitimately institutionalize the system of punishment, the need for a legitimate public authority was felt, for which people entered into a social contract among them to choose an appropriate authority.

The Social Contract

To institutionalize the system of just punishment to take care of the rottenness set in the society, people assembled to choose the chief as most favoured and capable person from among themselves.

> Now these, *Vasettha*, gathered themselves together and bewailed these things, saying: from our evil deeds, sirs, becoming manifest, in as much as stealing censure, lying, punishment has become known, what if we have to select a certain being, who should be wrathful, when indignation is right, who should ensure that which should rightly be censured and who deserves to be banished. But we will give him in return a proportion of the rice. (Appadorai 1992, 4)

From the above two things are manifested the need of a legitimate authority elected by the people as a whole with coercive power of punishment to the wrongdoer and the system of taxation in kind, in the form of the produce from people's economic occupation.

> 'Then *Vasettha*, those beings went to the being among them, who was the handsomest, the best favored, the most attractive, the most capable and said to him: Come now, good being, be indignant at that whereat one should rightly be indignant, censure that which should rightly be censured, banish him who deserves to be banished. And we will contribute to thee a proportion of our rice'. He acceded to their request and did so as they gave him a proportion of their rice. The person thus elected came to hold the titles of '*Mahāsammata*' (The Great Elect) implying the one chosen by the whole people, 'the first standing phrase to arise'—the *Khattiya*, 'Lord of the fields', the next expression to arise—the *Rāja*, who 'charms the people by norm' the *Dhamma*—the third standing phrase to arise. (ibid.)

The description made in *Dīgha Nikāya* seems to be the attributes of the stage of social development of disintegration of tribal society, 'giving rise to clash of interests between men and women; between the people of different races and colors; and between the people of unequal wealth' (Sharma 1991, 65). From this, the inference is made that the paddy cultivation was the basis of the economy of the people in the middle Ganga plains, the region of Buddha's sermons. It is to be noted that no other crop than paddy is mentioned in the text, although other crops find reference in subsequent *Jātaka*[6] stories and other texts but, nevertheless, paddy was the main produce. Originally the agreement takes place between a single *Kṣatriya* on the one hand and the people on the other, but at a later stage it is extended to *Kṣatriya* as a class. Towards the end, the *Dīgha Nikāya* talks about the circle of nobles, '*the Kṣatriyas mandala*'. 'This obviously is intended to justify and strengthens the rule of oligarchies, which existed in the middle Gangetic plains, in the age of Buddha' (Sharma 1991, 67).

Thus, we see that the state arises as a punitive institution with the aim of maintaining order in the society, as a result of agreement between the ruled and the ruler, in which the ruled transfers part of the sovereignty for specific purpose. The contractual relationship between the people and the state involves the institutionalized taxation on the condition of the state's obligation of the protection of life and property of the people.

> Unlike Hobbesian contract, the obligation is not one-sided but like Locke's contract the obligation is mutual. If one party violates the terms of the contract other party is not obliged to abide by it. But without the contract, there shall prevail anarchy as it existed before, therefore, neither have a choice outside it. (Gokhale 1969, 731–738)

The *Mahāsammata* was not a law giver or legislator but an executive head, which enforced the customary or the tribal conventions and a punitive authority against the transgressors. It can be compared to Lockean sovereign or commonwealth, who was not a lawgiver; he only interpreted, codified and enforced the natural laws that already existed. Thus, we see that the text refers to the ideal state of life to start with, followed by its degeneration due to emergence of evils like theft and falsehood and establishment of family and property by a series of agreements and finally establishment of state by electing the most gracious, capable and wise person from among them as the legitimate ruler, *Mahāsammata* to punish those who deserve punishment and cherish those who deserve to be cherished. The contract theory of the origin of state is the original contribution of ancient Indian thinkers, particularly Buddha. Ancient Greek thinkers, Plato and Aristotle, considered to be the founders of political science in the West did not envisage the origin of state as a result of contract between the people and the rulers. In Republic, Plato envisages the origin of state consequent to peoples' coming together for fulfilling the mutual needs that can be treated as some kind of contract by implication (Plato 1960, 221). The state is established by a lawgiver; subsequently people take oath in accordance with the common laws applicable equally to the ruler and the ruled. The contract theory in ancient India could be attributed to the existence of post-*Vedic* republics, which functioned through popular assemblies in the age of Buddha. In modern times, the social contract theories of state were propounded under monarchies, either to justify it (Hobbes); to limit it (Locke) or to overthrow it and replace it with the popular government in which the ruled is the ruler also functioning through the popular assemblies (Rousseau).

Thus, we see that in Buddhist theory, the state is a human institution arising out of state of nature, which is depicted synonymous with anarchy that was ended by popular election of a ruler for the establishment of order. The ruler is basically a punitive authority to deter people from wrong doing by inflicting punishment to a bandit or a miscreant. Thus, we see that in Buddhist discourse compiled in the *Aggaññasutta* of *Dīgha Nikāya*, the state arises as a contractual, punitive institution with the responsibility of making society orderly. The laws enacted by state emanate from an agreement between the ruler and the ruled, wherein the ruled transfer a part of their sovereignty to the state for a specific purpose. The relationship between the state and the subject is a contractual obligation in which one commands and the other obeys. The contract is symbolized by the institution of taxation, which is payment for specific work of maintaining the order in the society. The obligation is mutual, like in Locke's contract, if one party violates it unilaterally, the other is no longer obligated by the terms of that contract. The contract is a basic condition of organized human society and in the absence of such a contract before the birth of the state, anarchy prevailed. It is therefore existential, and neither the people nor the state has any choice outside it. The state is the central institution of the society, distinct from other social institutions typical of some stateless societies, such as chiefdoms. The state under a popularly chosen ruler is considered to be the mediator between various parts of the society.

Qualities, Functions and the Duties of Ruler

The 'anointed warrior *Rāja*', as described earlier, is not a dynastic or a divine king but a popularly chosen ruler.

> Well born on both sides; pure in descent as far back as seven generations both of mother and father, unchallenged and without reproach in point of birth; he is rich with great wealth and resources and his treasure and granaries overflow; and his strength is in four divisions of his army loyal and alert to commands; his minister is wise, intelligent; discreet, able to judge rightly the future from past happenings; and these four things ripen to his glory; and with the fifth quality of glory, wheresoever he abides where he himself has conquered. … (Appadorai 1992, 6)

The well-born aspect of the ruler's quality seems paradoxical as in the beginning of the discourse in the *Aggaññasutta* Buddha refutes the *Brāhmanical* view of superiority of birth to *Vasettha* and *Bhardwaj*, the *Brāhmaṇs* who seek admission to *Saṅgha* and depicts social division based on functional deeds. According to a Srilankan scholar, Sita Arunthavanathan; 'A ruler was expected to have 10 personal qualities, such as generosity, liberality, virtue and so on. A king had to possess four cardinal principles which were generosity *Dāna*, pleasant words *(piyavacana)*, welfare of the subjects, and equal treatment of all' (ibid., 9).

As mentioned above, Buddhist state as depicted in *Dīgha Nikāya* is basically a punitive institution, which inflicts punishment on bandits and malefactors through a contractual ruler, to deter others from wrong doing. In doing so, the ruler 'should lean on the norm, the "*Dhamma*" (the law of truth and righteousness)' (ibid., 9). This implies that the ruler should be truthful and righteous in governance. The sacred duty of the king was to observe *Dhamma*.[7] The ruler must use his discretion of analysing the crime reasonably and award punishment righteously in accordance with the crime. The government's other important obligation towards people is their protection from external as well as internal forces. The wrongdoers must be punished and no wrong doing should prevail in the territory. Another important duty of king is to provide wealth to poor, as poverty may lead to anarchy. Kauṭilya's *rājādhārma* of *Rakshana-Palana* and *yogakshema* meaning security protection and well-being of the people seems to be bearing the Buddhist influence.

Buddha said that the qualities of the subjects of a kingdom depend largely on the behaviour of the kingdom's ruler. He then outlined 10 qualities—'*Dasa-Rājā-Dhamma*' ('ten virtues of the ruler' to guide rulers and produce virtuous subjects:

1. ***Dāna*:** Literality, generosity. It is the duty of the government to look after the welfare of the needy subjects. The ideal ruler should give away wealth and property wisely without giving in to craving and attachment.
2. ***Sila*:** Morality, a high moral character. He must observe at least the five precepts and conduct himself both in private and in public life as to be a shining example to his subjects. This virtue is very important, because, if the ruler adheres to it, strictly, then bribery and corruption, violence and indiscipline would be automatically wiped out in the country.
3. ***Pariccaga*:** Making sacrifices if they are for the good of the people—personal name and fame; even the life. By the grant of gifts, etc., the ruler spurs the subjects on to more efficient and more loyal service.
4. ***Ajjava*:** Honesty and integrity. He must be absolutely straightforward and must never take recourse to any crooked or doubtful means to achieve his ends. He must be free from fear or

favour in the discharge of his duties. 'If a person maintains justice without being subjected to favouritism, hatred, fear or ignorance, his popularity grows like the waxing moon.'

5. ***Maddava***: Kindness or gentleness. A ruler's uprightness may sometimes require firmness. But this should be tempered with kindness and gentleness. In other words, a ruler should not be over harsh or cruel.
6. ***Tapa***: Restraint of senses and austerity in habits. Shunning indulgence in sensual pleasures, an ideal monarch keeps his five senses under control. Some rulers may, using their position, flout moral conduct—this is not becoming of a good monarch.
7. ***Akkodha***: Non-hatred. The ruler should bear no grudge against anybody. Without harbouring grievances, he must act with forbearance and love.
8. ***Ahimsā***: Non-violence. Not only should he refrain from harming anybody, but he should also try to promote peace and prevent war, when necessary. He must practice non-violence to the highest possible extent so long as it does not interfere with the firmness expected of an ideal ruler.
9. ***Khanti***: Patience and tolerance. Without losing his temper, the ruler should be able to bear up hardships and insults. In any occasion he should be able to conduct himself without giving in to emotions. He should be able to receive both bouquets and brickbats in the same spirit and with equanimity.
10. ***Avirodha***: Non-opposition and non-enmity. The ruler should not oppose the will of the people. He must cultivate the spirit of amity among his subjects. In other words, he should rule in harmony with his people.[8]

A *Dhamma Rājā*, the righteous ruler, relies just on *Dhamma* saying (to his subjects), 'Follow such practice in deed, not that other; follow such practice in word, not that other; follow such practice in thought, not that other; follow such livelihood, not that other' (Appadorai 1992, 7). Thus, the ruler, apart from maintaining the order by punishing the wrongdoer, protecting the people and ensuring their wellbeing, also performs the role of a teacher of the people teaching them to practice the principles of *Dhamma*, the righteous life in deeds, words and thoughts.

Conclusion

The Buddhist theory of the origin of state is a great ancient Indian contribution to the history of social contract theory. It rejects the prevailing *Brāhmanical* divine theory of state and divinely ordained hierarchal social division, the *varṇa* system. In this text, the origin and development of the caste systems are critically examined, which was considered by Buddha as the gravest social problem of the time. Dispelling the legends and myths shrouding the origin of caste by the *Vedic* thinkers, Buddha has explained how the caste structure gradually evolved on the basis of physical and occupational factors in a one-time equal community, which was made hereditary by *Vedic* thinkers in course of time.[9] By Buddha's time, the egalitarian communal life has disintegrated, the private property and family had been institutionalized and evils like theft had appeared. Buddha in his teachings, as contained in the 27th Sutta (section) of *Aggaññasutta* in *Dīgha Nikāya*, rejects the divine theory of the ruler being anointed by the God and propounds a social contract theory, under which the popular assembly chooses the most competent person among them to maintain the order in the society for which they pay him taxes in the form of a portion of their produce, rice. This social contract theory anticipates the thought experiment involving the interrelated concepts of the state of nature, natural laws and the social contract. This social contract is two-way contract, between the ruler and the people. If the ruler is unable to carry out his duty of maintaining order; protecting people's person and property and ensuring their wellbeing, the people may withdraw the consent and choose another ruler.

A king had to rule with justice and equity ensuring security. Here, it must be stressed that moral responsibility lay not only with the ruler but also with the ruled. Each person in the society had a share of responsibility so that the community could present a united front. According to *Cakkavatti Sihanada Sutta,* king's duty could be summarized as protection of the state, elimination of crime, effecting economic stability and ruling in consultation with the clergy (*samana-brahmana*) for watch, ward and protection righteously. According to *Cakkavatti Sihanada Sutta*, protection had to be provided not only to the subjects, army, religious bodies, etc., but even to beasts and birds.[10] To sum up, it may be said that Buddhist theory of State is a kind of democratic theory under which the ruler is popularly elected and could be recalled. This, in Buddha's time, was an advanced form of social contract theory of the origin of the state.

Summary

Buddhist theory of the origin of state is contained in the *Aṅguttara Sutta* of *Dīgha Nikāya,* one of the collections of Buddha's teachings. It refutes the prevailing *Brāhmanical* divine theory of the origin of state and propounds a social contract theory. According to this theory, the ruler is not anointed by God but is chosen by the people. State is not an eternal or a natural institution but historic that came into existence at a historic time for historical reasons. In the earliest times, there was no family and private property and no state. The emergence of state is intimately linked with the emergence of the institution of private property. The state of nature as depicted in *Dīgha Nikāya* is a pristine state in which people were perfect and lived in happiness and tranquillity. It refutes the *Brāhmanical* claim of their class superiority over other classes. The perfection of state of nature lasted for a very long time, after which the pristine purity got corrupted, as there set in evils. People started building shelters and occupying plots of lands for cultivation of paddy for their livelihood.

Thus, at last the pristine primitive communal life, where there were no private families and property, disintegrated. 'People gradually entered into a series of agreements among themselves and set up the institutions of family and property' (Sharma 1991, 65). This led to appearance of evils like theft and other forms of wrong doings, which demands punishments to deter others from indulging into similar unsocial acts. For this, people assembled to choose as a ruler from among themselves, who 'was the best favoured, most attractive and most capable'. They also agreed to contribute to him a portion of their paddy. He was supposed to punish those who deserved. The elected person had three titles, *the Mahāsammata*, the one chosen by the people; the *Khattiya*, the lord of the fields; and the *Rājā*, who ensures the observation of the *Dhamma*, the righteous principles of life. The ruler does not have only rights but duties to ensure protection and the well-being of the people.

Points for Discussion

1. Buddha's *Dhamma* was an alternative to the *dhārma* of the *Brāhmanical* political order. Give your views.
2. Discuss the features of Buddhist theory of origin of state and its functions.
3. Discuss the theory of kingship as described by Buddha in *Dīgha Nikāya.*

4. Critically examine the relationship between state and religion in *Dīgha Nikāya.*
5. Analyse the social contract theories described in *Dīgha Nikāya.*

Endnotes

1. The Life of the Buddha, www.buddhist-pilgrimage.com/life-of-buddha.html
2. *Saṅghas* are the most fundamental institutions of Buddhism. Monks and nuns, trained in them, are considered to be responsible for the preservation and dissemination of the Buddha's teaching and the guidance of people.
3. In epistemological and psychological senses, *Mokṣa* refers to freedom from ignorance: self-realization, self-actualization and self-knowledge.
4. Other *Nikāyas* are *Majjhima Nikāya*, *Samyutta Nikāya* and *Khuddaka Nikāya.*
5. The life of the Buddha, www.buddhist-pilgrimage.com/life-of-buddha.html
6. The *Jataka* stories are related to the former births of Buddha, probably narrated by some later Buddhist teachers and monks to illustrate Buddha's doctrines by appropriate examples. Appadorai (1992, 11).
7. The Buddhist religion that essentially meant righteousness.
8. www.lankalibrary.com
9. http://dlib.pdn.ac.lk/bitstream/123456789/3071/1/Rev.Pandith%20Kamburupitiye%20Ariyasena%201981.pdf
10. *Sita Arunthavanathan*, Buddhist political thinking, http://www.lankalibrary.com/Bud/politics.html

Glossary

***Dīgha Nikāya*:** *Nikāya* means collection, *Dīgha Nikāya* is one of the five collections of Buddha's teachings.

***Dhamma* (*Dhārma*):** Buddhist principles of righteous life.

***Saṅgha*:** The residential monastery of Buddhist education to the monks and nuns. The non-monarchical, republican states were also called *Saṅgha.*

***Mahāsammata*:** The great elect, the ruler chosen by popular consent.

***Mahājānpadas*:** The 16 big kingdoms that emerged around 6th century BC were known as 16 *Mahājānpadas. Jānpada* meant populated territory.

***Bimbisara*:** King of Magadh at the time of Buddha's birth.

***Ajatasatru*:** Son and successor of *Bimbisara* and king of Magadh at the time of Buddha's death.

***Vaishali*:** One of the republican states in Buddha's time, under whose leadership 12 republics had formed a military confederation.

***Vivaṭṭa Kappa*:** Opening up of the universe.

***Samvaṭṭa Kappa*:** Closing down of the universe.

***Rājā*:** The title of the ruler when he ensures the observation of *Dhamma.*

***Khattiya*:** The title of ruler when he acts as the lord of the fields

References

Appadorai, A. 1992. *Political Thinking in India through Ages.* New Delhi: Khanna Publishers.

Gokhale, Balkrishna Govind. 1969. *Journal of the American Oriental Society,* Vol. 89, No. 4 (Oct–Dec, 1969), pp. 731–738.

Plato, Republic, Book II, Quoted in Ebenstein. 1960. *Great Political Thinkers*. New Delhi: Oxford University Press.
Sharma, R. S. 1991. *The Aspects of Political Ideas and Institutions in Ancient India*. Delhi: Motilal Banarasidass.

Further Readings

Kulke, Hermann. 1995. *The State in India 1000–1700*. Oxford: Oxford University Press.
Sarao, K. T. S. and Geoffrey D. Long, eds. 2017. Buddhism and Jainism, Vol. 1. In, *Encyclopedia of Indian Religions*, edited by Arvind Sharma. Heidelberg and New York: Springer.
Sharma, R. S. 1989. *Origin of the State in India, D. D. Kosambi Memorial Lecture, 1987*. Bombay: University of Bombay Publication.

10 CHAPTER

Śānti Parva of *Mahābhārata*: Ideas on the Kingship and *Daṇḍanīti*

Varun Kumar Tripathi

CHAPTER OUTLINE

- **Introduction**
- **The Life Sketch**
- **The *Śānti Parva***
- **Origin and Nature of Ancient Indian State**
- **Kingship—the *Rājādhārma***
- **Code and Doctrine of Punishment—the *Daṇḍanīti***
- **Conclusion**
- **Summary**
- **Points for Discussion**

State, being vast machinery, can't be run by those who haven't conquered their minds.

—*Bhīṣma*, *Śānti Parva*

Reader's Guide

The word *Mahābhārata* refers to two things: the Great War that took place between two confederacies of *Kaurava* and *Pāṇḍava*, respectively, and the great epic narrating the story of the war, composed by the great sage *Vyāsa*. The epic is an encyclopaedic account of a vast range of subjects, such as the different regions and kingdoms of the *Bhāratavarṣa*, their kings and famous warriors, princes, meritorious women, sages, deities, demons, mountains, rivers, forests; the vast description of prosperity, people, clans, rituals, craftsmanship; and polity, governance, statecraft, morality, spirituality and unending range of war skills. The readers of the chapter will find some of the finest ideas pertaining to polity, kingship, statecraft and governance as vastly illustrated in the *Śānti Parva* of *Mahābhārata*. The readers may note that the author of this chapter has not chosen deliberately any theoretical framework to weave those ideas and analyse them or even initiate any theory laden criticism. It was chosen so to provide the reader almost a first-hand account of the political precepts as discussed in the treatise so as to facilitate him making an uncorrupted perception of those precepts.

More importantly, the readers may note that the political precepts discussed in the *Śānti Parva* are the summary of the views of ancient proponent of *rājaśāstra* (political doctrines), such as *Brahmā*, *Bṛhaspati*, *Viśālākṣa*, *Śukrācārya*, *Indra*, *Prācetas* Manu, *Bharadvāja*, *Gauraśirā* and others. *Bhīṣma*, after the end of the Great War when his body was pierced with arrows, was visited by *Yudhiṣṭhira* who wanted to learn from him the lessons of *rājaśāstra*. *Bhīṣma* acknowledges above ancient teachers and summarizes the doctrines for *Yudhiṣṭhira*. It suggests that *Bhīṣma* did not present as much of his views as of his ancestors. It also suggests that *rājaśāstra* was a subject matter of scholarly contemplation for ages in India much prior to the time of *Mahābhārata*. Accordingly, there might have been diversity in views too. So, if the readers find any apparent contradiction in the ideas, they may see it in the context.

The references are mostly taken from the *Śānti Parva* and relevant verses are translated from Sanskrit into English by the author, less literally and more illustratively. The endnotes of the chapters often indicate numeric, for example, 65/13-31, in which 65 would indicate the 65th chapter of the *Rājadharmānuśāsana Parva* of *Śānti Parva* of the *Mahābhārata* and 13 or 13-31 would indicate number or range of verses (*śloka*) from the chapter. Like in case of translations, the terms appearing in glossary are also defined to illustrate the best sense for the reader, instead of furnishing mere transliteration.

Introduction

For ages, there has been a prevailing opinion[1] that ancient Indian thinkers had least interest in polity and governance and even lesser in political theorization. However, such opinions were held much earlier to the discovery of Kauṭilya's *Arthaśāstra* (1922), and political scientific revision of other *Nīti* treatise in the latter half of 20th century, such as the *Mahābhārata* of *Vyāsa*, *Śukranīti* of *Śukrācārya*, ideas in Buddhist Pāli canon, or even the *Vedic* concepts such as *rāṣṭra*, *sabhā*, *samiti*, *bali*, *jana* and *janapada*, etc., and miscellaneous ideas from 18 *Purāṇa* and *Dharmaśāstra* or the *Smṛiti* of Manu, etc. Yet, to get woven the ideas into one or some theoretical schema would be a tedious task for a careful reader or researcher. While ignoring the enormous array of political ideas of Indian past would be to get disconnected from the ways of political thinking in the subcontinent and possibly to argue *ad ignorantiam* for the absence of any significant political thinking or statesmanship in the history of the land.

As for as the *Mahābhārata* is concerned, its *Śānti Parva* significantly deals with a range of affairs which indicate the complexity of political affairs. It also indicates that how the human minds have been inquisitive since ages towards political affairs and have always derived this inquisition from the generic inquisition for human happiness and peace. Yet, the description of the 'state of nature' across all Indian treatises would not confirm to the Aristotelian idea of *zoon politikon*, rather it would show that human beings have been totally apolitical in the 'state of nature' and becomes politically conscious when they experience a moral degeneration and social chaos thereupon, hence feeling the necessity of installation of a statecraft through which the life and affairs were hoped to be put to order. And there came a king.

To guide the king, the *dhārma* operated. The *dhārma* sets the ideal principle of action, as Kumārila Bhaṭṭa defines *rājādhārma* as the principle on which the state 'ought to function'.[2] The *Śānti Parva*, however, like other Indian treatise on polity does not confirm that the nature of kingship, state or governance principles has been same across various parts of subcontinent and various phases of time.

The Indian political thinking is not merely a concern for management of the political affairs and statecraft, but has been quite conscious of constructing political ideals in the light of which the justification of all political acts could be sought. As in Western political thinking, justice often becomes the highest political ideal, although sometimes replaced by the idea of democracy; in case of ancient Indian political thinking, *dhārma* becomes the highest political ideal. *Dhārma*, however, traverses in different realms of discourse, moral, spiritual, religious, social, etc., but when it comes to political realm it encompasses concepts like dutifulness, justice, equality, justified discrimination, professional duties and as far as doctrines of punishment. The term *dhārma* is used in all above senses in different contexts. The *Śānti Parva* touches almost all of them. The *rājādhārma—dhārma* of a king—is a further specified fraction of the *dhārma* in general, and when kingship is debated as a political idea, the *rājādhārma* becomes the highest ideal in the political schema of thinking and theorization. The *rājādhārma*, therefore, functions as a criterion, that is, if a political decision or act is according to the *rājādhārma*, it would be right, and if not then false and deplorable.

The Life Sketch

Vyāsa, also known as *Veda Vyāsa* (being compiler of *Vedās*) and Kṛṣṇa Dvaipāyana (Kṛṣṇa—having dark complexion and Dvaipāyana—being born on an island), is considered the author of the great epic *Mahābhārata*. He also compiled four *Vedās* and 18 *Purāṇas*. *Vyāsa* is a title for the compiler of the *Vedās* and is not confined to one person, but about 28 legendary figures have been named as *Vyāsa* in *Hindu* tradition. *Vyāsa* appears as the compiler of, and an important character in, the *Mahābhārata*. It is held by the *Hindu* mythology that Lord *Viṣṇu* himself incarnated as *Vyāsa* to compile all the knowledge treasure which was till then in oral form and transmitted among the teacher–disciple tradition of sages and hermits. He was the son of *Satyavatī* and the sage *Parāśara*. He was very much alive at the time of the Great War as he had met the *Pāṇḍava* during their visit to Pāñcāla kingdom and compiled the *Mahābhārata* when the Great War was over. There are two views about his birthplace, one that he was born at a place called *Vyāsa* in Nepal, and other that he was born on a river island of river *Yamunā*, in modern Uttar Pradesh.

After the Great War, *Vyāsa* took assistance from Lord *Ganesha*, who served as his scribe in writing the great treatise, which was originally known as Jaya (meaning victory) and later on named as *Mahābhārata*—the great story of Bharata dynasty (alternatively of Bhārata, the Indian subcontinent). *Vyāsa* himself mentions that there are different versions of *Mahābhārata* authored by him (*Ādi Parva* 1/1/101-106). For the benefit of human realm he wrote the treatise comprising 100,000 verses; the other of 24,000 verses; of 6,000,000 verses; of 3,000,000 verses for the realm of deities; of 1,500,000 verses for the realm of ancestors (*pitṛ*); and of 1,400,000 verses for the realm of *gandharvas*. Only the first one, that is, composed for the human realm, is popularly known as *Mahābhārata*. The significance of the treatise can be understood by the fact that it is recognized as fifth *Vedā* in *Hindu* mythology. And, the high place of *Vyāsa* in the hearts of *Hindus* can be understood by that fact that even today when a recitation session of *Mahābhārata* or *Purāṇas* is organized, the reciting teacher is called *Vyāsa* for the duration.

The *Śānti Parva*

The *Śānti Parva* is the 12th of 18 books of great Indian epic—the *Mahābhārata*. The canto is further subdivided into three sections, namely *Rājdharmānuśāsana Parva* (dealing with duties of a king), *Āpaddhārma Parva* (dealing with duties in situations of crisis) and *Mokṣa dhārma Parva* (a discourse on liberation). The three sections contain 365 chapters altogether. After the end of the Great War, *Yudhiṣṭhira*, the king designate, visits *Bhīṣma*, who was still alive pierced with arrows, for learning from him about polity, how to protect and up-bring the subject and what were the duties of a king—the *rājādhārma*. The canto reports a number of dialogues, such as between *Vyāsa* and *Yudhiṣṭhira*; *Indra* and *Māndhātā*; *Vasumanā* and *Bṛhaspati*; *Indra* and *Bṛhaspati*; *Utathya* and *Māndhātā*; and more; and several *upākhyāna*—narratives, such as narrative of *Paraśurāma*; *Kekayrāja* and a demon; *Indra* and *Prahlāda*; *Kālakavṛkṣīya* sage, *Janaka* and *Kṣemadarśī*; to quote a few. Through these numerous dialogues and narratives, as *Bhīṣma* tells *Yudhiṣṭhira*, a modern reader can build a large picture of polity and its doctrines—*rājaśāstra*, of ancient India. The very first chapter of the *Mahābhārata's* first canto *Ādi Parva* (1/1/90) eulogizes the *Śānti Parva* as the ultimate fruition of the *Mahābhārata* discourse.

Interestingly, it is not the case that the *Mahābhārata* is the first treatise that talks of state and statesmanship, but as it reports, there had been several great exponents of polity and their treatises as well, prior to the time of the Great War. As *Bhīṣma* says that he just summarized the teachings of the great ancient teachers like *Brahmā*, *Bṛhaspati*, *Viśālākṣa*, *Śukrācārya*, *Indra*, Prācetas Manu, *Bharadvāja*, *Gauraśirā* and others. It shows that ancient Indian lawmakers were significantly careful and industrious about engaging with issues related to the state and public affairs. It was not easy ever to establish a kingdom and rule the masses, as *Māndhātā*—a king much earlier to the time of the *Mahābhārata*—asks Indra as how should he rule his kingdom when it was populated by people of a variety of communities such as *yavana*, *kirāta*, *gāndhāra*, *chīna*, *śabara*, *barbara*, *śaka*, *tuṣāra*, *kaṅka*, *pahlava*, *āndhra*, *madraka*, *paundra*, *pulinda*, *ramaṭha* and *kamboja*, etc., and that too when many of them are engaged in deplorable professions like crime, robbery, etc., how could he engage them on the right path. Indra taught him the *dhārma* such as non-violence, truthfulness, protection of public property and advised him to rule the kingdom without any kind of vengeance.[3] The dialogue indicates the complexity of stately affairs, that too in a time much earlier to the age of Great War. It also shows how teachings of *rājaśāstra* started formulating, in different phases, by different people and with a range of doctrines.

Origin and Nature of Ancient Indian State

The *Śānti Parva* describes the origin of state, its nature, kingship, origin of code and punishment, duties of kings and their numerous matters pertaining to the statecraft. *Yudhiṣṭhira* asks *Bhīṣma* about the origin of state and is also curious as how a person from amongst the populace of a society, and who is like any other ordinary person of that society, becomes a king.[4] *Bhīṣma* replies that, at the start of the society there was no state, no king and no punishment. People were governed and protected by the natural virtues (*dhārma*), but gradually, due to the spread of unrighteousness (*moha*), people's understanding of natural duties and sense of mutual care and protection degraded and *dhārma* vanished.[5] *Bhīṣma* speculates the fundamental vices such as greed (*lobha*), desire (*kāma*) and attachment (*rāga*) as the contours of moral degradation which further led to the loss of the sense of discrimination between what was dutiful and what was not, among men. He describes in detail how moral degradation generated social disorder. As per his interpretation of the mythology, anguished by the social degradation on Earth, the deities went to *Brahmā*[6] and narrated to him their cause of anguish. The *Brahmā* created *Nītiśāstra*—a large treatise of moral code, describing *dhārma*, *ārtha* and *kāma* (*trivarga*) and the fourth was *mokṣa* (liberation or emancipation), the purpose of which was different from the former three. His *Nītiśāstra* also included discourses on epistemology, human action, punishment and most importantly kingship, statecraft, administration, war machinery, strategy and duties of a king. The treatise was received and summarized by several deities and masters and thereby it got into many editions like *Vaiśālakṣa*, *Bāhudantak*, *Bārhaspatya*, etc. After getting the treatise, the deities went to *Viṣṇu* who, after creating numerous *manasa-putra*, created *Vena*, who was given the knowledge of the code and oath for following the *dhārma* with full righteousness. Then, Pṛthu, the son of *Vena* became the king of men.

Pṛthu established *dhārma* on Earth and brought unprecedented prosperity for his people. Different communities of people accepted his authority as king. *Bhīṣma* says:

tena dharmottaraścāyaṁ kṛto loko mahātmanā
rañjitāśca prajāḥ sarvāstena rājeti śabdyate[7]

That is, by virtue of his establishing the *dhārma* and bringing comfort and happiness to his people, he was called a king—*rājā*—who delivers happiness to people. Being protector of people, he was called *kṣatriya*. The term is derived from the root, namely 'ksha' means 'wounds or injury' and the suffix 'trayi' means 'to protect'. The complete significance of the word is that 'one who protects from the injury or wound'.[8] Later on, the term became synonymous to 'warrior' and also designation of the warrior class. *Bhīṣma* further describes that whatever a king does with his mind and action is for the well-being of the subject alone, and there is no other reason but the divine virtues of the king on account of which he received acceptance of his authority by the subject.[9] As the king observes the *dhārma*, rule the subject according to the *dhārma*, he occupies right to punish those who violate the *dhārma*. And that is why the *Nītiśāstra* describes the doctrines of punishment—*daṇḍanīti*. The king is the epitome of *dhārma* and *daṇḍanīti*. By this unique virtue, he is treated as equivalent to deities—*devāśca naradevāśca tulyā iti viśāṁpate*.[10]

On account of above description, it is often held that the *Mahābhārata* propounds a divine origin theory of state.[11] Though such opinion is well grounded, at the same time the great epic also gives reference to certain practices of the *gaṇarājya*—republics, in Indian subcontinent. The *Mahābhārata* describes:

dharmiṣṭhān vyavahārānśca sthāpayantaśca śāstrataḥ
yathāvat pratipaśyanto vivardhante gaṇottamāḥ
putrān bhrātṛn nirgṛhṇanto vinayantaśca tān sadā
vinītānśca pragṛhṇante vivardhante gaṇottamāḥ[12]

That is, the reputed citizens of the republics behave according to *dhārma*, they always see what is right and always tend to progress. They punish their own sons and kin if they deviate from virtues, they educate and counsel them, if they find them righteous then they are accepted and well respected, that is why the republics tend to always progress. This description shows the high standards of conduct of republics and the importance of the citizens. The *Mahābhārata* also recognize the high virtues of the people of republics, they are brave warriors, wise, zealous and always ready to do anything for the progress of the state. They can be subjugated only in case if they act against each other out of anger, or they develop a tendency of pulling each other down. If they are united, there is no external threat that can terrorize them. It shows that the *gaṇa* communities knew the importance of unity and integrity. The republics were governed by prominent people and office bearers. The *Mahābhārata* does not indicate any specific house or dynasty of rulers in case of republics. Rather it indicates that having a strong confederacy, unity, trust and integrity as the only refuge of the republics. If the above virtues collapse, a republic collapses too. It prescribes a maxim for the strength of a republic—*ābhyantaraṁ bhayaṁ rakṣyaṁ asāraṁ vāhyato bhayam*[13]—if internal weakness is taken care of, external threats are meaningless, which applies to the endurance of any kind of state and statecraft.

The state needs certain grounds and efforts for its endurance. *Bhīṣma* further preaches *Yudhiṣṭhira* lessons from his predecessors'[14] on *rājaśāstra* (polity). They all taught protection and well-being of the subject as prime aim and *raison d'être* of the state. *Bhīṣma* says[15] deployment of information machinery and espionage, deployment of ambassadors to other states, timely and well payment of the officers and servants, rational taxation, non-confiscation of public property, keeping experienced and wise people in the councils, bravery, truthfulness and skill, helping the poor, rational use of punishment, possession and collection of objects and goods of utility, taking counsel only from wise men, giving suitable rewards and honours for the morale of the military, engaged contemplation of the welfare of the subject, enrichment of the treasure, protection of the cities and other settlements, conscious avoidance of any kind of grouping among people or council, and adherence to the *nītidhārma* are the indispensable factors for the endurance of a state.

Significantly, *Bhīṣma* gives much importance to quality of mind of the bureaucrats and kings who run the gigantic machinery of state:

rājyaṁ hi sumahat tantraṁ dharyate na akṛtātmabhiḥ
na śakyaṁ mṛdunā vodhumāyāsasthānamuttamaṁ[16]

A state is a huge machinery, and one who has not controlled one's mind cannot run the machinery. Cruel and unrighteous kings cannot control it. Even the tender-hearted ones cannot run it. For them, statecraft becomes a complex affair. A good king should have both the qualities, tenderness and toughness, and have a sense of timely use of the qualities.

A number of instruments for running of the statecraft and for the protection of state have been prescribed in the *Śānti Parva*, such as measures for confidence of ministers, appointment of ambassadors, qualities of princes, establishment of intelligence machinery, types of counselling, uses of diplomacy, types of treaties (such as *vitta-sandhi*, *satkāra-sandhi* and *bhaya-sandhi*), occasion and methods concurring enemies, three types of victories (*dhārma vijaya, ārtha vijaya* and *āsura vijaya*), classification and characteristics of ministers, states, forts, armies, treasure, etc., components and flanks of an army, different formations of army flanks and warfare. It also talks of certain subtle governance practices (*sūkṣma vyavahāra*) such as *kaṇṭaka-śodhana*—removal of obliterating factors and people from the governing machinery, right efforts and wisdom of right use of money and saving.

The *Śānti Parva* holds clearly that a state is run on wealth. That is why the *koṣa*—treasure—becomes an integral part of a state. For the *koṣa*, suitable taxation system is often mentioned in the treaties. It gives the analogy of a cow and honeybees. As milk is taken from a cow, protection of the cow is also obligatory; as honeybees take a little amount of nectar from several flowers, similarly a king should see his taxation principle. The purpose of taxation is to protect the subject.[17] In a dialogue between *Arjuna* and *Yudhiṣṭhira*, *Arjuna* says that without wealth there cannot be a kingdom; one cannot rule it and nurture *dhārma* either. It is the wealth that helps *dhārma* progress. He connects the acquisition, possession and right use of wealth with stately duties.[18] Therefore, right taxation is inevitable for the protection and well-being of people; for right action and *yajña*—religious rites; and for the endurance of the kingdom. The *Śānti Parva* prescribes that a maximum of one-sixth of people's income can be taken towards taxes and that too for the purpose of common good.

Kingship—the *Rājadhārma*

A state cannot exist without king and codes. The king's prime duty is to protect the people and work for their well-being. Despite presenting a monarchic model of state and kingship, the chief characteristic of the *Śānti Parva*'s polity is that it puts *dhārma* and people at the centre, not the king or the state. If people's well-being is ignored and *dhārma* (which is the integral principle of virtue, dutifulness and justice) is violated, both state and king fail. The *Śānti Parva* clearly states: *rājyaṁ sarvāmiṣaṁ nityamārjaveneha dhāryate,* [19] that is, state is a common property and it is for all and kings must keep it with purity and simplicity. It is clear that state is never treated as end in itself, it has an instrumental value. Given the nature of the state, the protection of state becomes the essential duty of kings. The great epic says:

yadyapyasti vipattiḥ syāt rakṣmāṇsya vai prajā
so'pyasya vipulo dharma evaṁvṛttā hi bhūmipāḥ[20]

That is, even if the king puts himself in a great peril or dies while protecting the subject, it will earn great merit to him, and that would rather be a standard of the kings.

A king is known by his excellence in the knowledge of and conduct according to the *dhārma*. If a washerman does not know how to wash or dye clothes he cannot be called a washerman; similarly, a king who does not know how to wash the errors of his conduct is not a good king.[21] The goodness of king lies in spreading of goodness in his dominion too. The *Śānti Parva* says that when a huge tree grows, it becomes shelter for a variety of birds and creatures; in the same way, a good king becomes shelter for a variety of skilled people. He protects good people and scholars and punishes criminals. If criminals roam around the kingdom freely, that means the king is overpowered by evil. To establish law and order, a king should distribute departments among able ministers as per their merit and does not humiliate them for their ignorable mistakes; when he does not forgive his own son for his folly; when he grants poor people social security; when he protects traders like his own family; in whom there reside both *nigraha* and *anugraha* powers; when he respects his priests and teachers; the king is said to have behaved according to the *rājādhārma*.[22] A king is compared with 1,000-eyed Indra[23]—*sahasrākṣa*—a symbolic of having knowledge of everything that happens in his territory, and also of having knowledge of *dhārma* and *daṇḍanīti*. A king is also prescribed to treat *dhārma* as above *arthasiddhi*—acquisition of wealth and growth in economy.

***Rājādhārma* and *varṇadhārma*:** Superiority of *rājadhārma* over *varṇadhārma* is emphatically held by the great epic in several chapters of its *Śānti Parva*[24] for the reason that observance of the *varṇadhārma* is possible only when the kings duly observe their *rājādhārma*. *Rājādhārma* or *kṣātradhārma* is also said to be superior to all other *dhārma* because if *kṣātradhārma* is not observed properly, the entire subject will be destroyed. The great epic defines *rājādhārma* as foundational to all *dhārma* as all other *dhārma* and professions of all other *varṇa* progress in assistance with the *rājādhārma* only.[25] All the *dhārma* residing in people of various professions gets nourished and realizes their climax of progress in assistance with *rājādhārma*.[26] When people of all *varṇa* and in all *āśhrama* perform their duties and since their residing in their own *dhārma* and performance of the duties are protected and assisted by kings, the kings' duties—*rājādhārma*—naturally earns greater merit than all of them.[27]

The *Śānti Parva* give significant weightage and emphasis to the purity of mind while performing the *rājādhārma* and dispensing *daṇḍa*. The purity of mind is explained in terms of its being bereft of attachment, personal affinity and hatred, vengeance or abhorrence and undue favour or biasness. *Bhīṣma*, through a beautiful metaphor, defines *rājādhārma*:

dharme sthitā sattvavīryā dharmasetuvatārakā
tyāgavātādhvagā śīghrā naustaṁ santārayiṣyati[28]

That is, *rājādhārma* is like a boat, the boat is rowed in the ocean of *dhārma*. The *sattva-guṇa* (the purer properties of mind) is the main mast; *dharmaśāstra* is the rope to be tied with it, sacrifice (*tyāga*) is the force of wind that helps sail the boat rapidly. The boat, if rowed properly, will help the king sail through the ocean of the world. The metaphor demonstrates all important components of an ideal state and the duties of the king accordingly. If the king fails to discharge any of them, the *rājādhārma* is obliterated. And that is why the kings are advised to keep all the modifications of mind (*cittavṛtti*) annihilated, maintain the utmost equipoise of mind, and keep purity on mind and senses (*antaḥkaraṇa*) for the sake of proper care and protection of people. *Ātmā jeyaḥ sadā rājñā tato jeyāśca śatravaḥ*[29]—a king should first conquer his own mind and later the enemies is the hallmark of the kings' conduct. If a king has not been able to overcome the mental weaknesses, he will not be able to conquer his enemies.

King—the indispensable: The importance of a king for the state is emphasized time and again. It is held in the *Śānti Parva* that where there is no king there is no *dhārma*, where there is no *dhārma* there is no social order. Without a king there prevails anarchy. It is the duty of people of a state to install a king for the protection of *dhārma* and social order. The miseries of anarchy are enumerated exhaustively to establish the inevitability of a good king. Similarly, there is no limit of merits when there is a good king in the state. The kingship is glorified as embodiment of people; king is the greater heart of people, their respect and happiness.[30] On the other hand, kings are prescribed to rule the subject with utmost control over senses, and with truth and harmony.

Despite glorifying the virtues of gallantry, evoking king's readiness for conquering the enemy and vast lessons on warfare, management of military, its supplies and intelligence, the *Śānti Parva* cautions the kings from being a war monger. *Varjanīyaṁ sadā yuddhaṁ rājyakāmena dhīmatā*[31]—a wise king should try his best to avoid war, for peaceful coexistence and for the welfare of people. This is a directive for kings. Being the supreme official of the judicial machinery, a king should always listen carefully to both the petitioner and the accused, and dispense justice without any bias. In the process, he should also seek counsel from the wise scholars appointed for the purpose in his court. Accumulation of all needful properties; just taxation; facilitation agriculture, husbandry, etc., construction of public infrastructure, wells, hospitals, etc., proper arrangement of medicines; fortification and deployment of soldiers, promotion of scholarship and skills, etc., are all enumerated as part of the duties of kings. If the aforesaid logistics are not well taken care of, people suffer and the *rājādhārma* is obliterated. Since, a king is accountable for everything that happens in his kingdom, if people commit crime the king also earns sins.[32] It shows that the king has to establish a just order and be always careful to protect it through right use of *daṇḍa*. It also works as a principle of check and control as people will not appreciate a king who is unable to establish order in society.

Observing the *dhārma* is not different from the *rājādhārma*. A king who protects and observes the *dhārma* becomes the embodiment of the *dhārma*. If a king walks away from *dhārma*, he is called a sinner.[33] If a king does not protect his people from wrongdoers and does not annihilate sinful tendencies from society, people incur great fear and the kingship also comes under fear of its sudden loss. People lose trust in a king bereft of his *dhārma*. *Dhārma* is the directive principle of *Śānti Parva*'s state policy. It defines the king, 'one in whom the *dhārma* resides is called a king; and the king who has dropped his *dhārma* the deities call him *vṛṣala*—fallen from *dhārma*.'[34] *Dhārma* is therefore both directive and imperative to the kings.

Two powers of the king—*nigraha* and *anugraha*: As stated earlier, *nigraha*—the power to command and control, and *anugraha*—the power of compassion—are two basic powers or strengths of a good king. Through *nigraha*, he punishes the criminals, traitors, miscreants and unscrupulous servants and officials; and through *anugraha*, he wins the trust of his people, ministers, scholars and teachers. *Nigraha* is called a special strength only when the right to use *daṇḍa* is exercised judiciously. An impertinent use of *daṇḍa* does not portray the *nigraha-śakti* of a king. The qualities of *nigraha* and *anugraha* are time and again emphasized in the *Śānti Parva*:

vyaktaścānugraho yasya yathārthścāpi nigrahaḥ
guptātmā guptarāṣṭraśca sa rājā rājadharmavit[35]

That is, a king who keeps compassion upon all subjects and whose *nigraha* is used on justified grounds that king is able to protect himself and the kingdom as well and is said to have knowledge of *rājadhārma*. It is clear that the above verse uses adjective *vyakta* (expressed) for *anugraha*, that is, the king's compassion should always express and be upon people, but *nigraha* has to be *yathārtha*—realistic and upon due examination of facts and truth.

***Āpaddhārma* of a king:** *Āpaddhārma* (*āpat* + *dhārma*) is a term used for what is dutiful in a situation of crisis and described in the *Śānti Parva* many ways. A king, when in crisis, is though not supposed to relinquish his *dhārma*, yet granted certain relaxations by the ancient lawmakers and great sages. *Āpat* or *āpatti* is an extraordinary and emergency situation when law and order fails for numerous reasons. The *āpatti* of a king or kingdom is when it is encircled by enemies; king's own people start betraying him; military and wealth are destroyed; when ministers go unscrupulous; then the *āpaddhārma* of a king is to use his wisdom in the best way. Through right means only should he increase his wealth, as upon the loss of wealth the strength of a king is lost. A king may impose additional taxation and take voluntary donations from people, provided he suitably does good to the people when good time comes. A king can also confiscate wealth of anyone excepting of *Brāhmaṇs* and ascetics.[36] In the detailed description of *āpaddhārma*, the *Śānti Parva* justifies such acts of the kings on the ground that if the state is protected, it will be possible for the king to reproduce happiness for the people. The *āpaddhārma* may also be justified on the *Śānti Parva*'s principle of flexibility, as it says 'in response to time and place what is proper may become improper and what is improper may become proper'.[37]

Code and Doctrine of Punishment—the *Daṇḍanīti*

In the *nītiśāstra* of *Brahmā*, the four *puruṣārtha* (*trivarga* and *mokṣa*) are enumerated which serve as the bases of all codes of life and all succeeding formulators of *nīti* drew inspiration from it. The group of the six—*ātmā*, *deśa*, *kāla*, *upāya*, *kārya* and *sahāyaka*—are enumerated as cause of progress and prosperity when used in the light of the code—*nīti*.[38] A king is supposed to have thorough knowledge of *daṇḍanīti*, rather the *Śanti Parva* claims that, 'after exhausting all merits (*puṇya*) in heaven, one descends to Earth and born as *daṇḍanīti-viśārada*—a king who is a great exponent of *daṇḍanīti*'.[39]

According to *Bhīṣma*, in the *nītiśāstra* of *Brahmā* the *daṇḍa* is as fundamental as code. *Bhīṣma* says:

trayī cānvīkṣikī caiva vārtā ca bharatarṣabhaḥ
daṇḍanītiśca vipulā vidyāstatra nidarśitā[40]

Trayī (three *Vedās* containing rituals), *ānvīkṣikī* (method of inquiry—epistemology), *vārtā* (agriculture, animal husbandry and trade) and *daṇḍanīti* (doctrines of punishment) are discussed in it. This is the broad classification of subject matters or schema of discourse under which a number of issues are discussed. *Daṇḍanīti*, however, literally means 'doctrine of punishment', but a range of affairs such as general governance, establishment of code and judicial procedures, communication, methods of settlement of disputes, etc., are included under this head. *Daṇḍa* is also enumerated among one of the five (*sāma, dāma, daṇḍa, bheda* and *upekṣā*) measures of protection of the state and running of the statecraft.

It is strongly held in *Śanti Parva* that *daṇḍa* is essential for governance and social order:

daṇḍena sahitā hyeṣā lokarakṣaṇakārikā
nigrahānugraharatā lokānanucariṣyati
daṇḍena nīyate cedaṁ daṇḍaṁ nayati vā punaḥ
dañḍanītiritikhyātā trīṅllokānabhivartate[41]

That is, *daṇḍa* protects the world, it is to restrain the antisocial elements and to protect the noble public, it puts the masses on the path of righteousness, and kings rule their kingdom according to the *daṇḍanīti*. This is the essential science for war and peace. It has large contribution in spreading of right conduct among masses. The *Śanti Parva* alludes that the order of the *varṇa* and *āśhrama* (*varṇāśhrama dhārma*) is also dependent upon the success of the *daṇḍanīti*:

majjet trayī daṇḍanītau hatāyāṁ
sarve dharmāḥ prakṣayeyurvibuddhāḥ
sarve darmāścāśramāṇāṁ hatāḥ syuḥ
kṣātre tyakte rājadharme purāṇe[42]

That is, if the *daṇḍanīti* perishes the *Vedās* will perish, if *Vedās* perish all the *dhārma* will perish (hence, *rājadhārma* will also perish), and if *rājadhārma* (also called *kṣātradhārma*) perishes the *āśhrama dhārma* will also perish. It suggests that the *Śanti Parva*'s *daṇḍanīti* does not prescribe uniform principles of treatment and punishment for the people. The punishments' principles are not only based upon the degree of violation of code—the *nīti*—but also vary according to the *varṇāśhrama dhārma*. Interestingly, the *Śanti Parva* proclaims that the *śūdra* are not punishable:

vāco daṇdo brāhmaṅānāṁ kṣatriyāṇāṁ bhujārpaṇaṁ
dānadaṇḍā smṛitā vaiśyā nirdaṇḍaḥ śūdra uccyate[43]

That is, *vāgdaṇḍa* (verbal punishment like public criticism, reprimand, etc.) is prescribed for *Brāhmaṇs*, a *kṣatriya* has to render suitable service in proportion to violation of code, a *vaiśya* is imposed monitory penalty and *śūdra* should not be punished.[44] The *Śanti Parva* sometimes also mentions that *Brāhmaṇa (Brāhmaṇs)* are also exempted from punishment.[45]

***Vyavahāra* and *bhartṛpratyayalakṣaṇa*:** *Daṇḍa* is also called *vyavahāra*[46] and the kings are prescribed to use the *vyavahāra* keeping a complete detachment from his personal preferences or hatred, liking or disliking and with an unbiased attitude. When a king uses *daṇḍa* in such a way, it becomes *dhārma* nevertheless. If *daṇḍa* is used rightly it naturally protects *trivarga—dhārma, ārtha* and *kāma*. The *Śanti Parva* glorifies *daṇḍa* as protector of social order and says if there is no *daṇḍa*, 'might is right' will prevail in society and people will destroy each other.[47] The great epic also claims that *daṇḍa* is a divine grant to the kings, that is, the authority to probe conflicts among people or examine allegations and dispense punishment (*daṇḍa*) is a prerogative granted by God (*Īśvara*) to the kings, the purpose of which is to protect the *dhārma*.[48] *Daṇḍa* is also called *bhartṛpratyayalakṣaṇa*[49] (ways of examining allegations) on account of its being based upon examination of the allegations against the culprit. It shows that punishment was not supposed to be dispensed blindly or on account of public perception or rumours, but only after a thorough examination of the allegation.

The *Śanti Parva*, through a mythological narrative, explains what will happen if there was no *daṇḍa*. According to the narrative, once *daṇḍa* disappeared from governance, as a result of which *varṇa*-order collapsed, people forgot the distinction between what was dutiful and right and what was not; what was eatable and what not; people started killing each other for petty reasons; public property was possessed by mighty people; and then prevailed a total social chaos[50]; then *Brahmā* requested *Viṣṇu*[51] to reveal and re-establish *daṇḍa* on Earth. The narrative indirectly advocates the importance of *daṇḍa* in governance for maintenance of social order. The *Śanti Parva* cautions[52] the kings time and again to use the *daṇḍa* judiciously and according to the *dhārma—bhūmipālo yathā nyāyaṁ vartetāneva dharmavit*. If the *daṇḍa* is not used judiciously, the kings lose their moral right to use it.

The treatise also gives details as how can one use the *daṇḍa* judiciously. It tells several sources of correct knowledge—*prameyasiddhi*, such as *pratyakṣa* (perception), *anumāna* (inference), *upamāna* (analogy), *āgama* (testimony), *arthāpatti* (postulation or presumption), *aitihya* (heritage or history), *samśaya* (doubt), *nirṇaya* (conclusion or decision), *ākṛti* (form or appearance), *saṅketa* (hint or sign), *gati* (motion or movement), *ceṣṭā* (inclination), *pratijñā* (resolve), *hetu* (cause or reason), *udāharaṇa* (example), *upanaya* (application) and *nigamana* (conclusion or derivation). A king should know these instruments of correct knowledge, or at least the first two, to become able to use the *daṇḍanīti* appropriately.[53] This is sheer evidence that kings have to learn a lot and be wise enough to be accomplished in *daṇḍanīti*.

Conclusion

Based upon the above discussion, it can be said that the *Mahābhārata* gives a vast account of views and practices pertaining to state, its executive and judicial functions, importance of a righteous king and the role of *daṇḍa*. The treatise depicts vast relationship among people, among the king and the subject and nature and man. The discourse begins with building a case with moral degradation of people in the *state of nature* and the need generated thereupon for a ruler who can re-establish the moral order. With the ruler there comes the state, its complicated machinery and a range of people and principles to run it. It would again demand a high moral standard and uprightness of the functionaries and the king himself. That is why there comes unending lessons of *rājaśāstra*. The discourse reveals an inherent paradox in the existence of state; on one hand it seeks its *raison d'être* in moral degradation in the *state of nature* and on the other hand it demands moral uprightness to run the machinery, almost as a prerequisite. That is why the discourse lays its conclusive focus on conquering the mind.

The kind of monarchy depicted in the great treatise may prompt one to hurriedly compare it with those which existed in medieval or pre-modern European world. No doubt, a king is the major centre of attraction in the *Mahābhārata* statecraft, but he does not seem to become a despot as he has a large range of considerations before his choices and decision-making. And the non-violation of *dhārma* occupies centrality among those considerations. A *Mahābhārata* king appears helpless in front of his council and councillors, the demands of the *rājādhārma*, wrath of people and sages, and forces of nature and internal insurgencies. There is no wonder that a king would always long for taking refuge in the forest for austerity having handed over the kingship to a suitable successor.

Summary

The *Śānti Parva* of *Mahābhārata* covers a range of political scientific issues, many of which constitute relevant field of discourse in contemporary political terms. It gives a vast framework of society and its structure, in which the people get their significant due. The proposed kingship does not sound tyrant or autocratic as the guiding principle—the *rājādhārma*—is always overarching the kingship. Although kingship is inevitable like a hub of the wheel of statecraft, it is always controlled by the *rājādhārma*, without which the kingship does not find its own definition. The political thoughts of *Śānti Parva* are formulated in a society with social stratification, with *varṇa*, *āśhrama* and a variety of clans and communities; the state and kingship endeavour their best to suit the aspirations of all, without any attempt to homogenize the society. And that is why it recognizes the social, religious and community entitlements of all strata of society; it endeavours to protect all professions excepting for those ignoble; and it facilitates different professions of people as per requirements. Given the case, different treatment for different professions of people, such as traders, warriors, priests, ascetics, craftsmen, etc., does not seem to be injudicious. The modern principles of equality also recognize the justified discrimination, what we call *principle of difference* in John Rawls' terminology. Accordingly, the state without much efforts recognizes and give due treatment to social, cultural and ethnic variety.

The state's prerogative of judicial rights and dispensing punishment is also tied with strict chain of *daṇḍanīti*. If a king violates the *daṇḍanīti*, he loses his own moral right to use it. The king's glory does not come that much from his gallantry or victory in war as it comes from his following the *dhārma* and *daṇḍanīti*. His prime task is to protect and uplift people, assist people pursue their *dhārma* and facilitate progress in their respective professions. His *āpaddhārma* is also tied with strict conditions and promises, and is not beyond the *rājādhārma*. One may ask what the guarantee of people's rights and entitlements is if a king tends to violate them all out of his own wild will. As per the total narrative of *Śānti Parva*, one can clearly see that such a king would lose public support, trust and loyalty of their ministers, and hence lose the habitual obedience of the masses, which is a key necessity of his kingship. His power to control people (*nigraha śakti*) would be lost as he would have already lost his compassion (*anugraha śakti*) by his wild will. The most important thing that the *Śānti Parva* teaches is that it keeps people in the centre of political affairs. The state is not an end in itself; rather it only has an instrumental value—instrumental in the well-being of people.

Points for Discussion

1. Do you think that *Śānti Parva* is an accord on political obligation and political values in ancient India? Justify your answer.
2. 'King is self-disciplined' in *Śānti Parva*. Discuss the attributes of *Veda Vyāsa's* ideal king in the light of this statement.
3. Critically evaluate the notion of *Rājādhārma* in *Śānti Parva* with special reference to the duties of the king.
4. Examine the *daṇḍanīti* of the *Śānti Parva* in the light of modern theories of punishment.
5. Do you agree that the attributes of *Rājādhārma* given in *Śānti Parva* are relevant in modern context? Discuss.

Endnotes

1. James Mill (History of British India, 1818), Ernest Barker, Hegel (The Philosophy of History), Max Weber (1958) 'there was no natural order of men and things in contrast to positive social order. There was no sort of natural law...All the problems which the concept of natural law called into being in the Occident were completely lacking.' (Weber 2012).
2. Derrett (1968, 100). Op. cit. p. 5. Bhattacharya (1993, 3–24).
3. 65/13-31, Shastri (2001, 4591–4592).
4. 59/5-12, ibid. p. 4570.
5. 59/14-16, ibid. p. 4570.
6. As per *Hindu* mythology, *Brahmā* is an elderly deity, called *pitāmaha* (grandfather) of all deities, and creator of the universe and different realms of existence. Deities would visit him for any situation of crisis or problem that they were unable to address, hoping that the *Brahmā* will have some solution or advice for their problems.
7. 59/125, Shastri (2001, 4577). However, there are several other words used to designate the hierarchy in kingship, such as *rājā/rājan, viśāṁpati, mahārāja, samrāṭ*, etc. As Hemchandra Raychaudhury has mentioned that in *Mahābhārata* Kṛṣṇa is lauded as *samrāṭ, virāṭ, svarāṭ* and *sura-rāja*. He further suggests that, as per *Śatapatha Brāhmaṇa*, one gets designation of *rājā* having performed the *rājasūya* sacrifice, and *samrāṭ* having performed *vājapeya* sacrifice (Raychaudhury 1996, 141).
8. *Mahābhārata, Śānti Parva* 59.1.25, p. 383, Sharma and Singh (2010, 383–398).
9. 59/130, Shastri (2001, 4577).
10. 59/144, ibid. p. 4578.
11. However, it is vastly debated; as R. S. Sharma says that 'the Cardinal Supposition of *Śānti Parva* in Chapter 67 is the appropriate theory of origin of state. It is scientific because it involves the King and people. The people's obligation to pay taxes and render military services to the King clearly implies the presence of the elements of *Koṣa* and *Daṇḍa*. Thus, four important elements of the state out of seven can be distinctly discerned in the statement of the contract theory of the origin of the state,' and Altekar observes that 'the state was regarded as a divine institution; the King's right to govern was partly due to his divine creation and partly due to the agreement of the subjects to be governed by him, in order to terminate anarchy.' Op. cit. p. 80, Garg (2004, 77–86).
12. 107/17-18, Shastri (2001, 4700–4701).
13. 107/28, ibid. p. 4701.
14. 58/2-4, ibid. p. 4567, enumerates Viśālākṣa, Śukrācārya, Indra, Prācetas Manu, Bharadvāja and Gauraśira as notable ancient teachers of polity—exponents of *rājaśāstra*.
15. 58/5-12, ibid. pp. 4567–4568.
16. 58/21, ibid. p. 4568.
17. 120/33-34, ibid. p. 4730.

18. 8/3-22, ibid. pp. 4438–4440.
19. 58/22, ibid. p. 4569.
20. 58/23, ibid. p. 4569.
21. 91/2-5, ibid. p. 4659.
22. 91/26-43, ibid. pp. 4660–4661.
23. Indra is an important *Vedic* deity and the king of all deities in the realm of heaven, who is of *kṣatriya varṇa*, hence worshiped by *kṣatriya* and kings for victory in war.
24. Eg. 63/23-27, Shastri (2001, 4586–4587).
25. 65/6, ibid. p. 4590.
26. 65/12, ibid. p. 4591.
27. 66/41, ibid. p. 4595.
28. 66/37, ibid. p. 4594.
29. 69/4, ibid. p. 4601.
30. 68/58-60, ibid. p. 4601.
31. 69/23, ibid. p. 4603.
32. 75/8, ibid. p. 4619.
33. 90/5-10, ibid. pp. 4656–4657.
34. 90/15, ibid. p. 4657.
35. 120/31, ibid. p. 4730.
36. 130/1-20, ibid. pp. 4753–4754.
37. *Shanti Parva*, 79. 31. Op. cit. pp. 12–13, Bhattacharya (1993, 3–24).
38. 59/30-32, Shastri (2001, 4571).
39. 59/133, ibid. p. 4578.
40. 59/33, ibid. p. 4571.
41. 59/77-78, ibid. p. 4574. The description is also similar to the Arjuna's statement that *daṇḍa* protects the subject, even when all fell asleep the *daṇḍa* is awake and that is why wise men call it as *dhārma* of kings (15/2, ibid. p. 4454).
42. 63/28, ibid. p. 4587.
43. 50/9, ibid. p. 4454.
44. Such a description cannot be taken as accidental occurrence as *Mahābhārata* also lays that a person who kills a *śūdra* is a sinner (34/7, ibid. p. 4507) and *śūdra* are prescribed lesser religious obligations and lesser expiation (*prāyaścita*) too (35/32-34, ibid. p. 4511).
45. *adaṇḍyatvaṁ ca viprāṇāṁ yuktyā daṇḍanipātanam*, 59/69, ibid. p. 4574.
46. 121/8-9, ibid. p. 4733.
47. 121/34, ibid. p. 4734.
48. 121/42, ibid. p. 4734.
49. 121/50, ibid. p. 4735.
50. 122/19-21, ibid. p. 4737; also see 65/24, ibid., p. 4591, which suggests that is *daṇḍanīti* is destroyed (due to its injudicious use), the *rājādhārma* is also negated and as a result people forget the distinction between what is dutiful and what is not.
51. *Viṣṇu* is an important *Vedic* deity who is responsible for sustenance of creation and establishment of social order on Earth.
52. For example, 122/54, Shastri (2001, 4739).
53. 24/10-11, ibid. p. 4473.

Glossary

***Anugraha Śakti*:** The capacity of a king to extend protection and welfare to people.

***Āpaddhārma*:** The duties and entitlements of a king in the situation of emergency.

***Arthasiddhi*:** Acquisition of wealth/economic growth.

Bhartṛpratyayalakṣaṇa: The ways of examining allegations.

Daṇḍanīti: The principles of examination of allegations and dispensing punishment.

Daṇḍanīti-viśārada: One who is a great master of *daṇḍanīti*.

Dhārma: The general moral code proscribed in various *śāstra* and also the natural law.

Gaṇarājya: A republic, that is, which is ruled by council of elected members/elected king.

Janapada: A province, the initial form of state, which had its own governance.

Kaṇṭaka-śodhana: Removal of obliterating factors from the government machinery.

Kṣātradhārma: The duties of a *kṣatriya*, that is, to protect people.

Mahābhārata: A great epic authored by *Veda Vyāsa*; a great war.

Nigraha Śakti: The capacity of a king to dispense punishment.

Nītiśāstra: An ancient treatise authored by *Brahmā* prescribing moral codes; moral philosophy.

Puruṣārtha: The four cardinal virtues, that is, *dhārma*, *ārtha*, *kāma* and *mokṣa*.

Rājādhārma: Duties and obligations of a king.

Trivarga: First three *puruṣārtha—dhārma*, *ārtha* and *kāma* (*mokṣa* was added later on).

Varṇa: The four *varṇa* of ancient Indian society: *brāhmaṇa, kṣatriya, vaiśya, śūdra.*

Varṇadhārma: The duties of the *varṇa* as per their station in society; their professional morality.

Vyavahāra: The *daṇḍanīti* is also known as *vyavahāra*.

References

Bhattacharya, Sibesh. 1993, December. 'Pluralism and Visible Path (Pratyaksha Marga) and Early Indian Idea of Polity.' *Social Scientist* 21(12): 3–24.

Derrett, J. D. M. 1968. *Religion, Law and the State in India*, 100. London: Faber & Faber.

Garg, Sushma. 2004, January–March. 'Political Ideas of Śānti Parva.' *The Indian Journal of Political Science* 65(1): 77–86.

Raychaudhury, Hemchandra. 1996. *Political History of Ancient India*. Oxford: Oxford University Press (First published in 1923 by University of Calcutta).

Sharma, Susheel Kumar, & Vinod Kumar Singh. 2010, April–June. 'Indian Idea of Kingship.' *The Indian Journal of Political Science* 71(2): 383–398.

Shastri, Ramnarayandatta (Tr. in Hindi). 2001. *Mahābhārata*, Vol. V (*Śānti Parva*). Gorakhpur: Gita Press.

Weber, Max. 2012. *The Religion of India: The Sociology of Hinduism and Buddhism*. New Delhi: Munshiram Manoharlal Pub. (Originally Published in 1958 by Free Press).

Further Readings

Altekar, A. S. 1949, 2001. *State and Government in Ancient India*. Delhi, Varanasi: Motilal Banarsidass.

Badrinath, Chaturvedi. 2006. *The Mahabharata: An Inquiry into Human Condition*. New Delhi: Orient Longman.

Das, Gurcharan. 2012. *Difficulty of Being Good*. New Delhi: Penguin.

McGrath, Kevi, and Gregory Nagy. 2017. *Raja Yudhisthira: Kingship in Epic Mahabharata*. Hyderabad: Orient BlackSwan.

Raychaudhury, Hemchandra. 1996. *Political History of Ancient India*. Oxford: Oxford University Press (First published in 1923 by University of Calcutta).

Shastri, Ramnarayandatta (Tr. in Hindi). 2001 *Mahābhārata*, Vol. I (*Ādi Parva*, etc.). Gorakhpur: Gita Press.

11 CHAPTER

Kauṭilya: A Pragmatic Thinker

Ramakrushna Pradhan

CHAPTER OUTLINE

- **Introduction**
- **The Life Sketch**
- ***Arthaśāstra*: Science of Statecraft**
- ***Dhārma* and *Daṇḍanīti***
- ***Saptanga* Theory of State**
- **Theory of *Mandala***
- **Foreign Policy**
- **Ethics and Politics**
- **Kauṭilya and Machiavelli**
- **Conclusion**
- **Summary**
- **Points for Discussion**

Prajaa Sukhe Sukham Rajyah, Prajanam Cha Hiteh Hitam (In the welfare and happiness of the people lies the king's welfare and happiness).

—Kauṭilya (Chanakya Nīti)

Reader's Guide

We all know that an effective and pragmatic leadership is a sine qua non in statecraft. This chapter thus is an attempt to peep inside and ponder the real political persona of Kauṭilya better known as Chanakya. It provides a vivid account of Kauṭilya with an emphasis on his treatise on *Arthaśāstra*, *dhārma* and *daṇḍanīti*, *saptanga* theory of state, ethics and politics and theory of *mandala*.

Introduction

Kauṭilya, the great diplomat, was the minister in the Kingdom of Chandragupta Maurya during 317 BC–293 BC. He has been considered as one of the shrewdest ministers of the times and has explained his views on state, war, social structures, diplomacy, ethics, politics and statecraft very clearly in his book called *Arthaśāstra*. The Mauryan Empire was larger than the later British India which expanded from the Indian Ocean to Himalayas and up to Iran in the West. After Alexander left India, this was the most powerful kingdom in India and Kauṭilya was minister who advised the King.

Before Kauṭilya, there were other philosophers in India who composed the *Śhāstras*, but Kauṭilya's work was robust and encompassed all other treaties written previously. This chapter considers Kauṭilya for three reasons. First, it wants to highlight the patterns of thinking in the East long before Machiavelli who wrote his *Prince*. Second, Kauṭilya's ideologies on state, statecraft and ethics are very realistic and vastly applicable in today's context. Third, it feels Kauṭilya's work on diplomacy is greatly underrepresented in the Western world and is quite apt to analyse his work in that area.

Kauṭilya's work is primarily a book of political realism where state is paramount and king shall carry out duties as advised in his book to preserve his state. Kauṭilya's work is so deep rooted in realism that he goes to describe the gory and brutal means a king must adopt to be in power. This could have been one reason why *Ashoka*, the grandson of Chandragupta Maurya whom Kauṭilya advised, renounced violence and war thus taking the path of *dhārma* or morals.

This chapter will primarily focus on Kauṭilya's thoughts on war, diplomacy and ethics. A section in this chapter has been devoted to compare Kauṭilya with great philosophers like Aristotle and Machiavelli. Kauṭilya's work is then seen in the light of today's politics and ethics. As Max Weber puts it aptly in his lecture, 'Politics as a Vocation', he said Machiavelli's work was harmless when compared to Kauṭilya's *Arthaśāstra*.

The Life Sketch

Kauṭilya, better known as Chanakya and less known as Vishnu Gupta, was a pragmatic thinker. Historically speaking, he was the Prime Minister of King Chandragupta Maurya and the founder of realist paradigm in Indian political tradition. A practical statesman, Kauṭilya could be able to solve the problems confronting the world. His monumental work *Arthaśāstra* is a practical manual of statecraft and administration not only for the Mauryan times but for all times and for any kingdom. For that reason, many used to compare and call him as the Machiavelli of India. In fact, in political tradition the name of Kauṭilya comes much before Machiavelli. It would not be an exaggeration to call Kauṭilya as the father of Indian political traditions and Machiavelli as Italian Kauṭilya. In simple words, he is an Indian teacher, philosopher, statesman, economist, jurist and a royal advisor.

Born to a poor maga *Brāhmaṇa* family in the village of Chanak in the Gola district of Magadh, Kauṭilya was called Chanaky by his father's name *Ṛiṣhi* Chanak while the title Kauṭilya derived from his gotra 'Kotil'. It is believed that Kauṭilya studied in Takshashila in 325 BC (Das and Patro 1995). His father *Ṛiṣhi* Chanak was also a teacher, after whom he came to be known as Chanakya.

Ṛiṣhi Chanak, being a teacher himself, understood the importance of education and, hence, he started teaching his son Kauṭilya in early age. He had extensively studied *Vedās*, mathematics, geography and science along with religion. Right from his childhood, Kauṭilya's wisdom and shrewdness were visible and effective. His favourite subject was politics.

He received his education at the University of Nalanda. After completion of education, he started teaching in Takshashila at Nalanda University. It is believed that in this University, Kauṭilya met Chandragupta Maurya who had come there for education. He developed a very good impression about Chandragupta and was convinced that he had all the qualities to be a true king. During this time, Kauṭilya left for Pataliputra—a prosperous city ruled by *Dhanananda*—on an assignment to become the President of Sungha or Trust which was controlled by Royal charity. However, *Dhanananda* removed him without any reason. Utterly insulted by this move, Kauṭilya promised him to dethrone. He nurtured Chandragupta with this aim and defeated *Dhanananda* only to establish the famous Mauryan empire ushering a golden era in Indian history. Unfortunately, the details about Kauṭilya's life education and career are unknown. What was told to us to be genuine is not proper. Hence, the only reliable source is the tradition and history which proclaims that Kauṭilya was the religious preacher and *guru* of the mighty king Chandragupta Maurya of Magadha.

Although Kauṭilya is known for his masterpiece *Arthaśāstra*, his glory extends far and wide with monumental writings like *Arthaśāstra* and *Nītiśāstra* which are also known as Chanakya *Nīti*. All works of Kauṭilya are special because of their logical approach and unembarrassed advocacy of politics. Kauṭilya gained extraordinary fame over 2,300 years ago for two reasons: (a) his Sanskrit writings on politics and (b) the practical counsel to Chandragupta who established a big empire under his guidance. His books are translated into various languages like English, French, etc. His literature shows the depth of study of *Bharatiya* way of life. In his books, he had touched all points of life.

While his work *Arthāŝastra* (science of material gain) was written at the end of the 4th century BC, it was rediscovered only in 1905. Kauṭilya described his political ideas into the *Arthāŝastra* which is called the oldest treatise in the world of political thought and command in society. It includes encyclopaedic information about political economy and aspects of government, monetary and fiscal policies, coinage, commerce, forests, welfare, weights and measures, agriculture, law, international relations, methods of defeating kingdom, military strategy and duty of king, qualification of ministers, formations of villages, punishments and protection of citizens. Kauṭilya's *Arthāŝastra* is considered as the first systematic book in economics.

Nītiśāstra is Kauṭilya's second famous work. It is variously translated as *The Science of Morality*, *Common Sense* or *Ethics*. *Nītiśāstra* is a treatise on the perfect way of life's principles and very simple conduct in all works of life. In other words, the real aim of *Nīti*, indeed the aim of life is to realize one's eternal position. It is a collection of facts of practical wisdom for living a life with Indian culture and code of conducts. Kauṭilya teaches us how to be happy in general life. Kauṭilya also developed *Neeti sutras* about behaviour. There are 455 *Sutras* in it. Kauṭilya used 216 *Sutras* to train Chandragupta in the art of ruling kingdom.

Arthaśāstra: Science of Statecraft

The *Arthaśāstra* is the title of the book written by Kauṭilya. It is an ancient Indian treatise on statecraft, economic policy and military strategy. Written in Sanskrit, composed, expanded and redacted between the 2nd century BCE and 3rd century CE, the *Arthaśāstra* was influential until the 12th century when it disappeared. It was rediscovered in 1905 by the great historian R. Shamasastry, who published it in 1909. The first English translation was published in 1915 (Rangarajan 1987).

The title *Arthaśāstra* which is in Sanskrit language often translated to 'the science of politics', but the book *Arthaśāstra* has a broader scope. It includes books on the nature of government, law, civil and criminal court systems, ethics, economics, markets and trade, the methods for screening ministers, diplomacy, theories on war, nature of peace and the duties and obligations of a king. The text incorporates *Hindu* philosophy, includes ancient economic and cultural details on agriculture, mineralogy, mining and metals, animal husbandry, medicine, forests and wildlife.

The *Arthaśāstra* explores issues of social welfare, the collective ethics that hold a society together, advising the king that in times and in areas devastated by famine, epidemic and such acts of nature, or by war, he should initiate public projects such as creating irrigation waterways and building forts around major strategic holdings and towns and exempt taxes on those affected. The text was influential on other *Hindu* texts that followed, such as the sections on king, governance and legal procedures included in *Manusmṛiti* (Roy 1993).

It should be noted here that *Arthaśāstra* is more than a book. Guidance for his royal master, a manual for statecraft, an anthology on polity, in its own sphere, the book is an ideal and utopia. The contents of the book are elaborated in detail as below.

1. The *Arthaśāstra* provides a brief description of the different aspects of administration and *Hindu* society. It deals with the branches of knowledge which were in existence in those times. The human knowledge was divided into four branches: (a) *Anvikashki* (Philosophy), (b) *Tryi* (Theology), (c) *Varta* (Economics) and (d) *Daṇḍanīti* (Polity). It shows that *Hindus* showed equitable regard to the sciences making material progress and those conducive to spiritual culture.
2. It is a manual of administration. It lays down certain practical suggestions for the functioning of administration. In the words of eminent scholars, the *Arthaśāstra* is more a manual for the administration than a theoretical work on polity discussing the philosophy and fundamental principles of administration. It is mainly concerned with the practical problems of government and describes its machinery and functions both in peace and war with an exhaustiveness, not seen in later work with the possible exception of *Śukranīti*.
3. The book superseded the works of all the predecessors. In this book references have been made to *Manusmṛiti* and *Yājñavalkyasmṛiti*.[1] The conclusion is supported by the data of *Arthaśāstra* of Kauṭilya, for innumerous places it refers to and discusses the views of *Vishalakha*, *Indra*, Manu, *Parasara*, *Bharadvāja*, Gaurasivas and other scholars of sciences of polity that are referred to in *Arthaśāstra* (Keith 1921).

Dhārma and *Daṇḍanīti*

In the *Arthaśāstra,* the word *dhārma* is used in various senses. To understand this political thought, it is quite essential to comprehend them. At least three meanings of *dhārma* can be distinguished:

1. *Dhārma* in the sense of society;
2. *Dhārma* as moral law based on truth; and
3. *Dhārma* as civil law.

According to Kauṭilya, an accomplished king must be devoted to *dhārma*. He is called as the promulgator of *dhārma*. Even if, mendicants and ascetics engage in improper proceeding, the punishment by the king should be carried out in accordance with *dhārma*.

Kauṭilya argues that when all *dhārmas* perish, the king becomes the promulgator of *dhārma* for the establishment of the fourfold *varṇa* system and protection of the morality. Hence, in concrete terms, the kings' maintenance of *dhārma* signified nothing but the defence of the social order based on family, property and *varṇa*. The dominant ideal that moved the kings in ancient India was the attainment of *dhārma* (righteous performance of one's own duties), *ārtha* (acquisition and preservation of wealth) and *kāma* (fulfilment of sexual or worldly desires). The chief duty of the king was the upholding and implementation of *dhārma* making it as the constitution of the state. So far as the elucidation of the concept of *dhārma* was concerned, he had accepted the views of the *Brāhmaṇas* and the *Upaniṣhads* that *dhārma* was the source of law and more specifically of moral and civil law. Kauṭilya believes that there are four sources for settling a legal controversy. The first is *dhārma or* law. The second is *vyavahara* or evidence. The third is the *charitra* or history and conduct of reputed persons. The fourth is the *rajashasana*. But out of all these, *dhārma* is the outstanding source which settles all legal and institutional conflicts. Kauṭilya made it clear that *dhārma* is fixed in truth, *vyavahara* in witness, *charitra* in judicial precedence and *rajashasana* in the edicts of the king. The *Arthaśāstra* begins with the examination of the end of societies in order to determine the place of *trayi* (theology), *anvikshiki* (philosophy), *varta* (economics) and *daṇḍanīti* (science of politics) in the scheme of human existence as these are the light of all knowledge and an easy means for accomplishment of great acts and the sources of a life of virtues. Distinction is made between natural and artificial disciplines, between *dhārma* and *adhārma*, *nyaya* and *anyaya*, expedient and inexpedient.

Kauṭilya is the staunch champion of the *Varṇaāśhrama dhārma*. In fact, *varṇaāśhrama* is elaborated as the foundation of the social order and duties common to all are prescribed like the practice of harmlessness, truthfulness, purity, absence from cruelty, tolerance and forgiveness; for the observance of one's duty leads one to *svarga* and infinite bliss *anantya*. He believes that Swami who is well educated and disciplined and devoted to good government of his subjects will likewise enjoy the earth unopposed. It is this philosophy of kingship, to ensure observance of *varṇaāśhrama dhārma* and to contribute to the increase of virtues essential to all which explains and also justifies the ever-increasing role of the king in the life of men. Some of the lapses or violations of the *Varṇaāśhrama dhārma* were certainly justifiable and could be punished in the court of law. Kauṭilya was against inter-*varṇa* marriage and interchange of occupation among different *varṇas*. He recommended punishment for those who took to asceticism prematurely without making due provisions for his dependents (Chandrasekaran 2006).

According to Kauṭilya, the sources of law are *dhārma* (*Dharmaśāstra*), *vyavahara* (judicial precedence), *sannistha* (customs) and *nyaya* (equity). The last should not be understood to mean the edict of the king for which Kauṭilya has another term *rajashasana*. But Kauṭilya does not include *rajashasana* as a source of positive law. As a matter of fact, according to traditions *dhārma* (law was independent and even anterior to king and *daṇḍanīti*) was given to the king to enforce and the latter had not created it.

Saptanga Theory of State

Kauṭilya's *Arthaśāstra* deals with the art of administration in detail than with political theory. This treatise covers political and economic matters of administration as also morality, education, social problems, responsibilities of the king and subjects, international relations, army, spy system, etc. The book has 6,000 *ślokas* and 15 chapters each dealing with one department of running a state. The chapters are on discipline of the prince, qualifications of ministers and duties of the king, departments of ministers, civil laws, criminal laws, removal of dangers to the state, elements of kingship and policy threats to the welfare of the state, military campaigns, corporations, theory of conquest, devices for advancing the interests of the state, etc.

Kauṭilya puts out clear views on the state but mentions at one place that state originated when people got tired of the law of fish (*matsyanayaya*) and selected Manu as their king with the decision that he would receive one-sixth of the grain and one-tenth of the merchandise and gold as his share (of taxes) which would enable him to ensure the safety and security, and law and order of the state and punish the wrongdoers. Kauṭilya adopts the seven limbs theory of the state of Indian tradition or *saptanga* which are: (a) *Swami*, (b) *Amātya*, (c) *Jānapada*, (d) *Durga*, (e) *Kośa*, (f) *Daṇḍa* and (g) *Mitra*. He suggests, a state can only function when all these elements or limbs of a body politic are mutually integrated and cooperate well with each other (Roy 1993).

1. ***Swami* (the sovereign king)**: The king here was referred to as the Lord or *Swami* and placed at the top of the body politic. Kauṭilya says a perfect king should have the following qualities:
   (a) He should have an inviting nature (*Abhigamika Guna*).
   (b) He should have qualities of intellect and intuition (*Pragya Guna*).
   (c) He should have great enthusiasm (*Utsaha Guna*).
   (d) He should have qualities of self-restraint and spirit (*Aatma Sampad*).

   In addition, Kauṭilya mentions the king should be from a high family, be non-fatalistic, endowed with strong character and should be religious and truthful. He should be free of passion, anger, greed and fickleness and capable of self-management, observing the customs taught by elderly people and have the capacity to make judgements like when to go to war and when to seek peace through a treaty. He should have a sense of sovereignty and owe allegiance to anybody and be the king of one whole political organization and not part of it (Chandrasekaran 2006).
2. ***Amātya* (ministers):** By *Amātya*, Kauṭilya refers to higher officials of the state like ministers and not necessarily just ministers. He says the qualities of a high official should be as follows: he must be a native of the county that he is an official of, come from a good family, be adequately trained, have foresight, eloquence, dignity, enthusiasm, have administrative ability, knowledge of scriptures and high character, a morally and ethically pure character, steadfastness and devotion.
3. ***Jānapada* (people and territory):** Territory and people constitute the third limb of the state in Kauṭilya's *Arthaśāstra*. Kauṭilya gives a clear-cut description of what an ideal territory would be like. He says the territory should be free from muddy, rocky, saline, uneven and thorny areas and from wild beasts. There should be lands that are fertile with a lot of timber and forests. There should be plenty of arable land, and richness of cattle and the land should be wholesome to cows and men. The territories should not be dependent on rains too much and have waterways. Also, there should be roads and good markets capable of bearing the army and taxation. The people populating a state should have the qualities of being hostile to the foes, be powerful enough to control the neighbouring kings and consist of people who are pure and devoted. The people should respect the rule of law and the government. They should be industrious agriculturists and economically productive *Vaiśya* and *Śūdras* (Karad 2015).
4. ***Durga* (fort):** Kauṭilya identifies forts as the fourth limb and mentions four kinds of forts that a king needs. He says the four kinds of forts that are necessary are: *Audak* (surrounded by water), *Paarvat* (built on the top of hill), *Dhaanvana* (built on barren or waste land) and *Vana* (surrounded by forests). The water and hill forts are suitable for defending the population and the desert and

forest forts are suitable as headquarters for wild regions and to serve as places to run away to in case of emergency. Kauṭilya says the power of a king depends on the forts which should be fit for fighting and to defend the state (Roy 1993).

5. ***Kośa* (treasury):** Kauṭilya puts great stress on the economic resources of a state and mentions that the success of a state depends upon its treasury size which should have enough gold and silver for the king through long periods of calamity. The treasury should be legitimately acquired by the king or his predecessors. The treasury is easily increased when (a) there is opulence of the industrial department run by the state, (b) there is a propensity for commerce and (c) abundance in harvest. In cases of emergency, Kauṭilya finds no problem with the king raising revenue even through means such as a higher assessment on first class and fertile land and heavy taxes on merchandise, etc. He also condones in emergencies for the king to exploit the superstitious and religious sentiments of the people.
6. ***Daṇḍa* (army or force):** Kauṭilya mentions the *daṇḍa* or army as the limb that the king needs to control both his own people and his enemy. Kauṭilya talks about six types of army: (a) *Maul Bala* (hereditary forces), (b) *Bhrit Bala* (hired troops), (c) soldiers of fighting corporations, (d) *Mitra Bala* (troops belonging to an ally), (e) *Amitra Bala* (troops belonging to the enemy) and (f) *Atavi Bala* (soldiers of wild tribes). Interestingly, the best of the six according to Kauṭilya is the hereditary army composed of members of the *Kṣatriyas* caste for they are most loyal to the king and are committed to serve the king through weal and woe and have powers of endurance and superior fighting skills because they have fought many battles.
7. ***Mitra* (allies):** Kauṭilya finally stresses on the need for political friends in the other states because no state functions in isolation. Kauṭilya classifies allies into two kinds: *Sahaj* (natural) and *Kritrim* (acquired). The *sahaj* ally is one who is close by territorially and has been inherited as a friend from fathers and grandfathers and the *kritrim* ally is one who is resorted to temporarily for the protection of wealth and life. Kauṭilya prefers the *sahaj* ally over the *kritrim* one if the *sahaj* ally is free from deceit and is capable of making large scale preparations for war quickly and on a large scale.

In Kauṭilya's view the above seven elements are necessary for maintaining and perfecting the sovereignty of the king. Kauṭilya classifies the functions of the state basically into four:

1. **Protection**: The first function of the state is guarding the state against internal as well as external threats. Internally people and their property have to be protected from thieves and dacoits, etc. and also externally from outside the state, there may be threats from invasions that have to be dealt with.
2. **Maintaining the law**: It is expected by the people that the King and the state will maintain the customs and laws of the land. The king, according to Kauṭilya should settle legal disputes in conformity with the sacred principles and laws in consultation with learned *Brāhmaṇs.*
3. **Preserving social order**: Kauṭilya saw it is the duty of the king to protect the *dhārma* of the land by which he meant the social order. It is the duty of the king to deliver justice and to help people of different *varṇas* to preserve their professions or in other words help to maintain *varṇaāśhrama dhārma.*
4. **Promoting the welfare of the people**: The king, according to Kauṭilya, should function on the goal that it is in the happiness of his subjects that his happiness lies. The state should control

the whole of social life. It should promote religion and spirituality and in doing so regulate the age and conditions under which one might renounce the world. Kauṭilya advised the state to provide support to the poor, pregnant women, and to their children, to orphans, to the aged, the afflicted and the helpless.

Theory of *Mandala*

For Kauṭilya, the principle of foreign policy—that nations act in their political, economic and military self-interests—was a timeless truth of his science of politics or *Arthaśāstra* (Boesche 2003). Kauṭilya is most famous for outlining the *Mandala* theory or the circle of the states which consists of 12 kingdoms as

1. *Vijigishu* (*Rājā mandala*): Desirous for or would be, world conqueror.
2. *Ari* (enemy state): Whose territory is contagious to *Vijigishu*, is a natural enemy.
3. *Mitra* (ally): It is ally of *Vijigishu* whose territory is immediately beyond the enemy or *ari*.
4. *Arimitra* (enemy's ally): Enemy's ally indirectly is enemy, who is immediate beyond ally.
5. *Mitra-Mitra* (ally of friend): It is ally immediately beyond the enemy's ally.
6. *Ari Mitra-Mitra* (ally of enemy's ally): It is ally of enemy's ally situated at immediate beyond *Mitra–Mitra*.
7. *Parshnigraha* (rearward enemy): The enemy, in the rear of the *Vijigishu*. Means Heal catcher when *Vijigishu* would be on the expedition in front.
8. *Akranda* (ally of *Rājā Mandala*): *Vijugishu's* ally in the rear behind that of *Parshnigraha*.
9. *Parshnigrahasara* (ally of a rearward enemy): Enemy's ally, the ally of *Parshnigraha* behind *Akranda*.
10. *Akrandsara* (ally of Akranda): The ally of *Akranda* behind *Parshnigrahasara*, ultimately an ally.
11. *Madhyama* (middle king): The middle king with territory adjoining those of *Vijigishu* and *Ari* and stronger than both.
12. *Udasina* (neutral): The kingdom lying outside or neutral and more powerful than that of *Vijigishu*, *Ari* and *Madhyama*.

Kauṭilya explained further that there are four principal states—*Vijigishu*, *Ari*, *Madhyama* and *Udasina*—each of these has an ally and ally's ally along with five material constituents each, thus making 12 kings and 60 material constituents, conforms the circle of 72 elements in all. These schemes are based on assumptions derived from the practical experiences found everywhere that two neighbouring states sharing their borders are hostile to each other. And the hostile state to the enemy, that is, the enemy's enemy is a natural ally. The *Vijigishu* is situated at exactly the centre of this circle. It does not give the fixed account of the numbers of the kingdom in this *mandala*, but refers to a number of possible relationships that may arise when *Vijigishu would* be in the quest of suzerainty (Karad 2015).

The neighbouring princes, *samantas* (*feudal lords*), may normally be supposed to be hostile but it is possible that some may have friendly feeling towards the *Vijigishu*, while others may even be subservient to him. Neighbouring states of this kind fall into three categories—*Aribhavin*, *Mitrabhavin* and *Bhrytbhavin;* the last are, of course, vassals of *vijigishu* (Kangle 1965).

Mandala theory is the plan, the blueprint of the expedition with the intention of world conquest because Kauṭilya believes in strength and power. For him, 'Power is the possession of strength' and it is in three forms: (a) *Mantra Shakti*: power of knowledge, that is, power of counsel; (b) *Prabhu Shakti*: power of might, that is, power of treasury and army; and (c) *Utsaha Shakti*: power of energy, that is, power of valour. Likewise, success is also threefold. By this theory, Kauṭilya indicates towards reality, and alerts the king to be a conqueror or suffer conquest. All his discussion revolves around the desire of victory over enemy and world conquest to establish unified, sovereign world empire that is the concept of *Chakravarti*—imperatively the Indian territories in between the Himalaya and the sea. G. P. Singh argues that the *Mandala* theory is ancient India's most notable contribution to political theory (Karad 2015). Singh analysed the *mandala* theory as a 'balance of power' but Bosche contradicted this statement by stating that 'it was not offering modern balance of power arguments where the ultimate status quo and peace is the purpose of such inter-state activities in modern time' (Boesche 2003). Moreover, this theory provides geo-strategic analysis of inter-state relations; therefore, it is the theory of geopolitics.

Foreign Policy

Kauṭilya set the goal of foreign policy before the *Vijigishu* that it is not mere preservation of the state but its expansion as well. It is the goal of world conquest and pertaining to this goal he propounded the theory of *Mandala* or circle of the states along with the six-fold policy. The king is suggested to follow the right means at the right time with the flexible planning and complete determination. Kauṭilya preaches that there is nothing like ethics and moral in foreign policy but the goal and self-interest only; after all, end justifies the means.

Shadguna Sidhanta, that is, Six Measures of Foreign Policy

This doctrine is about the six principles of foreign policy like a formula for attainment of one's national interests and goals at the level of international politics based on political reality. It is the archetype of foreign policy acting as a guiding force for the *Vijigishu* to become a world conqueror. It contains six basic principles as follows:

1. ***Sandhi* (making treaty containing terms and conditions):** The general principle in foreign policy is that, when one is comparatively weaker than that of his enemy, the policy of peace, that is, *Sandhi* should be employed. When making a treaty one may be required to surrender troops called *Dandopanta sandhi* or treasury called *Kosopanta sandhi* and territory called *Desopanta sandhi*, respectively. Kauṭilya advised the king to enter into the treaty, thwart the strong enemy when fulfilling the conditions of the treaty and after biding his time till he becomes strong to overthrow the strong enemy. It means this is the policy to seek or spare the time to become strong and waiting for weakening of enemy, till then, one has to hold patience for right opportunity. It is practical opportunism (Karad 2015).
2. ***Vigraha* (policy of hostility):** If one is stronger than the enemy, policy of hostility should be adapted. This policy has two dimensions: (a) defensive and (b) offensive. While in first case, one who is sure about its strength to repel attack of enemy should resort to *Vigraha*. And in the second case, one who feels from the secured position can ruin the enemy's undertakings or can seize enemy's territories, because he is engaged in the war on another front, can go for *Vigraha*. But Kauṭilya is very anxious about the profit and losses as he recommends *sandhi* instead of *Vigraha*

when both are supposed to lead to the same result. Obviously, there are comparatively more losses, expenses and troubles in hostility (ibid.).

3. ***Asana* (a policy of remain quite, not planning to march):** Asana is the state in which one is to wait in the hope that the enemy would get weaker or find himself in difficulties or in calamities, get involved in war on other front and one would be stronger than enemy. Naturally, this policy is often a concomitant of the policy of the *sandhi*. But, at the same time, it can be corroborated with the policy of *vigraha*. For example, by seducing enemy's subjects from their loyalty by the means of dissension and propaganda, one will try to weaken enemy secretly (ibid.).
4. ***Yana* (marching on an expedition):** The policy of *yana* is much clear and explicit among all of others, which can be persuaded in the situation when one is surely strong than his enemy. 'Normally, *yana* and *vigraha* are parallel but in *yana*, one is expected to be completely dominant in the strength' (ibid.). However, even *sandhi-yana* is recommended. This is to be obvious; it involves a downright breach of faith with one with whom one is at peace having entered into treaty with him. 'The joint expedition would be based on sharing benefits is also recommended in this policy' (ibid.).
5. ***Sansraya* (seeking shelter with another king or in a fort):** This policy is particularly recommended for a weak king who is attacked or threatened to be attacked by powerful enemy. The discussion about the king with whom the shelter should be sought is included in book 7, Chapter 2, verse 6–25 and *Sansraya* conforms to the status of Protégé, one's protection is assured thereby (ibid.).

   It is also implied that the king would be making continuous efforts to recoup his strength and independence. The shelter at one's own fort is also a suggestion. But if none of these remedies would help, then the weak king should resort to the last means of surrender, this is vassalage. He should be watchful for opportunity to strike back and obtain his previous position.
6. ***Dvaidhibhava* (the double policy of *sandhi* with one king and *vigraha* with another at a time):** It is obviously a policy of dual purpose, where *Sandhi* is for seeking help in the form of treasury and troops from one king to wage hostility towards another king. This policy is referred for the king who is equally strong to enemy and he cannot win the battle without additional strength of his ally (ibid.).

Four *Upayas*:

These are the tactics or means of overcoming opposition mentioned as:

1. *Sāma*: conciliation
2. *Dāma*: Gifts
3. *Bheda*: Dissension
4. *Daṇḍa*: Force.

First two are suggested to be used with subjugate weak king and last two are to overcome strong kings. *Gunas* are concerned only with foreign policy while *upayas* have wide applications (ibid.).

Diplomacy

Kauṭilya finds the diplomacy also as an apparatus of war. 'For Kauṭilya, all ambassadors were potential spies with diplomatic immunity' (Mujumdar 1960). He argued that diplomacy is really a subtle act of war, a series of consistent actions taken to weaken the enemy and get advantage for oneself all with an eye towards eventual conquest. 'In entire circle he should ever station envoys and secrete agents becoming a friend of the rivals, maintaining secrecy when striking again and again' (Boesche 2003).

Geopolitical Analysis

American scholar Bruce Rich compared Kauṭilya's geopolitical analysis in modern perspectives, with the concept of groupings of civilizations by Samuel Huttington and Brzvenski's explanation of the changing geo strategies of world powers, especially Eurasian. In his view, he explained, after Cold War, world politics is divided among nine geopolitical groups, like the elements of *Mandala* in Kauṭilya's theory. On this basis, we would be able to analyse the current problems at international level. 'A number of treatise on post-cold war geopolitics published in 1990s and in early 2000s, unconsciously evoke Kauṭilya's analysis, accept that the entire planet is now the arena of play for the *Mandala* of states rather than as in Kauṭilya's time, the Indian subcontinent' (Rich 2008).

As a practical statesman and a realist, Kauṭilya realized that every state acts in order to enhance its power and self-interest; therefore moral, ethical or religious obligation does not have any scope in the international politics. 'War and peace are considered solely from the point of view of the profit' (Dikshitar 1987). Kauṭilya assumes that every move of the king desirous for victory towards its ally or enemy should have to be based on its own interests. As Bruce Rich says, 'Kauṭilya's foreign policy was the ruthless realpolitik, intrigue and deception… Kauṭilya's cold blooded realism and treachery added with some remarkable enlightened policies'. Most scholars of political history, especially Westerners, blame Kauṭilya for his so-called immoral recommendations in foreign policy. But at least, he is honest with his arguments and teachings, unlike those who are the idealist of daylight and opportunist in the dark. The fault of *Arthaśāstra*, as that of Machiavelli, 'lies in openly saying something that has always been actually practiced by states everywhere' (Kangle 1965). Was Kauṭilya immoral? The answer is obviously no! He just followed principles which were actually in practice at inter-state level at that time, and it is still being followed now. He 'was unmoral not immoral; unreligious, not non-religious, in his political teachings' (Sen 1920).

Ethics and Politics

In the *Arthaśāstra*, a great deal of writing has been devoted towards ethics (*dhārma*) and politics. Kauṭilya has defined ethics in various ways and used to call it as *dhārma*. The term again has been variously used as:

1. Sense of duty
2. Moral law based on truth and
3. Civil law

For Kauṭilya, the king must be apostle of *dhārma* and must promulgate the same. All the actions and convictions of the king must be carried on in accordance with *dhārma*. The important moral duty before the king is to maintain the social order by upholding the idea of attainment of *dhārma*, *ārtha* and *kāma*.

The pursuit of (the people's) welfare as well as the maintenance of the philosophic tradition, the *Vedās* and the economic well-being (of the society) are dependent on the sceptre wielded by the king. The maintenance of law and order by the use of punishment is the science of government. By maintaining order, the king can preserve what he already has, acquire new possessions, augment his wealth and power, and share the benefits of improvement with those worthy of such gifts.

The progress of this world depends on the maintenance of order and the (proper functioning of) government. A well-considered and just punishment makes the people devoted to *dhārma*, *ārtha* and *kāma* (righteousness, wealth and enjoyment). When, no punishment is awarded (through misplaced leniency and no law prevails), then there is only the law of fish (i.e., the law of the jungle). Unprotected, the small fish will be swallowed up by the big fish. In the presence of a king maintaining just law, the weak can resist the powerful (Rangarajan 1987).

Kauṭilya has well mentioned the sphere of *dhārma* and duties of the king for the betterment of the state in his treatise *Arthaśāstra*. He is of the view that the King should be in control of the state if the state has to progress. For that maintenance of internal peace, he believed in a just and realistic rule of law. His definition of a state was one which had power and wealth and hence he put property rights and protection of wealth as one of the important themes in his jurisprudence. In fact, he advocated that one could get rid of corporeal punishment by paying off fines. Kauṭilya also attaches great importance to human rights on how the invaded ruler and his ministers should be treated. He shows a deep understanding of criminal justice and war justice. Surprisingly, for a harsh and realistic man like Kauṭilya he shows mercy towards the people defeated in a war and recommends humanity and justice towards them. He thinks that this is important to preserve the *mandala* structure of war and peace. He advocates that defeated king shall be treated with respect and he should be made an ally.

Kauṭilya believes that law should be in the hands of the King and punishments need to be awarded to those who are guilty so that King can protect himself from the social unrest and unhappiness. He believes that punishment is a means to an end and it needs to prevent the commission of the crime. Kauṭilya also was a reformer where he thought punishments could reform a person and hence a society. Kauṭilya's view on crime and justice is very elaborate and goes on to differentiate between various crimes. He advocates different punishments, if they were crimes committed while in public office, civil crimes, sexual crimes, religious crimes, etc. This shows that he had a great grasp to customize the rule of law depending on both the offence and the structure of the society. He believed that the structure and peace are preserved in a society by effective jurisprudence. In today's context, some of his ideas might be irrelevant but it shows that the ancient *Hindu* jurisprudence was codified and actually more resembled the common law (Chandrasekaran 2006).

Kauṭilya's understanding of justice, war, diplomacy and human rights makes him unique in his times. In ancient India there is no one comparable who could have stood the test for justice being a tool for statecraft. Kauṭilya believed that while it is as much important for the state to wage a war and conquer, it is also important to maintain law and order within the state in order to make it more powerful (ibid.).

Kauṭilya and Machiavelli

Kauṭilya's *Arthaśāstra* has much that is common with the content and tenor of the *Prince*—a manual written by Niccolo Machiavelli for the guidance of rulers based upon the principles set forth by him in '*The Discourses*'. The two books are perhaps the world's most famous treatises on the art of kingship.

And both writers have realistically analysed the methods by which a king can rise to supreme power and maintain it against all odds. As a matter of fact, Kauṭilya lived and wrote at least 1,000 years before Machiavelli. In that way, Kauṭilya undoubtedly was Machiavelli's predecessor in theory and reality both. Kauṭilya and Machiavelli both commend to statesman to set policies that are expedient and practical. Their in-depth analysis of given historical events demonstrate facets of universal validity which can be applied in comparable situation. Their writings were in fact down to earth, whereas Kauṭilya's *Arthaśāstra* reads like a meticulous note of an official with an all-round experience based on practical knowledge, the *Prince* is concerned with the practical question of the precise methods which a prince or monarch must employ to govern society efficiently. It seems Machiavelli has drawn heavily from Kauṭilya's *Arthaśāstra* without even acknowledging the same.

However, the attitude of Kauṭilya and Machiavelli to history reveals interesting resemblances and contrasts while both of them wrote for rulers rather than for ruled ones. The realist account of '*Arthaśāstra*', a vivid analysis of the statecraft, a guide to the foresight of the ruler, while 'The *Prince*' on the other hand is a handbook of sovereignty which provides concreteness to the reign of the rule by establishing supremacy both inside and outside the state.

Conclusion

Kauṭilya was brave and systematic, never forgetting his goal in life, simple and uninterested in pomp, intelligent and sharp, devoted and selfless. Works of Kauṭilya have been used today, although it was constituted over 2,000 years ago. His whole life was mysterious but spotless. He fought against *Adhārma* like Lord *Krishna*. He had chance of becoming an Emperor but he never thought to become an Emperor. He was loyal to Chandragupta till his death. He would change all the circumstances in his favour. Indeed, Kauṭilya had a brilliant personality.

In Delhi, *Chanakyapuri* is situated; it means 'the city of Chanakya'. *Chanakyapuri* is one of the posh areas of Delhi. It reminds us of Chanakya. Kauṭilya was the first patriot in India who succeeds in his aim and whose vision is relevant today. Kauṭilya reminds us that he is not just history but he created history. His life, teaching and works will continue to guide us and inspire to follow him.

Summary

Kauṭilya's *Arthaśāstra* is one of the greatest compositions on political science in ancient world. It is the book on political realism which explains how the political world works actually, than that of it ought to be. It continues to recommend even immoral, brutal and cruel means to preserve own state and the prosperity of its subjects. At long before the realistic discussions of Machiavelli, Kauṭilya as the first great political realist (Boesche 2003, 5). He was the chief adviser to Chandragupta Maurya, who united India and the subcontinent in the form of a great empire at around 300 BCE, and at the same, time Kauṭilya wrote his *Arthaśāstra*, rendered as a 'science of politics' (Kangle 1965, 1). *Arthaśāstra* has two-fold aims: (a) Preservation of state, means internal security and general wellbeing of subjects by good governance and by the law and order and (b) acquisition of the territories from others by expansion through excellent code of foreign policy.

This text contains 15 books, 150 chapters and 180 sections, along with 6,000 *ślokas*. Out of these books, the first five books deal with internal administration, that is, *Tantra*; and the next eight books are concerned with the foreign policy, that is, *Avaap*, while remaining two are miscellaneous in nature. Kauṭilya's foreign policy is like the modern realist's foreign policy that is 'unregulated competition of states in which the parameter of the success is strengthening the state' (Waltz 1979, 117). Also, it is 'struggle for power' as mentioned by Morgenthau (1985, 195). Whereas the Greeks are pioneers of political philosophy, Kauṭilya stands there as a first political realist.

Kauṭilya is an expansionist who advised not only the preservation of the state but also to conquer territories of others. It is the *Mandala* theory which is the basis of Kauṭilya's foreign policy. In other words, it is a theory of world conquest. He has paved the way for *Vijigishu*, that is, 'the king who is desirous or aspirant to world conquest,' how to be a *Chakravartin*, that is, world conqueror.

Points for Discussion

1. Examine Kauṭilya's *Mandala* theory and its significance in the context of modern nation state.
2. 'Kauṭilya made politics autonomous'. Examine.
3. Do you agree that Kauṭilya's conception of State in *Saptanga* theory and *Yogakshema* is 'surprisingly modern' in character? Elaborate your response.
4. Discuss Kauṭilya's concept of *Dhārma* and *Daṇḍanīti*.
5. Explain the elements of Kauṭilya's *Saptanga* theory of state.
6. Discuss Kauṭilya's foreign policy and analyse its contemporary significance.

Endnote

1. The *Yājñavalkyasmṛiti* is one of the many *dhārma* related texts of *Hinduism* composed in Sanskrit. It is dated between the 3rd and 5th century CE, and belongs to the *Dharmaśāstra* tradition.

Glossary

Arthaśāstra: *Arthaśāstra* is regarded as the oldest treatise in the world of political thought and command in society. It includes encyclopaedic information about political economy and aspects of government, monetary and fiscal policies, coinage, commerce, forests, welfare, weights and measures, agriculture, law, international relations, methods of defeating kingdom, military strategy and duty of king, qualification of ministers, formations of villages, punishments and protection of citizens. Kauṭilya's *Arthaśāstra* is considered the first systematic book in economics.

Daṇḍanīti: *Daṇḍanīti*, the science of law enforcement, is the name given in the *Mahābhārata* to the mythical original work of this kind, said to have been handed down by *Brahmā* himself at the time of creation. *Daṇḍa*, meaning rod or staff, stands for the sceptre wielded by rulers; it also has many other meanings. For example, the army is called *daṇḍa*. It is also one of the four methods of dispute settlement and connotes the use of force.

Dhārma: *Dhārma* not only signifies an absolute and immutable concept of righteousness but also includes the idea of duty which every human being owes to oneself, to one's ancestors, to society as a whole and to universal order. *Dhārma* is law in its widest sense—spiritual, moral, ethical and temporal.

***Dharmaśāstra*:** According to Kauṭilya, *Dharmaśāstra* is the source of all law. It has been used in various senses by Kauṭilya. It can be understood at least in three ways: as sense of social duty, as cannons of civil law and as moral law based on truth. Whenever there is disagreement between customs and *dhārma* the matter shall be decided on the basis of *Dharmaśāstra*.

Diplomacy: Kauṭilya finds diplomacy also as an apparatus of war. For Kauṭilya, all ambassadors were potential spies with diplomatic immunity. He argued that diplomacy is really a subtle act of war, a series of consistent actions taken to weaken an enemy and get advantage for oneself all with an eye towards eventual conquest and in entire circle he should ever station envoys and secrete agents becoming a friend of the rivals, maintaining secrecy when striking again and again.

Ethics and politics: In the *Arthaśāstra*, a great deal of writing has been devoted towards ethics (*dhārma*) and politics. Kauṭilya has defined ethics in various ways and used to call it as *dhārma*. The term again has been variously used as: sense of duty, moral law based on truth and civil law. For Kauṭilya, the king must be apostle of *dhārma* and must promulgate the same. All the actions and convictions of the king must be carried on in accordance with *dhārma*. The important moral duty before the king is to maintain the social order by upholding the idea of attainment of *dhārma*, *ārtha* and *kāma*.

Foreign policy: Foreign policy was given highest priority by Kauṭilya in his *Mandala* theory. This doctrine is about the six principles of foreign policy like a formula for attainment of one's national interests and goals at the level of international politics based on political reality. It is the archetype of foreign policy acting as a guiding force for the *Vijigishu* to become a world conqueror. It contains six basic principles: (a) *Sandhi* (making treaty containing terms and conditions), (b) *Vigraha*: (policy of hostility), (c) *Asana* (policy of remaining quite, not planning to march), (d) *Yana* (marching on an expedition), (e) *Sansraya* (seeking shelter with another king or in a fort) and (f) *Dvaidhibhava* (the double policy of *Sandhi* with one king and *Vigaha* with another at a time).

Geopolitics: Geopolitics, derived from the German term Lebensraum, means space consciousness. It signifies the importance of geography on foreign policy. Unconsciously, Kauṭilya through his Mandal theory has evoked the idea of geopolitics much before its modern connotation.

***Mandala* theory:** The only thing they can recall is the '*mandala*' theory, based on the principles: 'Every neighbouring state is an enemy and the enemy's enemy is a friend'. Kauṭilya explained further that there are four principal states—*Vijigishu*, *Ari*, *Madhyama* and *Udasina*, each of these has an ally and ally's ally along with five material constituents each, thus making 12 kings and 60 material constituents, conforms the circle of 72 elements in all. These schemes are based on assumptions derived from the practical experiences found everywhere that two neighbouring states sharing their borders are hostile to each other. And the hostile state to the enemy, that is, the enemy's enemy is a natural ally.

Realism: Realism also known as realpolitik or political realism explains how the political world works actually, instead of how it ought to be. It continues to recommend even immoral, brutal and cruel means to preserve own state and the prosperity of its subjects. Kauṭilya's *Arthaśāstra* is one such doctrine of political realism which explains the science of statecraft.

***Saptanga* theory of state:** *Saptanga* theory of state emphasizes on every organ of the state as most relevantly significant towards the working of the government, integrally relating every part of the state with the organs of the human body. Kauṭilya adopts the seven limbs theory of the state of Indian tradition or *saptanga:* (a) *Swami*, (b) *Amātya*, (c) *Jānapada*, (d) *Durga*, (e) *Kośa*, (f) *Daṇḍa* and (g) *Mitra*. He suggests a state can only function when all these elements or limbs of a body politic are mutually integrated and cooperate well with each other.

State: State is a political organization having seven important limbs: (a) *Swami*, (b) *Amātya*, (c) *Jānapada*, (d) *Durga*, (e) *Kośa*, (f) *Daṇḍa* and (g) *Mitra*. The effective and harmonious functioning of all these organs enables the state to perform well.

Statecraft: Statecraft is the art of management of the affairs of the state. The *Arthaśāstra* of Kauṭilya has been widely regarded as the best-known treatise on statecraft in which rules, regulations, principles and duties and responsibilities of King and the subjects are vividly mentioned.

***Varṇaāśhrama dhārma*:** Kauṭilya is a staunch champion of *varṇaāśhrama dhārma*. It is elaborated as foundation of social order and duties common to all are prescribed. This philosophy prescribes contribution of virtues to the society by all by performing their allotted duties as per their *varṇaāśhrama*. This in turn brings peace, prosperity and harmony in the society.

References

Boesche, Roger. 2003. *The First Great Political Realist: Kauṭilya and His Arthashastra*. New York: Lexington Books.

Chandrasekaran, Pravin. 2006, May 5. *Kauṭilya: Politics, Ethics and Statecraft, Munich Personal RePEc Achieve*. Cambridge, MA: Harvard University.

Dikshitar, V. R. Ramchandra. 1987. *War in Ancient India*. New Delhi: Motilal Banarsidass.

Kangle, R. P., trans. & ed. 1965. *The Kauṭilya Arthashastra: Part I, II & III*. New Delhi: Motilal Banarsidass.

Karad, Satish. 2015. 'Perspectives of Kauṭilya's Foreign Policy: An Ideal of State Affairs.' *Modern Research Studies—An International Journal of Humanities and Social Sciences* 2(2): 322–332.

Mujumdar, B. K. 1960. *The Military System in India*. Calcutta: Firma KLM.

Rangarajan, N. R. 1987. *Kauṭilya: The Arthaśāstra*. New Delhi: The Penguin Classic.

Rich, Bruce. 2008. *To Uphold the World: The Message of Ashoka & Kauṭilya for 21st Century*. New Delhi: Viking.

Roy, Chittaranjan. 1993. *Indian Political Thought, e-book*. New Delhi: Pragati Publications.

Sen, A. K. 1920. *Studies in Hindu Political Thoughts*. Calcutta: Oxford University Press.

Further Readings

Ghoshal, Upendra Nath. 1923. *A History of Hindu Political Theories*. London: Oxford University Press.

Keith, A. B. 1921. *Foreword to Studies in Ancient Hindu Polity*, ed. N. N. Law, v–vi. London: Oxford.

Morgenthau, Hans. 1985. *Politics Among Nations: The Struggle for Power and Peace*, 6th ed. New York: Knopf.

Mujumdar, B. K. 1960. *The Military System in India*. Calcutta: Firma KLM.

Rich, Bruce. 2008. *To Uphold the World: The Message of Ashoka & Kautilya for 21st Century*. New Delhi: Viking.

Singh, G. P. 1993. *Political Thought in Ancient India*. New Delhi: D. K.

Waltz, Kenneth N. 1979. *Theory of International Relations*. New York: McGraw Hill.

PART II

Medieval Indian Thought and Traditions

12 CHAPTER

Medieval India: State, Society and Religion

Ritu Sharma

CHAPTER OUTLINE

- Introduction
- Debates About Classification of Medieval Period
- Nature of State and Salient Features of Administration
- Economic and Social Reforms in Medieval Period
- Religious Traditions in Medieval Period
- Land Policy and Economic Scenario During Medieval India
- Akbar's Contribution
- Conclusion
- Summary
- Points for Discussion

India has natural abundance and fertility of soil. India has no mines of gold or silver. There has been a constant influx of gold and silver in exchange for the natural productions of the country. It has been a regular and uninterrupted accumulation. Conquest and plunder are the only expedients to bring back into circulation this super abundant wealth.

—Col Alexander Walker

Reader's Guide

The purpose of the chapter is to highlight the debates about the classification of medieval period. Medieval period was an important period of Indian history. This chapter is an attempt to highlight the major changes and development of this period as well as also elaborating the reforms during this era. This chapter also discusses the reforms initiated by Akbar and their impact on society. The impact of medieval India on modern India is also narrated in this chapter.

Introduction

Medieval period is an important period in the history of India because there were major developments during this era in the field of art, languages, culture and religion. This era also witnessed the impact of other religions on the Indian culture. Medieval period is also referred as post-classical era. This period lasted from 8th to 18th century with early medieval period from the 8th to the 13th century and the late medieval period from the 13th to 18th century. This era witnessed many wars among regional kingdoms and *Muslim*'s invasions by *Mughals*, Afghans and Turks. By the end of the 15th century, many European companies in the form of traders started doing trade and around mid-18th century they became a political force in the country marking the end of medieval period. There are different arguments regarding this theory. Some are of the opinion that start of *Mughal* Empire is the end of medieval period in India (Seshan 2007, 15).

The period of the 8th to 12th century in political life of India is particularly dominated by the presence of a large number of states. The bigger ones tried to establish their supremacy in northern India and the Deccan. The main contenders in this struggle for supremacy were the *Pratiharas*, the *Palas* and the *Rashtrakutas*. In the south, the most powerful kingdom to emerge during this period was that of the Cholas. The Cholas brought about the political unification of large parts of the country, but the general political picture was that of fragmentation particularly in northern India. It was in this period that India's contact with the new religion of *Islam* began. The contacts began late in the 7th century through the Arab traders.

Later in the early 8th century, the Arabs conquered Sindh. In the 10th century, the Turks emerged as a powerful force in central and west Asia and carved out kingdoms for themselves. They conquered Persia but their lives were richly influenced by Persian culture and tradition. The Turks first invaded India during the late 10th and early 11th century and Punjab came under Turkish rule. Another series of Turkish invasions in the late 12th and early 13th century led to the establishment of the *Sultanate* of Delhi. Within a few centuries after rise of *Islam* in Arabia, it became the second most popular religion in India with followers in every part of the country.

The establishment of the *Sultanate* marked the beginning of a new phase in the history of medieval India. Politically, it led to the unification of northern India and parts of the Deccan for almost a century. The rulers of *Sultanate* separated from their native place from which they had come. The *Sultanate* disintegrated towards the end of the 14th century leading to the emergence of a number of kingdoms in different parts of the country. Some of these like *Bahmani* and *Vijaynagar* Kingdom became very powerful. Emergence of new social groups took place. New social groups like the Turks, the Persians, the Mongols and the Afghans besides the Arabs emerged. There were important changes in economic life also. Trade and crafts received a stimulus and many new towns arose as centres of administration, trade and crafts. New elements of technology were also introduced during this period.

Debates about Classification of Medieval Period

Periodization in history is generally considered to be a tool in understanding and reconstructing the past rather than an end in itself. Historians in this process have divided history into various periods like ancient, medieval, modern and contemporary, in which certain predominant characteristics are found.

Ideological polarization has confounded further the confusion in the matter of periodization. While the ancient period of European history, in which slavish mode of production was predominant, has been reckoned to have come to an end with the downfall of Roman Empire, the medieval period of European history began with the downfall of the Roman Empire and was characterized by feudal mode of production. This period came to an end with the downfall of Constantinople of Roman Empire in 1453. The modern period in European history is deemed to have started after that. The periodization of European history does not suit Indian history as it has been unanimously agreed by the historians. Therefore, while dealing with Indian history, especially medieval India, one has to be familiar with the various trends in periodization and also different conclusions arrived at by historians. The historians who tried to analyse the nature of medieval Indian society and economy employed several conceptual frameworks. A survey of these attempts is done here in this section (Seshan 2007, 15).

1. **Oriental despotism:** James Mill considered the traditional institutions of India bearing in mind the 19th century utilitarianism and judged them as static, retrogressive and conducive to economic backwardness. Eminent philosophers of history of the time provided intellectual support to the idea framed by him for the pre-modern history of India. Hegel remarked on the absence of dialectical change in Indian history, and consequently dismissed Indian civilization as being static, despotic in its orientation and outside the mainstream of relevant world history. The theory of oriental despotism was the underlying current of this view of the pre-modern history of India. This was implicit in Mill's History. Montesquieu accepted the theory of oriental despotism, while Voltaire and others doubted the correctness of its assumptions. Richard Jones endorsed the theory of oriental despotism.
2. **Asiatic mode of production:** Karl Marx, despite his movement, was not averse to the idea (oriental despotism) with its emphasis on a static society and an absence of change. He worked out the theory of Asiatic mode of production for the pre-modern Asian society. According to Henry Maine and Karl Marx, the earlier Indian society had been stagnant because it had at its base the self-sustaining village community. They, therefore, declined to find such historical developments in India as noticed in the West. However, the material on which they based their theory of stagnant society was mostly the administrative reports prepared by the officers of the British East India Company. Therefore, they had limitations in the sense that they were not contemporary testimony.

   The absence of private property in land was central to the concept of Asiatic mode of production. The structure was seen in the form of a pyramid, with the king at the apex, and self-sufficient, isolated village communities at the base. The bureaucracy collected the surplus from the cultivators. The process of redistribution led to it being appropriated, substantially by the king and the court which paved the way for the fabulous wealth of oriental courts. The state monopoly of the irrigation system or the hydraulic machinery maintained the control over the peasant communities. This control was crucial in arid lands dependent on artificial irrigation (Wittfogel 1957).

   S. A. Dange, who tried to prove the existence of slavery in North India, during ancient times criticized the theory of stagnant society by applying the theory of dialectic development of human society formulated by Marx basically on the models of social development in European countries. D. D. Kosambi, another Marxist scholar, however, questioned the mechanical application of Marx's theory to India and tried to explain the development of feudalism in India by using his unique idea of 'feudalism from above and feudalism from below'[1] (Kosambi 1956).

3. **Feudal mode of production:** The notion of feudalism had entrenched itself firmly in Indian historiography between 1956 and 1965 with the appearance of D. D. Kosambi's *An Introduction to the Study of Indian History* and R. S. Sharma's *Indian Feudalism*, respectively. Primarily, however, Indian feudalism was envisioned as the state's creation through land grants; it was not seen as a mode of production even when its protagonists were avowedly Marxist.

   R. S. Sharma made an effort to verify the development of feudalism in India by connecting it with the increase of land grants made by Gupta rulers. He writes:

   > Unlike Europe, in India the decentralization of political power was not the result of fiefs granted to comrades-in-arm: the most important factor which contributed to this development was the practice of land grants made to priests and temples. It is clear that foreign invasion did not play any appreciable 'within the process of feudalisation, as was the case in Europe.' (Sharma 1980)

   He further states:

   > Feudalism in India, therefore, was characterized by a class of landlords and by a class of subject peasantry; the two living in a predominantly agrarian economy' marked by decline of trade and urbanism and by drastic reduction in metal currency. The superior state got its taxes collected and authority recognized by creating a number of inferior power blocks or even states (that is landed priests, *mathas*, *viharas*, temples, etc.) which generated the necessary social and ideological climate for this purpose. West European feudal lords granted land to their serfs in order to get their own occupied land cultivated. But Indian kings made land grants sometimes to get the taxes (surplus) collected and in other times for religious purposes.

Nature of State and Salient Features of Administration

The history of medieval period started after the end of ancient age in 550 AD and it continued till 18th century after which the *Mughal* empire collapsed. Medieval history is often interpreted after the demise of Gupta dynasty. This phase is called early medieval period. The gap between this phase, from the fall of Gupta's to the emergence of *Sultanate* is called early medieval period. The period that comprises mainly that of the reigns of the *Sultanate* and the *Mughal* period is generally considered as late medieval period, of course with regional variations. In the early medieval period there were many regional and local powers because there was not a single paramount force of power in India. During this era, there were several kingdoms which fought wars for expansion of territory. In the late medieval period, high level of centralization was found. This is a contrast between these two phases.

When the Guptas empire came to an end, the country witnessed decentralized political fragmentation as well as a sort of administrative and bureaucratic polity suspended above the society. During this era, kings were dependent on feudals and the government system working under the king's supremacy. The bureaucratic system with the support of feudals operated the whole system. The practice of granting tax free land was also given to the officials through royal proclamations. The bureaucracy at this time was guided by ministers who directly reported to the King. The ministers were selected from noble families; basically it was a hereditary system. The central administrative system was divided into various departments. These all departments were supervised by the Prime Minister who was chief of all. Land revenue was the main source of income during medieval period. Separate departments were established for the collections. The landlords were lifeline for this system and collected revenue. The peasants were under obligation to pay all form of taxes imposed upon them.

The era of medieval period witnessed the upliftment in the advancement of war technologies also. There were remarkable changes in the war technology during this era. Art flourished in full speed. *Mughal* era was the golden period of art under the rule of Jahangir. A new form of architecture was established during *Sultanate* and *Mughal* period. Many new forms came into format regarding sculptures and architecture.

Economic and Social Reforms in Medieval Period

During medieval period many reforms were introduced in all sectors. Agrarian administration received the closest attention of various governments established in the subcontinent throughout history. Only when anarchy or disorders made efficient government impossible, did agrarian administration receive a setback. Sher Shah tried very honestly to solve the problems; therefore, Akbar did not have to search very far for previous traditions. He, however, increased its efficiency and introduced some far-reaching reforms. Agrarian system was protected, encouraged and helped. The level of agricultural production was to be not only maintained but also continuously increased.

It was taken for granted that the state was a sharer in the produce; its right to demand a portion of the yield was universally accepted. This tradition precedes the dawn of history in the subcontinent. The recent discovery at Mohenjo-daro of a large building for storage has led archaeologists to believe that there was a large pool of grain which could not but be common property, perhaps of the government, would be impossible without a well-obeyed government. It does not seem beyond the pale of probability that this was the share of the government in agricultural produce. The '*jātakas*' which certainly embody a good deal of ancient traditional folk lore take such a demand for granted. The earliest literature, whether in the form of the *Nītiśhāshtras* or records of a secular nature, also does so. When the Muslims entered the subcontinent, they found the tradition well established. As the concept was embedded in their own tradition, they did not question it.

The social reforms in medieval India were mainly the product of certain economic and political developments. Some specific castes increase their pride by birth which became the chief characteristic in the early medieval period. For example, by the constant transfer of lands to the *Brāhmaṇa* class, *Kṣatriyas* advanced the monopoly of *Brahmanism*, thus accelerating the pace of rigidity in the society. Due to the matrix in every religion, multiple social reforms movements emerged. As with other social problems, the status of women was not so well like in ancient era, where they were worshipped. From the early medieval period to late medieval period, the status of upper caste women declined gradually.

A major development in the context of early medieval period social reforms was *Bhakti* Movement. It was exposed by both *Shaiva* saints called *Nayanaras* and *Vaishnava* once known as *Alvars*. These both sects enriched the process of social movement with propagation of their faith, debate with the rivals. They sang and danced as well as composed beautiful lyrics in the praise of their deities. The *Bhakti* movement was very helpful in changing the social attitude towards caste system. There is no doubt that Kings during this era were even handed in their attitudes to the various religions, but so were those with partisan views boarding on bigotry.

In the late medieval era *Islam* came to India. *Islam* was unable to associate itself with *Hinduism* despite its principle of universal brotherhood. The main reason behind this was that *Islamic* people were annoyed with the rituals, polytheism and idolatry of *Hinduism*. Of course, they did not try to understand the *Hindu* philosophy and the *Islamic* religious preachers and the rulers' primary aim were to propagate their religion. They considered *Hinduism* infidels and eventually they declared *Jihad* on the eve of war against *Hindu* rulers. At this critical hour, the *Sufi* movement emerged and tried to established love between these two different religions. The *Sufi* movement was basically socio-religious movement. They studied the *Vedāntic* philosophy and were impressed by its values. They propagated many theories of *Hindu* religion in their speeches and texts. They criticized the orthodox *Muslims*. The union of human soul with the God through devotion and love was the essence of the *Sufi* saint teachings. They established singing and dancing as a form and method to bring people nearer to realization of god.

Religious Traditions in Medieval Period

The Department of Religious Affairs was under the *sadr-u's-sudur*.[2] The offices of the *quadi-u'I-qudat*,[3] the chief judge of the empire, and of the *sadr-u's-sudur* were generally combined during *Mughal* era. In case they were kept separate, the *sadr-u's-sudur* took precedence and was responsible for the judicial administration and religious affairs of the realm and the *quadi-u'I-qudat* simply held court as the chief judge (Naqvi 1990, 207). The office of the *sadr-u's-sudur* originated with the institution of the post of the *sadr-u's-sudur* under the Abbasids when Imam Abu Ysuf was given the 'authority to appoint the *qadis*'[4] outside the capital. In the *Sultanate* of Delhi, however, the office existed from the beginning. The *Mughals* not only continued it but, in the beginning, they also attached the same importance to it as had been by the *Sultans*. *Abu-'l-Fadl* writing of the appointment of Shaikh '*Abdu'n-Nabi* in the 10th regnal year says that,

> It is important that a person distinguished for his wisdom, foresight, truthfulness, integrity and understanding should be appointed to the exalted post of the *sadr*. He should be one who has the virtues of faith, sincerity and kindness, so that through him the poor, the deserving and the needy may attain the good fortune of kissing the sublime threshold and receive, in accordance with their condition and talent, stipends and grants from the emperor.

Four categories of persons were considered deserving to get aid from the state through the *sadr-u's-sudur*. The first were 'the seekers of wisdom who do not distinguish the night from the day in acquiring true knowledge' and 'who have withdrawn their hand from everything else'. The second consisted of persons 'who had declared war on their own desires' and 'in search of spiritual advancement had turned their faces away from the people of the world'. The third were 'helpless persons who did not have the capacity of earning a livelihood'. The fourth were 'people of good birth who through their short-sightedness had not learnt a profession'. Thus the learned, the religious recluses, those incapable of work and persons of good birth lacking the necessary training for earning the means of sustenance were the concern of the *sadr-u's-sudur*.

The grants were given in various forms. If given in cash, they were called *wazifah*; if a grant of land was made it was called *suyurghal*, though the older names of milk and *madad-i-ma'ash* were used more often. These lands were hereditary and, the grants were not conditional upon service, hence they come to be called milk or property, unlike *jagirs* which were assignments on revenue and represented only a method of the payment of the salary attached to the rank or the office. *Madad-i-ma'ash* described the real purpose of the grant, because the term means 'assistance in subsistence'. These 'lands were also called *imah* and the grantees were known as *imahdars*, means holders of grants'.

The Department of Religious Affairs dealt with only one aspect of charity, it has been mentioned that stipends and land were given through it to men of learning and persons of gentle birth who were incapable of earning a livelihood; in particular, ladies left without support were considered deserving of such help. The *Mughals*, however, found other ways and means of helping the poor and the destitute. The department, however, exercised considerable influence upon education. In all *Muslim* countries, education was not controlled by the state and any person who was qualified and felt the urge could set himself up as a teacher. The jurists have laid it down that the *muhtasib* should not permit ill-qualified or disreputable persons to act as teachers. Beyond this, there seems to have been no interference by the government. Every educational institution recruited its own teaching staff and ran its affairs as it liked. Many of these institutions were run by private donations or pious endowments. Quite a few, however, received aid in one form or another. Very often the institution as such received only a modest grant, but the members of its teaching faculty were given grants in their individual capacity and could, therefore, devote themselves to teaching and academic pursuits. In all *Muslim* educational institutions, no fees were charged and deserving students were supplied not only with books but also with all means of sustenance. The Department of Religious Affairs provided grants for the maintenance of such institutions if an endowment did not exist already for the purpose.

Culture was sustained by tradition as well as by prosperity. The population of the subcontinent under the *Sultanate* and *Mughal* era has been estimated at 100,000,000. There was no shortage of cultivable land. Indeed, the anxiety of the state to ensure the expansion of cultivation shows that there was comparatively a shortage of peasants. This is readily understood, if it is remembered that during this era empires were self-sufficient in all their needs and exported not only raw produce but finished materials as well.

Land Policy and Economic Scenario during Medieval Period

Every inch of land in the empire belonged to the King. Any grant of land that he made would be a life grant. Within that period he could take away the land whenever he wanted, for example, 'at the death of the landholder', the land would revert to the crown. His children might or might not get the land, as the king wielded absolute authority. The system of tenure was *Ryotwari*, that is to say, peasants were the tenants of the crown. They were tenants-at-will. To sum up, all the land was vested in the king. He could give and take back land whenever he liked. Vested interest in land, therefore, could not arise.

The 'Divine Right' theory which believe in the absolute authority of the king, assess the cultivators. There was no idea of rent in those days and even if; the idea would not have been put into practice. The crown's demand on land was therefore a tax levied on the peasant 'what the peasant can bear'. The revenue payments in the empire were set by the '*Zabt*' which fixed cash rates and took one-third gross produce as the share of the crown during the *Mughal* era. The charge was on cultivation and not on occupation. Stress was laid on the officials being paid in cash and dealing directly with the individual peasant cultivators. The settlement was based on measurement, and classification of lands, and fixation of rates.

Collectors were to make yearly reports on the conduct of their subordinates. Monthly returns were to be transmitted to the imperial exchequer. Special reports were to be sent up of any special calamities, hail, flood or drought. The collectors were to see that the farmers got receipts for their 'payments, which were to be remitted four times in the year, at the end of that period no balance should be outstanding.

Payments were, if possible, to be voluntary, but the standing crops were theoretically hypothecated, and where needful, were to be attached. Above all, there was to be an accurate and minute record of each man's holdings and liabilities.

In the medieval period the king was the sole banker. He advanced big loans and financed industries. As he would not deal in small sums and as he would give money only to those whom he liked, so a need for other institutions which would take up small businesses, issue *hundees* (bills) and exchange old coins for new coins at a fixed discount was keenly felt. The latter part of the business, namely the exchange of old coins was done by the Kings. The King's business was confined to the capital. In other places, he would deal only through' his governors.

A few banking houses came into existence in order to take up those businesses which the king would not do. They were immediately pounced upon by the officials who put an end to their business. They pleased these officials and approached the Emperor who, after consulting his officers, allowed them to carry on their business within certain limits. The limits imposed were three:

1. They should not compete with the State.
2. They should always consult the king's officials, if they intended introducing any new business; and
3. The rates fixed by the king would be observed by them, that is to say, rates determined by the laws of supply and demand would be ignored and only the king's rates would determine the market tone.

The kinds of business that fell to their lot were:

1. That kind of money lending which king would not do.
2. Exchanging old coins for new coins at a certain discount fixed by the king; and
3. Issuing and discounting of *hundees* at rates sanctioned by the king.

Taxation was recognized as a definite source of income to the king. It was levied everywhere in a haphazard manner. Taxation was viewed purely from the revenue standpoint. Foreigners were taxed less than the subjects of the empire and were further given concessions which hit indigenous industries hard. This was done not with a view to enable the foreigners to destroy the Indian manufactures but to keep the foreigners fighting among themselves. Certainly, this was the chief reason for the English getting better terms than the 'Portuguese'. Agra was anxious to cripple the growing power of the Portuguese and it wanted the English to fight with them. To make one class fight with the other so as to maintain the balance of power seems to be the destiny of India. This central arch of class war in the magnificent edifice of administration is a prime necessity in India as all her rulers have realized.

Akbar's Contribution

The *Ain-i-Akbari,* or the 'constitution of Akbar', is a 16th century classic with detailed document, a record of Akbar's works. This is the third volume of the *Akbarnama* which contains information about Akbar's noble works regarding administrations, gazetteers etc. The first volume contains the history of the Timurs' family and the reigns of Babar, the kings of Sur dynasty and Humayun. The second volume is related to the history of the 46 years of Akbar's life and works. Since it was written around the year of 1590, it also contains details of *Hindu* religion and practices as well as history of India during that era.

Akbar had to fight against odds from the very beginning. He would entreat God for help and beg the favours of saints. When he won his struggles, the religious emperor began to think his success the results of a 'Special Favour of God'. Successive victories and repeated escape from danger developed the idea that he was 'the Chosen of the Lord'.

Akbar was interested in religious discussions. He had filled his court with *Ulema*. When Badauni, an 'alim', was presented in the court, in 1573, he was introduced as a smart debater, 'a mace for the head of *Haji* Ibrahim Sarhindi', the chief of the court scholastic debaters. Akbar asked Badauni to assail certain views of *Haji* Ibrahim and the *Haji* was to defend them. The emperor himself played the judge. The same fondness for scholastic debates led the emperor to order the construction of the *Ibadatkhana* in 1574. The building was completed next year, and debates began to take place therein right earnest. Akbar was zealous in worship and considered the discussion of religious topics a part of worship. But he had begun to play with dangerous material.

Scholastic, legal and religious discussion, where the sole authority is explaining and interpreting writers of the past, may yield a very elastic form of argument. Most of the priestly classes were too proud of their scholarship to accept one another's views. The respect and influence they enjoyed as religious pontiffs had corrupted many of them. The weight of their support when given being amply rewarded, many of them in the court service would not hesitate to distort 'the clear rulings of religion' to confirm Royal actions. Set against them were those courageous spirits who would make no concession to the emperor's wishes. There were, moreover, the usual petty jealousies of human nature and the tactlessness of the martyrs. All this soon caused trouble and led to Akbar's estrangement from the priestly class.

Akbar formulated a religious policy for the *Mughal* empire that can in some ways claim to be a forerunner of the secular aspects of modern Indian polity, is now almost a historical cliché; that he founded a new religion that serious historians have long been trying to eradicate without much success. It is almost certain that, though encouraged by Akbar himself, as his Happy Savings reproduced in the *Ain-i-Akbari* show, his illiteracy was more or less a myth. Akbar's early measures of tolerance, and the abolition of the pilgrimage tax-*Jizya* in the early 1560s were episodic and of little immediate significance. Writing later, Abul Fazl probably exaggerates their importance. On the other hand, Akbar soon initiated a vigorous '*Islamic*' policy, illustrated by the *Fathnama-I Chittor*, the proclamation on the fall of Chittor in 1568, where the infidels are reviled; the reimposition of *Jizya* in 1575 is also symbolic of this policy. It was probably here, in the realm of relations between political sovereignty and theological law, that the contradiction germinated, which later on led to a complete reformulation of Akbar's religious views (Ahmad 2009, 73–79).

Akbar's idea of God was heavily influenced by pantheism: God creates visible differences whereas the reality is the same. 'One heart-ensnaring beauty, lights up thousands of curtains (*pardah*)'. Akbar, indeed, protests that to ascribe evil to Satan (as is done by conventional *Muslims*) is really to limit the absoluteness of God. The evil of Satan too comes from God. At the same time, he is no believer in divine incarnations. He makes a wry dig at this belief of popular *Hinduism*, when he says that in India no one claimed to be a prophet because all would be prophets claimed to be 'God'. Akbar thus expressed a positive disbelief in any visual appearance of the creator in any from whatsoever. Akbar saw a close relationship between the divine sovereign and the temporal sovereign. Akbar not only felt free of any restraint of *Islamic* law; he could also freely criticize it. It is interesting to read his criticism of how daughters are treated in *Islamic* law.

The conclusion that emerges is that Akbar, in pursuit of empire and under the light of an exceptionally brilliant mind, evolved a set of mutually consistent religious ideas derived from a multiplicity of sources but processed and refined by a considerable application of reason. The sincerity with which the beliefs once evolved came to be held was accompanied by an anxiety to provide them with practical application to which we may apply the term *Sulh-i-Kul*. In this application, there was an extension in the opening of doors to the *Hindus* and to *Shias*, as far as the ranks of the nobility were concerned; and there was a withdrawal of patronage to a class particularly hostile to Akbar's own views and policies, the *Muslim* orthodoxy. Given India's variegated culture and multiplicity of religious beliefs, what Akbar was attempting to secure was an integrated ruling class. That he also thereby took a step which could later on be invoked by India's modern nation-builders is not only a tribute to the breadth of his vision but also an illustration of the way in which historical processes occur achieving ends which in earlier times would have been only dimly grasped, or would perhaps have remained totally undiscerned.

In India, during the medieval period, a number of changes occurred. Feudalism was one of that; the feature of this society is that the dominant position in society is held by those people who are the sole centre of power without working on the land. Caste system also existed during this span of time. Due to these evils mostly rulers during medieval period were forced to find a new way of belief and system to establish a peaceful and just society.

Akbar was possessed of an inquisitive mind and was a good physiognomist. If by education, we understand the bringing out of all the faculties latent in man and developing them, then Akbar was highly educated. All his faculties were well developed and well-coordinated. He possessed, in an unusual degree, common sense, that most uncommon thing in the world (Ali 2006). As early as 1566 AD when he was 24, he realized the secret of a stable empire. He was the *Mughal* king who saw the vision of a united India where the two great religions *Hinduism* and *Islam* would be merged in his *Dīn-e Ilāhī* (the divine faith). He developed his ideas in this direction till the date of his death. His one obsession was to combine the monotheism of *Islam* with 'the symbolic and ritualistic worship of *Hinduism*'. He saw that if the empire was to last, it must be based on a religious coalition of the Indian races.

Akbar never pinned his faith to any dogmas and ritualism and gave the first place in religion to reason. He used to say that every religion was based on 'truth' though obscured by weeds of dogmas and ritualism. Therefore, remove the noxious growths and understanding will follow. He was always very fond of discussing religions with men of 'letters and fame'. In his court one might find men of all religions—*Hindus*, *Muslims*, *Christians*, *Parsees* and others—with ample liberty to stress the truths of their religion and criticize the others.

Conclusion

Medieval period has been a turning point wheel in the history of India. This era's impact can be seen till today on all the various dimensions of religion, society and administration, etc. The system which evolved during this era has been a path of life for coming generations and decades of our country. The reforms of Lodi, Khilji, Tughlak and all other dynasties are still relevant. *Mughal* era deeply impacted the fabrics of Indian society, noble works of Akbar are applauded in this century also. Various reforms were started by many *Bhakti* movement saints and *Islamic Sufis*. They talked about one god and one religion. Religious narratives created a harmonious bond between all the sections of society, thus resulting in a secular society. This aspect is relevant in modern world also without any dispute. These all reforms in the medieval period can create equal and better world enriched with peace. These social reforms measures for weeding out the evils of both the *Muslim* and non-*Muslim* societies. These social measures including religious toleration that were introduced during the medieval period give us an impression of a new world or modernism.

Summary

Medieval period has a great importance in Indian history. During this ear many reforms were initiated which changed and impacted the society as well as religion, politics and administration on a broader scale. In this chapter, classification of medieval period and nature of the state has been discussed. Many social reforms occurred and many religious traditions were established during this period. The nature of administration and its scope are also discussed in this chapter. The contribution of the medieval period is versatile in nature. The great *Mughal* ruler Akbar's contribution in each field which discussed in this chapter are praiseworthy.

Points for Discussion

1. Explain the various narratives regarding classification of medieval period.
2. Discuss about the dimensions of economy during medieval period.
3. Critically analyse the nature of State and feature of administration during the medieval period.
4. Discuss the religious aspect of medieval period.
5. Examine the various land policies during the medieval period.
6. Evaluate the contribution of medieval period to modern India.
7. Discuss the role and importance of Akbar as a reformist.

Endnotes

1. Feudalism from above and feudalism from below: it is based on the relatively optimistic belief that a clear division between federal and state authority can exist. This theory believes that authority between natural and state could be treated equally.
2. The *sadr-u-sudur* exercised supervision over the lands granted by the Emperors. His duty was to protect the laws of *Shari'ah*.
3. *Quadi-u'I-qudat* means the Chief Justice of the Empire (Chief Justice of Highest Court).
4. Qadis is the magistrate or Judge of the *Shari'ah* Court.

Glossary

Asiatic Mode of Production: The theory of the Asiatic mode of production was derived by Karl Marx around the early 1850s. Engels was also a commentator on the Asiatic mode of production. They both focussed on the socio-economic base of the society. This theory is basically related to mode of production regarding Asia.

***Dīn-e Ilāhī*:** It means religion of God and it was propounded by the *Mughal* Emperor Akbar in 1582 AD.

'Divine Right' Theory: It is a political-religious doctrine of royal and political legitimacy.

Feudalism: It is a system of land ownership and duties. It came into limelight in medieval age.

Oriental Despotism: Oriental deposition is a particular idea, especially used in the writings of Montesquieu. It is an oppressive form of despotic government.

***Ryotwari* System:** *Ryotwari* system was introduced by Thomas Munro in 1820. In this system, peasants were given the ownership and proprietorship of the land so they could make direct payment to state as 55 per cent of the production.

***Sulh-i-Kul*:** *Sulh-i-Kul* means, peace with all or universal peace. This term is derived from a *Sufi* mystic principle. It was applied by *Mughal* emperor Akbar.

References

Ali, Athar M. 2006. *Mughul India: Studies in Polity, Ideas Society and Cultures*. Delhi: Oxford University Press.
Ahmad, Bashir. 2009. *Akbar: The Great Mughal, His New Policy and His New Religion*. Delhi: Aokar Books.
Kosambi, D. D. 1956. *An Introduction to the Study of Indian History*. Bombay.
Naqvi, H. K. 1990. *History of Mughal Government and Administration*. Delhi: Kanishka Publishing House.
Seshan, Raohika. 2007. *Medieval India, Problems and Possibilities*. Jaipur: Rawat Publications.
Sharma, R. S. 1980. *Indian Feudalism, C 300–1200*. Delhi: Macmillan Publishers.
Wittfogel, K. 1957. *Oriental Deposition*. New Haven: Yale University Press.

Further Readings

Alam, Muzafir and Sanjay Subrahmanyam. 1998. *The Mughal State (1526–1750)*. Delhi: Oxford University Press.
Altekar, A. S. 1967. *Rashtrakutas and Their Times*. Oriental Book Agency.
Chattopadhyaya, B. D. 1994. *The Making of Early Medieval India*. Oxford University Press.
Chaudhuri, K. N. 1990. *Asia Before Europe: Economy and Civilisation of the Indian Ocean from the Rise of Islam to 1750*. Cambridge University Press.
Habib, Irfan. 1963. *The Agrarian System of Mughal India*. Oxford University Press.
Habib, Irfan. 2007. *Medieval India: The Story of a Civilization*. Delhi: National Book Trust.
Hasan, S. 2005. *Nurul Religion, State and Society in Medieval India*, edited and introduced by Satish Chandra. Oxford: Oxford University Press.
Herman, Kulke. 1995. *The State in India 1000–1700*. Oxford: Oxford University Press.
Kosambi, D. D. 1965. *Culture and Civilization of Ancient India in Historical Culture*. Delhi.
Kulkarni, A. R. 2008. *Maharashtra in the Age of Sivaji*. Dimond Publications.
Majumdar, R. C. and S. A. Altekar. 2006. *Vakataka Age—The Gupta Age Circa 200-550 AD*. Motilal Banarsidass Publications.
Nilakanda Sastri, K. A. 1997. *A History of South India from Prehistoric Times to the Fall of Vijayanagar*. Oxford: Oxford University Publication.
Nizami, K. A. 1985. *State and Culture in Medieval India*. New Delhi: Adam Publishers and Distributers.
Noboru, Karashima. 2014. *A Concise History of South India: Issues and Interpretations*. Oxford: Oxford University Press.
Sharma, R. S. *Indian Feudalism Stein Burton, Peasant State and Society in Early Medieval South India*.
Veluthat, Kesavan. 1993. *The Political Structure of Early Medieval South India*. New Delhi: Orient Longman.

13
CHAPTER

Ziyauddin Barani: Ideas on Good *Sultan* and Ideal Polity

Santosh Kumar Mallik and Ramesh Chandra Mahanta

CHAPTER OUTLINE

- Introduction
- The Life Sketch
- Writings of Barani
- Kingship
- Ideal Polity
- Ideal *Sultan* and His Qualities
- Advices to *Sultan*
- Conclusion
- Summary
- Points for Discussion

Should the king consider the payment of a few tankas (standard of exchange) by way of jiziya (religious taxes) as sufficient justification for their allowing all possible freedom to the infidels to observe and demonstrate all orders and detail of infidelity, to read the misleading literature of their faith, and to propagate their teachings, how could the true religion get the upper hand over other religions, and how could the emblems of Islam be held high? How will the true faith prevail if rulers allow the infidels to keep their temples, adorn their idols, and to make merry during their festivals with beating of drums and dhols, singing and dancing?

—The Reḥla, Iban Batuta, Āg̱ẖā Mahdī Ḥusain, Oriental Institute (1953, 261)

Reader's Guide

The chapter is designed to focus on the contribution of Ziyauddin Barani (1283–1359) who was the most important political thinker of the Delhi *Sultanate*, particularly during the reigns of Alauddin Khalji, Muhammad bin Tughluq and Firoz Tughluq. The reader will get an idea how Barani represented the idea of political expediency in the *Islamic* history. The chapter also intends to provide information regarding Barani's *Fatwa-i-Jahandari* (AD 1357), written as *nasihat* (advices) for the *Muslim* kings, a classic work on statecraft which can be compared with Kauṭilya's *Arthaśāstra* and Machiavelli's *Prince*. The reader will be acquainted with Barani's idea about kingship, ideal polity, ideal *Sultan* and his qualities.

Introduction

Ziyauddin Barani was a great political thinker of Delhi *Sultanate*. He was the greatest among all the contemporary historians of the early medieval India. He has given a clear picture about the polity and administrative mechanism through his notable works, such as *Fatwa-i-Jahandari* and *Tarikh-i-Firuz-Shahi*, which led the future monarch towards benevolence and good governance (Afzaluddin 1956, 119). Barani was a close associate of Amir Khusrau and scratched with the highest of the nobility in the *Sultanate*. According to him, the class of order system is determined on the basis of occupational and social orders. Barani sought for stability and justice in the society around him and believed that this cause only be achieved through the ruling institution of *Sultanate* when managed by a properly instructed *Sultan*. However, his political theory had some personal ambition attached to it (Rosenthal 1985, 107).

Barani was the favourite courtier of Muhammad bin Tughluq for 17 years. However, he was out of favour with *Sultan* Firoz Tughluq, who banished Barani from the court and even imprisoned him for some time in Bhatner after which he spent his life in poverty (Syros 2012, 549). Barani was a great author; he wrote two important books, such as *Fatwa-i-Jahandari* and *Tarikh-i-Firuz-Shahi*, in which he has given his emphasis on mapping the political and administrative history of Delhi *Sultanate* (Aḥmad 1949, 107).

The Life Sketch

Ziauddin Barani, born at Baran (Buland-Shahr) in 684 AH (Hijira Era)/1258 AD, was the first Indo-Persian historian to be born and brought up in India. He completed his *Tarikh-i-Firuz-Shahi* in the year 758 AH/1359 AD, at the age of 74. No record is available about Barani's early education. He gives the names of 46 renowned teachers of Alauddin's time whose learned discourses and associations elevated his mental dimensions. Being deeply influenced by the audience of Shaikh Nizamuddin Auliya as a mask of devotion took up his abode at Ghyathpur where the Shaikh lived. He was on equally good terms with Amir Khusrau whom he calls the greatest of all ancient and modern poets (Al-Azmeh 1997, 87).

His youth passed in luxury and pleasure, a gorgeous life after the fashion of the great nobles of the time (Vrolijka and Hogendijk 2007, 241). He was faithful and the favourite courtier of Muhammad bin Tughluq but at times was extremely critical of his policies. When Muhammad bin Tughluq's died, the heyday of Barani's life also came to an end (Chandra 1996, 175). His life lost all glamour and prosperity.

Period of gloom and misery took him, and he almost became a pauper. The alignment of Barani with Khwaja Jahan after the death of Ghiyath al-Din Tughluq was enough to make the relations between Barani and Firuz Shah Tughluq which was further aggravated by rival opponents in the court. Barani's frantic attempts to prove his loyalty to the *Sultan* proved futile (Syros 2012, 560).

Barani belonged to an aristocratic family of the earliest Turkish immigrants to India. His maternal grandfather was a distinguished Nobel of Balban, and his father Muwaidul Mulk was on the personal staff of prince Arkali khan, the second son of Jalaluddin khalji. Barani's uncle Alaul Mulk was a friend of Alauddin Khalji; he was the right-hand man of the latter in planning the Deogiri expedition and the conspiracy to murder Jalaluddin (Vrolijka and Hogendijk 2007, 243). After Alauddin's usurpation of the throne, Alaul Mulk was rewarded immediately with the governorship of Kara and Oudh, and soon after, invited to Delhi to be the chief counsellor of the *Sultan*. Barani was brought up in the capital in an affluent environment and highly aristocratic traditions of the day; he joined the imperial court under Muhammad bin Tughluq and enjoyed his patronage for 17 years. The *Sultan* held him in high esteem as an intellectual (Al-Azmeh 1997, 87).

Barani's misfortune makes him a victim to a sudden change in the court politics. Muhammad bin Tughluq died childless at Thaffa (*sind*), where he had gone to suppress a revolt. When the news of his death reached the capital, Khwaja Jahan, who ran the central administration in the absence of the *Sultan*, raised a young boy to the throne without knowing the fact that Firoze Tughluq (a cousin of Muhammad bin Tughluq) had already been declared *Sultan* by the army officers in Sind (Sarkar 2006, 329). The Khawaja and his associates lost their lives for this misadventure, and Barani, who had extended moral support to them, was also thrown into the prison. Barani lost the royal patronage and suffered confiscations of his assets and properties. He became a pauper overnight, disowned by friends, neglected by relatives and despised by enemies; he died a broken-hearted man in the Khanqah of Sheikh Nizamuddin Auliya (Sarkar 2006, 328).

Barani had remarkable intellect, superb wit, versatile temper and enlivened the parties he attended during his heydays, with his quick wit and humour. He left behind numerous works of which *Sinai-Muhammedi*, *Salavat-i-Kabir*, *Enayet-Namah-i-Ilahi*, *Maathir-i-Saadat* and *Akhbar-i-Barmakiyan* have been prominently mentioned by contemporary and later authors (Chaurasia 2009, 191). All the works have been lost to oblivion except *Tarikh-i-Firuz Shahi* and *Fatwa-i-Jahandari* which bear ample testimony to Barani's talent and scholarship (Syros 2012, 48). It is a pity that Barani is known and acknowledged only as a historian despite the fact that he was endowed with poetic gift of considerably high merit. He exercised his hand on almost all forms of versification, but they did not stand the test of time. We find some of his poetic compositions in *Tarikh-i-Firuz Shahi* (Crone 1980, 108).

Writings of Barani

Tarikh-i-Firuz Shahi

Barani's *Tarikh-i-Firuz-Shahi* personifies the history of the Delhi *Sultanate* for one full century, from 1259 to 1352. Barani's write-up, excluding the narrative of Firoze Tughlug, constitutes a standard work of history which establishes his reputation as a premier historian of his age (Sarkar 2006, 333). Barani's description of Muhammed bin Tughluq's reign is unfair and he distorted the facts deliberately, and works with a biased mind. Barani also described of Alauddin Khalji's war in and Malwa and the Deccan campaigns of Malik Kafur (Syros 2012, 59).

Barani is usually credited with eight historical works, most of which cannot be traced at present. The two most well-known works of Barani are *Tarikh-i-Firuz-Shahi* and *Fatwa-i-Jahandari*, which provide valuable information about the history of that period (Collins 2000, 184). He completed his work *Tarikh-i-Firuz-Shahi* in 1357 and dedicated the same to the ruling Sovereign. It may be noted that the book does not exclusively deal with the reign of Firoz Shah. It begins with Balban and ends with the sixth year of Firoz Shah (Sarkar 2006, 350). His account of Balban is based on what he learns about Balban from his ancestors.

While on the one hand, he shows great admiration for the intellectual accomplishments, scholarship and qualities of head and heart of Muhammad bin Tughluq, on the other hand he also criticizes the *Sultan's* capricious temper and high handedness (Sarkar 2006, 352). However, while narrating the events of the reign of Muhammad bin Tughluq, Barani does not present the various events in their chronological order (Elliot and Dowson 1867, 129). Barani himself was aware of this shortcoming in his work and said: 'I have written in this history the principle of *Sultan* Mohammad's administration and have paid no heed to the sequence and order of events' (Habib 1981, 78). Barani displays himself a shameless flatterer when he describes Firoz Shah. He finds divine attributes in the person of Firoz Shah and considers his court as the court of *Allah*. 'He lavishly praises the *Sultan* for his various works of public welfare. If we judge Barani by the canons laid down by him in the preface to *Tarikh-i-Firuz-Shahi*, he stands condemned as a historian' (Habib 1981, 76).

One can notice a number of defects in the historical writings of *Tarikh-i-Firuz-Shahi*, and these include (a) description of events, which were not of his liking, in brief, and overplay of the thing which he liked; (b) his narration lacks chronological order. His account of the reign of Mohammad bin Tughluq is an evidence of it; (c) his work lacks order and arrangement; (d) his vision was coloured and he interpreted the various measures and polices in terms of his religion; (e) he deals with personality and character of the *Sultan* and other *Amirs* in detail and does not provide detailed accounts of the wars, battles and the life of the people; (f) he makes contradictory statements which make a proper assessment difficult (Fleischer 1986, 99). For example, 'he lavishly praises *Sultan* Alauddin but dubs him as a *pharsh*. As a result, it is difficult to judge whether Alauddin was a liberal ruler or a despotic tyrant (Hardy 1978a, 132). In spite of the above shortcomings, Barani's works have great historical value. 'Though he had his prejudices, drawback, weakness and obstructions, his account of the *Sultan* is reliable. Compared with others, he is more authentic especially for the Khilji period' (Syros 2012, 548).

Fatwa-i-Jahandari

His other historical work *Fatwa-i-Jahandari* was compiled after *Tarikh-i-Firuz-Shahi*. It analyses the qualities, virtues and talents that a good monarch should possess (Jackson 1999, 312). He also describes the principles of administration and ideals of government and illustrates them by examples from the history of Iran and other *Muslim* countries. Barani held that his work was superior to the work of earlier writers (Rosenthal 1985, 109). He says' 'old writers had many works on administration, but the way in which I have explained the principles and ordinances of administration for the guidance of kings, ministers, *Maliks* and *Amirs* has not been done so far by any writer' (Hardy 1978b, 202). The detailed account provided by Barani about the *Sultan*, their courts and how they framed their polices as well as the description of the contemporary conditions of immense value in forming an idea about the social and economic conditions of the people in the 14th century cannot be denied (Kumar 2007, 98).

Barani's *Fatwa-i-Jahandari* provides an example of his extreme views on religion. He states that there is no difference between *Muslim* kings content in collecting *Jizya* (poll tax) *Khiraj* (tribute) from the *Hindu* (Morris 2009, 279). Instead, he recommends that a *Muslim* king should concentrate all his power on holy wars and completely uproot the false creeds. According to him, a *Muslim* king should establish the supremacy of *Islam* in India only by slaughtering the *Brāhmaṇs*. He recommends that a *Muslim* king should make a firm resolve to overpower, capture, enslave and degrade the infidel (ibid., 281).

This work appears to have been a kind of supplement to his *Tarik-I–Firuz shahi*. What Barani has merely hinted in the *Tarikh-i-Firuz-Shahi*, he has said plainly in the *Fatwa-i-Jahandari*. It describes certain ethics of administration and important ideas of government (Marlow 2007, 35). It begins with an account of the creation of world and the prophets and their teachings. It analyses the good qualities, virtues and talents that a monarch should possess. It suggests ways and means to propagate *Islam* to destroy the infidels (*Hindus*) and tells about *din Panah* (Protector of religious *Sunni* faith) and *din parwari* (observance of the *Sunni* faith) (Hardy 1978b, 209). It explains the advice that a ruler should seek and follow glories and principles of administration, judiciary, crimes and punishments, state treasury, army and its composition, military expeditions, revolts and measure to suppress them, fiscal policy and market regulations, etc. (Persram 2007, 39). Barani himself writes about the *Fatwa-i-Jahandari*. 'Old writers had written many works on administration, but the way in which I have explained the principles and ordinance of administration for guidance of king, Ministers, *Maliks* and *Amirs* has not been done so far by any writer' (Sarkar 2006, 330).

The *Fatwa-i-Jahandari* can be divided into two parts: (a) principles of ideal administration and (b) examples from history to illustrate them. In this work, Barani has stated that the *Sultan* Mohammad of Gazni was an ideal and extraordinary ruler (Nizami 1981, 122). He possessed all the kingly virtues and talents and other *Muslim* rulers should follow them. He has substantiated them by giving examples from the history of Iran and quoting events from the history of other *Muslim* countries (Pacey 1991, 26).

The economic policy that he initiated in the *Fatwa-i-Jahandari* is the same as followed by *Sultan* Alauddin Khalji. He desired that the prices of articles of consumption should be fixed by the state authorities; none should be allowed to sell articles at higher rates than those fixed by the state authority. Market inspectors and officials should be appointed to enforce the market tariff rigidly (Stowasser 1983, 186).

As *Hindus* had enjoyed the monopoly of trade and commerce, Barani had at many places initiated the principle of depriving the *Hindu* merchants and traders of their wealth and humiliating them socially (Pipes 1981, 133). As *Brāhmaṇs* were well to do and had enjoyed good social status, Barani advocated the principles of robbing them of their wealth and annihilating them. According to Barani, this was an easy way to acquire wealth and enrich the poverty-stricken *Muslims* (Al-Ashmuni 1961, 279).

The following are the other important works of Barani:

1. *Salvat-I-Kabir* (The Greater Prayer)
2. *Sana-I-Muhammadi* (Praises of Prophet Muhammad)
3. *Hasratnama* (Book of Regrets)
4. *Tarikh-I-Barmaki*
5. *Inayat Nama-I-Ilahi* (Book of Good Gifts)
6. *Maasirsaadat* (Good Deeds of the *Sayyids*)
7. *Lubbatul Tarikh*

Kingship

Ziyauddin Barani argues about the theory of kingship that the rulers, who maintained glory and grandeur of court by impressing royal people, in fact, create fear among their subjects which consequently raise the status and prestige of a king (Prasad 1936, 6). Therefore, it was necessary for the rulers to create fear by showing their power and glory among the common people as well as the nobles. He also said that the *Sultan*, though he was not an educated man and did not study books, had been careful to prevent rebellions against him (Puri and Das 2003, 182). He always implemented rules which were in favour of common people in one way or the other (Habib 1999, 32). If people did not obey the *Sultan's* order and ignored laws, *Sultan* took stern action against them because their main concerns were to maintain peace and order for the welfare of people. As Barani stated that both Balban and Alauddin following their own concept of kingship, successfully ruled over the people.

Mohammad Habib wrote of the Delhi *Sultanate*, 'It was not a theocratic state in any sense of the word. Its basis was not the *Shari'at* of *Islam* but the *zawabit* of state laws made by the king; and not only that, *Muslim* jurists were equally uncertain about the foundations of *Islamic* political power in a post-Caliph world' (ibid., 22). In a *Sunni* context, and in relation to the power and authority of God's caliph (*khalifat Allah*), *Sultans* were the right hand of God's caliph (*yamin-i khalifat Allah*). They were in an absolute sense the arbitrators of justice and punishment, nothing less than God's shadow on earth (*zill Allah fi'l-'ard*) (ibid., 23). This idea of *Islamic* power and authority was invented and sustained in prominent writings produced in the 5th to 11th century. It contributed to the understanding of the Delhi *Sultanate* not as 'expediency', but as an ideal of *Islamic* power embodied and united in the figure of the *Sultan*. On the other side of the legitimacy debate, some scholars have staked out a 'shari'ah position' (Raverty 1881, 497.).

Bold proclamations such as, 'The *Sultanate* of Delhi was a theocracy and not a secular state are frequently found in secondary literature on the subject' (Habib 1999, 26). A lack of recognition of fundamental ambiguities in the Delhi *Sultanate* authority has led to a polarized understanding of the relationship between religious authority and political power in a variety of historical contexts (Rizvi 1978, 375). To better investigate the relationship between religion and power, one must look at its historiography, the dominant literary mode utilized in presenting the image of *Sultan*, in the Delhi *Sultanate* (Syros 2012, 571). The crafters of history employed certain kinds of historiography to draw up an idea of the *Islamic* heritage that replicated, reinvented and reinterpreted conceptions of *Muslim* authority. On a fundamental level, they were the architects of the rhetoric of the *Islamic* empire (Rosenthal 1985, 106).

To seek legitimacy, some like Iltutmish, Muhammad bin Tughluq and Firoz Shah Tughluq got a letter from the Caliph at Baghdad; Iltutmish even declared himself to be the 'Helper of Caliph'. Balban's kingship ideology was based on Iranian theory that the king was semi-divine and only answerable to God (Sarkar 2005, 289). He underlined the theory that the *Sultan* was the shadow of the almighty '*Zil-i-Allah*', and emphasized it by insisting people to perform *Sijada* and *Pabos*, which according to theologians were reserved alone for God. But, otherwise, the rulers tried to find legitimacy through literature and *Muslim* historiography. They have often tried to bring references from *Shari'ah* or, sometimes, by even opposing it (Syros 2012, 574). In *Fatwa-i-Jahandari* of *Ziyauddin Barani*, state legislation or *zawabit* was seen to be totally opposed to *Shari'ah* (Sarkar 2005, 312). On the other hand, in the literature produced in the Persian world, the *adab* or later *akhlaqi* literature had Greco-Hellenic shadows and talked about kingship in that manner (Hardy 1978a, 130). Following that, many of the rulers declared themselves as descendants of some mythical king who, in certain cases, might not even have existed (Aquil 2008, 171).

Ideal Polity

The major book on the political philosophy of the Delhi *Sultanate* is the principle of government (*Fatwa-i-Jahandari*) by the historian *Khwaja Zia-uddin Barani* (Afzaluddin 1956, 119). In the period of Tughlugs, Barani complained of the appointment of *Hindus* and men of low birth to high offices. He definitely looked at *Muslim* government from the perspective of his aristocratic class and he very much resented the *Muslim* slaves (*Sultani*) in the government and hated *Hindus* even more. His bias was so strong that he even considered religious piety the privilege of good birth. He argued that state offices should be hereditary. Barani also hated philosophers, scientists, heretics and low-born *Muslims* as well as *Hindus*, against whom he advocated war (Syed 1974, 86).

In his work on government, *Fatwa-i-Jahandari*, Barani used the *Sultan* Mahmud of Ghazni as his spokesman and thus was not able to give examples later than the 11th century. Barani emphasized the importance of good counsel and listed the conditions of good Counsellor, who should be permanent, aware of state secrets and have perfect security (Sen 2013, 70). The king should begin by keeping his opinions secret, and discussion should be held before eating, in order to have clear heads, and anonymous decisions by the counsellors are recommended. To avoid tyranny, the king should make correct determinations for the general welfare and avoid weakness in carrying them out (Sherwani 1945, 165).

Barani had his own concept of how society should be organized. The *ashraf* (elite) alone should enjoy high positions in the government as well as in society. But how was this possible? Barani solved this problem by suggesting that knowledge should not be given to people of the lower sections of society; he appreciated Iltutmish's terminating the services of some officers who were found to have affiliations with 'lower classes' (Rizvi 1978, 357).

It is not possible to agree with K. A. Nizami when he opines that, 'This class-consciousness ultimately developed into a complex, and embittered his attitude towards the lower sections of society; the source of this bitterness was political, not religious or social' (Nizami 1981, 122). During the *Sultanate* period, even to think of social equality or justice was totally out of the question. It was not only Barani who held this opinion. It was the feeling of the time. In *mulukiyat*, one cannot even think of social equality. It may be *Hindu*, *Christian* or *Muslim*, monarchy condition is one and the same (ibid., 418). Barani complains that talented people do not enjoy the status due to them. But, at the same time, he reminds us about the attitude of *Ulema* and *mashaikh* (Siddiqi 1983, 183). He quotes Balban who said that;

> You have not seen those *ulema* and *mashaikh* whom I had seen in the company of *Sultan* Iltutmish, and I had heard their sermons. Now, such type of God-fearing *ulema* and *mashaikh* are not there, who could dare to tell the truth in front of the *Sultan*, even though it would not be liked by him? Here, Barani is appreciative of the role of those *ulema* who were learned, pious and also courageous. (ibid., 184)

Barani considered the perfection of scholarship to remain independent and free from all pressures. But he himself served as *nadeem* (secretary) of Muhammad bin Tughluq, and when he was not given any position by Firoz Shah, he made an issue of it. It shows that Barani was not able to live up to his own principles (Stowasser 1983, 186).

Barani was not only against *Hindus* but also firmly hostile to non-*Sunni Muslims*. Barani believed that one should condemn *Muslims* who are anti-*Sunni*; no non-*Sunnis* should be allowed to hold any position in the government (Barani 1983, 105). This approach was also the result of the conversion of *Islamic* republic to *Mulukiyat*. *Sunnis* always held power and controlled the governments in different countries, and they did not allow non-*Sunnis* to share power (ibid., 106).

As far as Barani's attitude towards *Hindus* is concerned, it is clear from his writings, 'They (*Sultans*) should eradicate paganism and idol-worship and if they are not able to do it because of the overwhelming population of *Hindus*, for the sake of *Islam*, these rulers should keep *Hindus* at a low level' (Nizami 1981, 19). 'For the sake of *Islam*, they should not allow a single pagan to lead an honourable life'.

Barani examines the problems of *Sultan*. A position that is achieved on the basis of power is not easy to hold. One had to do away with the old guard of the earlier *Sultans*. Until Iltutmish had not killed Qazi Sad, Qazi Hisam and some other Ghauri nobles, he would not have succeeded in getting full control over the government (Siddiqi 1983, 180). While *Turkan-i-Chahalgani* was holding power, they had killed so many people, with the result, some old and powerful families were ruined totally. Balban followed the same policy as a *malik* when he became the *Sultan*. First of all, Balban killed Tughril, and his supporters were hanged. During the period of Kaiqubad, many people were killed. Barani's statement about the elimination of the favourite nobles of the late *Sultan* (Muhammad) is more comprehensive in the first version (ibid., 181). Many confidants of the *Sultan* were either put to death or thrown into prisons. It clearly shows that he revised his statement in the second version in the light of the circumstances. Although Barani eulogizes Firoz Shah Tughluq, there is some implicit criticism of the new *Sultan*. Describing the good qualities of Firoz Shah, he indirectly refers to the elimination of the favourite nobles of Muhammad bin Tughluq, because they were quite close to their master ideologically, or carried out his orders strictly. These killings of the nobles took place during the period of the crisis of succession and also later on (Rizvi 1978, 356).

In an *Islamic* set-up or in a monarchy, the *sultan* was the only powerful person. Everything revolved around him. *Muslims* who were writing the history of the age shifted to the history of kings. Some of these historians, who had a long record of their family member's association with the *Sultans* of Delhi, had its impact on their writings. Delhi became a major centre of learning and became richer after the sack of Baghdad in 1258 AD. *Ulema* migrated from other parts of the *Muslim* world and settled down in Delhi, which was the safest capital for *Muslims*. There, they got patronage and financial support from the *Sultans*.

Ideal *Sultan* and His Qualities

Barani is especially emphatic about the importance of the ruler's carrying out his decisions. The sovereign ought to possess correct determination (*azm-i durust*), which is the element that distinguishes true kingship from tyranny and despotism. He enjoins the ruler to exhibit correct determination in the tasks of the government and to permit no weakness or disorder in the management of state affairs so that he can implement his plans faster and with greater efficiency (Rosenthal 1985, 105). As Barani phrases it, faith in the firmness of the will of the sovereign is one of the main foundations of an effective ruler, which creates a lasting impression on the minds of those both far from and close to him as it instils fear in his rivals, and enhances his subjects' confidence that he will persist in an enterprise until it has been accomplished. However, if a ruler gains the reputation of being weak and unstable, the people will sense his vacillation and inconstancy in the administration of the state; his supporters will lose their confidence in the permanence of his favours; his enemies will have no fear of him; and his subjects will have no assurance about the execution of his orders and prohibitions and no respect for his words (Syros 2012, 566).

For Barani, strong resolve is a key virtue for the model ruler: Socrates, Plato, Aristotle, Diogenes, Hippocrates and all wise men concurred on the notion of kingship as the embodiment of strong resolve. But strong resolve is the mark not only of a competent ruler but also of the prophets, saints and wise men who have resisted material temptations. A sovereign who lacks strong resolve, lofty determination and a desire for greatness will fall short in his attempts to execute fully the duties associated with his position (Habib 1958, 212). His benefits will not reach the people, and he will fail to inculcate in his subjects respect for his dignity and greatness. While the ruler's dignity is founded on his possession of treasures, valuables, horses, camels, mules and sumptuous palaces, strong resolve leads him to be generous in the distribution of benefits (Syros 2012, 568).

Barani underscores the link between strong resolve and the ruler's reputation: strong resolve correctly executed and aimed at an achievable goal is conducive to the public welfare and to other beneficial ends and enhances the ruler's reputation. But if the end of princely conduct is mischievous, evil or impossible to attain, then ruin, public hatred, distress, and misfortune will result, and these are signs of despotism and tyranny. Resolve, strength, greatness and the desire for greatness are at odds with parsimony, avarice and miserliness (Syros 2012, 569). A rapacious ruler is likely to be tempted by everything valuable or costly that his subjects possess. Then, loath to spend his revenues, he will seize the property of his people. True kingship can exist and flourish only when the king is superior to his fellow men in dignity, power and status. Ultimately, strong resolve allows the ruler to build and sustain his reputation and to secure the backing of the people. Barani stipulates specific practices and behaviour that instil a proper mix of hope and fear in people's hearts and thereby promote the ruler's public persona and allow him to carry out his policies (Habib 1958, 256). Elaborating on the Greek idea of the mean, he contends that the best actions follow the middle path and that moderate conduct and the balanced use of pleasure and fear are crucial to a ruler's success (Marlow 2007, 35). Extreme demands and heavy taxation are detrimental to the stability of the state, and a sagacious leader ought to treat his subjects with leniency and meekness. The ruler in his relations with his officials, courtiers, soldiers and subjects ought to follow the middle course. If he seeks to please his subjects, his prestige will suffer; if he is harsh and ill-tempered or if he makes extreme and severe demands, he will incur hatred. The ruler ought to operate like a physician who puts ointment and cauterizes when necessary (Syros 2012, 559).

One element that sets Baranī's work apart from previous advice books for princes is that he refrains from projecting the ruler as an ideal individual. Instead, he sees him as susceptible to passions and irrational desires (Habib 1999, 35). A ruler therefore decide the affairs of his realm in consultation with his advisers and is ought to solicit the counsel of experienced and wise persons before embarking on important enterprises and promulgating laws. Specifically, Baranï recommends that before making any decisions about a particular enterprise or policy and announcing it, the ruler ought to reflect on the likelihood of its success and failure and its implications for his own position, the religion of the state, the military and the people. In private deliberations with his advisers, he should discuss the various aspects of each enterprise: its beginning, termination and effects; its advantages and risks; and the consequences of persistence and retreat. The ruler ought then to publicize his decisions and persist in them so as to reach his objectives as soon as possible (ibid., 25).

Baranï lays out a series of requirements for the process of deliberation and counselling: (a) Counsellors ought to express their opinions frankly and should be able to say whatever comes to their mind, put forward reasons and arguments, and engage in honest deliberations with one other. (b) Counsellors ought to be permanent and equal to each other in experience, loyalty and status before the ruler. (c) All counsellors should be acquainted with the secrets of the state in order to be able to proffer right advice, just as a physician cannot prescribe a proper remedy unless he knows the diseases of the patient. (d) The ruler should conceal his opinions and first listen to the suggestions of his advisers. For, if he reveals his own views at the outset, his counsellors are likely to endorse his decisions intentionally or unintentionally, will lack the courage to oppose or give reasons against his decisions, and will refrain from expressing their own views (Hardy 1978a, 131).

Barani emphasized the importance of grading the ranks of the officials in order to elevate the worthy nobles. Kings are obligated to appoint intelligence officers in their court (Rizvi 1978, 356). The rulers should control the prices according to the costs of production. A king must recognize the rights of the people. The ruler should be capable of virtues, truthfulness, keeping promises, protecting other classes, loyalty, justice, gratitude and fear of God (Rosenthal 1985, 108).

Justice, for Barani, is the bedrock of social organization and political order. Accordingly, he visualizes the ruler as the custodian of justice and identifies power and authority as the two major components of an efficient ruler. He vividly explains: if the wise men of the earth try to govern a village or even a household through mere policy or on the basis of the precepts of wisdom, without power, they will not succeed (ibid., 109). The justification for the supremacy of kings lies in their power and dignity, which enable them to apply justice. Through his authority and prestige, the ruler ought to prevent the strong from oppressing the people. By safeguarding justice, he should create the conditions for every art and profession to flourish and the whole world to become inhabited and prosperous (Siddiqi 1983, 183).

Advices to *Sultan*

A king must recognize the rights of the people. The king should not interfere with the punishments of *Islamic* law (*Shari'at*), but the death penalty in political trials should only be inflicted in extreme cases. The king must also establish and enforce permanent state laws. First, there must be religion of Islam. Second, sins and shameful deeds must be suppressed. Third, rules of the *Shari'at* must be enforced. Fourth, justice must be enforced. Barani considered non-Muslims as enemies and could be plundered by force (Aquil 2008, 170). The king should be characterized by high resolve, which Barani meant generosity not miserliness. He warned that if the king afflicts his subjects with exactions, they will be unable to comply and will rebel. The king must have contradictory qualities in order to be able to handle the virtuous and the wicked. The king should avoid the qualities of changeability, deception and wrath and false promotion of the unjust. Barani wanted to establish *Islamic* truth at the centre and he also urged prohibiting the education of the lower orders lest they become more capable (Data 2008, 193).

Barani's political theory is premised on the notion that the ruler is constantly exposed to attempts to overthrow his power. People nourish resentment against the ruler and seek to take revenge. In order to quench their wrath and to satisfy their desire for vengeance, they seek to undermine his rule. Therefore, Barani admonishes the ruler to be on his guard against deception and conspiracies. Wise leaders, ancient and modern, have always surrounded themselves with guards and watchmen in order to be safe from rebels and assassins. Barani underscores the importance of an elaborate intelligence network as one of the main pillars of efficient leadership. In the event of a rebellion in the capital or the provinces, or if rebels come from outside, the ruler should dispatch spies and informants to gather intelligence about the number, strength and unity as well as the plans and methods of the rebels. If intelligence about a planned rebellion reaches the ruler in time, he can quash it in such a way that he will not need to murder the rebels (Aquil 2009, 79).

If potential conspirators know that no conspiracies can be concealed from the ruler, they will often be frightened and refrain from plotting. Barani's account of the benefits derived from the study of history: knowledge of historical events which enables the *sultans*, kings, ministers and other great men to remain firm in case a disaster falls from the sky, to learn from similar situations that occurred in the past, and to apply remedies used by their predecessors for the various maladies affecting ruler and social life in general. Barani's pronouncements on the nexus between history and government echo ideas found in medieval historiography and *akhlãq* literature, a body of treatises intended to proffer moral advice (Foltz 1998, 17).

Unlike previous *Islamic* theorists, Barani is not concerned solely with determining the causes of dissent and of the decline of kingship. Rather, he displays a profound understanding of the variety, severity and duration of political crises and military challenges and adds depth to earlier debates on the origins and effects of various forms of contingencies. He discusses epidemics and famines, the confidence of the subjects and enemy onslaughts (Zakharia and Cheiban 2007, 229). When famines break out, the ruler ought to provide relief to his subjects by reducing the tribute and poll tax or by offering loans from the treasury, distributing gifts to the poor and subsidizing merchants so that they can import grain from abroad and sell it at the cheapest possible prices. If the famine is more serious, Barani enjoins the ruler to remit the tribute and poll tax and to order rich men to support the needy (ibid., 231).

The factors that lead a ruler to lose public support are: severe demands, bad temper, harsh measures, excessive censures and punishments, lack of mercy, failure to redress grievances and maladministration, low salaries and excessive taxation, and policies whose implementation causes great affliction to the subjects or is impossible (Yamanaka 2003, 17). The characteristics of salutary ruler are friendliness, affection, kindness and mildness. Barani expects the ruler to perceive the moral principles underlying rulership and to treat his subjects with kindness and moderation if he wants to secure his domain and gain a long-lasting reputation. If the sovereign imposes orders to which the subjects are not accustomed, their implementation will entail difficulties and hardships; and if the ruler persists in carrying them out, his subjects are likely to rebel and challenge him (Bosworth 1996, 530). The loss of the subject's goodwill constitutes for Baranï a chronic disease, because it results from the ruler's own character and conduct and is therefore hard to cure. If the subjects figure out the ruler's true character and intentions, even if he decides to abandon his policies and to change his character and comportment, they will keep distrusting him, their hatred will not diminish, and they will ascribe his change of character to trickery and deceit (Lambton 1971, 421). In such cases, some rulers decide to step down, relinquish power to their sons or brothers and retreat from political life to be safe from murder and disgrace or they commit suicide.

An enemy superior in military power, dignity and resources invades the ruler's realm, and no opposition or resistance is possible. In this case, the ruler should try to postpone military confrontation by resorting to conciliatory methods, for example by sending gifts to the invader and his entourage. In the meantime, he should build up his defences and reorganize his military forces (Dahlén 2009, 21). If he offers a monetary tribute to the invader, his reputation will suffer irrevocable damage. Many kings preferred wars and battles that led to total destruction rather than submission to the enemy and payment of tributes. The ruler ought to sacrifice everything to repulse the invading forces. Another solution is marriage with the aim of forging an alliance with the enemy, provided that the two parties follow the same religion. A third option is to win over the enemy's senior officers and military commanders (Fleischer 1986, 99). In case the enemy continues its inroads despite all efforts (sending presents and secretly bribing officers of the enemy), the ruler should transfer his capital to another territory and select skilled warriors to defend it from the enemy's attacks, although such a solution is nearly impossible to implement because emigration is difficult (Rizvi 1978, 354).

It may happen that the ruler is established in his capital with his army and treasures, and two enemies equal to him in power attack his realm simultaneously from opposite directions. If confronting them simultaneously is not possible, he should focus on protecting the capital and the key strongholds until the campaigning season is over and both enemies retreat. If the ruler has exhausted all his equipment and, before he can acquire additional military supplies, an enemy of equal strength marches against him, the ruler should provide for the defence of the capital and seek refuge in forts (Fleischer 1986, 98). The ruler may have established his power over a newly conquered territory but may not yet have managed to consolidate his rule or overcome the hostility and opposition of the army officers of the conquered territory. If at that moment an enemy attacks his kingdom, Barani advises the ruler to not launch war but, rather, to seek refuge in his forts, protect the capital and to try to gain time (Chandra 1996, 180). If an enemy of equal power attacks and the ruler does not possess sufficient forces to repel invaders, he is entitled to take his subjects' property as a loan and prepare his troops for combat. If an enemy invades his country and the ruler's forces do not match the enemy's, making it impossible for him to build up a stronger army, he should mobilize the whole population (ibid., 182).

Conclusion

Ziyauddin Barani was a political thinker of Delhi *Sultanate* during the reign of Muhammad bin Tughluq and Firoz Shah Tughluq. Barani was the first Indian to write in Persian the chronicle of *Turko–Afghan* kings. Prior to his attempts, *Taj-ul-Maathir*, and *Tabaqat-i-Nasiri* had been written by authors who had migrated from abroad to India while Barani was born and brought up in India (Essid 1995, 38). Barani could not help employing the words of indigenous origin in his writings. Nizami goes as far as to remark that 'a careful study of Barani's *Tarikh-i-Firuz Shahi* creates the impression that the thought was in Hindi but he wrote in Persian'. The following words of Hindi have been used by Barani in his *Tarikh*: Supari, Bhatti, Reori, Paek, Kewani, Kahar, Dhanek, Payadah, Chabutarah, Rawat, Mawas, Thug, Mandahar, Mandil, Dugla, Morah, Bang, Chandheri, Patwari, Manda, Bhatt, Thana, Dhawah, Boriyah, Math, Chhappari, Kaudi, Deotha, Bira, Seth, Dholak, Ghhati, Hajjam, Jolaha, Lakh, Karor, Piyaz, Tika, Bhangi, Bhangri, Mahent, Dhakkar, Qhol, Balahar, Sondhar, etc. Following names of fruits and grains of Indian origin have been referred to: Janheri, Ponds, Peepul, Jamun, Badhal, Khirni, Lemun, Jhawanek, Mothi, Kunjad (Alam and Subrahmanyam 1998, 117).

Barani as a historian had certain advantage over other writers of the period and is established by the following facts: Barani's father and uncle held reliable posts in the Court of reigning monarchs. He himself was attached to the Court of Muhammad bin Tughluq for 17 years and had the opportunity to witness the affairs of state. Even in the case of his predecessors he had first-hand authority in his father and uncle (Syed 1974, 86). Barani's *Tarikh-i-Firuz Shahi* is the only authoritative account which gives full information about the first two Tughluqs. Later writers have based their writing on Barani who, though obsessed by his orthodox mentality, supplies valuable details. History was a favourite subject of Barani. He made extensive studies in this branch of learning. The idea of history according to Barani is

> to record the good and evil, justice and injustice, rights and their opposite virtues, sins, vices and weaknesses of the ancients, so that posterity may take their lessons to the heart and see the good of

justice and the evils of injustice so far as political statecraft is concerned, and they may adopt virtuous ways and refrain from evil doing. (Barani 1983, 138)

Consequently, Barani not only records his events but judges them in the light of/own ideas and draws conclusions which often lead the reader astray.

Barani belonged to that school of *Ulema* who approved only those who followed the formulae of the orthodox school and condemned them who did not act according to the set rules (Aigle 2007, 19). That is the reason, the rationality and far-sightedness of Alauddin do not deserve any praise in the eyes of Barani and he expresses his indignation. His mental make-up was such that he judged the king according to his own values and presented him to the readers as his eyes saw him (Subtelny 2009, 56). Although Barani is always lacking in dates and has a faulty method of arrangement, his record is considerably accurate and honest. He can be relied upon. In the preface of his work he writes that 'history is a record of events and a historian should write nothing but truth; if he is unable to do so openly, he should employ hints and codes to serve his purpose' (Sherwani 1945, 165). On the one hand, he believes truth to be inevitable for historians and on the other he is unable to tolerate those who do not agree with him. He denounces low-born persons and notwithstanding their talents deprives them of every right to education and rank. He extols the privileged class and undermines the *Islamic* concept of universal brotherhood and equity.

But Barani finds it difficult to read the actions of leading persons in the context of community interests and considers them as isolated performers. Barani's frankness and honesty are appreciable. Even Ishwari Prasad remarks that 'he was sincere in his condemnation of the *Sultan's* measure' (Chandra 1996, 180). His only fault lies in that he was obsessed by the idea that Islam was being ruined by the *Sultan's* policy and it was this mental obsession which prevented him from seeing things in their proper perspective. His attitude is precisely that of an orthodox Brahman Pandit attempting to write a history of modern India with its multifarious problems. He is blamed of opportunism by Ishwari Prasad, who quotes Barani's confession to the effect 'I did not speak (at times) what was right and true on account of fear and greed. I do not know what will happen to me in future' (ibid., 179).

Ishwari Prasad warns us to accept the observance of such an author with care and caution. But we must understand Barani's state of mind at the time of writing the book. He might have been an opportunist at times as he confesses. But at the time when he wrote the book, he had lost all glory and was at the brink of death, with no hope and no aspiration. At the stage when he was remorseful of his past actions and repentant of his greed, we cannot blame him to be indulging in falsehood for the sake of availing himself of opportunities. He is never accurate in figures and dates as, for instance, the number of soldiers accompanying Taghi is given as 30,000–40,000, leaving it to the whim of the reader to make out any number ranging from 30,000 to 40,000. Barani gives details of economic measures of Alauddin, but mostly writing from memory, he has kept Delhi in the limelight ignoring the provinces, small towns and villages. Despite all his shortcomings, no other historian of the period comes anywhere near him (Barani) and, in spite of all discrepancies, *Tarikh-i-Firuz Shahi* still remains the most important source of the history of the period covered by it.

Summary

Barani's prominence lies in his theory of narration and its steady application in dissimilar aspect of society of his time resulting in his theory of statecraft which made him exclusive and unfathomable. In fact, it will not be erroneous to say that he mobilized all his acquaintance and undergoes for the past and the events of his time to serve the interests of the *Sultanate*. The prominent elements of his theory were his conviction in the transmissible status of the aristocracy, championship of political feasibility on the part of monarchy and nobility, and contempt for the downtrodden. Thus, the complete assumption of Barani had a clear-cut concentration. On the facade, his *Fatawa* or *Tarikh* may look like a collection of contradictions, but underneath it lies the steadiness of his interest—the fortification, integration and expansion of the *Sultanate*, and the methods applied to achieve these aims. Fundamentally, a conventional member of the aristocracy in his outlook, he imprinted for stability but was surpassed by the altering situation of his time, and relegated by the course group whom he preferred to characterize.

Points for Discussion

1. Analyse the thoughts of Ziyauddin Barani in the circumstance of Indian politics during the *Sultanate* period.
2. Evaluate the 'Theory of Kingship' and good governance as recommended by Barani during the *Sultanate*.
3. What is the political consolidation and intervention of Barani's thoughts on ideal polity of *Sultan*?
4. Discuss the fundamental thoughts of Ziyauddin Barani
5. How far Barani's work *Tarikh-i-Firuz Shahi* is important as far as polity and administration is concerned?
6. How Machiavellian ideology is revealed and reflected in Barani's thoughts?
7. Critically analyse Barani's advice for a good *Sultan*.

Glossary

***Chachnama*:** An account by an anonymous writer which describes the conquest of Sindh by the Arab general Muhammad bin Qasim in 712 CE. It also gives us detailed account of Sind, about its people, flora and fauna, agriculture, trade and commerce.

***Quasidas*:** Genealogies composed by Arabs in praise of gods and goddesses in the pre-Islamic days.

***Devnagiri*:** A North Indic script descended from *Brahmi*; used to write Sanskrit and a range of north Indian languages.

***Malfuzats*:** Conversations between a Sufi teacher called the *Murshid* and the *Sufi* disciple called the *Murid*; contains explanations of Sufi ideas and doctrines.

***Tabaqat-i-Nasiri*:** A book written by *Minhaj-us-Siraj*, refers to the account of Bakhtiyar Khalji's march to the kingdom of Lakhnauti and the eventual defeat of Lakshman Sen, the last *Hindu* Sen ruler.

***Qiran-us-Sa'dain*:** Written by Amir Khusrau; a historical account which starts from the time of Balban's death.

***Tarikh-i-Mubarak Shahi*:** A book by Yahya-bin-Ahmad Sirhindi furnishes an account of Timur's invasion and the plunder of Delhi in 1398.

***Khair-ul-Majlis*:** One of the most important Malfuzats; about Nasiruddin *Chirag-i-*Dehlavi, the famous Chishti Sufi saint, who lived in Delhi in the time of Alauddin Khalji and provides information about his reign.

***Minhaj-us-Siraj*:** A historian who came from Jurjan in Central Asia; lived in the court of Iltutmish; the first example of Persian style of writing history.

***Fatwa-i-Jahandari*:** A political treatise by Ziyauddin Barani dealing with the characteristics of the *Sultanate*.

References

Afzaluddin, Afsar. 1956. *The Fatawa-i-Jahandari of Zia ud-din Barni: Translation with Introduction and Notes*, 119. London: School of Oriental and African Studies, University of London.

Aḥmad, Muḥammad. 1949. *Azīz: Political History and Institutions of the Early Turkish Empire of Delhi (1206–1290 A.D.)*, 107. Lahore: Muhammad Ashraf.

Aigle, Denise. 2007. 'The Conception of Power in Islam Mirrors of Persian Princes and Sunni Theories (11th–14th centuries).' *Medieval Perspectives* 31: 17–44.

Al-Ashmuni. 1961. *Hashiyat al-Sabban sharh al-Ashmuni ala Alfiyat ibn Malik*, 279. Dubai: Maktabat al-Safa.

Al-Azmeh, Aziz. 1997. *Muslim Kingship: Power and the Sacred in Muslim, Christian, and Pagan Polities*, 87. London and New York: I. B. Tauris Publishers.

Alam, Muzaffar and Sanjay Subramanyam. 1998. *The Mughal State, 1526–1750*, 117. Delhi and New York: Oxford University Press.

Aquil, Raziuddin. 2008. 'On Islam and Kufr in the Delhi Sultanate: Towards a Re-interpretation of Ziya'al-Din Barani's Fatawa-i Jahandari.' In *Rethinking a Millennium: Perspectives on Indian History from the Eighth to Eighteenth Century: Essays for Harbans Mukhia*, edited by Rajat Datta, 168–97. Delhi: Aakar Books.

Aquil, R. 2009. In the Name of Allah: Understanding Islam and Indian History. New Delhi: Penguin Viking.

Bosworth, C. E. 1996. *The New Islamic Dynasties*, 530. Columbia: Columbia University Press.

Chandra, Satish. 1996. 'Impact of Central Asian Institutions on State and Society in Medieval India (10th–14th Centuries).' In *Historiography, Religion and State in Medieval India*, Saiyid Nurul (Ed.), 174–84. New Delhi: Har-Anand Publications.

Chaurasia, Radhey Shyam. 2009. *History of Ancient India: Earliest Times to 1000 A. D*, 191. New Delhi: Atlantic Publication House.

Collins, Randall. 2000. *The Sociology of Philosophies: A Global Theory of Intellectual Change*, 184–5. Harvard: Harvard University Press.

Crone, Patricia. 1980. *Slaves on Horses: the Evolution of the Islamic Polity*, 208. Cambridge: Cambridge University Press.

Data, R. 2008. *Rethinking a Millennium: Perspective on Indian History from Eight to Eighteenth Century: Essays for Harbans Mukhia*. Delhi: Aakar Books.

Dahlén, Ashk P. 2009. 'Kingship and Religion in a Mediaeval Fürstenspiegel: The Case of the Chahār Maqāla of Niẓāmī 'Arūẓī.' *Orientalia Suecana* 58: 9–24.

Elliot, H. M. and J. Dowson. 1867. *Táríkh-i Fíroz Sháhí of Ziauddin Barani, The History of India as Told by Its Own Historians. The Muhammadan Period*, Vol. 3, 129. London: Trübner.

Essid, Yassine. 1995. A Critique of the Origins of Islamic Economic Thought. Leiden-New York-Köln: E. J. Brill.

Fleischer, Cornell H. 1986. *Bureaucrat and Intellectual in the Ottoman Empire: The Historian Mustafa Ali (1541–1600)*, 99. Princeton, NJ: Princeton University Press.

Foltz, Richard C. 1998. *Mughal India and Central Asia*, 170–90. Oxford and Karachi: Oxford University Press.

Habib, Irfan. 1958. *The Agrarian System of Mughal India (1556–1707)*. London: Asia Publishing House for Department of History, Aligarh Muslim University, 1963.

Habib, Irfan. 1981. 'Barani's Theory of the History of the Delhi Sultanate.' *Indian Historical Review* VII(1–2): 99–115.

Habib, Irfan. 1999. 'Ziya Barani's Vision of the State.' *Medieval History Journal* 2: 19–36.

Habib, Mohammad. 1961. 'Life and Thought of Ziyauddin Barani.' *Medieval India Quarterly* 3(3–4): 197–252.

Hardy, Peter. 1978a. 'Unity and Variety in Indo-lslamic and Perso-lslamic Civilization: Some Ethical and Political Ideas of Diyā' al-Dïn Baranï of Delhi, of al-Chazâlï and of Nasïr al-Dïn Tusï Compared.' *Iran* 16: 127–35.

Hardy, Peter. 1978b. 'The Growth of Authority over a Conquered Political Elite: The Early Delhi Sultanate as a Possible Case Study.' In *Kingship and Authority in South Asia*, edited by John F. Richards, 192–214. Madison, WI: University of Wisconsin-Madison, Department of South Asian Studies.

Jackson, Peter. 1999. *The Delhi Sultanate: A Political and Military History*, 312–7. Cambridge: Cambridge University Press.

Kumar, Sunil. 2007. *The Emergence of the Delhi Sultanate*, 98. Delhi: Permanent Black.

Lambton, A. K. S. 1971. *State and Government in Medieval Islam: An Introduction to the Study of Islamic Political Theory*. (Reprint 1981). Oxford: Oxford University Press.

Marlow, Louise. 2007. *Cambridge Studies in Islamic Civilization: Hierarchy and Egalitarianism in Islamic Thought*, 35. Cambridge: Cambridge University Press.

Morris, C. W. 2009. *Mind, Self and Society: From the Standpoint of a Social Behaviourist*, Vol. 13, 279–81. Chicago, IL: The University of Chicago Press.

Nizami, Khaliq Ahmad. 1981. *A Comprehensive History of India: The Delhi Sultanat (A.D. 1206–1526)*, 122. New Delhi: People's Publishing House.

Pacey, Arnold. 1991. *Technology in World Civilization: A Thousand-Year History*, 26–9. Cambridge: The MIT Press.

Persram, Nalini. 2007. *Post-colonialism and Political Theory (Global Encounters: Studies in Coomparative Political Theory)*, 39. Lexington, KY: Lexington Books.

Pipes, Daniel. 1981. *Slave Soldiers and Islam: The Genesis of a Military System*, 133. New Haven and London: Yale University Press.

Prasad, Ishwari. 1936. *A History of the Qaraunah Turks in India*, 5–6. Allahabad: The Indian Press.

Puri, B. N. and M. N. Das. 2003. *A Comprehensive History of India: Comprehensive History of Medieval*, 182. New Delhi: Sterling Publishers.

Raverty, H. G. 1872 and 1881. *Ṭabaḳāt-i-Nāṣirī: A General History of the Muhammadan Dynasties of Asia*, 497. London and Calcutta: Asiatic Society of Bengal.

Rizvi, Saiyid Akthar Abbas. (1978). *A History of Sufism in India*, Vol. I, 357. University of California/New Delhi: Munshiram Manoharlal.

Rosenthal, Erwin. 1985. *Political Thought in Medieval Islam: An Introductory Outline*, 106–9. Westport, CT: Greenwood Press.

Sarkar, Nilanjan. 2005. *The Political Identity of the Delhi Sultanate, 1200–1400: A Study of Zia Al-Din Barani's Fatawa-I Jahandari*, 65. London: University of London.

Sarkar, Nilanjan. 2006. 'The Voice of Mahmud: The Hero in Ziyã Barani's Fatãwã-i Jahãndãri.' *Medieval History Journal* 9: 327–56.

Sen, Sailendra. 2013. *A Textbook of Medieval Indian History*, 68–102. Calcutta: Primus Books.

Sherwani, Haroon Khan. 1945. *Studies in Muslim Political Thought and Administration*, 165. Delhi: Muhammad Ashraf.

Siddiqi, Iqtidar Husain. 1983. *Authority and Kingship under the Sultans of Delhi: Thirteenth-fourteenth Centuries*, 180. New Delhi: Manohar Publishers and Distributors.

Stowasser, Barbara Freyer. 1983. *Religion and Political Development: Some Comparative Ideas on Ibn Khaldun and Machiavelli*, 186. Washington, DC: Center for Contemporary Arab Studies, Georgetown University Press.

Subtelny, M. E. 2009. *Agriculture and the Timurid Chaharbagh: The Evidence from a Medieval Persian Agricultural Manual*. (Reprint 1997). Attilio: Petruccioli.

Syed, Ameer Ali. 1974. *A Short History of Saracens*, 86. New Delhi: Kitab Bhawan.

Syros, Vasileios. 2012. 'Indian Emergencies: Baranī's Fatāwā-I Jahāndārī, The Diseases of The Body Politic, And Machiavelli's "Accidenti".' *Philosophy East and West* 62(4): 545–73.

Vrolijka, A. and J. P. Hogendijk. 2007. *O Ye Gentlemen: Arabic Studies on Science and Literary Culture, in Honor of Emke Kruk*, 241. Leiden: Brill.

Yamanaka, Yuriko. 2003. *History and Kingship Through the Looking Glass: A Comparative Study of Specula/Jiàn in Oriental and Occidental Literatures*, 17. Delhi: Aakar Books.

Zakharia, Katia and Ali Cheiban. 2007. *Savoirs et Pouvoirs: Genèse des Traditions, Traditions Réinventées (Knowledge and Powers: Genesis of Traditions, Reinvented Traditions)*, 129–31. Paris: Maisonneuve & Larose.

Further Readings

Afzaluddin, Afsar. 2011. 'An Urban Imaginaire, ca 1350: The Capital City in Ziya` Barani's Fatawa-i Jahandari.' *Indian Economic and Social History Review* 48: 407–424, esp. 408–410.

Al-Azmeh, Aziz. 1983. *Historical Writing and Historical Knowledge: Introduction to the Craft of Historical Writing in Arab-Islamic Culture* (in Arabic), 151. Beirut: Dar alTaliʿa.

Al-Azmeh, Aziz. 2018. 'The Muslim Canon from Late Antiquity to the Era of Modernism, Canonization and Decolonization.' In *Canonization and Decanonization*, edited by A. Van Debeek and Karel Van Der Toorn, Vol. 82, 191–2. Leiden: Brill.

Bosworth, C. E. 1973. 'Barbarian Incursions: The Coming of the Turks into the Islamic World.' In *Islamic Civilisation 950–1150*, edited by D. S. Richards, 14–5. London: Oxford.

Brown, James. 1949. 'The History of Islam in India.' *The Muslim World* 39(1): 11–25.

Davis, Richard. 1994. 'Three Styles in Looting India.' *History and Anthropology* 6(4): 293–317.

Digby, S. 1975. 'The Tomb of Buhlūl Lōdī.' *Bulletin of the School of Oriental and African Studies* 38(3): 550–61.

Dixit, Prabha. 1980. 'Prof. Mohammad Habib's Historical Fallacies.' In *Bias in Indian Historiography*, edited by D. Devahuti, 201–13. Delhi: D. K. Publications.

Eaton, Richard M. 2001. 'Temple Desecration and Indo-Muslim States Part II.' *Frontline* 5: 70–7.

Epigraphia Indo-Moslemica. 1937–1938. *'Alā' al-Dīn: Inscription of Sultan Balban from Bayana, Bharatpur State*, 5–6. Calcutta: Office of the Superintendent of Govt Printing in India.

Frye, Richard M. 1991. 'Pre-Islamic and Early Islamic Cultures in Central Asia.' In *Turko-Persia in Historical Perspective*, edited by Robert L. Canfield, 35–53. Cambridge: Cambridge University Press.

Habib, Irfan. 2002. *Essays in Indian History.*

Habib, Mohammad. 1961. 'Life and Thought of Ziyauddin Barani.' *Medieval India Quarterly* 3(3–4): 197–252.

Habib, Mohammad and Afsar Umar Salim Khan. 1961. *The Political Theory of the Delhi Sultanate: Including a Translation of Ziauddin Barani's Fatawa-i Jahandari, Circa, 1358–9 A.D.* New Delhi: Kitab Mahal.

Habibullah, A. B. M. 1945. *The Foundation of Muslim Rule in India.*

Hardy, Peter. 1983. 'Force and Violence in Indo-Persian Writing on History and Government in Medieval South Asia.' In *Islamic Society and Culture*, edited by Milton Israel and N. K. Wagle, 165–208. New Delhi: Manohar.

Irwin, Robert. 1986. *The Middle East in the Middle Ages: The Early Mamluk Sultanate 1250–1382*, 186. London & Sydney: Croom Helm.

Islam, R. 1997. 'A Note on the Position of the non-Muslim Subjects in the Sultanate of Delhi under the *Khaljis* and the *Tughluqs*.' *Journal of the Pakistan Historical Society* 45: 215–29.

Islam, R. 2002. Theory and Practice of Jizyah in the Delhi Sultanate (14th Century).' *Journal of the Pakistan Historical Society* 50: 7–18.

Jackson, Peter. 1990. 'The Mamlūk Institution in Early Muslim India.' *Journal of the Royal Asiatic Society of Great Britain & Ireland* (New Series) 122(2): 340–58.

Khan, Iqtidar Alam. 1972. 'The Turko-Mongol Theory of Kingship.' *Medieval India: A Miscellany* 2: 8–18.

Kulke, Hermann and Dietmar Rothermund. 1998. *A History of India*, 187–90. London and New York: Routledge.

Lambton, A. K. S. 1965. 'Reflections on the *iqṭā*.' In *Arabic and Islamic Studies in Honor of Hamilton A. R. Gibb*, edited by George Makdisi, 358–76. Leiden: E. J. Brill.

Majumdar, R. C. and K. M. Munshi. 1990. *The Delhi Sultanate*, 189. Bombay: Bharatiya Vidya Bhavan.

Majumdar, R. C., H. Raychaudhuri, and K. K. Datta. 1951. *An Advanced History of India*, 134. London: Macmillan.

Mehta, V. R. 1992. *Foundations of Indian Political Thought.*

Ramratan and Ruchi Tyagi. 1999. *Indian Political Thought.* New Delhi: Mayur Paperbacks.

Roy, N. B. 1941. 'The Transfer of Capital from Delhi to Daulatabad.' *Journal History* 20: 159–80.

Siddiqui, I. H. 1989. 'Fresh Light on Ḍiyā' al-Dīn Baranī: The Doyen of Indo-Persian Historians.' *Islamic Culture* 63(1–2): 69–94.

Singh, M. P. and Himanshu Roy. 2011. *Indian Political Thought: Themes and Thinkers.* Pearson Publication.

Subtelny, Maria-E. 2001. 'The Making of Bukhara-yi Shanf: Scholars, Books and Libraries in Medieval Bukhara (The Library of Khawaja Muhammad Parsa).' *Studies on Central Asian History Honour of Yuri Bregle* 115: 87–8.

Tripathi, Ram Prasad. 1998. 'The Turko-Mongol Theory of Kingship.' In *The Mughal State, 1526–1750*, edited by Muzaffar Alam and Sanjay Subrahmanyam, 115–25. New Delhi: Oxford University Press.

14

CHAPTER

Abul Fazl: Views on Governance and Administration

Sumit Mukerji

CHAPTER OUTLINE

- Introduction
- The Life Sketch
- Conception of State
- Kingship, Sovereignty and Ideal Ruler
- Administration and Governance
- Religion and Religious Syncretism
- Conclusion
- Summary
- Points for Discussion

Man's nature does not always receive wisdom. An independent counsellor is required who, without consideration of his own interest, will represent in private chambers what is proper for the time without any mixture of flattery.

—Abul Fazl (Akbarnama, Vol. III, p. 450)

Reader's Guide

The purpose of this chapter is to familiarize a reader with the works and sociopolitical and religious ideas of Abul Fazl who occupies a prominent place in the history of medieval Indian political thought. This chapter would also provide a comprehensive account of *Mughal* administration and state structure.

Introduction

In the history of medieval political thought, Abul Fazl occupies an eminent place. Just as Ziauddin Barani provided an exhaustive account of the state system, governance and administration of the Delhi *Sultanate*, Abul Fazl produced a detailed and incisive study of the *Mughal* state and machinery of administration. His work was more authentic and well documented than that of Barani. It was intellectually more organized and based on a new methodology which he sought to apply in practice. His interpretation of history was integrally linked to the political, social, economic and religious realities of the period. Abul Fazl was a champion of rational thinking and his appeal to reason was visualized as a bulwark against religious and cultural traditions which threatened to stymie freedom of thought. At the beginning of the *Mughal* period, India was divided into many small kingdoms which proved to be a source of chronic instability. This ended with the victory of Babar over Ibrahim Lodi in the first Battle of Panipat in 1526. The *Mughals* conquered a large chunk of India and established an integrated empire with a hierarchical administrative structure, strong monetary policies, centralized system of governance and new methods of military organization. This created an integrated, syncretic culture incorporating elements from both *Hindu* and *Muslim* thought derived from the legacy of *Bhakti* and *Sufi* movements which transmitted the message that no religion is inferior to others and that God can be found without blind and dogmatic adherence to superstitions. They further postulated the basic equality of human beings and the gospel of unity and equality in all religions.

Abul Fazl was a courtier, historian and also a friend of *Mughal* emperor Akbar. His magnum opus *Akbar Nama* and *Ain-i-Akbari* together constitute his most authentic work which he finished by the end of the 16th century. It represented a significant departure from the contemporary historiography demolishing its *Islamic* moorings and constructing an alternative teleology of universal history where Akbar is the heir not of Prophet Muhammad and Caliphs but of Adam himself, the first human being and is the ruler of all humanity. He is thus the symbol of a powerful sovereign and a centralized state structure. The first part of the book *Akbar Nama* contains an account of Akbar's ancestors. The second part gives a detailed account of Akbar's reign up to the 46th year in chronological sequence. The work was undertaken in 1595 and completed in 1602 after five revisions. The *Ain-i-Akbari*, the third part of the book, is a compilation of the system of administration and control over the various departments of government. It provides a veritable mine of information on the extent, population, resources, condition, industry and wealth as well as an account of the religious and philosophical system of the Hindus and also their social customs and practices. No medieval historian before him had tried to recapture the historical developments of his age in such a wide canvas. Abul Fazl's work is thus considered the most comprehensive account of the *Mughal* system of administration and state structure.

Abul Fazl adopted a rational and secular methodology which he applied not only to collect facts but also to articulate them on the basis of critical investigation. After amassing a huge quantum of facts, he selected the important ones and presented them clearly and systematically. He never took any source on trust and verified its validity by ascertaining whether it measured up to the principles of historical enquiry formulated by him. He thus produced a new Philosophy of History that is a definite concept of the nature and purpose of history, principles for its interpretation and the critical equipment for the collection and selection of the facts of history. Like a genuine historian, Abul Fazl assigned priority to original sources. He did not limit himself to a single source to ascertain a fact but obtained as many versions of the same as possible. Thereafter, he subjected them to critical scrutiny before acceptance. His source material consisted of accounts of events written by eye witnesses.

Reports, memoranda, imperial *Farmans* and other records were also duly consulted. It is remarkable how in those distant times Abul Fazl evolved a methodology conducive to the verification of the authenticity of conclusions. It is of enduring relevance to researchers in present-day India who can take a leaf out of Abul Fazl's book.

The Life Sketch

Abul Fazl (1551–1603) was the second son of Shaikh Mubarak Nagauri, a reputed *Islamic* scholar and the younger brother of poet Faizi. Abul Fazl was born in Agra when the *Mughal* Empire was yet to be regained by Humayun who had been driven out by Sher Shah. Trained by his father, Abul Fazl could read and write Arabic by the time he was 5 years of age and memorized all conventional learning before he reached the age of 10. This clearly testifies that he was extraordinarily gifted and talented. To quote his own words, 'At a little over one year I had the miraculous gift of fluent speech and at five years of age I had acquired an unusual stock of information and could both read and write.' This clearly proves that he was a Wonder Child. Noted for his erudition by the time he had reached 20, he developed a singular capacity of providing new interpretations to old problems. Although Abul Fazl grew up in the capital during the period when Akbar was re-establishing *Mughal* authority in north India, he was not initially attracted to court service, as had been his older brother Faizi, Akbar's famous poet-laureate. Instead, he applied himself to rigorous life of study, and by the age of 15 he had extensively read Arabic, Greek philosophy and *Sufism*. His precociousness seems to have made him something of a social misfit, however, and by the time that he was 20 he had already embarked on a life of ascetic withdrawal which was unusual for his age.

Meanwhile, the leading members of the *Mughal* '*Ulema*' were mounting an intense campaign against Shaikh Mobārak, because the latter had publicly defended a member of the Mahdawī sect. In 977/1569–70 Abul Fazl stirred a hornet's nest by challenging in public the opinions of one of the leading *Ulemas*. The atmosphere at court became tense. Shaikh Mobārak, accused of being a Mahdawī and a *Shia* himself, was driven with his family from home to home seeking refuge. For a while he lived in Delhi. The events surrounding his father's persecution made a profound impression on Abul Fazl; he devoted a major part of his autobiography to describing these traumatic experiences, and he dedicated his subsequent career to exposing what he considered the narrow-minded bigotry of the '*Ulema*'. In 981/1574 Abul Fazl made his first appearance in Akbar's court. He favourably impressed the emperor and soon thereafter entered court service.

His reputation for forming his independent judgements based on his own observations came in for much opprobrium, particularly from his peers who were accustomed to *taqlid* or blind emulation. His mindset was objective and free from bias which was conducive to dispassionate history writing. His refusal to be browbeaten by authority prompted him to publicly refute a powerful *Alim* in the *Mughal* court which enraged him so much that he started a vendetta campaign against Abul Fazl and his father. Abul Fazl rose to prominence in the court of Akbar where he was introduced in the theological debates that took place in the *Ibadatkhana* at Fatehpur Sikri during 1576–1578. Championing a more liberal brand of Islam he outwitted most of the *Ulemas* in court. Soon the nature of the *Mughal* polity underwent a significant change and the body politic was radically transformed so as to produce a redefinition of *Mughal* political culture which persisted for more than a century. Akbar abolished the *Jizyah* tax much to the chagrin of the *Ulemas* and soon promulgated the doctrine of *Suhl-i-Kul* to emancipate himself from the control of the *Ulemas*. This is largely attributed to the influence of Abul Fazl. Abul Fazl translated the Bible and also the *Panchatantra* in Persian and wrote an introduction to the Persian translation of *Mahābhārata*. Because of his intimacy with Akbar he was in the bad books of his son Salim who had assassinated him in 1603 apprehending that he was inciting hatred in the mind of Akbar. Moreover, Abul Fazl had opposed Salim's accession.

Conception of State

Abul Fazl defined the state in the context of the needs of society. He categorized human beings into warriors, artificers and merchants, the learned that is the religious classes like the *Brāhmaṇs* and *Ulemas* and finally the labourers and husbandmen. He relegated this class to the third position, thereby striking at the root of their self-opinionated pretensions. Jalaluddin Dawwani, who influenced Abul Fazl, placed the learned ahead of the merchants but below the warriors. He classified human beings into noble, base and intermediate. The nobles possessed intellect, sagacity, administrative capacity, eloquence and courage for military duty. The other two classes were self-centred. Abul Fazl's view of the base or ignoble classes reflected the prejudices of the contemporary upper classes. It implied that those belonging to the lower order of society should not aspire for a share in state power and administration should be the exclusive preserve of those belonging to the noble families and upper castes. Prevalence of evil sections justified royal despotism, for only a king who possessed the necessary qualities could control these sections. He had to ensure social stability by preventing sectarian strife and he was also duty bound to put each section in its proper place. Stability and even dignity meant the maintenance of one's due station in life. Akbar was of the opinion that when a menial takes to learning, it is at the expense of one's duty. Here one can clearly hear reverberations of Plato and Bradley who were of the opinion that each person should specialize in his allotted station of life. According to Abul Fazl, the noblest souls are those pledging absolute, unquestioning loyalty to Emperor Akbar. Just below them are those whose loyalty is commensurate with tangible gain. The worst are those who are disloyal and rebellious.

Abul Fazl compares the body politic to a living organism. Just as the equilibrium in any animal constitution depends on the balance between the four elements of fire, water, air and earth, similarly equilibrium in the body politic is maintained by a judicious division of ranks; each rank contributing to the prosperity of the whole. If any rank transgresses its functions, the equilibrium is upset. At the apex of the administrative hierarchy, there is the *nuwinan-i-dawlat* who comprises the highest nobility whose devotion illuminates the battlefield. They resemble the element of fire. Next comes the *auliya-i-nusrat* that is the revenue officials who resembles the wind enabling the administration to breathe. This is followed by *ashab-i-suhhat* or advisors of the king who represent water. Perceptive, experienced and well versed about human nature, they irrigate the body politic with their moderate views contributing to world prosperity. Conversely, they inundate the world with deluge and calamity. In the fourth category are the personal attendants of the king resembling earth. If they are free from dross, they can be like elixir but otherwise they can be like dust in the face of success. To Abul Fazl, the efficiency of administration depended upon the coordination of the four elements (Fazl 1897a, 9).

Kingship, Sovereignty and Ideal Ruler

Abul Fazl was categorical on the point that the term *Badshahat* signified a powerful, established owner whom none can eliminate. The *Badshah* was the supreme superior in the empire, the complete repository of social, economic, political and juridical powers. In the words of Abul Fazl, '*Badshahat* is the light derived from God which has been sent by God himself. God throws his kindness on *Badshah* who works as the agent of God' (Fazl 1897b, 255). This signified a continuation of the legacy of the Delhi *Sultanate* where rulers like Balban projected them as representatives of God on earth. Abul Fazl was of the decided view that a *Badshah* must consider himself the father of his subjects whom he should treat as his children. It was thus his effort to make every effort to ensure the welfare of his subjects and take care of every aspect of their life—economic, social, religious, political and so on. He should treat his people equally to ensure peace and harmony in the empire (ibid., 255). It is known from Abul Fazl that Akbar made it a point to establish the overriding authority of the *Badshah* over all other elements of the state. In 1579, he promulgated a decree called *Mazhar* which conferred on him the authority to interpret law. However, he was not satisfied with this and lost interest in the position of King of Islam. Abul Fazl impressed on him the idea of the king being an agent of God who worked on his behalf. Sovereignty was a divine light (*farr-i-izidi*) which replaced the traditional concept of King as the shadow of God (*Zill-i-Ilahi*) (Athar 2006, 125). The *Sultanate* theory of Kingship viewed the ruler as an intermediate authority between the *Rasul Allah* (messenger of God) and *Khilafatal-Rasul* (deputy of the Prophet that is the Caliph) on the one hand and the Umrah on the other. The *Sultan's* authority was conditional upon his satisfactory performance as the *amir al-mominin* that is leader of the faithful in defence and promotion of his faith. Allegiance is thus not automatic and is retractable. Abul Fazl, however, was categorical on the point that a ruler endowed with *farr-i-izidi* does not need the intermediate assistance of anyone and men in his presence, bend in submission (Fazl 1897b, 255). At the same time, while the *Badshah* wielded absolute power and the people were duty bound to obey his orders, yet Abul Fazl was of the opinion that if the Emperor discriminated on the basis of caste, religion, class, etc., he could not be considered a good king. All rulers are not necessarily endowed with *farr-i-izidi* by the mere fact of their holding authority. Political power is characterized by a large treasury, a considerable military force, wise counsellors, loyal followers and skilful workmen. Selfish rulers enjoy control over these temporarily while the rightful ones enjoy them all through. They consecrate themselves to the mission of suppressing cruelty and promoting the well-being of the people (ibid., 255). The selfish ones, in contrast, are obsessed with the external forms of power that feed their vanity. This leads to insecurity, strife and oppression. Providing a rationale for royal Omni competence, Abul Fazl says that

> No dignity is higher in the eyes of God than royalty and those who are wise, drink from its auspicious fountain. Royalty is a remedy for the spirit of rebellion and the reason why the subjects obey. If royalty did not exist, the storm of strife would never subside nor selfish ambitions disappear. Mankind, being under the burden of lawlessness and lust, would sink into the pit of destruction; this world this great market place would lose its prosperity, and the whole world becomes a barren waste. (Embree 1992, 425)

Abul Fazl uses the analogy of bride for the world and bridegroom for the ruler and says that the world becomes the worshipper of the king. In this way he elevates the king to the highest pedestal. He, however, adds perceptively that silly and short-sighted men cannot distinguish between a true king from a selfish one as both have in common, a large treasury, a numerous army, an abundance of wise men, a multitude of skilful workmen and a superfluity of means of enjoyment. However, men with deeper insight, note the difference. In the case of the former, the aforesaid advantages are lasting but in the case of the latter they are transitory. This is because the former is detached from these things and his objective is to remove oppression and ensure common good. The latter is a prisoner of the external forms of royal power, vanity, slavishness of man, etc. Royalty is a light emanating from God just like a ray from the sun. It is the illuminator of the universe, the receptacle of all virtues. This divine light is communicated by God to kings without the intermediate assistance of anyone. The qualities which flow from it are first, a paternal love towards the subjects. With his ripened wisdom the king can judge the spirit of the age and shape his plans accordingly. Second, the king is large-hearted. The sight of anything disagreeable does not unsettle him. His divine firmness gives him the power of requital. The wishes of great and small are attended to and their claims are met without delay. Third, he has an everlasting trust in God and when he performs an action, he considers God as the doer and himself as his medium. Finally, he is committed to prayer and devotion. The success of his plans will not make him complacent and adversity will not make him forget God and repose his trust in man. He puts his desires in the reins of reason and never permits himself to be trodden down by restlessness. He makes wrath the tyrant pay homage to wisdom, so that blind rage does not overpower him. He sits on the eminence of propriety, so that those who have gone astray have a chance to return without their evil deeds being exposed in public. He endeavours to promote the happiness of all creatures in obedience to the will of God but never seeks to please anyone in contradiction to reason. He is essentially a truth seeker (ibid. 1992, 426–427). It is clear from this that the ideal king to Abul Fazl is a truly enlightened man comparable in some respect to Plato's Philosopher King who with his ripened wisdom is best fitted to rule the society. In making his case for the ideal ruler who works only for the highest perfection of happiness, Abul Fazl followed the footsteps of Al-Farabi, but unlike him, he did not speak of the happiness of *Sunni Muslims* alone and instead included all people regardless of their sect. In his opinion, the ideal ruler is not merely one who adheres to the *Shari'at* to be on the right path but he is rather an *Insan al-Kamin* or Perfect Man capable of observing the connection between spiritual and temporal things and preserving both of these high matters in their proper place. He does not totally ignore the *Shari'at* but is at liberty to disregard it if it jeopardizes the welfare and happiness of his subjects (Rizvi 1975, 356). This was not only a radical but almost revolutionary proposition. Abul Fazl was of the decided view that kingship was a gift of God. Neither lineage nor access to resources or support of the people makes a sovereign. The ideal ruler must possess qualities like magnanimity, benevolence, endurance, exalted understanding, innate graciousness, natural courage, rectitude, justice, proper conduct, thoughtfulness, willingness to overlook the trivial, etc. If the monarch is not sufficiently wise to overpower desires, he is not fit for his lofty office (Fazl 1897b, 289). It may be noted here that the aforesaid view of good kingship largely resembles the Buddhist view of exalted kingship. Here, we can discern a continuity and convergence of ancient and medieval thought.

Enunciating the concept of *Jahanbani* or world rule, Abul Fazl says that this in the nature of guardianship on behalf of the creator who bestows that sovereign authority whom the ideal ruler worships by preserving or restoring peace and stability. A true ruler always prevails over any force that challenges the peace and stability of the empire. A great fire cannot be extinguished by a little water and evil doers and mischief makers are undone by their own evil deeds. According to Abul Fazl, military action and expansion are inevitable for uprooting all dissension and obstreperous elements. This is like a cleansing operation comparable to clearing of weeds in a garden (ibid., 122). Abul Fazl also focuses on the concept of Justice which he does not define in terms of Islam. Following the paradigm of *Akhlaq-i-Nasiri*, he advocates the notion of universal justice. To him, foresight, reason and forbearance were the essential attributes of broad-based justice. Rulers rich in these qualities could never be motivated by narrow personal considerations and would never distinguish between friends and strangers in matters of justice. Abul Fazl took the irrevocable stand that a sovereign who did not uphold the gospel of universal peace and did not regard all sects in the same light was not worthy of the exalted dignity of kingship (Rizvi 1975, 364). While advocating equality of treatment for all, Abul Fazl did not make the naïve assumption that all people were alike. He classified subjects of the Emperor into five heads. First, there were the commendable men who did only what was proper and necessary and was most suitable for consultation in state affairs. Second, there were the men of good intentions who were themselves of good conduct but were less reliable in advising what was right conduct for the other people. Third, there were those who were neither good nor evil who should be encouraged to do good. Fourth, there were inconsiderate men who were themselves evil but did not harm others. They should be subjected to good counselling and severe rebuke. Finally, there were the vicious ones whose evil spread like contagion who should be isolated from the rest. If that does not work, he should be banished from his house. If even that does not pay off, then he should be blinded or have his limbs amputated as a deterrent rather than retribution. Thus, Justice was corrective and not retributive. Just as the gardener extirpates bad trees and chops off some branches, in the same way just and far sighted kings light the lamp of wisdom by regulating and instructing their servants (Fazl 1897b, 323).

In the era of the *Sultanate*, the king was the final authority in governance, administration, agriculture, education and other fields but he had no say in the sphere of religion. Akbar, however, arrogated to himself the power to arbitrate in religious disputes vis-a-vis *Imam-I-Adil* because he followed the order of God and was thus infallible. Abul Fazl eulogized Akbar as the ideal king who could do no wrong. In *Akbarnama,* Abul Fazl mentioned that Akbar always worked for the welfare of the people. He was imbued with tolerance, broadmindedness and a sense of justice. He ensured both stability and good governance to the *Mughal* state along with economic prosperity, peace and safety. He also provided a moral justification for Akbar's policy of imperialist expansionism.

Administration and Governance

Abul Fazl was born at a time when the *Mughal* Empire was yet to be re-established by Humayun. Humayun did not have the time to revise the old administration and it was Akbar who gave it a structure of government and administration more or less along lines of the Delhi *Sultanate*. The question is what was innovative which made the *Mughal* Empire stronger? A strong and well-planned administrative structure is the key to good governance as well as welfare and peace and is also the surest guarantee against attack by an enemy. This would have been impossible to achieve without loyal and intelligent officers and an efficient army. The *Mughal* polity was not a continuation of the legacy of the Delhi *Sultanate* as Akbar changed the designation of the officers and developed a provincial administration patterned on the central system of government. Elaborate rules and regulations were framed for better control. Abul Fazl in his views on administration, assigned priority to advocates who he said, should possess qualities necessary to solve the problems of the king, both public and private. Just as in the *Arthaśāstra*, the state was divided into many levels and each level had officers of various kinds. All of them were responsible for the administration of the state and directly answerable to the ruler and were thus compulsively committed to the betterment of the condition of the people. Akbar divided his empire into *Sarkars* and *Mahalls*. He established a chain of ministers at various levels who were controlled by ministers at the centre. The system was thoroughly secular, and the religion of the officers could not interfere with administrative work. Akbar left no stone unturned to centralize and systematize his administration. There were small landlords under the king who were called *Zamindars* or *Jagirdars*. The King often used their forces to curb other chieftains. There was also a class called *Bhumia* who got some land from the *Jagirdars*. They were owners of land and did not have to pay any duty for it, but his land was inferior to that of *Jagirdars*. There was also *Khalsal* and in the vicinity of the capital which was under the direct control of the king. The *Mughals* did not disturb this system which prevailed from the days of the *Sultanate* because the landlords kept the lands with those who were allied with the king of Delhi (Mehta 1996, 149).

The *Mughal* state was based on a centralized patrimonial system where ranks and hierarchies borrowed from the *Mansabdari* system of Persia were bestowed. Each rank had two parts, *zat and sawar.* The former meant rights and the latter meant a force of horses to command. Sixty-six ranks were enlisted by Abul Fazl in *Ain-i-Akbari.* Gifts were granted to the deserving and each *Mansabdar* reported directly to the ruler. They collected revenue on behalf of the ruler and received salary in cash. Abul Fazl has referred to three *Mansabs* who had 500 and above, 400–200 and 150–10 *Mansabs.* It created a military hierarchy which was like a status symbol (Fazl 1897a, 250). Akbar had a strong army which was maintained by *Mansabdars.* Monsterat testified in 1581 that there were 45,000 cavalries, 5,000 elephants and many thousands of infantries all paid directly from the royal treasury (Chandra 2007, 162–165). While Abul Fazl was a believer in hierarchy, he was also concerned about the need for talent irrespective of social background. Akbar was acutely conscious of this and promoted common soldiers to the dignity of Grandee on the basis of talent. The *Mughals* did not interfere with the caste system and left unchanged, the basic framework of the Indian society. Abul Fazl wanted *Hindus* and *Muslims* to co-exist peacefully but found that the *Hindus* remained isolated and very few of their matters came up in court. The Panchayat and caste courts were there and the *Zamindar* enjoyed a paternal image.

As regards Land Revenue system, Akbar divided all provinces into *Sarkars* and *Parganas.* Each *Sarkar* was divided into a number of *Parganas.* There was a *Shiqdar* and *Amil* for the collection of revenue and there were posts of treasurer, *Qanungo*, etc. A large group of people was entrusted with looking after production that is the produce at the time of harvest and the state's share in it. *Dashsala* or a 10-year system was the basis of Akbar's revenue policy which was the logical culmination of the system introduced by Sher Shah. The productivity and local prices during the last 10 years were averaged in cash on the basis of information. Land revenue was the heaviest demand on peasants, and they were under constant threat of penal action. Unlike collection of tax on collective basis, Akbar collected tax from the farmer based on his individual harvest. Earlier the farmer had to pay the tax irrespective of whether he had a good harvest. The system of Akbar did not however redound to the benefit of the farmer because they were exploited by the collecting authorities like landlords who did not spare them even during natural calamities in violation of Akbar's directive. Akbar thus took preventive measures against this exploitation of farmers. He kept a watch on the landlords to identify the exploiters. He was able to return the money to the farmers who had been forced to pay the tax. However, it was not possible for him to monitor the system entirely and exploitation remained (ibid., 147, 157).

Religion and Religious Syncretism

Abul Fazl was never a blind supporter of *Islam.* He was in favour of participation of the *Hindus* in governance and administration. He was a votary of composite culture and contended that the *Hindus* like *Muslims*, subscribed to the doctrine of monotheism but *Muslims* because of their ignorance of scriptures, misunderstood them. Unlike Barani, Abul Fazl never believed in the superiority of *Islam* over other religions. Thus, he was maligned as *Kafir, Hindu and Agnipujak* (Hassan 1983, 129). His outlook was secular espousing the equality and fraternity of all religions and based on the doctrine of *Suhl-i-Kul* or universal peace. He was an intellectual with catholicity of outlook who was a sworn enemy of dogmatic orthodoxy. His counterpoint was that if traditions were sacrosanct then why Prophet Muhammed of all persons went for new thoughts. To him, changes in law and religion must be initiated attuned to the requirements of the age. His refreshingly modern outlook was reflected in Akbar's doctrine of *Dīn-e Ilāhī*. Abul Fazl assiduously adhered to the doctrine of *Suhl-i-Kul* believing from the core of his heart that the king who was the agent of God could not discriminate between various faiths. A doctrine justifying tolerance was the desideratum. Sovereignty was not limited to any particular faith as all religions were same in essence, only their paths diverged. Abul Fazl thus did not subscribe to Barani's plea for the overarching sovereignty of Islam. He was of the decided view that in a poly religious country like India, monarchical sovereignty was more relevant. Thus, he supported Akbar who with his rationalist attitude, wanted to create a *Hindustan* which could stand out in the world with greater confidence. In his quest for a more inclusive order, Akbar needed to end the monopoly of the incumbent *Muslim* elite without transgressing the limits of the *Islamic* order. Abul Fazl provided the theoretical foundation for this mission.

Abul Fazl addressed the seminal question as to what constituted the *Islamic* order. He contended that while the benchmark of the former was the enforcement of the laws of *Islam*, yet there was no rigid consensus on *Islamic* law. The *Qur'an* was open to multiple interpretations and there was no monolithic *Shari'at* which had to be upheld everywhere. Laws were meant to regulate human behaviour in such a manner that man remained on the *Sirat al-Mustaqim* that is the straight path leading to God. Whether an order was *Islamic* or not, depended not on the enforcement of any individual law but the criteria were its conformity to the essence of Islam. Abul Fazl's understanding of the *Islamic* order emanated from the transcendentalist theory of *Wahdat al-Wujud* or unity of being developed in the 12th century by the Andalusian philosopher Ibn al-Arabi. According to it, the *Khaliq* or the Creator and *Khalq* or creation, were not distinct entities but the divine element pervades all creation and there is no being who is not a part of the higher being. According to Abul Fazl, *Khair-i-Mahaz* or pure good was the essence of divine majesty and absolute goodness permeates his entire creation. To him, a good life did not simply consist of prayer and invocation but demanded an attitude of service to the whole of mankind rising above sectarian differences (Chatterjee 2016, 96).

Abul Fazl justified Akbar's abolition of the hated *Jizyah* tax saying that the *Hindus* were equally loyal having bound up the waist of devotion and service and exerted themselves for the advancement of the dominion. This action was motivated to strike at the root of the aspiration of *Ulemas* for predominance (Chandra 2007, 168). Commenting on the religious debates which took place in Akbar's *Ibadatkhana*, Abul Fazl says that it served one purpose, that is to publicly demonstrate the bigotry of the *Ulemas* (ibid., 177). Abul Fazl related Akbar's *Dīn-e Ilāhī* with the concept of the Emperor as the spiritual guide of the people. He identified two tendencies of man, one class inclined towards *Din* that is religion and the other to worldly thoughts that is *duniya*. It is necessary to find a common ground between the two taking into account the all-encompassing nature of God. It was necessary to check blood thirsty fanatics who superficially resembled human beings. If anyone mustered courage to openly proclaim his enlightened thoughts, these elements would immediately think of heresy and atheism and contemplate his murder. Faced with this menace, the people would naturally look to the king on account of his high position and accept him as their spiritual leader as well. Abul Fazl quotes two sayings of Akbar in this connection. 'by guidance is not meant indication of the road, not the gathering together of disciples'. 'To make a disciple is to instruct him in the service of God, not to make him a personal attendant' (ibid., 180). Akbar's liberal outlook incurred scornful reaction from orthodox people like Badauni who even went to the extent of alleging that because of such abuses of *Islam*, many *Muslims* were leaving the country in disgust. In the face of such virulent diatribe, Abul Fazl steadfastly defended Akbar by projecting him as a benevolent ruler whose instruments of control were favour and affection. He was a righteous ruler who had ruled for decades through the aid of heaven. Thus, while steering clear of religious dogmatism, Abul Fazl used religion to glorify and fortify the ideological foundations of the *Mughal* state under Akbar by representing him as a recipient of divine benediction. In this sense, his secular outlook was not irreligious but was free from all traces of religious narrowness. Perhaps there was an incipient Machiavellian element here because like Machiavelli who separated the domain of the politics from that of religion, advocated that religion could be used to augment the power of the state, Abul Fazl too deified Akbar using the idea of divine sanction.

Conclusion

The political thought of Abul Fazl championed the integration of *Hindus* and *Muslims* in the empire of Akbar. In articulating the imperial ideology, Abul Fazl refused to step into the shoes of his predecessors. He did not emphasize on the sacrosanctity of the *Shari'at* but at the same time did not compromise on the basic principles of the *Islamic* order. He provided an *Islamic* rationale for equal treatment of *Muslims* and non-*Muslims* in the polity thereby laying the foundation of a political dispensation where religious affiliation was secondary to the political allegiance of the subject. This new political culture characterized by catholicity of outlook, endured almost till the modern period. While the principle of equality was not always honoured by the *Mughal* state, yet Abul Fazl delineated the contours of a political ideology where discrimination on the basis of sectarian identity was absent. One main reason behind his affinity to Akbar was his freedom from religious bias which suited Akbar's own inclination. Abul Fazl was essentially a secular rationalist as apparent from his conviction that 'He is a man who makes justice the guide of the path of inquiry and takes from every sect, what is consonant to reason.' Benoy Sarkar has stated that Abul Fazl was the precursor of Raja Ram Mohan Roy and sought to remove strife and animosity among diverse races. He was a bridge builder and peacemaker. His logic was unchallengeable in theory and fruitful in practice. Perhaps no one from Megasthenes to Nivedita has flattered the Hindus in so dignified a manner. He was truly speaking one of the first creative specimens of *Hindu–Muslim* cultural fusion. It was he who tried to emancipate the *Muslim* mind through the enfranchisement of the intelligence consummated in the Christian mind by the Renaissance which was to attack the *Hindu* mind two centuries later in and through Ram Mohan (Sarkar 1935).

Abul Fazl has been rightly criticized for his lack of objectivity as his sole purpose was to glorify Akbar. His single-minded aim was to extol and justify all the activities of Akbar. He has rarely referred to Akbar's shortcomings and yet the essential bedrock of his thought was rationality which commands respect. In a way he was the forerunner of the sage Sri Ramakrishna who discovered some truth in all religions and said that there are as many paths as there are viewpoints. He refused to step into the shoes of Barani who was vehemently anti-*Hindu* and instead emphasized on communal amity. He ruthlessly pulverized the *Bigots* who represented fanaticism at its worst, and it is here that Abul Fazl most resplendently reflected the spirit of broadmindedness, which was the quintessence of the Indian culture. This is of enduring relevance even today as it is the surest guarantee against sectarian and religious conflict and recrimination in modern India where the threat of ignition of communal conflagration still hangs over the head like the sword of Damocles.

Summary

Abul Fazl was one of the trusted confidantes of Emperor Akbar and his works contain a veritable repository of information on the life and work of Akbar, particularly his policy in social, economic, administrative, religious and political matters. Abul Fazl accumulated vast quantum of data and subjected them to searching analysis on the basis of an objective methodology. He was much more broadminded than Zia Barani and epitomized the spirit of liberal pluralism which Akbar incarnated. This was a departure from the culture of the Delhi *Sultanate* where despite occasional moves by the *Sultans* to empower the Hindus, there was no concerted attempt at integration at the religious and philosophical level. The gestures towards the Hindus were actuated by political motives but Abul Fazl in contrast, visualized integration at a deeper, philosophical level. His own persecution, in the hands of *Bigots* and zealots, was instrumental for this catholicity of outlook. His depiction of Akbar as the ideal ruler amounted to almost an eulogy and has been criticized by scholars, but despite lack of objectivity here, Abul Fazl was the exponent of a legacy of tolerance and amity which is relevant even today as India grapples with the communal challenge.

Points for Discussion

1. Explain Abul Fazl's concept of state and sovereignty.
2. How did Abul Fazl challenge the predominance of *Ulemas* in administration?
3. To what extent did Abul Fazl's political thought mark a departure from that of the Delhi *Sultanate?*
4. Explicate Abul Fazl's view of Ideal Ruler. How did he portray Akbar as the Ideal Emperor?
5. How did Abul Fazl describe the socio-economic and religious life of Medieval India?

Glossary

Agnipujak: One who worships fire.

Alim: All-knowing.

Badshah: Emperor.

Bigot: Dogmatist.

Farman: Order.

***Ibadatkhana*:** House of worship.

***Jizya*:** A per capita yearly tax historically levied by *Islamic* states on certain non-*Muslim* subjects.

Kafir: Infidel, an Arabic term (from the root K-F-R 'to cover') meaning 'one who covers the truth'. The term alludes to a person who rejects or disbelieves in God according to the teachings of the *Islamic* prophet Muhammad.

Mazhar: Phenomenon.

Monotheism: Worship of single deity.

***Suhl-i-Kul*:** Universal peace.

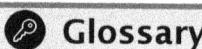

Syncretism: A union or attempted fusion of different religions, cultures or philosophies.

Ulema: A body of *Muslim* scholars who are recognized as having specialist knowledge of *Islamic* sacred law and theology.

References

Athar, M. Ali. 2006. *Mughal India: Studies in Polity, Ideas, Society and Culture*. New Delhi: Oxford University Press.

Chandra, Satish. 2007. *Medieval India: From Sultanat to the Mughals, Mughal Empire, Part 2*. New Delhi: Har Anand Publication.

Chatterjee, Kingshuk. 2016. 'Abul Fazl and the Politics of *Wahdat al Wujud (1551–1603)*.' In *Indian Political Thought and Its Contemporary Relevance*, edited by Sengupta Lopamudra, 96. New Delhi: Atlantic Publishers.

Embree, T. Ainslee, ed. 1992. *Sources of Indian Tradition*. India: Penguin Books.

Fazl, Abul. 1897a. *Aini-Akbari*, Vol. 1, translated by H. Blochmann. Calcutta: Calcutta Royal Asiatic Society.

Fazl, Abul. 1897b. *Akbarnama*, translated by H. Beveridge. Calcutta: Calcutta Royal Asiatic Society.

Hassan, Mohibbul. (1983). *Historians of Medieval India*. New Delhi: Meenakshi Publications.

Mehta, V. R. 1996. *Foundations of Indian Political Thought*. New Delhi: Manohar.

Rizvi, S. A. 1975. *Religious and Intellectual History of the Muslims in Akbar's Reign*. New Delhi: Munshiram Manoharlal Publishers.

Sarkar, Benoy Kumar. 1935. *The Ain -I-Akbari as a Semi Moslem and Semi Hindu Arthashastra*. Kolkata: Calcutta University Press.

Further Readings

Burn, Richard. 1937. *The Cambridge History of India*, Vol. 4. Cambridge: Cambridge University Press.

Mukhia, Harbans. 2005. *The Mughals of India*. Oxford: Blackwell.

Nizami, K. A. 2002. *Religion and Politics in India during the Thirteenth Century*. New Delhi: Oxford University Press.

15
CHAPTER

Islamic Tradition: A Tradition of Human Affairs and Classical Heritage

Iftekhar Ahemmed

CHAPTER OUTLINE

- Introduction
- Origin and Evolution of the *Islamic* Tradition
- Delhi *Sultanate* and *Islamic* Tradition
- *Mughal* Empire and *Islamic* Tradition
- Revivalism in *Islamic* Tradition
- Conclusion
- Summary
- Points for Discussion

It (Islam) has always been willing to accept ideas and institutions from those it vanquished. But in acceptance it has adapted and transformed its inheritance. Not always able to work the various strands into a harmonious whole, Islam has never yet lost its identity, even if instead of fusion and synthesis there resulted only fruitful and peaceful coexistence. This holds good for every manifestation of Muslim life and thought.

—Rosenthal (1962, 1)

Reader's Guide

The purpose of this chapter is to examine the trends of *Muslim* political thought in medieval India. Here, the author has tried to discuss the *Sufi* tradition, the orthodox tradition, the imperialist-liberal tradition and the revivalist tradition. Despite the paucity of exclusive treatises on political thought during this period, enough material is available for deducing the prevailing thought of the author and of the time. However, it is very important that the medieval India witnessed not only the establishment and consolidation of the *Muslim* rule in the land but also saw the evolution of appropriate political thought to buttress the political system.

Introduction

Islam, being a complete way of life, has grown into a distinct cultural unit. But in the process of its emergence in the Indian subcontinent, it has been influenced by the dominant Indian tradition, that is, the *Hindu* tradition. It is a well-known and well-documented fact that Indian civilization has a unique capacity to assimilate incoming foreign traditions. So, with the advent of *Islam*, Indian traditions experienced and encountered the onslaught of the just entered *Islamic* tradition. It began a new process of engagement, generating stress and strains on both sides of the divide. But, finally these cleavages were bridged and the famous assimilation process started to crystallize. This process was strengthened by the emergence of two great traditions. On the side of *Islam*, it is emergence and spread of the *Sufism* and on the other side, the *Bhakti* movement, contributed immensely to the assimilation process. The result was the emergence of a composite culture of India. These two movements constitute two important strands of Indian traditions.

When we look at the medieval *Muslim* tradition, we can easily recognize the strands or streams having distinct *Islamic* marks. Sometimes, due to political compulsions, *Muslim* political thoughts have accommodated *Hindu* traits to make it more realistic to the peculiar situation in India. Thus, one of the main currents of the medieval Indian *Islamic* tradition was the growth of *Sufism*. Its spread was the result of the spiritual bent of mind of Indian people. It got a fertile ground in India due to religious orientation of Indian masses. Second, its emphasis on love, service and secular attitude towards all (even the men of other faith) attracted people towards it. It gained unparalleled and unprecedented sociopolitical outreach in Indian subcontinent. However, its impact was most pronounced upon the *Muslim* masses. It became one of the most influential factors in luring the masses to the acceptance of *Islamic* mores and mentality. There were thousands of *Sufi* masters (*Pirs*) and each one of them was virtually a magnet, attracting people within his reach towards a view of life which is consistent with *Islam*. They are the most effective and influential factors in the spread of *Islam* in India. The history of medieval India is replete with their narratives of myriad achievements and adventures. *Sufi* influence was all-pervasive, engulfing almost all strata of Indian *Muslim* society. Even the *Ulemas* were attracted to it and got co-opted by it. It penetrated the peasantry, military establishment and the administrative machinery of the state. *Sufi* masters were revered and given patronage even by the rulers and the bureaucrats.

Origin and Evolution of the *Islamic* Tradition

Muslim political thought was deeply affected by the growth of *Sufism* in the Indian subcontinent. It acted as a cementing force or a buckle that joined the apolitical masses with the state and its machinery. *Sufi* saints, with their immense social power, exerted deep and lasting impact on the affairs of the realm. They possessed a sort of soft power that permeated deep enough to dominate the moral and mental landscape of Indian society in general and *Muslim* society in particular. Their influence was to be seen and observed on both the elites as well as the masses, of whom they acted as the articulator of interest with the former.

Sufism shaped the contours of political culture of *Muslim* society in medieval India. It gave a particular shape to the cognitive orientation of the people who already possessed a deep spiritual bent of mind. Their effective and evaluative orientations also got a particular form under the *Sufi* influence. Views of people regarding the regime, rulers or officers were influenced by the views of *Sufi* master of the locality. *Sufi* viewpoints on the policies and actions of the rulers acted as the source of public opinion. *Sufism* successfully developed elaborate social network which acted as the 'institutional sinews with an entire parallel social organisation' (Black 2001, 128). *Sufi* shrines became focal points for people of the locality. Both *Muslims* as well as non-*Muslims* flocked to these shrines and tombs in large numbers. One can witness this phenomenon which continues to fascinate people till today. Birth or death anniversaries of famous *Sufi* saints (e.g., Khwaja Moinuddin Chisti of Ajmer and Nizamuddin Auliya of Delhi) known and observed as annual *Urs* have attracted people from far and wide places transcending the boundary of state and religion.

The organizational set up of *Sufism* was informal with excessive emphasis on strict personal allegiance to the *Sufi* preachers known as *Pirs*. Its basic social ethos was authoritative, fraternal and benevolent. It is a type of *Guru–Chela* (teacher–disciple) relationship between the *Pir* and the *Murid* (disciple). In *Sufi* masters, the society witnessed a new type of religious leadership to whom the disciple owed unquestioning obedience and allegiance. This created a sort of spiritual elitism in the society. *Sufi* organization tends to the elitist approach to spirituality.

Sufism is linked to the political thought in a unique way. It filled the void created by political disengagement of the masses. *Sufism* acted as the link between apolitical populace and political dispensation. *Sufi* masters, in spite of harbouring usually quietist and non-political stance, played important role of social and political nature. Most of the *Sufi* saints were specially committed to helping the poor and downtrodden (so, the title of *Garib Nawaz* was given to Khwaja Moinuddin of Ajmer), thereby becoming spokespersons for popular grievances. They acted as effective and important channels of 'interest articulation' and 'interest aggregation' between the common man and the governing elites. There are certain instances where *Sufi* leadership provided a pathway to power and acted as a de facto local leader. Sometimes, *Sufi* masters played important roles in the government establishment. Instances are many, when the regime looked for support and blessings of a highly popular *Sufi* Shaikh in order to gain a foothold in the area. It has been observed that the support/blessings of a *Sufi* saint of the locality clinched the issue of succession to the realm. Thus, *Sufism*'s engagement with politics is a well-established and well-documented fact. Trimingham has cited instances of *Sufi* leaders 'aspiring to political power, revolting against the established authority and sometimes actually founding a dynasty' (Trimingham 1971, 239).

Sufism stood for a brand of spiritualism that was broad-based, liberal, hugely tolerant and secular to such an extent that they even integrated wholeheartedly people of other sects and faiths (e.g., *Shias* and *Hindus*). Their cosmopolitan and liberal approach to life was responsible for wide acceptance of *Islamic* mysticism in India. Here lies their real contribution to the *Muslim* rule in a predominantly *Hindu* society. They not only helped in the spread of *Islam* in India but also provided supportive structure and legitimacy to the *Muslim* rule in medieval India.

Besides these positive contributions, *Sufism* has a negative side also. It was responsible for widespread innovations in Indian *Islam*, which is the result of its liberal incorporation of some *Hindu* mores and practices in its mystic practices. Second, its concept of knowledge and its sources was mystical, known as *ma'rif* or gnosis. It is a gift of God and can be achieved by a select few who can communicate this to others by discipleship. To them, knowledge is not a result of rational enquiry but of intuition. This popularized the belief in mystical phenomena, such as dreams, astrology, miracles, etc. As Gibb has pointed out rightly, that 'especially in its popular forms, *Sufism* came more and more to equate God's indwelling in the world with animistic idea of divine powers inherent in material objects and persons' (Gibb 1962, 212). Its resultant effect was manifested in the decline of almost all branches of knowledge, that is, law, science, technology, political philosophy and political science in the medieval *Muslim* India. This explains the contrast between non-availability of treatises on science, technology, politics and philosophy (which are horribly few) with the highly organized social penetration of *Sufi* saints and their *khanqahs*.

Delhi *Sultanate* and *Islamic* Tradition

Barani (1285–1357) was the most reflective and representative thinker of the Delhi *Sultanate* period. No other work on politics can be compared to Barani's (*Fatwa-i-Jahandari*) during this period. V. R. Mehta points out that, 'there is no other work on political thought in the whole period which can rival it in both depth and subtlety of political ideas, notwithstanding his fads and foibles and strong antipathies to thunders' (Mehta 2017, 138). Similarly, commenting on his other work on history Habib says that, 'in spite of all its shortcomings, *Tarikh-i-Firoz Shahi* remains the greatest book that has survived to us from the *Sultanate* period. Its eminence in this respect is unchallengeable' (Habib 1958, 252).

Barani was probably the first thinker who made an attempt to resolve the contradictions between *Islamic* and *Iranian* view of the government. Although the basic premise of his thought is *Islamic*, he tried to solve the issue with the help of Greek thought, of which he was well aware. Due to his conservatism, Barani firmly believed in the absolute sovereignty of the divinely decreed sovereign. The king is the vicegerent of God on earth, if he performs two things sincerely, such as enforce the *Shari'ah* severely and rule with justice. According to him, God created everything in pairs, such as truth and falsehood, peace and disorder, good and evil, day and night, light and darkness. In this world of opposites, the king is responsible for conducting the affairs of state in such a way that truth and justice prevail over falsehood and injustice. He was very particular about two ideas, that is, justice and moderation. To him they are the key to success in both the worlds. The king must see that the truth is established in the centre which actually means the overpowering of untruth by the truth (Barani 1957, 60). He identifies truth with the greatness of *Islam* and falsehood with the local religions (i.e., *Hinduism*). This explains his antipathy to *Hinduism* in general and *Brahminism* in particular.

Barani gives justice a central place in his whole scheme of thought. It is the main reason for which kings are appointed by God. The rule by the king with justice will make this life heavenly while the opposite (injustice by the king) will make the life miserable, like life in hell. Justice is required to prevent oppression and protect the weak. There can be no religion without it. He opines that 'religion and justice are twins'. Justice requires 'a strong Ruler among the people' possessing 'force and authority' (Fatawa 3, 16 and 34). Therefore, it demands a strong government with the king combining in him the quality of severity and mercy. King was an absolutist, but his absolution is mixed with benevolence.

Barani gave a lot of importance to the secular law which he calls *zawabit*, which are in addition to the religious *Islamic* Laws (*Shariah* Laws). In other words, he admits that there exists the need of secular law to fill the gaps in the religious laws and to meet the demands of real politic. To him, since law making is a difficult and delicate task, it is not desirable to leave the responsibility to the king alone so as to minimize possibility of errors in law-making. Second, keeping the *Qur'anic* injunction of consultations, Barani advices that there should be a King's Council to perform as the legislative wing of the state. Its members are to be selected by the king with care, presumably in accordance with some clear-cut principles and transparent method. The king should also be present in its deliberations. The council should have full freedom to discuss every aspect of the matter. If there is unanimity and consensus on the matter, the advice should be accepted, otherwise it should be deferred for a rethinking and fresh discussion on a later date (Habib 1958, 250). Barani has advised the king to pay utmost attention to three things, namely good counsellor, effective army and good intelligence. The king should be very careful and vigilant towards the nobility who are disloyal, least they may cast their lot with the enemies and conspirators. The king should pursue a policy of zero tolerance to the corruption and injustice. This will result in the development of the state and happy life of the people.

Mughal Empire and *Islamic* Tradition

The *Mughal* Dynasty, which came to India from the Central Asia, created the largest Indian state after Asoka the great. Displaying political realism, the *Mughals* embarked upon building, a multi-credal empire through innovation and adaptations. They set out to bring *Hindus* (who were a vast majority) and *Muslims* into a single political community by adopting the liberal policy of religious toleration and secularism. This gave the *Mughal* Empire its distinctive political identity. The aforesaid policy was initiated by none other than the very founder of the dynasty, that is, Babur, who instructed his son and successor Humayun in these words.

> That realm of *Hindustan* is full of diverse creed .... It is but proper that thou, with heart clean of all religious bigotry, should dispense justice according to tenets of each community ... And the temples and abodes of worship of every community under imperial sway, you should not damage .... The progress of Islam is better with sword of kindness, not with sword of oppression. And bring together subjects with different beliefs in the manner of four elements, so that the body politic may be immune from various ailments. (Mehta 1936, 340)

Thus, the principle of toleration, liberation, moderation and secularism continued to be the guiding philosophy of the *Mughals* till the last. Akbar, with remarkable open-mindedness, realized that effective rule over *Hindustan* can only be possible by the cooperation of the *Hindu* princes and the masses who constitute the vast majority of his subjects. In this project, he was fortunate in getting the support and advice of Abul Fazl (1551–1602), who became a close friend and intellectual ally. Abul Fazl, in his *Ain-e-Akbari* and *Akbarnama* actually reflected, articulated and stimulated Akbar's ideas on various political and social issues concerning the Empire. The purpose was how to deal with the vast majority of *Hindu* subjects without unnecessary violence. Vanina has summed up the point by saying that the purpose was that 'hostility towards (the *Hindus*) might abate and the temporal sword be swayed a while from shedding the blood; that dissensions within and without be turned to peace and the thornback of strife and enmity bloom into a garden of concord' (Vanina 1996, 63).

It was a time when the need of the dynasty coincided with the broader religious and philosophical developments. Much before this, *Sufism* had already prepared the ground for *Hindu–Muslim* symbiosis. Abul Fazl, taking cue from the great *Sufi* philosopher Ibn Arabi, developed the theory that by a combination of dialectical reason and spiritual exercise, one can attain directly and independently the knowledge of the divine. Then, by fitting Akbar to that slot, he projected the Emperor as the embodiment of Perfect Man (*Momin-e-Kamil* or *Mard-e-Kamil*). The masses, already predisposed to the idea through *yogic* and *Sufi* thoughts, readily accepted the projection. This, in turn, brought an important change in emotional climate of the Indian subcontinent. The net result was the desired solidarity and increase in the strength of the empire.

Akbar professed application of reason to the religious matters. As a creed, it subscribed to the view that blind submission to any human being as a moral and intellectual authority is slavish. Taqlid to Imams (following one of the four schools of *Islamic* jurisprudence) was thought to be unnecessary and deplorable. One should be free to apply his independent rational judgment in following the *Islamic* Laws. Here, some criticize Akbar, following individual whims and passion of the Emperor in the grab of rationalism. Another pillar of Akbarism was religious toleration and integration of the nobles of other faiths by giving them high place in the Court life. He abolished *Jizyah* (poll tax imposed on *Hindus* and other non-*Muslims*), allowed non-*Muslims* to build and repair their places of worships and gave them status at par with *Muslim* subjects. This has its desired effect on the Indian society in the form of weaving a rich and colourful tapestry in which people of all faiths were brought together under a single imperial allegiance.

Akbar in his zeal to make the empire strong and imperial sway more effective, issued the 'Infallibility Decree' in 1579. Officially called as the *Mazhar*. The decree stated that:

> Should in future a religious question arise, regarding which the opinion of the highly qualified religious jurists differ and His Majesty in his penetrating intellect and clear wisdom be inclined to adopt, for the benefit of the people and for the betterment of the administration of the country, any of the conflicting opinions which exists on that point, he should issue an order to that effect. We do hereby agree that such a decree shall be binding on us and on the whole community. (Black 2001, 243)

Akbar got the endowment of many senior *Ulemas* who signed this decree. He thus assumed the position of the supreme religious authority of the *Muslim* Community, who can legislate as well as adjudicate matters pertaining to religious nature. Emboldened by the successful promulgation of the decree Akbar went ahead a step further to propagate a new religion known as *Dīn-e Ilāhī* (The Religion of the God). In the new religion, Akbar assumed the role of the religious leader (just like a *Sufi* master, or *Pir*) with others as his disciples. Those who accepted the new faith were mostly senior officials who were inducted through an elaborate oath-taking ceremony by saying that:

> I liberate and dissociate myself from the traditional and imitative *Islam* which I have seen my furthers practice....and join the 'Religion of God' of King Akbar, accepting the four decrees of devotion, which are sacrifice of property, life, honour, and religion. Thus, Akbar tried to elicit unqualified and unconditional loyalty to the throne in the form of *Dīn-e Ilāhī*. Newer rules were made in which usury, gambling, wine and pork were made lawful defying the *Islamic* ban on them. Cow-slaughter, purdah, circumcision were forbidden, while law relating to marriages were amended. However, there were few takers of this new religion whose acceptance was limited to the high-ranking court officials only. It has no mass following and died with the emperor. (Streusand 1989, 150)

As far as the *Muslim* masses are concerned, Akbarism was nothing but apostasy. The *Muslim* masses, who harboured orthodox orientation towards *Islam*, developed a disdain and antipathy for it. According to Ishwari Prasad, 'The Emperor's disregard for the religion of the Prophet, which was manifest in the rules and regulations issued by him further exasperated the learned in the law and produced a great uneasiness in the minds of the *Muslims*' (Prasad 1974, 248). Akbarism can be termed, at best, as a variant of political realism and, at worst, as Machiavellism, which was both narrowly local and narrowly dated.

Revivalism in *Islamic* Tradition

Another noteworthy political tradition during the medieval period was the Revivalist tradition. It owes its origin to the irreligiosity of Akbarism. It arose as a reaction to the imperialist tradition propounded by the Emperor and his band of intellectuals led by Abul Fazl and Faizi. Its core was rooted in the orthodox tradition of *Islam*. Mainly led by the *Ulemas*, this new school rose to the occasion and valiantly opposed the state ideology, fully aware of the consequence of such a move. It developed itself into a movement by the untiring effort of its main ideologue Shaikh Ahmad Sirhindi (1564–1624). An erudite scholar with a *Sufi* upbringing in the Naqshbandi order, Shaikh Ahmad steadfastly stood in continuous and consistent opposition to the ideological enterprise of Akbar and Abul Fazl.

Shaikh Ahmad Sirhindi gave a clarion call to 'return to the basics and fundamentals' of *Islamic* values in public life. According to him, the prevalent degradation was the result of the corrupt *Ulemas* who surrounded the Emperor (Akbar) and misled him. To purge the Indian *Islam* of its un-*Islamic* strands, he started a movement which he called by the name of 'Jehad by persuasion.' He established close contacts with many politically active figures in Jehangir's Court and made an attempt to prevail upon the latter to appoint a body consisting of honest and upright *Ulemas* and religious doctors (*Muftis*) to act as the highest court of arbitration and interpretation in place of the 'Infallibility Decree.' He got the support of important dignitaries, such as Mirza Aziz-uddin, Khan Jahan Khan Lodi, Khan Khanam Mirza Abdur Rahim, Mirza Darab and Qaleej Khan. However, the attempt ended in a failure and the Emperor interned him in the Gwalior fort.

The Mujaddid unleashed a tirade against the theory of *Wahdat-ul-Wujud* (The Unity of Being) and *Hama Ost* (All in Him) that has misled the masses to eclecticism. He popularized the alternative theory known as the *Wahdat-us-Shuhud* (Unity of Manifestation) which was based on correct *Islamic* premises, launched the movement against the innovations in religious practices, and revolutionized the *Muslim* society.

Sirhindi's well-conceived plan to reform and renovate bore fruits and impacted far-reaching consequences on the long run. While on the one hand, it led to the ascendancy of Aurangzeb to the *Mughal* throne, on the other hand the reform movement got fresh air of *Islamic* resurgence with the emergence of Shah Wali Allah and a chain of religious scholars.

> These scholars and activists contributed heavily to the growth of religious awakening and spiritual regeneration of Indian Muslims through teaching and preaching of the *Kitba* (the Holy *Quran*) and the *Sunnah*.... They caused a chain of educational institutions to be set up, reframed *Muslim* society of its un-*Islamic* customs and usages, awakened the spirit of *Jehad*, and made India a centre of *Islamic* learning, particularly of Hadith. It was, thus, through the efforts of the Mujaddid that India became the focal point of *Islamic* thoughts and a harbinger of its call. (Nadwi 1993, 155)

With the death of Aurangzeb, the *Mughal* Empire started to disintegrate. Aurangzeb was followed by weak successors, who were lacking in the original thought and praxis that resulted in the making and sustenance of the great empire for more than two centuries. Provincial governors declared their independence and hitherto subjugated rebellious people of many regions became active, thereby resulting in the disintegration of the empire. This instability was further aggravated with the invasion of foreign powers, first by Nadir Shah (1739) and then by Ahmad Shah Durrani (1957–1961). Delhi was ransacked on both the occasions. In this turbulent times, Shah Wali Allah of Delhi (1703–1763) rose to illuminate the dark sky with such brilliance and fresh approach which was never seen by the Indian *Muslim* society. He lived to see the reign of 10 *Mughal* kings who followed one another in quick succession. He was very much pained by the decadence of sociopolitical condition of the time. He wrote with the purpose of reviving the lost ground and glory of *Muslims* in the subcontinent. Thus, he became one of the pioneers of *Islamic* resurgence in India.

His contribution to the *Muslim* political thought is remarkably fresh and original. His thoughts have a revolutionary impact on the *Muslim* traditions of India. First of all, he stressed the use of *ijtihad*, that is, individual rational judgment. Its implied purpose was to interpret *Islamic* Laws (*Shariah* Laws) in light of the original circumstances of its inception and adapting it to the needs of the present-day world. This was a remarkably modern idea, which he forcefully enunciated in his magnum opus *Hujjat Allah Al Baligha* (The Conclusive Argument from God). The second remarkable effort was to resolve the conflict between *Ulemas*' legalistic-juristic approaches versus the *Sufi's* informal-mystic approach to the religion. He stressed reconciliation and moderation in resolving these doctrinal differences. The main point is, to him, 'one should take into account that all of them were adapted to the spirit of the time' (Baljon 1986, 202). He advocated tolerance in ritual variations as long as the basic spirit remains the same.

Wali Allah's most important and original contribution to political thought is his theory of *Irtifaqat*, that is, the theory of human social development. He developed this theory in order to substantiate his above-mentioned thesis that the law would vary from time to time. According to him, human beings are the best creations in that they possess some special traits which are not to be found in other animals, such as (a) a universal outlook, (b) an aesthetic sense and (c) among the people of intelligence and awareness the capacity to 'discover the appropriate support of civilization'. Towards the march for a civilized living, human beings progress through a four-stage developmental process. These stages remarkably correspond to 'moments' in Hegelian thought.

To begin with, the first stage is related to the rudimentary development associated with the language, agriculture, posturing, clothing, tools building, house building and female monogamy relating to the beginning of family life. This stage is the most common and found in human beings of all races and all places. The second stage is associated with refinements and development of science of testing in these spheres. Through the knowledge derived from correct experience in every field, one should select correct mores and practices resulting in the development and refinement in techniques and art of living. Here the guiding principle for selection is a natural law, that is, the principle of utility. Men discard those things which brings pain and sufferings while adopt those which results in pleasure and happiness. This starts the process of crystallization of proper customs relating to eating, defecating, clothing, dwelling, sexual and marital life, etc. It also includes development of proper manners relating to household management and economic transactions, exchange processes, cooperation, division of labour, means of earning, contract, partnership, hire and lease, borrowing, witnessing, etc. It also leads to development of different professions and division of society according to functional specialization. This stage is the stage of formation of the 'Civil Society' in Hegelian philosophy.

The third stage is associated with the development of political nature of man. It is the stage in which the science of ruling and administration comes into existence. When people living in close proximity interact with one another, disagreement and conflicts crop up. Man's reason forces him to set up a king to judge among them with justice, restrain the rebellious … and collect taxes to spend as they should be spent. Therefore, people felt the need of establishing the state and the government led by a strong and powerful personality whom he calls the *Imam*.

The fourth stage is the establishment of a supra-national or international state. It is a sort of world-state. As the conflict and quarrel between individuals led to the setting up of state, similarly conflict and wars between states will pave the way for establishment of an international body or a world-state with the function and task to regulate and adjudicate affairs of the states inter se. The states will be 'forced to appoint a *Caliph*', with an army and equipment which will clothe it with strength and power to control the warring states. According to Wali Allah, the leader or the *Imam* should be elected by the wise and headmen of the community. He should be a man of good character, brave, strong-willed, tolerant and an able administrator and always anxious for the welfare of the people. He should know the art of wining the hearts of the people and should make himself acceptable by his sincerity and performance.

Reflecting on state activities, Shah Wali Allah opines that state's responsibility does not end with the ensuring of safety and security of its citizen, rather it is also responsible for the happiness and the progress of the society. He particularly stresses that the state should see to it that the time, talent and energy of people are utilized for the above-said purpose. The state should carefully organize the society by properly distributing the people into different occupational groups. Thus, he says that, when the occupations are not fairly distributed amongst the different sections of a society, its culture receives a setback (Wali Allah, vol. I).

Analysing the factors responsible for decline of the state (especially, the *Mughal* Empire), he highlights two important causes. First, the state suffers heavily when people abandon their own allotted occupation and become parasites on the government, thereby increasing the stress on the political system. For example, soldiers, *Ulemas*, poets, clowns, etc., receive regular donations, gifts and rewards from the court as matter of past customs, without contributing anything to the welfare of the society and state. The sooner the state gets rid of these parasites, the better. Second, he was very critical of exorbitant tax rate on the peasants, traders and artisans. The matter becomes worse when taxes are collected forcibly and cruelly by the insensible government officials. The people groan under the burden of heavy taxation while their economic condition deteriorates at an alarming speed. This causes ruination of the state (ibid, 44).

Wali Allah was a revolutionary thinker. For him state is a means to an end. Therefore, 'he holds that the possessions of coercive power cannot be defended regardless of the end to which it is devoted' (Sharif 1993, 1562). If the government is within the limit of law and performs justly and according to the mandate, then it is the highest obligation of the citizen to be loyal and supportive to such a regime. But when the government transgresses the constitutional limits and disregards public good, then it brings greater obligation on the people to revolt against the oppressive regime. It is an important duty of the people. When the society and the government become corrupt beyond proportions, revolution becomes a necessity. These sociopolitical institutions must be removed in order to cure the state. But revolution is not easy, as it demands great sacrifices. Sometimes, the goal may be achieved through protests and demonstrations while sometimes it may require actual armed struggle.

The most noteworthy thing in Wali Allah's thought is the analysis of human nature that led to the establishment of social organization and then unfolds itself in the form of establishment of the body politic in an ascending order. His naturalistic depiction of human nature, which is reflected in morality, law, society and polity, makes him singularly unique thinker in the whole of *Muslim* political thought. He was thus, 'the only *Muslim* to conceive of a natural moral law of the kind which transformed moral ideas in Europe between thirteenth and eighteenth countries' (Black 2001, 252).

Wali Allah was untiring in his effort of reforming the *Muslim* society and restoring the *Muslim* power to its days of pristine glory. He exerted tremendous influence on the posterity. His thought inspired Shah

Ismail Shahid and Syed Ahmad Barelwi (1786–1831) to start the *Mujahideen* movement that appeared as a spring thunder and attempted to liberate *Muslim* from the *Sikh* rule in Punjab. Later on, this movement got transmuted into the first anti-British movement which was crushed by the latter with a difficult and long-drawn effort. However, it continued well past the famous First War of Independence of 1857. His influence is also seen in the thoughts of Iqbal and other theorists of *Islamic* resurgence in the modern period.

Conclusion

The contact of India with *Islam* is almost a millennium old. It started with Arab conquest of the Sind in the beginning of the 8th century. Today, more than 60 million *Muslims* live in India. Thus, historically as well as in magnitude, *Islam* is an important and sociologically very meaningful cultural tradition in India. Both *Hinduism* and *Islam* represent two varieties of traditional world views, and assimilate with the tide of times. Moreover, the pattern of cultural syncretism between *Hinduism* and *Islam* on the one hand and the process of the spread of *Islam*, which may be called *Islamization*, on the other, are significant social movements which have a bearing on the contemporary dynamics of culture in India and must be analysed. An evaluation of these processes should be undertaken first to bring out the contribution that the great and the little traditions of *Islam* have made towards cultural changes in India. These changes might either be in the form of new syncretic patterns emerging through interaction with the indigenous Indian traditions or they might be in the form of endogenous changes in the very tradition of *Islam* itself.

Summary

To sum up, the chapter deals with the political trends prevailing during the *Muslim*-ruled medieval India. To begin with, the *Sufi* tradition successfully popularized the new ideas and mores of *Islam*. *Sufi* movement also contributed to the strength of newly established *Muslim* brotherhood and the regime. The next important strand was the conservative tradition represented by the famous thinker Barani, who stressed that the *Muslim* rule in India is divinely ordained, mandated to overpower untruth and falsehood. Barani's emphasis on justice, moderation and secular law is indeed commendable. The next was the rationalist tradition espoused by Akbar and Abul Fazl. They emphasized on integration and inclusiveness in order to strengthen and increase the state power. Religion was relegated to the background and made subservient to the demands of the political order. This was by and large the only instance of a secular political thought. This was followed by the now famous revivalist tradition, initiated by Shaikh Ahmad Sirhidi and later on popularized by Walli Allah's school of thought. The main thing in this tradition is their call of 'back to the basics' and restoration of the lost political greatness of *Islam* and *Muslims* in the subcontinent. Therefore, this tradition may also be called as the fundamentalist tradition. However, the positive side of this tradition is its latter transmutation into anti-British and anti-imperial tradition.

Points for Discussion

1. Examine the different streams of *Islamic* traditions in India.
2. Discuss the origin and evolution of *Islamic* traditions in India.
3. Write an essay on the *Mughal* tradition of the medieval India.

4. Illustrate the basic perceptions of *Islamic* traditions in relation to the emergence of syncretic tradition.
5. Critically evaluate Barani's contribution to *Islamic* tradition.
6. Write an essay on Walli Allah's school of thought.

Glossary

***Dīn-e Ilāhī*:** The new religion initiated and propagated by Akbar.

***Khanqahs*:** Hospices, teaching centres maintained by Sufi masters.

***Pirs*:** Sufi masters.

***Shari'ah* Laws:** Laws derived from the *Qur'an* and the *Sunnah*.

***Sufism*:** The concept and practice that professes the mystic principles for attaining the gnosis of God.

Theory of *Irtifaqat*: Social development.

Theory of *Wahdat-ul-Wujud*: Unity of being.

***Ulemas*:** Religious scholars.

References

Baljon, J. M. S. 1986. *The Religion and Thoughts of Shah Wali Allah Dihlavi*. Leiden: Brill.

Barani. 1957–68. The Fatawa-i-Jahandari, trans. *Medieval Indian History Journal*, III(January–April): 151–196.

Black, Antony. 2001. *The History of Islamic Political Thought from the Prophet to the Present*. Edinburg: Edinburg University Press Ltd.

Gibb, H. A. R. 1962. *Studies on the Civilization of Islam*. Princeton, NJ: Princeton University Press.

Habib, Mohammad. 1958. 'Life and Thought of Ziauddin Barni.' *Medieval India Quarterly*, (January): 197-252.

Mehta, N. C. 1936. 'An Unpublished Testament of Babur.' *The Twentieth Century*, January, pp. 339–344 at p. 340.

Mehta, V. R. 2017. *Indian Political Thought*. New Delhi: Manohar Publishers.

Nadwi, Abul Hasan Ali. 1993. *Saviours of Islamic Spirit*, Vol. III. Lucknow: Academy of Islamic Research and Publications.

Prasad, Ishwari. 1974. *The Mughal Empire*. Allahabad: Chugh Publications.

Rosenthal, E. I. J. 1962. *Political Thought in Medieval Islam: An Introductory Outline*. Cambridge: Cambridge University Press.

Sharif, M. M., ed. 1562. *A History of Muslim Philosophy*, Vol. II. New Delhi: Low Price Publications, p. 1562.

Streusand, Douglas E. 1989. *The Formation of the Mughal Polity*. New Delhi: Oxford University Press.

Trimingham, J. S. 1971. *The Sufi Orders in Islam*. Oxford: Oxford University Press.

Vanina, Eugenia. 1996. *Ideas and Society in India from the Sixteenth to the Eighteenth Centuries*. New Delhi: Oxford University Press.

Wali Allah. 1979. *The Hujjat Allah Al Baligha*, Vol. I. Lahore: Shaikh Ghulam Ali and Sons.

Further Readings

Appadorai A. 1987. *Indian Political Thinking in the Twentieth Century: An Introductory Survey*. New Delhi: South Asia Publisher.

Iqbal, Muhammad. 1955. *Reconstruction of Religious Thought in Islam*. Chicago, IL: Kazi Publications.

Easton, Richard M. 2003. *India's Islamic Traditions*. Delhi: Oxford University Press.

Verma, V. P. 1971. *Modern Indian Political Thought*. Agra: Laxmi Narayan Aggarwal Educational Publishers.

Mehta, V. R. 2008. *Foundations of Indian Political Thought*. Delhi: Manohar Publishers.

16
CHAPTER

Sufi Tradition: A Tradition of Spiritualism and Tolerance

S. M. Azizuddin Husain

CHAPTER OUTLINE

- **Introduction**
- **Origin and the Salient Features of *Sufism***
- **Growth of Major *Sufi Silsilahs* and Society**
- ***Sufism* and Society in Medieval India**
- ***Hindu-Muslim* Interaction**
- **Summary**
- **Points for Discussion**

> Sufism is not a religion or a philosophy, it is neither deism nor atheism, nor is it a moral, nor a special kind of mysticism, being free from the usual religious sectarianism. If ever it could be called a religion, it would only be as a religion of love, harmony, and beauty.
>
> —Hazrat Inayat Khan

Reader's Guide

The purpose of this chapter is to familiarize the reader with the growth and features of *Sufism* in India. In fact, the *Islamic* political thought in India was deeply affected by the growth of *Sufism*. After reading this chapter, the reader will be able to understand the significance of *Sufi* tradition and its impact on Indian society.

Introduction

A dictionary of Islam defines *Sufiyah* as a man of the people who professes the mystic principles of *Tasawwuf*. Such men in popular parlance were known as the *Sufis*. The origin of the word *Sufi* can be traced to various roots, for example to the *Arabic Suf* which means wool; this was on account of the woollen dress worn by the Eastern ascetics or from Arabic *Safu*, meaning purity, with reference to the effort to attain to metaphysical purity or according to the *Ghiyaasu-l-lughaat* it is derived from the *Sufah*, the name of a tribe of *Arabs* who in the time of ignorance separated themselves from the world and engaged themselves exclusively in the service of the Makkah Temple (Hughes 1993, 608–609). It would not have been very easy to engraft mysticism over the *Quranic* lessons. However, it is generally admitted by the *Sufis* that one of the great founders of their system, as found in Islam, was the son-in-law of the Prophet and the fourth Caliph, Ali-ibn-Abu-Talib. All the *Sufi silsilahs* with the exception of Naqshbandiya start with Ali because he never discriminated between the *Arabs* and non-*Arabs* and behaved truly impartially towards them. He was also very sympathetic towards the downtrodden in the society and he lived an exemplary simple life. It was for this reason Ali became the attracting point for the *Sufis* who traced their source of inspiration in him. Ali shifted the capital of *Islamic* state from Arab-dominated town of Madina to Kufa. Kufa was a military cantonment and also the most planned urban centre and was thus confluence of people belonging to different religious and social groups. More than 50 per cent of population was of non-Arab origins who were mostly slaves or liberated slaves. Most *Sufis* accept that their religious system had always existed in the world, even prior to the rise of *Islam*. Indeed, mysticism as a way of religious emotionalism and simple spirituality can be traced in other religions as well, like the *Bhakti* stream of *Hinduism* or the writings of the old academics of Greece, such as Plato (Ibid.).

Origin and the Salient Features of *Sufism*

Rise of *Sufism* in Arabia was prompted by its own sociocultural nuances. However, among reasons of political hue, one issue was that Islam believed in democracy and democratic functioning of the state which continued up to Ali, the fourth Caliph, but in 661 AD, Muawiyah converted *Caliphate* into *mulukiyat* (absolute monarchy). After the assassination of Ali, Muawiyah laid the foundation of Umaiyad rule. Yazid, the son and successor of Muawiyah, openly violated the tenets of Islam. In 681, Imam Husain protested against this and he along with his family members and companions was killed. In 682, Madina and Mecca were attacked and plundered, and the result was rape and massacre of innocent people. Abdullah bin Zubair was executed. Kufa and Basra were the main targets of the barbarity and tyranny since 661. It is likely that *Sufi* movement originated in these very towns as a fallout of challenging political, sociocultural circumstances. It is obvious that diverse inter- and intra-religious systems have their own powerful mechanisms for confirming a particular belief. Often the confirmation comes from the past experiences of the community or communities in question. In such cases, the present starts manipulating the past; this could happen through a systematic way of selection, reduction or enhancement of evidences and facts. There might be overplay or underlay of incidents that may come in handy in justifying a current demand or situation. Development of consciousness and identity are not casual things and their evolution cannot be studied with simplistic ease. Exactly why and how religious philosophers feel and think in a certain way, at a certain point in time may remain unclear, but what sometimes is comparatively clear and probably more important is the positive impact of their thought process. The cognitive science of religion is a new approach to the scientific study of religion. Cognitive science is the set of disciplines that investigate the mind–brain process involved in human thought and behaviour. Scholars in the cognitive science of religion explain features of religious thought and behaviour that recur across cultures and eras in terms of mental processes involved in their production and transmission. Religion, along with other forms of culture like music, art and literature, is understood by cognitive scientists as a natural by-product of the way our mind–brain functions. Cognitive scientists of religion are primarily interested in explaining religion, which they distinguish from theology. Religion for them is a set of actual religious concepts people have in their heads and behaviours they perform. Theology is the set of creeds that clergy instruct people to believe in. *Islamic Sufism* is an interesting mix of this 'religion' and 'theology'. The early *Sufis* of Arabia were probably designing, consciously or unconsciously, an emotional revolt against exploitation of religious systems for perpetuating imperialism, separatism and corruption. Their mission was to establish peace and harmony in society.

Sufi scholars like Shaikh Ali Hajweri (b. 1072 AD) the author of *Kashful Mahjub*, Shaikh Muhiuddin Ibn-i-Arabi (b. 1248 AD) author of *Futuhat-i-Makkiya* and *Fususul Hikam*, Shaikh Shahabuddin Suhrawardi (b. 1234 AD) and Maulana Jalaluddin Rumi (b. 1273 AD) created a treasure of philosophy of religious emotionalism. The *Sufis* divided the universe into their *vilayats* (spiritual territories) and India was one of those. They played a significant and positive role in the Indian society.

The famous doctrine of Mohiuddin Ibn-i-Arabi's *Wahdatul Wujud* (Unity of Being) was quite a revolutionary doctrine as far as harmony between the followers of different religions was concerned. This doctrine implied that the entire mankind is one and it reflects the glory of God. It meant that essentially the Being is one and we all are manifestation of this Being. When put to practical and emotional use, the doctrine of *Wahdatul Wujud* inculcates a sense of unity among all human beings. It also induces respect for nature and other objects in the universe as everything in the universe is a reflection of Divine glory. Ibn-i-Arabi's verses have always fascinated the students of his thought

My heart can take on any form:
A meadow for gazelles,
A cloister for monks,
For the idols, sacred ground,
Ka'ba for the circling pilgrim,
The tables of the Torah,
The scrolls of the Quran.

My creed is Love;
Wherever its caravan turns along the way,
That is my belief,
My faith

Thus, the doctrine of *Wahdatul Wujud* was instrumental in promoting communal harmony by eliminating all formal differences of faiths; this attitude was of great importance in the context of the Indian subcontinent because of the heterogeneous religious milieu of the place.

Shaikh Ahmed Sirhindi refuted the doctrine of *Wahdatul Wujud* and instead propounded that of *Wahdatush Shuhud* (Unity of witnessing). What was implied was that though we witness such unity, in fact, it does not exist. Existence does not emanate from God, since He is divinely distant and transcendent. However, it was the all-embracing and all-inclusive *Wahdatul Wujud* which was the accepted popular notion in India and *Wahdatush Shuhud* could never compete successfully with it. Although Shah

Waliullah tried to work out a synthesis of the two divergent philosophies, even the synthesis did not find many takers. It remained confined to a small section of scholars. Akbar's policy of *Sulh-i-kul* (Peace with all) was also based on *Wahdatul Wujud* Abul Fazl and Faizi's religious outlook was also based on *Wahdatul Wujud* and this implies that the popularity of this notion had cut across class structures; the commoners as well as the most brilliant scholars of the age were touched by it.

Maulana Jalaluddin Rumi sums up the substance of the story in his own characteristic way.

'The religion of love is apart from all religions. The lovers of God have no religion but God alone.' Hafiz Shirazi echoes it in his own superb way:

'The good of this world and that can be summed up in a few words: that is kindness towards friends and hospitality towards enemies.'

The noted Persian and Urdu poet Mirza Ghalib (b. 1797) highlighting the doctrine of unity of Being and one creed is 'to renounce all formalities of faith within different communities, when obliterated, became ingredients of everyone's faith'.

Mir Anis (1805–1874), a famous *Marsiya* poet, sums up the essence of *Wahdatul Wujud* in his 'Rubai' on which shii mujtahids of Lucknow who were *usulis* asked Mir Anis to give an explanation of his religion because Maulana Dildar Ali (b. 1752), a shii *alim*, had declared *sufis* as *kafirs* in his work *Shihab-i-Saqib* because *Sufis* believed in *Wahdatul Wujud* Mir Anis was also a descendent of the famous *Sufi* Saiyid Muhammed Gaisu Daraz of Deccan. That is why, Anis says—

Har Rang Main Jalwa Hai tri Qudrat Ka
Jis Phool Ko Soughta Hou Bu Teri Hai

Each colour bears the splendour of your essence, whichever flower I smell, the fragrance is yours.

So *Sufis* never hesitated to assimilate the spiritual insights from other faiths. They were more akin to the Quranic verse 'for everyone there is direction to which one turns, so view with each other in good deeds.' Once Shaikh Nizamuddin Auliya went for a morning walk in Ghiyaspura along the river Yamuna where he saw some *Hindu* women worshipping the rising Sun. He, on seeing these women in the act of worship, told his poet disciple Khusrau.

'For every people there is religion and direction to which they turn to pray.' These words were literal translation of the *Quranic* verse quoted above and deeply reflected Nizamuddin Auliya's approach towards other religions. Nizamuddin Auliya used to recite very often.

(He who is not my friend—may God be his friend! And he who bears ill will against me, may his joys increase. He who puts thorns in my way on account of enmity, may every flower that blossoms in the garden of his life, be without thorns).

Sufis adopted an attitude of sympathy and understanding towards all creeds. They said.

O you who sneer at the idolatry of the *Hindu*,
learn also from him how worship is done.

Growth of Major *Sufi Silsilahs* and Society

The last phase of *Sufism* was the establishment of *Sufi Silsilahs* like Sulurawardi, Kusram, Chisti, Firdausi, Nagshbandi and Chists. They all draw inspiration from Hajrat Ali and call him as *Imam-i-Arhia*. These *Silsilahs* came to India and worked in different parts of the world. In India they worked in Kashmir,

Kerala, Gujarat and Assam. They followed the policy of resignation with worldly interest. They clashed with *Sultans* of Delhi, Gujarat, Malwa, Bengal and Kashmir because their policies had nothing to do with *Islam*. They divided whole India into their milayet. They opened Madrasas in Qesbas and towns to teach people belonging to any section of society. Their primary claim was to educate people. It created healthy society. Their *Khanqahs* were open to *Hindus*. A platform of harmony was also created to settle down the clashes of *Hindus* and *Muslims*. *Sufis* believed that all the people of the world are the creation of God as Prophet Muhammad said that all the people are *Ayal Allah*. They fought against discriminations. During this struggle, some *Sufis* were also killed but that did not affect their movement. *Sufis* kept distance from *Sultans* and did not like their company. Sheikh Nijamuddin Auliya had to face a lot of problems from some *Sultans* of Delhi. So the survival of *Sufis* during *Sultan* period was not so easy.

Sufism and Society in Medieval India

Sufis believed in universal brotherhood and never made any individual distinction between the people of different creeds, races, communities and sects. The concept of God, people and existence of the universe is very clear and lucid in the *Quran*; this enlightened and influenced the *Sufis* and they put it into use through preaching and practice. As Jami has explained:

> Jami you have become the slave of love, so you just forbade pride in genealogy because in the path of love, you are the son of such and such is meaningless.

The fundamentals of *Sufi* ideology rest on the relationship of Love that exists between God and man. They helped in developing a more humanitarian approach in religious life with stress on service to mankind and a belief that love of God was not possible without the love of mankind.

Sufis, unlike the *Ulema*, did not keep themselves aloof from Indian masses. They knew Arabic and Persian, but they adopted local idiom and preached the message of love and universal brotherhood in local languages. They also adopted local customs and traditions and thus drew Indian masses near Islam. Thus, they played a much greater role in spreading universal values of Islam than the doctrinaire *Ulema*. As Ibn Hujveri had rightly commented:

> You will not find God in the books on jurisprudence; see the mirror of your heart, because no book is better than this.

Islam, as practised by the *Sufis*, was somehow more influential than the *Islam* of the ambitious Turkish conquerors. *Sufis* believed in equality and fraternity of mankind. They abjured narrowness of mind and opposed communal, sectarian and caste barriers, which cause conflict and destroy social harmony.

The outstanding *Sufis* who played a revolutionary role in the social, cultural and religious life of India were Khwaja Moinuddin Chishti of Rajasthan, Shaikh Fariduddin Ganj-i-Shakar of Punjab, Shaikh Bahaduddin Zakariya of Punjab, Shaikh Nizamuddin Auliya of Delhi, Mir Saiyid Ali Hamedani of Kashmir, Saiyid Muhammed Gaisu Daraz of Deccan, Shaikh Latif, Shaikh Jalal Thanesri and others. These *sufis* had divided the whole north India and some parts of south up to Deccan into their *vilayats* (spiritual territories). *Sufis* worked in Kashmir, Sindh, Punjab, Bihar, Bengal, Gujarat, Maharashtra, Awadh and Deccan. Through their unparalleled moral standards and sweet spiritual voice, they propagated *Islam* in India and opened a new epoch in *Islamic* history for a better understanding of other religions, cultures. Human values and good inter-religious relations were stressed upon.

Shaikh Fariduddin Ganj-i-Shakar established his *khanqah* at Ajodhan, a town of Punjab. He was the first Indian *Sufi* who had cordial relations with the *Hindu* thinkers. He wrote excellent poetry in Arabic, Persian, Punjabi and local Hindavi dialect. His *ślokas* and *Shabads* have been incorporated in the *Guru Granth Saheb* by the fifth Guru, Arjun Singh. Baba Farid adopted Punjabi and vice versa Sikhs adopted Persian. Baba Farid's poetry was a means of creating congenial moral atmosphere in Punjab. His *ślokas* and *Shabads* won the hearts of Punjabi people. His Punjabi and Hindavi poetry became immortal and even today his verses are being sung in Punjab.

Amir Khusrau (1253–1325), born of an Indian mother and the Turkish father, personified the diffusion of two cultures, imbibing the best of both. Extremely proud of being an Indian, intensely devoted to *Hindavi*, he occupies a prominent position among the spiritual benefactors of mankind by his love towards the common people of India. Khusrau endeared to transform the common speech of the people into a literary language *Hindavi* which he regarded as not being second to either Arabic or Persian. Khusrau also brought about a synthesis of Indian and Iranian music.

In the socio-religious life of Deccan Burhanuddin Gharib, Saiyid Zainuddin Daood, Shaikh Ainuddin Bijapuri, Saiyid Muhammed Gaisu Daraz and Shaikh Sirajuddin Junaidi played a significant role. One of the most celebrated figures in the early history of *Sufism* in Deccan was Saiyid Muhammed Gaisu Daraz, who played a very conspicuous role in the Deccan. Hindus also frequently visited him and stayed in his *khanqah* without any inhibition (Husaini 1983, 7). He also read Sanskrit books to know the mythology of *Hindus*. Saiyid Muhammed Gaisu Daraz's father Saiyid Yusuf composed *Manan Suhagan Nama* in *Dakkani* Gaisu Daraz also wrote Mairajul Ashiqin in *Dakkani*, which is a symbol of composite culture and social integration. The liberal attitude of *Sufis* created pleasant atmosphere and their *khanqahs* became the centres of cultural synthesis and communal harmony. That is why a new language known as *Dakkani* originated in the *khanqahs* of the *Sufis* of the *Deccan*.

Shaikh Muhammed Baba of Shirgonda of Ahmednagar district gave his message in Marathi. With Marathi, the *Sufis* established a dialogue with and within the entire Marathi knowing community of Maharashtra. Shivaji's grandfather Maluji's wife was barren and he went to a *Sufi*, Shah Sharif, and sought his blessings for children and subsequently two sons were born to her which he named after the *Sufi* as Shahji and Shivaji. The 19th century reformer M. G. Ranade holds opinion

> Some Mohammedan fakirs have been ranked with the *Hindu* saints in general veneration and there are some saints who are venerated by both communities alike. These features of tolerance and moderation have been developed in the course of centuries and they constitute some of the most stable elements and national character. (Namade 1980, 8)

Sufism had a deep impact on Sindhi life and literature, with its humanist outlook and harmonious approach, especially through the liberal poetry of our *Sufi* poets like Qazi Qadan, Abdul Karim, Shah Inayat, Shah Latif, Sarmast, Sami, Bedil, Bekas, Dalpat and others of mid-16th to mid-19th centuries. All these poets had condemned communal hatred and religious bigotry and preached communal harmony and social integration. Shah Latif (1690–1750) and Sachal (1739–1829) were very influential and are household names for both Sindhi Muslims and Hindus till today. Sachal was a multilingual poet of Sindhi, Persian and Urdu, and has used Persian prosody also along with indigenous forms. He boldly spoke in favour of a classless and peaceful society, which would form a base for communal harmony. He warned the people against the rising British power as well. He had said, '*Hindus* and *Muslims* unite in bond of love. Before it is too late and the Sun sets in the west'. And indeed, Sachal's fears proved true because we did suffer many losses due to the 'policy of divide and rule' which the British administrators followed in the Indian subcontinent.

Through *Padmavat*, Jaisi tried to open the eyes of all those who advocated separation between followers of different religions. He said that '*Viyog*' of Ratna Sen for *Padmavati* was the same as that of Alauddin for her. The text evokes emotions and feelings for the different characters, irrespective of their caste, colour or religion. Jaisi asserts that all humans emote in the same way; the basic human responses to situations do not have much to do with formal religions. During the course of humanitarian interaction, bonds of religion, caste, sect and nationality break down automatically and there emerges a perfect being whose heart is tender, liberal, permissive and powerful. Jaisi wrote thousands of verses in Avadhi but in Persian script. His description of events smoothly goes on without any modification at the cultural and social level. Jaisi followed the tradition of Khusrau's masnavis in *Chaudayan.*

Shaikh Qutban of Jaunpur wrote a book *Mirgawati* (1503), an epic of love and romance. Shaikh Qutban has properly utilized *Hindu* mythology, astrology and many a religious symbol to weave a wonderful tale which culminated to preach oneness and the unity of God.

In retrospect we can see that just as the basic ideas and attitudes of *Sufism* were translated from Arabic to Persian, so were they expressed in Hindavi, Rajasthani, Punjabi, Maharashti, Sindhi and Dakkani.

The *Sufis* promoted communal harmony with their devoted activities and attracted the caste-ridden and oppressed lower sections to their organizational fold. Titus (2005) rightly said, 'It was through *Sufism* that Islam really found a point of contact with *Hinduism* and effective entrance to *Hindu* heart'. R. K. Megh holds opinion, 'We can thus conclude that whenever there is a crisis of cultural identity, or the romantic sprit is resurrected, the *Sufi* heritage would speak with a thousand tongues to us all'.

We see that immediately following the death of Muhammed Ghori, the Ghorid Empire broke up. His favourite slave, Yalduz, succeeded him at Ghazni, while another slave, Qubecha, seized control of Multan and Uchh. Qutubuddin Aibak became the *Sultan* of Delhi in 1206 and India was divided. But the dream of united India was seen by a *Sufi* Shaikh Bahauddin Zakaria of Suhrawardi order. After the death of Aibak, Iltutmish became the *Sultan* of Delhi in 1210, Shaikh Bahauddin Zakariya who had his *Khanqah* in Multan invited Iltutmish to attack Multan. Iltutmish followed the direction given by the *Sufi* and Qubecha was defeated and the whole of Punjab came under the direct rule of Delhi (Khizer 1991). So we see that *Sufis* played an important role in uniting India and Punjab during 13th century.

Some poets joined the romantic band of liberal poets of love and beauty. Such a manifestation of the eternal feminine is a radical departure from the feudal cultural system. They believed that love is not realized without beauty and one must sacrifice oneself, in the fire of love. Yet, they were clearly against lust; they transformed their '*Ishq-i-Majazi*' into '*Ishq-i-Haqiqi*' and elevated the woman of pleasure and dance into a spiritual symbol. Among such romantic rebels of the 18th and 19th centuries, prominent ones were Bodha (18th century), Thakur (18th century) and Ghananand (19th century). Almost all of them were under the deep influence of the *sufis*. *Ishq Nama* by Bodha and *Ishq Lata* by Ghananand are glowing examples. It appears that the *Sufi* influence had become a strong archetype in our cultural pattern. *Rubaiyat-i-Umar_Khaiyam* is popularly tinted with *Sufi* thought and they have been variously translated by Hindi poets of different schools and period. Bhagwati Charan Verma and Jaya Shankar Prasad have intimately drawn from *Sufi* idioms. They refrained from hallow argumentation and lived a life of poverty, piety, trust, patience, resignation and love. They practised and preached these values and thereby created a peaceful and progressive society. They shared the life of the downtrodden.

The *Sufis* has never been sectarian because they never identified with any particular sect. All the *Sufi* poets had condemned communal hatred and religious bigotry and preached communal harmony and social integration. *Sufis* stood for cultural coexistence—*Sufi* idea of cultural coexistence became the norm of mutual relations during medieval period in India. This is the great legacy which *Sufis* have left for the succeeding generations in India. Respect for cultural diversity is perhaps the greatest contribution of *Sufis* to Indian civilization.

Today, when we are facing a great challenge from the communal and divisive forces bent upon promoting conflict in the name of creed, sect, caste, it is necessary to revive the spirit of *Sufis* and the *Bhakti* saints. Real spiritualists can always play a vital role in the spiritual evolution of a pluralistic society which will promote peace, harmony and humanitarianism. We need them again.

Hindu–Muslim Interaction

When Taimur invaded India, most of the *Sufis* migrated from northern India and shifted to Gujrat, Bengal, Malwas and Deccan. *Mughal* emperors were the sovereign rulers, so they did not like that anyone should work independently. They believed that *Sufis* should also work for them and some *Sufis* joined them. But a section of *Sufis* kept themselves from *Mughal* emperors. So from *Mughal* period we find decay in its values as were enjoyed by the earlier *Sufis* during the 13th and 14th centuries.

In India, there was not a common place where *Hindus* and *Muslims* could sit together. With the establishment of *Khanqahs*, its gates were opened to all people belonging to any religion, caste or sex. That provided an opportunity to sit together and discuss various aspects of life. *Khanqah* gave birth to *Hindavi* language, a medium to talk. *Sufis* also learnt regional languages like Punjabi, Gujarati, Kashmiri, Bengali and Deccan. With this language they came much nearer to each other.

Summary

Sufism played an important role in medieval India and created an environment of communal harmony. It created a new culture of understanding between the followers of different religions which reflect from the verses of *Sufis* and *Bhakts*. Sheikh Farid Uddin sauji-i-shakar, a *Sufi* of Punjab, was an eminent poet of Punjab. His verses are incorporated in *Guru Granth Sahib*.

Points for Discussion

1. Critically examine the origin and growth of *Sufism* in India.
2. Discuss the major beliefs and practices that characterized *Sufism*.
3. Analyse the impact of *Sufism* on *Hindu–Muslim* interaction in Indian society.

Glossary

Communal harmony: Social and religious harmony among different sections of the society.

***Sufism*:** The concept and practice that professes the mystic principles for attaining the gnosis of God.

***Ulemas*:** A body of *Muslim* scholars who are recognized as having specialist knowledge of *Islamic* sacred law and theology.

References

Hughes, Thomas Patrick. 1993. *Dictionary of Islam*. New Delhi: Pub. Rupa.

Husaini, Syed Shah Khusrau. 1983. *Saiyid Muhammed Gaisu Daraz*. Delhi: Idarah-I Adabiyat-I Delli.

Khizer, M. M. 1991. 'Sufism and Social Integration.' in Sufism and Communal Harmony, edited by A. A. Engineer, 102–123. London: George Allen and Unwin.

Megh, R. K. *The Influence of Sufism in the Growth of Hindi Poetry*.

Namade, B. 1980. *Tukaram*. New Delhi: Sahitya Akademi.

Rauade, P. V. *Binocular Glossary of Vedanta and Tasawwuf of Shaikh Muhammed*.

Siddiqi, M. Sulaiman. 1977, July. 'Origin and Development of Chishti Order in the Deccan.' *Islamic Culture* I(3): 209–219.

Titus, Murray T. 2005. *Islam in India and Pakistan: A Religious History of Islam in India and Pakistan*. New Delhi: Munshiram Manoharlal Publishers.

17

CHAPTER

Kabir: An Indian Mystic Saint

Prabira Sethy

CHAPTER OUTLINE

- Introduction
- The Life Sketch
- Kabir's Views on Socio-religious Dogmas and Economic Inequalities
- Syncretism in Kabir's *Bijak*
- Comparison between Kabir Das and Ravidas
- Conclusion
- Summary
- Points for Discussion

Harsh words is worst of all
Burns its target to ash
Sweet word is like Heaven's nectar
It pleases, cools, does not harass.

—G. N. Das (1991, 120)

Reader's Guide

The chapter begins with an attempt to reconstruct Kabir's biography by analysing where Kabir was born, who were his parents and when he was born, which have been shrouded in the mists of mystery. Second, it has taken up the task of illuminating the different kinds of social inequalities which was prevalent during Kabir's period, such as intense religious bigotry, political upheaval, rampant exploitation, social discrimination, etc. Third, the chapter then goes on to exhibit Kabir's philosophy about syncretism by bridging the gap in between rich and poor, higher and lower castes and the *Hindus* and the *Muslims* by his message to maintain equality, love, affection and cooperation in place of enmity, jealousy, egotism, disparity and has shown the way to the human beings to live for one another. Finally, the chapter has made an attempt to make a comparative study in between Kabir and Ravidas which recognizes how much they had in common from their birth place to progressive ideas about the society.

Introduction

Sant Kabir is widely regarded as one of the most outstanding religious figures of medieval India. He was a reformer and a versatile preacher of religious truth. He pointed out every disorder in the society as he was determined to change the society. He was a good observer of the society. He was always seized with several problems of the society and found some solutions to them. He wanted to bring the people out from their mundane life by showing them the right path. He counselled like friend, enlightened like teacher and showed the right path like preacher. He had talked of social evils like what Raja Ram Mohan Roy, Mahatma Gandhi and B. R. Ambedkar talked about several centuries later. He is considered as a people's poet, *Vaishnava* reformer, one of the founders of the deistic movement in India, man of radical social critic, messenger of inter-faith harmony, an anti-caste evangelist and a benign humanist, etc., in one way.

Kabir strongly denounced asceticism, fasting, bathing in rivers and becoming *Sanyasis* without a sense of personal devotion to God. He also laid emphasis on a sternly ethical code of life for both *Guru* and the householder. He criticized laying emphasis on the external of religion and said that it was not confined to the *Brāhmaṇs*, but extended equally to the *Muslim*, *Shaikhs* and *Mullahs* for their empty insistence on *roza*, *namaz*, etc.

Kabir was strongly opposed to reliance on religious authority and revealed scriptures. For him, the only true path was reliance on constantly repeating the name of One God whom he identified as *Rāma, Hari, Govind, Allah, Khuda, Sahib*, etc. Tara Chand says that Kabir's mission was to 'preach a religion of love which could unite all castes and creeds'. Kabir certainly believed that God is one and different religions were different paths to him. His own path of love and devotion to God was one which could be followed by all irrespective of their religions.

An even more important aspect of Kabir's teaching was his emphasis on human equality. He denounced inequality based on caste, race or wealth, and criticized the wealthy and the powerful for their pattern of life. This strain is largely missing in the writings of the *Sufi* saints of *Hindu* for whom God was the creator of everything. According to them, he created the rulers and the slaves, and the rich and the poor. This resignation was not for Kabir. Therefore, he voiced the sentiments of the poor and the oppressed. He wanted a change in their lives through the message of love and fortitude (Chandra 1996, 141–142).

The Life Sketch

Sant Kabir Das has been acclaimed as one of the most outstanding of the saint-poets of *Bhakti* cult (devotion) and mysticism of medieval India. The period in which he lived is also not yet confirmed by the historians. Some people believed that he was born in 1398 AD and some others in 1440 AD. There are different opinions among the scholars about his birthplace. Some scholars say he was born in Banaras and others say he was born at Maghar 200 km away from Banaras. There are different versions about his birth story. According to some people, he was found on a full-blooming lotus leaf in a tank in Banaras, while others say that he was the son of a *Hindu Brāhmaṇa* widow who to hide her shame left him immediately after his birth. He was brought up by *Muslim* weaver-couple Niru and Nima who christened him Kabir, which means the great in Arabic and it is the 37th name of God in *Islam*. Since Kabir had received no schooling—formal or informal—it is said that he was a born saint-poet. Kabir adopted the profession of his Godfather, but being a man of sober and serious mood, he spent most of his time in solitude and meditation. This child grew up to be the celebrated Saint Kabir who gained popular support because of his large number of his uttering of *Dohas* (couplets) and *Bhajanas* (devotional songs) of great spiritual fervour and poetic quality. Thus, he was mystically oriented from his early life. Mysticism appears to have been an inborn element in his nature.

Kabir was remarkable for his spiritual earnestness and this was apparent in him from the very outset. His discipleship was the first step to it. Ramananda, the great saint of the Order of Ramanuja, accepted only *Brāhmaṇs* as his disciples. All entreaties to relax the rule proving futile. Kabir one day hid himself under the steps of the *Ghat* at Banaras, where Ramananda used to go very early in the morning for a bath. Unknowingly as he passed his foot fell on Kabir to the great joy of the latter. The Master, in sheer agony of having crushed one of God's own creatures, cried out, 'Rāma', 'Rāma'. Kabir took it as his initiation *Mantra*. Since then he called himself the disciple of Ramananda, and began to recite Rāma. When Ramananda saw the earnestness of Kabir he accepted him as a disciple, and with his *Guru* he associated for long. It was with him that he learned the worship and practice of the Impersonal Aspect (*Nirguna*) of the Lord (Behari 1991, 222–223). Under Ramanand's influence Kabir adopted a number of *Hindu* notions, though much of his own doctrine and some of the language were borrowed from the Nestorian Christianity of South India.

Kabir had married twice, and his wives were ever obedient to him and ministered to his special mandates to feed every mendicant who came to his door. Several legends name Loi as his wife whose parentage is however unknown. Dr Ramkumar Verma has advanced a theory based on internal evidence in Kabir's writings that Kabir had two wives, one homely, the other pretty. The second wife was called Dhania or Ramjaniya. However, it is generally accepted that Kabir had a son named Kamal and a daughter named Kamali. Among the contemporaries with whom Kabir was said to have matched his wits or engaged in friendly controversy were Gorakhnath (who in fact, lived long before him), Nanak, the emperor Sikander Lodi (who later persecuted him) and Sheikh Taqqi.

Kabir's insistence on speaking truth without caring for its consequence invited troubles for him. For the so-called high class, he was too big for his boots. He was humiliated. It is said that miscreants set his thatched hut on fire. Thus, the plain speaking of Kabir and his general disregard for the conventions of the society raised up enemies on every side. According to Kabirpanthi tradition, it was Shaikh Taqqi who voiced the feelings of *Muhammaedans*. The famous *Pir* came before the emperor Sikandar Lodi and accused Kabir of laying claim to Divine attributes. Furthermore, the orthodox *Brāhmaṇs* called him irreligious and carried tales of his intimacy with a woman of ill fame.

Popular with the masses but persecuted by the ruling classes Kabir was exiled from Banaras, and his subsequent wanderings took him from Bukhara to Kalighat. Kabir travelled widely on pilgrimages in India is proved by many references. Acharya Kshitimohan Sen has referred to Kabir's journey to Gujarat. *Khulasatuttavarikh* says that he had been to Ratanpur. *Ain-e-Akbari* mentions that Kabir had been to Jagannath Puri in Orissa and *A History of the Maratha People* records his travel up to Pandharpur in south Maharashtra. He visited Persia, Afghanistan and other places in the Middle East before settling down to end his days in Maghar in Northern India. It was commonly believed that those who died in Banaras received salvation, while those died in Maghar went to hell. Kabir deliberately chose to die in Maghar to show his contempt for such puerile superstitions. About the year of his death, there are different views: some place it in 1447, some in 1511 and some in 1517. Anantadas maintains that Kabir lived a long life of 120 years. Dharmadas presumes that Kabir died in 1463. Dr Shyamsundar Das believes that Kabir died in 1517. Sir W. W. Hunter gave Kabir's dates in his *Indian Empire* (1892) as 1380 to 1420. Dr Haraprasad Shastri put it as 1398–1518. The legend says that when he died his body was covered with a sheet. His *Hindu* disciples wanted to take it for cremation, and his *Muslims* disciples wished to bury it. So they argued and quarrelled. But when they lifted up the sheet they found the body for the possession of which they were quarrelling had disappeared and in its place there was a bunch of fresh flowers. The *Hindus* burned half the flowers at Banaras, and the *Muslims* buried the remaining half at Maghar (Walker 1983, 506–507).

Kabir's simple couplet compositions *Doha* (two liners) and *Chowtai* (four liners) are very popular among the peoples. His writings—*Bijak, Sakhi, Granth, Kabir Granthawali* and *Anurag Sagar*—prove his universal view of spirituality. He transcended the bounds of religion, rose to greatest heights in his spiritual thoughts and broke into spontaneous lyrics and *bhajans*. Kabir expressed his poems orally in vernacular *Hindi* language. He used native language with local idiom and popular expressions. He used the simple and crisp language of everyday usage and revealed astonishing truths with accuracy and persuasiveness. His works are read with a lot of reverence by *Hindus, Muslims* and *Sikhs*. He is universally recognized as a unique person. After his death, the followers of Kabir, both *Hindus* and *Muslims*, became known as *Kabirpanthis*. The devotees as well as the priesthood of the *Kabirpanth* retain their distinct identity up till this day. His followers number about half a million and are mostly found in Uttar Pradesh.

Kabir's Views on Socio-religious Dogmas and Economic Inequalities

As a social and ethical reformer, Kabir claims the attention of modern radicals in as much as he, like Buddha, denounced the folly of social inequity and injustice perpetrated in the name of caste. He ridiculed the orthodoxy of both *Hindus* and *Muslims* and challenged them like any later scientific rationalist to justify their sham and hypocrisy. Challenging the superiority of *Brāhmaṇs* based on their birth, he lashed out at them that if they were superior by birth why did they enter the world like others? Why were not they born differently?

Kabir denounced hoarding and show of wealth and was against any kind of luxury and indulgence in intoxicants. He preached simplicity and contentment and believed that everyone should do physical labour and stick to his own profession and no one should steal another person's property. He did not spare royal greed and political aggrandizement. He asks the question: 'Gathering forces and besieging castles and showing off his prowess—is this the only job of a *Badshah* (Monarch)? When the emperor dies, what remains of this game?' 'Crores of rupees and many elephants may be there with a king, such a miser's wealth is of no use.'

Kabir was a bitter critic of all kinds of sectarian and narrow creeds and outlooks. According to him, 'Neither the *Brāhmaṇa* is high-caste, nor is the *Śūdra* low. Why hate one another? Hatred is folly'. To Kabir eternal rituals are meaningless. Besmearing the body with ashes, taking a ritual bath three times a day, keeping fasts and going on pilgrimage, flaunting rosaries, repeating God's name loudly and indulging in physical mortification are a butt of great ridicule for Kabir.

'If by wearing a holy thread a person could be called twice-born, why not call the iron-wheel in the well that always wears a rope a *Brāhmaṇa*?' 'Why does the *Kazi* shout so loudly, standing on the top of the minaret at his morning prayer? Has *Allah* gone deaf?' 'The goat eats grass and is skinned. What will happen to those who eat the goat?'

> Look at these foolish people who worship the dead. After cremating the dead body at the burning *ghat*, they make a show of great love and attachment. They beat with *daṇḍa* (stick) the living elderly people; when dead they put Ganges water in their mouth. They starve the elders when living; when dead they feed the ancestors with rice-balls. The old while alive are always abused and cursed; when dead, there is the ceremony of showing honour and respect (*shraddha*). Kabir says I wonder how what is fed to the crow is conveyed to the dead old ancestors. (Kabir Granthavali)

Kabir saw how the social conventions had hardened into blind beliefs. He also noticed how people indulged in greed, hypocrisy and selfishness under the cover of religion. He refused to keep quiet. In an age when freedom of speech was unknown, he dared to speak freely. He hit at the outer rituals ruthlessly. He defied all that tended to hide the truth and divide people. With this end in view, Kabir addressed his poems to the people trapped in ignorance. He quizzed *Mullah* for crowing from the top of a Mosque as if God lived somewhere far off.

Kabir was a great reformer. He preached against religious differences as well as caste systems. He criticized the *Brāhmaṇs* and the *Maulvis* for their closed minds. He said,

> Vain too are the distinctions of caste. All shades of colour are but broken arcs of light; all varieties in human nature are but fragments of humanity. The right to approach God is not the monopoly of *Brahmins*, but if freely granted to all who are characterised by sincerity of heart.

Kabir was a bold preacher. He criticized the outer modes of religions. His satires were aimed at the orthodox *Maulvis* and *Pundits*. He asked, who is the Lord of the earth if *Allah* stays inside the Mosque? Who is looking after the world if *Rāma* is inside the image? To Kabir, *Hari* does not exist in the east and *Allah* in the west. They, as one, are inside the human heart. Divinity was existent in all men and women. It was impossible to know the God's will. Man's duty was to surrender himself to the will of God (Das 1991, 125).

Criticizing superstitions, Kabir said with courage: 'If by worshipping stones one can find God, I shall worship a mountain: better than these stones (idols) are stones of the flour mill with which men grind their corn'. To the *Muslims*, he asked, what good was the pilgrimage to *Mecca* if the pilgrim marched with an impure heart? He said:

> It is not by fasting and repeating prayers and the creed
> That one goes to the heaven:
> The inner veil of the Temple of Mecca
> Is in man's heart, if the truth be known.

Kabir was a firm believer in the unity of mankind and brotherhood. To him, *Allah* and *Rāma*, *Karim* and *Keshab*, *Hari* and *Hazrat* were the various names of the one and the same God. It required inner eye to realize him (Das 1991, 126).

The words of Kabir touched the human heart. He preached the messages of love and unity. If God created all men, He did not certainly desire difference between man and man. To Kabir, division of men into different religions was unnecessary and unnatural. He declared '*Hindu* and Turk were pots of same clay, *Allah* and *Rāma* were but different names'. For real believers, there could be no caste. As he said 'it is needless to ask of a saint the caste to which he belongs'.

Kabir believed in the sameness of *Hinduism* and *Islam* as far as the love of God was concerned. To him, the true love of God could be achieved only through devotion or *Bhakti*. This devotion should come from within the heart, not from eternal shows. He criticized the formalities of all religions. Worship or prayers in temples or mosques were meaningless without true devotion. By emotional *Bhakti*, man could come nearer to God. Although Kabir was born in a *Muslim* family, he attacked *mullahs* as well as *pundits* and was against ritualism and questioned inequality on the basis of caste. His Doha says:

Worship, libations, six sacred rites,
this dharma's full of ritual blights.
Four ages teaching Gayatri, I ask you, you won liberty?
You wash your body if you touch another,
tell me who could be lower than you?
Proud of your merit, puffed up with your rights,
No good comes out of such great pride
How could he whose very name
is pride-destroyer endure the same?
Drop the limits of caste and clan,
seek for freedom's space,
destroy the shoot, destroy the sced,
seek the unembodied place. (Omvedt 2012, 21)

During Kabir's period the division of wealth was very unequal. The gold and silvers were gathered to the vassals and the rich, and the ordinary people had very little money and resources. Generally, the condition of the lower classes, especially the condition of the *Hindu Śūdras,* was very pathetic. People were overwhelmed by 'tax'. The *Hindus* were suffering from '*Jizya*' tax, and they were taxed on agriculture, trade or any other income and they had to send the goods of the produced to the royal treasury at the proportionate rate. It was that there was both movable and immovable property, but over the land the *Sultanate* had the right. The slaves were counted as movable property and they were also bought and sold. The king's exploitation and nature's wrath broke the waist of the people. The money collected from the people for the fulfilment of the royal treasury was used for pleasure of the king.

Most of the people in the society were poor and used to earn their bread as farmers and labourers. The number of rich farmers was very less. Most of the farmers, who used to farm, used to run their families in some way, despite day and night of hard work. In proportion to the yield of cultivable land, the government levy was so high that it was difficult to spend the entire year for them. Apart from the farmers and the working classes, there was also a business class, who used to run their livelihood through trading. The market-*hat* was the main means of their livelihood. In addition to all this, there were communities like beggars and nomadic monks as well as slaves, who were bought and sold; despite being human they were deprived from respect of humans. The *sultans*, kings, government officials and employees and big traders were living in luxurious accommodations in high-rise palaces. They used to wear precious clothes and jewellery and enjoyed their life in pleasure. The ruling classes had immense wealth that was accumulated by the exploitation of the general public.

Kabir condemned the inequality of the then society in which the wealthy was the respected person of society and poor people were despised. There was no respect of poor people in the society and Kabir said: The devotees of *Rāma* living in a broken hut are better than the rich ones. The high temples should be burnt, where there is no devotion and love for *Rama*. There was no sympathy of the wealthy for the poor in the society. They were exploiting the poor by paying money at the interest rate. In Doha Kabir says:

Says Kabir,
Save only that wealth
That later may be useful
And if you carry it on head in a bundle
To others will not be visible.

It means the spiritual wealth being invisible to the eye is not subject to theft or burglary. Kabir indicates that man should collect and save that wealth and not the worldly riches. The former will bring him emancipation, while the latter only worries and miseries (Das 1991, 108). In other words, nobody can carry on their head the accumulated wealth after their death. The wealth which they can carry along with them (good deeds, fame, etc.) should be collected by them. On the contrary, the people are engaged in saving the worldly riches. Kabir said the tendency of saving only wealth is wrong and opposed the *Mahajans* (capitalists) because they were exploiting the poor by paying money at the interest rate.

Syncretism in Kabir's *Bijak*

The dictionary meaning of syncretism means it is an attempt to unify or reconcile differing schools of thought. Here, it can definitely be said that the synthesis of different and contradictory ideologies is the base of syncretism. From this point of view, Kabir tried his best to bridge the gap between the king and subject, rich and poor, higher and lower castes and the *Hindus* and the *Muslims* in medieval India. Kabir has given the message to maintain equality, love, affection and cooperation in place of enmity, jealousy, egotism, disparity and has shown the way to the human beings to live for one another. Thus, Kabir's apparently simple *Dohas* contains the essence of the great philosophical ideas of syncretism which have immense significance in the contemporary times.

1. **Criticize the caste system:** In his crusade against everything that was meaningless and unreal, Kabir naturally uttered strong denunciatory words against the caste system. It has been acknowledged unanimously that the strongest indication of *Islamic* influence on Indian thought is the rejection of caste system by some Indian mystics, such as Namdev, Ramananda, Nanak, Appar, Basava and Kabir. But unlike some *bhaktas*, Kabir rejected the caste system for social reasons. It is in this sense that Kabir is regarded as the revolutionary of medieval Indian society. Kabir simply could not tolerate the division and distinction between man and man. He urges us to forget our sense of distinctions between man and man and become humble like an ant. He says:

   Jaati napucho sadhu ki puchlijiye sab gyan,
   Mol karo talwar ka padi rehan do myan

It means we should not enquire about the caste of the saints but seek their wisdom. Sharpness of a sword counts more than the metal with which it is made of.

Thus, Kabir as a reformer and saint fearlessly preached the gospel of social equality, imparting with force and preaching by practice the gospel of his Guru, Ramananda:

Jati pati puchai na koi
Hari ko bhaje so Harika hoi

It means none shall inquire into thy caste. He who shall recite the name of the Lord will be claimed by Him.

There are verses which Kabir directed against the *Brāhmaṇs* who consider impurity and caste defilement in almost everything. The *Brāhmaṇs* censured Kabir for not giving due attention to caste rules. There are many stories told about Kabir's confrontations with the *Brāhmaṇs* on the question of the caste. One of these stories is told with regard to Kamali, Kabir's daughter. It is stated that when she was 20 years of age, she was one day drawing water from a well. A *Brāhmaṇa* named Har Deva, asked for a drink, but was afterwards horrified to know that he had taken water from a weaver's daughter. The matter was referred to Kabir. The *Brāhmaṇa* complained that the girl had defiled his caste. On that Kabir said the *Brāhmaṇa* to have fallen at the feet of Him and to beg his forgiveness and to be received by him as his disciple. Kabir accepted him, and Kamali was given to him in marriage.

2. **Raised voice against *Sati* and child marriage:** Kabir concerned himself not only with the matters of religion simple and pure but also with those social evils which the *Hindus* used to practise in the name of religion. One such superstition which obtained wide currency in the *Hindu* society of those days was the practice of *Sati*, that is, burning of a widow on the funeral pyre of her deceased husband. Kabir rejected the idea of salvation by *sati*, and condemned the practice. Thus, Kabir raised his voice against the custom of *Sati* and child marriage, the two evils which were purely social in character.
3. **Concept of universal humanism**
   a. *Equality of all men*: Following on his view of one God, Kabir preached equality of all men. Egalitarianism is the second great principle of *Islam* which Kabir accepted under the influence of *Sufism*. When the low-caste weaver Kabir began preaching to men of high caste, the principle of equality of all men, he was reproached for his daringness.
   b. *Unity of human beings*: Kabir took great pains for articulating his views about the unity of human beings. According to him, while the religious differences are only fortuitous, the essential humanity is always the same. In Kabir's word 'all have come from the same country', that is, it was all one human, thus one nation, 'but the evil influences of this world have divided us into innumerable sects'. His conception of the oneness of human beings is in uniformity with that of the Qur'an. Hence, he says:

O' Saints! I have seen the ways of both. In their
Pride the Hindu and the Turk don't recognize me....
The way of the Hindu and Muslim is the same.
The Satguru (God) has revealed it to me.
Hear what Kabir says?
Rama and Khuda are one and the same. (Bijak, Sabda-10)

c. *One human race*: In accordance with his concept of one human race, Kabir forcefully and with reason argued to denounce the *Hindu* caste system. In his efforts to convince the *Hindus* about the reality of humanity, Kabir traced the beginning of the human race to Adam and says:

Adam who was first did not know
whence Mother Eve came.
Then there was no Turk (Muslim) nor Hindu ...
Then there was no race, no caste,

If thou think the Maker distinguished castes:
Birth is according to these Penalties for deeds.

Born a Sudra, you die a Sudra;
It is only in this world of illusion that you assume the sacred thread.

If you mix the milk of black and yellow cows together,
Will you be able to distinguish their milk. (Bijak, Ramaini-62)

4. **Monotheism**

a. *Emphasis on the unity of God*: According to Kabir, the supreme reality is one, although it has been called by different names, such as *Sahab*, *Allah*, *Khuda*, *Rāma*, *Rahim* or *Brahmā*. Wisdom consists in getting at the basic unity underlying the multiplicity of names. After his spiritual awakening, one of the fundamental ideas which Kabir expressed in clear terms is his concept of God. It is generally held that under the influence of *Sufism*, Kabir denounced idolatry, image worship and polytheism, and adopted the strong monotheism of *Islam*. As a result, he at first taught and emphasized the unity of God. Hence, Kabir says:

He is one: there is no second (BijakSabda - 43)
Rama, Khuda, Sakti, Siva, are one: tell me,
How will you distinguish them? (BijakSabda - 48)
The one Name, like the tree of life, Seventh mankind,
They who are regenerated by God shall never alter,
Saint Kabir, I have recognised God's name.(Adi-Granth, Gauri-37)

Kabir believed in the oneness of God, irrespective of the names by which the human beings addressed Him. Having given a simple description of the oneness of God, Kabir tells us that the different appellations of God are only experiences of one and the same truth. According to him, it matters little by what name we call Him. Thus, he says:

> Brother! From where have the two masters of the universe come? Tell me, who has invented the names of Allah, Rama, Keshab, Hari and Hazrat? All ornaments of gold are made of a unique substance. It is to show the world that two different signs are made, one is called Namaz, while the other is termed Puja. Mahadev and Muhammad are one and the same; Brahma and Adam are one and the same, what is a Hindu? What is a Turk? Both inhabit the same earth. One reads the Veda and the other the Qur'an and Khutbah: One is a Mawlana (Mawlawi/Mullah) and the other a Pandit. Earthen vessels have different names, although they are made from the same earth, Kabir says: both are misled, none has found God. (BijakSabda-30).

In another *Doha* he says:

Hindu says Rama is dear to him
Muslim says Rahim

Both Quarrel, fight and kill each other
Not knowing the root of things.

It means the *Hindu* proclaims that *Rāma* is the God dear to him, while the Turak (*Muslim*) declares Rahim as his God, but not knowing that fundamentally both are one and the same, they quarrel over this, fight each other and court death. God of the universe is only one and the different names given to Him in different faiths cannot create more than one God. Both *Hindus* and Turaks should realize this and refrain from hostilities over inessential matters (Das 1991, 102).

b. *Hindus and Muslims are the children of One God*: The entry of Kabir into the fold of the *Bhakti* movement proved most fruitful in bringing about reconciliation between the *Hindus* and the *Muslims*. Kabir addressed mixed gatherings, consisting of *Hindus* and *Muslims* and made disciples from both. Kabir's idea of one God and one humanity is truly *Islamic*. As a matter of fact, this is the key conception of Kabir according to which he refused to find any distinction between *Hindus* and *Muslims* and on the basis of this unity in principle and substance he tried to find a *modus vivendi* between the two communities. By using terms employed by both systems, Kabir tells us that it is only the difference in names. Finally, in the *Upanishadic* style, Kabir tells us that the *Hindus* and the *Muslims* are only different manifestations of the same substance. Therefore, they are the children of one God.
c. *God is omnipresent*: Sant Kabir elaborates the theme of God's omnipresence and condemns the narrow-mindedness of the two communities, that is, the *Hindus* and the *Muslims*—who try to keep God confined to their respective places, whereas Kabir asserts that God is universal and is present everywhere especially in the human heart. Thus, he says:

If God dwelt only in the Mosque, to whom
belonged the rest of the country?
They who are called Hindus say that God dwelt in an idol: I see not the truth is sect. O' God,
Whether Allah or Rama, I live by Thy name, O' Lord show kindness unto me.
Hari dwelt in the South, Allah has his place in the west.
Search in thy heart, search in thy heart of hearts; there is His place and adobe.

(Adi-Granth, Prabhati-2)

In other words, it means if God is in the mosque only, then to whom does the rest of the country belong? If God be inside the mosque and *Rāma* within the image, then what lies outside? If *Hari* is in the south and *Allah* is in the west and look within your heart for there you will find both *Karim* (the merciful *Allah*) and *Rāma*.

5. **Transcended religious differences:** There is no reason to doubt that he transcended religious differences as he never showed any preference for either of the two religions. But his use of different names for God, mostly *Hindu* names, and his mention of some *Hindu* deities and narrations of stories connected with them simply indicate his acquaintance with both the religions. Having transcended religious differences, and in his intense desire to see all religions united, Kabir did not make any distinction between the two faiths, and thus accepted all *gurus* and *pirs*. For the synthetic nature of his teachings, Kabir has won an undisputed recognition as the best representative of the trend engendered by the interaction of *Hindu–Muslim* ideas. In doing so, he kept himself completely free from sectarian outlook and dogmatic mentality.
6. ***Bhakti* or devotion should be emotional and unalloyed:** According to Kabir, the ultimate reality is formless and yet the master of this universe. His consort *maya* has distracted

everybody. A loving devotion to him will bring deliverance from *maya* by his grace. In view of that, the basis of *bhakti* can be obtained by the fusion of all the men and women of the world who are the living forms with the formless, that is, God. The *Bhakti* or devotion should be emotional and unalloyed. The repetition of his name need not be done with the help of an objective rosary, but it should be an internal and intermittent affair. The search for the divine should be conducted not outside but inside one's own self. Consequently, worshipping a stone idol or shouting in the mosque is meaningless. Ritualism, pilgrimage to holy places and *hajj* are all useless. What is needed is the purity of emotion, fear of the Lord, moral conduct and an attitude of fraternal affection for all and not violence and bloodshed in the name of religion. In the search for the divine within oneself he has recognized the value of exercises prescribed by *hatha yoga*. He rejects the spiritual significance of dance and music as practised by the *Sufis* and recommends instead listening to the *nad* or music within. Nor does he attach any merit to scriptural learning (Pandey 1990, 335).

7. **Asked Hindus to give up centuries-old practising:** Turning to the *Hindus*, Kabir asked them to give up what *Hinduism* had been practising for centuries, such as ceremonies, sacrifice, lust for magical powers, image and temple worship, repetitions of mantras, pilgrimages, fasts, innumerable Gods and Goddesses, bathing in the holy waters, religious monopoly of the *Brāhmaṇs*, prejudices concerning untouchability and food, penances and yoga and sectarianism. He unequivocally condemned the doctrine of incarnation (*Avatarabad*). In Kabir's view it is neither rewarding to offer worship to the stone idols in the temple (instead of the God within) as do the *Hindus* nor to take shelter of God for attaining salvation (as do the *Muslims*). He holds that God who dwells in the heart of every being is the one whose shelter has to be sought by complete self-surrender to him (Das 1991, 107). Although his vocabulary is replete with *Hindu* spiritual concepts, he strongly opposed dogmas prevalent in all religions. In the ripe old age, Kabir decided to go to Maghar and die, just to break the blind belief that when people die in Maghar, they go to hell.
8. **Laid stress on religious toleration:** Kabir was one of the most outstanding *Bhakti* reformers who did his best to bring the *Hindus* and the *Muslims* close to each other in all walks of life. Kabir laid stress on religious toleration and taught a lesson of brotherhood to the *Hindus* and the *Muslims*. He suggested that people should speak in a palatable manner avoiding any kind of friction and disharmony:

   Aisee vani boliye, man kaa apa khoye
   Apna tan sheetal kare, auranko such hoye

   It means speak such words which will keep mind and body composed and give the listener joy.

   Kabir's poetry solely aims at bringing an attitudinal change in the individual and thus reforming the society. In one of his couplets, Kabir says that the individual should not blame others and indulge in mud-slinging act but should clean one's own self. As he said, I went on the search for the bad guy, but guy, I could not find. When I searched my mind, then no one is as bad as me (Krishna 2016, 108–110).
9. **Earning livelihood by the sweat of brow:** Kabir was not in favour of renouncing the world and going to forests or hills in search of true knowledge or salvation; instead he advised his followers to earn their livelihood by the sweat of their brow and perform all the duties as householders while leading an honest, noble and dedicated life. Kabir's idea was to educate the individual and wean

him away from illusion, ego, and thirst for wealth. Kabir also does not believe in earning more money than required. Through his *doha*, he exhorts:

Sai itna dijiye, jamei kutumb samaye
Main bhi bhukha na rahu, sadhu bhukha na jaye

It means God give me this much wealth, just enough to take care of my family, I do not remain hungry and the saints coming to me should not go hungry. Likewise, Kabir advises us not to daydream and chase mirages.

10. **Believed in service to the mankind:** Sant Kabir believed in the purity of the soul and service to the mankind. What use is a date palm which grows tall? It gives no shade and its fruits are quite far off and inaccessible. Kabir asks what good is our so-called eminence, if it is neither compassionate nor helpful to others. He emphasizes that we should shed our greed, selfishness and insecure tendencies and establish ourselves in such a way that we should be willing to give and share. Only then will we be blessed and become a blessing to others. Kabir compares such a vainglorious person with a date palm which though very tall is of no avail to anybody (Shekhar 2016, 113).

    Similarly, with regard to charity he says in *Doha* that:

    Amassed wealth should be taken in hand
    And given away in charity
    There is no market ahead for spending it
    On purpose better than bounty.

    It means amassed wealth is best spent on charity to the poor and needy. There is no use hoarding wealth with the hope of spending it later. After death one will have no chance to lay his hands on it (Das 1991, 95).

11. **Concerning the marriage:** Marriage is a sacred institution. Kabir's outlook towards the social institution such as marriage was the reflection of his medieval patriarchal social behaviour. Kabir has criticized the Muslims for having their marriage relationships within the family and among the near and dear relatives. However, neither has he opposed the child marriage nor has he supported the widow marriage or opposed the custom of polygamy which was prevalent among the people of higher classes in that society.
12. **Opposed to economic inequalities:** The disparity of economic distribution was fully reflecting in the utterings of the Mahatma Kabir. The state's exploitation, the tendency of luxurious life, undue tax, natural calamities, foreign plunderers, distinction of *Varṇadhārma*, lack of equal opportunities, slave system, etc., can be counted as causes of economic disparity. Kabir saw these situations minutely. His aim was to reform the so-called society which was not possible without the prevention of disparity. Kabir himself was poverty stricken who listened to the pains and the sufferings of the dalits and the exploitive peoples and prepared to solve it before the society by his own utterings. Kabir points out that the humble and small man should not be disparaged because of his humble and low position; he should be given due respect and honour as any other man. In his couplets, Kabir cautions not to oppress the weak as his sigh of sorrow is capable of causing ample harm to the oppressor elsewhere.
13. **Property not as an individual's right:** In Mahatma Kabir's perspective it is injustice to link property with individual's rights. He also very categorically said that it is very much stupid and ignorant to keep the feeling of mine and thine with property. It is an evil to feel proud on the basis

of property. It is your due right to possess property as required for your maintenance and safety. From Kabir's point of view, the tendency of gathering more and more property creates obstacle in making an individual honest. According to him, wealth is the main reason for all the evils. Kabir implies that man should not hanker after wealth in excess of the minimum need. He said that one should not feel sad and happy having seen the property. He wanted to give equality and respect to the poor and the rich, respectively. He also wanted to bring an end to egoism which is linked with the possession of property, position and power. According to him, the material wealth and prosperity cannot make a man happy and contended. So, Kabir says in *Doha*:

Save only that wealth
That later may be useful
And if you carry it on head in a bundle
To others will not be visible.

It means spiritual wealth, being invisible to the eye, is not subject to theft or burglary. Kabir indicates that man should collect and save that wealth and not the worldly riches. The former will bring him emancipation, while the latter only worries and miseries (Das 1991, 108).

14. **Kabir's path of resolution:** From Kabir's expression it seems that in order to overcome economic asymmetry, Kabir was giving a message to another noble rich class to become sympathetic to fulfil the needs of poverty and social harmony. Here is a sign of Gandhi's concept of trusteeship. Kabir was conveying the devotion to life, the momentous life and omnipresent creator to conquer the feelings of freedom and devotion to God. In the place of the second and on any economic-social reorganization, to be praying for God to fulfil the basic needs—food, clothing, bed, etc.

Kabir was neither a revolutionary communist like Marx, who wanted to redistribute the means, nor like Gandhi to use his property as a trustee. Simplified life wished only to meet the minimum basic requirements in the tradition of higher thought. The list of the requirements of Kabir included two tablespoons of flour, puffed whole ghee, a little salt, half a sherd dal, and a cot, pillow and blanket. Kabir had the impression that wealth, glory, luxury and power-ego carry man away from God. Therefore, as much as necessary to live a life, one should wish for the same amount of money. Therefore, Kabir's statement is:

O my Master, give me that much
For my family which's enow;
I mayn't have to live in hunger,
Nor should the righteous hungry go. (Karki 2001, 70)

Kabir neither talks of revolution or rebellion nor advises to beg for help to anyone because 'begging is equal to death'. Advocating living the life of diligence and honesty while relying on God, Kabir says that it does not help if you cry for 'hunger'. The Lord, who has placed a body in the form of a pitcher, will also manage food.

Why dost thou shout 'I am hungry?'
And let people listen thee shout,
One who has forged this (body) pot,
The same (God) will feed through the mouth. (Karki 2001, 70)

In the words of Kabir: Asserting the factor of economic inequality and depravity, in the hands of the creator of creation, Kabir was urged that if wealthy or poor is not in his hand, then no one should be proud of getting wealth or authority. Money, position or power is not permanent; it can come at any time. On the other hand, no person in the world can escape death. The king who builds the palace and the Babri goes away leaving everything right here. Therefore, Kabir warns the people of *Sultan*-Rana and Jagadar-Amir, who are involved in pleasure and egoism. So do not take pride and temptation of the officials and monopoly rights and riches. Remember the transience of life, improve your conduct and life and do not do injustice and atrocities against those who are helpless and poor.

Raskin had entrusted the responsibility on the state of the development of the most backward and the downtrodden people of the society in his book 'Unto This Last' (translated by Gandhi as Antyodaya). Kabir also emphasized the importance of the weakest and common man in the society. Kabir implies that the humble and small man should not be disparaged because of his humble and low position, he should be given due respect and honour as any other man (Das 1991, 96). Accepting the fundamental equality of humans, Kabir used to deny the distinction between the king and the people, or the wealthy and poor. His idea was that every person is equal. All are made of God, so all of them have the same value and importance. Kabir was the forerunner of these marginal classes and low castes, who challenged discrimination on the basis of class and caste, and prohibited discrimination between man and man.

Comparison between Kabir Das and Ravidas

Traditions say that both Kabir Das and Ravi Das were born in Banaras in low-caste hierarchy. Kabir's putative birthplace is located at Laharatala, on the western outskirts of the Banaras city and Ravi Das is said to have been born in the largely low-caste village of Mandua Deehin, the west of Banaras. Both were *Vaisnavites* because they were worshipping *Viṣṇu* and his avatars *Rāma* and *Krishna*. Both were the exponents of the *nirguna Bhakti* tradition and pupils of Ramananda. Both also breathed their last in Maghar.

Both have rejected the caste system categorically. Ravidas preached against the caste system and strongly condemned the four *varṇas*. Ravidas categorically rejected traditional *Hinduism*. In India we come across the traditional fourfold division of time into the *Krta*, *Treta*, *Dwapar* and *Kali* Ages. Ravidas did not agree with this scheme of periodization. He pointed out that the confusion was created by the *Vedās* and the *Purāṇas* because these led one to think as to what was to be done and what not.

He says 'I cannot perform thine adoration and worship according to *Hindu* rites'. He strongly condemned idolatry. He did not even approve of *Arati* (waving of lights before the images) because it amounted to idol worship. He felt that uttering his name was the right path and people had forgotten his name. He was particularly harsh on those who took delight in listening to the legends of 18 *Purāṇas*.

Like Kabir, Ravidas repeatedly declared that there was no use of pilgrimage if the heart was not cleansed of pride. The object of pilgrimage was not without but within oneself. One needed only to search it within one's heart and not at *Kailash* or *K'aba*. 'With the idea of the temple being within oneself, comes the repudiation of idol-worship'. According to Ravidas, *brat* (fasts), *tirathishnan* (holy dip) and pilgrimage only wash the dirt of body, not the soul. Inward spirituality could be attained by listening to the inner word.

Thus, he denounced offering rituals of worship, religious ceremonies, pilgrimage, etc. Ravidas preached inward spirituality and believed in one formless God who was omnipresent. Sant Ravidas, again like Kabir, denunciated the *pandit* too. In many of his compositions, he has asked the *pandits* many questions. All references to religious ceremonies, rituals and pilgrimage are invariably a dig at the *pandits*. Not only the *Hindu* priests, but the *Mulla* (*Muslim* priest) also had to suffer his wrath.

Conclusion

The preceding discussion suggests that Kabir is one of the greatest mystic saints of India. He was born in Varanasi (then Banaras) in the year 1389 nearly about 600 years ago. According to a legend, a newborn fair child was noticed floating on a giant lotus leaf in the Lahara Tala Lake on the outskirts of Banaras by a *Muslim* couple, Niru and Nimma by name. They picked the infant up and decided to rear him as their foster child. The story says that after Kabir's death his body was transformed into flowers—ensuring he was neither cremated by *Hindu*s nor buried by *Muslims*, each of whom claimed him as their own.

With filial attachment to both the religious communities, Kabir was free from religious prejudice against either. He rubbed shoulders with *Bhakti* reformers as well as the *Sufi* saints. Although intensely religious in outlook, he was not a slave of either *Hinduism* or *Islam*. He was a man of absolutely independent thoughts and boldly criticized the evils of both the religions. He denounced the *Brāhmaṇs* and the *Mullas* alike to be the sole custodians of their religious orders and took them to task for their orthodox and exploitative attitude. He refused to accept the sanctity of the *Vedās* as well as the *Qur'an* to be 'the revealed scriptures' (Mehta 1990, 193).

Kabir raised his voice against the custom of *sati* and child marriage and these two evils which were purely social in character. Kabir strongly opposed idol worship, caste system and untouchability as practised by the *Hindus* and simultaneously condemned the orthodoxy and the meaningless rituals of the *Muslims*. He exposed the futility of offering five daily prayers in the Mosque without the purity of the heart and sincere dedication to God. Kabir's teachings have more relevance even today in India when dissenting views are often exiled and forced out of the public sphere by state interference and by religious and social groups within the civil society. It is suffice to say that Kabir's teachings were in perfect harmony with the social and religious needs of the times and he identified himself completely with the concept of an integrated Indian society and won the hearts of millions. Thus, Kabir's concept of syncretism has contemporary relevance to the modern society which is torn to pieces in the name of sectarianism, racism, caste system and gender discrimination.

On his death, *Hindu* influences found their way back into Kabir's sect. The use of the rosary was introduced, though he had been against it. He opposed idolatry, yet his image and his book are both worshipped. He rejected the doctrine of divine incarnation, yet he himself is now regarded as an incarnation of the Supreme. The views of Kabir are not very systematic or well-reasoned out for he was no learned philosopher. On the contrary, there are even contradictory statements. But his attacks on social and religious evils are sharp and telling. Although his diction is not urbane or polished, the turns of phrases coined by him are saved from drabness by his high genius. Some of them are indeed marvellous and truly mystical. Some of his statements are couched in paradoxes whose correct meaning is difficult to unravel.

Summary

Son of a *Brāhmaṇa* widow, Kabir was brought up in a *Muslim* weaver's family at Banaras. A legend states that he was actually the illegitimate son of a *Brāhmaṇa* widow who abandoned him, and that he was found by a *Muslim* weaver named Niru who adopted the boy and taught him the weaver's trade.

Kabir spent much of his time in the company of ascetics, saints and *Muslim Sufis*. Feeling a strong urge for the devotional life, Kabir became a disciple of the Ramananda. This he was supposed to have done by recourse to a trick, lying across the path of Ramananda one morning while it was still dark, so that as the latter stumbled over him and he involuntarily uttered the words, *Ram, Ram*, which Kabir claimed constituted an initiation. Ramananda accepted the zealous youth as a disciple.

According to Kabir, God is formless, *nirguna*. It is necessary to have a preceptor to realize Him. He is to be found neither in the temple nor in the mosque, neither in Banaras nor in Mecca, but only in the heart of his devotees. So, in *Doha* he says:

I am neither in temple nor in mosque,
I am neither in Kaaba nor in Kailas;
Neither am I in rites and ceremonies
Nor Yog and renunciation
Lamp burns in every house, O Blind One
And you cannot see them...
Your Lord is near, yet you are climbing the Palm tree to see Him
Yoga and the telling of beads
...these are naught to me (Chopra et al. 1974: 89-90)

Kabir attaches no importance to caste. Kabir emphasized on the unity of God and preached the path of love, devotion and *Bhakti*. He permitted the adoration of *Viṣṇu*, *Rāma*, *Hari* (a form of *Viṣṇu*), *Govinda* (*Krishna*) and *Allah*, which he said were merely names for the One supreme deity. He accepted *karma* and transmigration, but like Ramanuja found a way out of the remorseless bonds of *karma* by preaching that the love of God can bring salvation. He upheld a high moral code, stressing truthfulness, mercy and self-control (Walker 1983, 507). Thus, he has tried to bring out the fundamental unity of *Islam* and *Hinduism*.

Kabir imbibed the tenets of both the religions; *Hinduism* and *Islam*, stood for *Hindu–Muslim* unity and declared that '*Allah* and *Rama*' were the names of the same God. The people of both the religions should not fight and kill each other. Both religions' essence is same. A number of people felt strongly attached towards him and many *Hindus* and *Muslims* became his followers.

Kabir pours ridicule on idolatry, polytheism, priest craft (*Qazis* and *Brāhmaṇs* both deserve hell), world renunciation and religious ceremonial in a number of apothegms called *Sakhi* which are still current and popular in his doctrinal poems known as the *Ramaini*. A collection of these called the *Bijak* (treasure) forms the scriptures of the Kabir *Panth*. He questioned the validity of the *Vedās* and *Purāṇas*, and was critical of parts of the *Quran*. According to him, the *Vedās* are empty words. He dubs the *Brāhmaṇs* and the *Mullahas* as ignorant, credulous, vain and misguided and exhorts them to accept the truth.

Points for Discussion

1. Discuss the notion of syncretism in Kabir's thought.
2. Analyse Kabir's concept of equality with special reference to caste and gender equality.
3. Discuss the relevance of Sant Kabir Das's syncretism in the contemporary times.

4. Examine Kabir's views on prevailing inequalities in his contemporary society.
5. Attempt a comparison between Kabir Das and Ravi Das.

Glossary

***Atma*:** A Sanskrit term for the self or soul, which is imperishable, beyond time and eternal. In the *Ṛigvedā*, the term means breath, or vital essence. It is formless, boundless and changeless. It is synonymous with God. The seat of the soul is between and behind the eyebrows.

***Avatarabad* (Incarnation):** The incarnation of a deity, especially of *Viṣṇu* on earth. It also means descent, advent or manifestation. In *Hinduism*, the God *Viṣṇu* is most commonly associated with *avataras*. *Avataras* of all kinds are said to descend to earth from time to time to guide people on the right path.

***Badshah*:** A *Muslim* designation for an emperor or ruler.

Banaras: A preeminent *Hindu* place of pilgrimage.

Bhajanas: A devotional song in praise of God. It is a term normally used for songs praising *Hindu* deities. *Bhajans* are compositions like songs, and may include several ragas. In other words, it is meditation that leads to inner hearing.

***Bhakti*:** It means devotion, passionate love for God. In other words, it means to keep faith and union with God through love. It implies worship, total surrender and personal love of God in any form. Forgetting everything and everyone else, the devotee yearns for a glimpse of God, and finally for total union.

***Bijak*:** Treasure.

***Brahmā*:** The *Hindu* God in charge of creation. In other words, the first of the Trinity is supposed to be the creator of the universe. His name is derived from the root word '*Brimh*' means 'to expand' implying the vast seed or womb (the *Prakriti*). The *Hindu* divinity most directly associated with process of creation.

***Brāhmaṇ*:** The highest caste in *Hindu* society traditionally composed of specialists in ritual and learning.

***Dohas*:** Couplets.

Fakir: Penniless and wandering merchant.

Gayatri: It is often called the most important *mantra* or sacred verse in the *Ṛigvedā*; *Brāhmaṇs* have a sacred duty to recite it morning and evening. It is addressed to the sun as Savitr, the generator, and so it is called also Savitri. Personified as a Goddess, Savitri is the wife of *Brahmā*, mother of the four *Vedās*, and also of the twice-born or three superior castes.

***Ghat*:** It is a Sanskrit term. *Ghats* are located at sacred sites near rivers and temples, and consist of stairs which lead down to the water. Devotees can use these to enter the water and perform religious rites, or to bathe.

***Ghata*:** Kabir uses for the body.

***Gorakhnath*:** He is master Yogi and wonder-worker famous in northern and western India from medieval times. He founded the NathPanth, a still powerful sect of ascetics who practice *Hatha Yoga* and are known as the *kanphat* ('split ear') Yogis because they pierce their ears and wear large earrings. It was a popular belief that the practice of *Hatha Yoga* could lead to physical immortality.

***Guru*:** Spiritual preceptor of *Hindu* faith. *Guru* is a religious teacher belonging to the *āśhrama* system of education in India. Kabir deifies the guru so a true guru is like a deity or God.

***Hari*:** Other name of *Viṣṇu*, *Krishna*, or *Rama*, frequently interpreted as meaning 'the one who takes away' sin or evil.

***Hatha Yoga*:** A system of *Yoga* or union with the divine described in various texts. It is merely a different approach to *Yoga*, and consists of first purifying the physical and subtle body through *Asanas* or physical postures, and *Pranayama* or breathing techniques, before going on to higher techniques of concentration and meditation.

***Kabba*:** The principal place of *Islamic* pilgrimage in Arabia. Another name for *Mecca*.

Kabir: *Nirguna* poet-saint.

Kabir *Panth*: The 'path of Kabir', the group that identifies itself as adhering to Kabir's teachings.

***Karim*:** The merciful *Allah*.

Magahar: Town near Gorakhpur in Uttar Pradesh where Kabir is said to have spent his last days.

***Maya*:** It is originally a word of Sanskrit language has been adopted by English dictionary. *Oxford Universal Dictionary Illustrated* defines '*Maya*' as 'illusion', 'a prominent word of *Hindu* philosophy. *Maya*, feminine in gender, is an abstraction but is mostly personified. The word thus means: love, affection, familial ties or attachment, mother, father, wife, son, daughter, pride, fame, worldly possessions and so on. In common parlance, the word is used to denote excessive attachment to a person (woman) or property (riches)'.

***Nada*:** A Sanskrit word meaning 'primal sound' or 'tone'. *Nada* can be both external and internal. External or audible sounds, such as music, can lead to God, while internal sounds indicate a contact with the divine.

Namdev: Low-caste poet-saint of west India particularly from the Maratha region.

Nanak: *Nirguna* poet-saint whom *Sikhs* regard as their first and foremost *Guru*.

Niranjan: A name for God or *Brahman* meaning one who has no stain/spot/mark.

***Nirguna*:** A term that means beyond attributes and applies to the formless deity, the absolute. The view that God cannot be positively conceived and should not be worshipped through images or other visual forms. In *Hinduism*, *Brahmā* is said to be *Nirguna*, or that which is without attributes, beyond form and image or specific qualities, can also take on attributes, and become *Saguna*, with qualities. Or a name of the God *Viṣṇu*.

***Nirguna Brahma*:** The attribute less absolute reality.

Pandit/Pundit: A term for a holy or learned man. In the times of Kabir, *Brāhmaṇa Pundits* were reading scriptures and they were instrumental in perpetuating rituals which Kabir satirized.

***Pir*:** A *Sufi* saint; the leader of a *Sufi* order. A spiritual preceptor of *Islamic* faith.

Puja: The act of worship in *Hinduism*, which may take place in a temple or at home. Prayers, along with offerings, such as fruit, flowers or incense, are made to the image of a deity, or to a symbol of the divine. *Puja* may be done according to prescribed rituals, or in a spontaneous way.

***Purāṇas*:** Sanskrit texts sacred to *Hindus*, which include myths, legends, methods of worship, geographical and historical details and a lot more. *Purāṇas* literally means 'old'. The term *Purāṇas* indicating a class of texts written primarily in Sanskrit that recount primordial events such as those having to do with the Gods.

***Qazi*:** *Muslim* judge or magistrate.

***Rahim*:** Name of God of kindness in *Islamic* theology.

***Rāma*:** Name of God incarnated as '*Rāma*' according to *Hindu* mythology. He is the eldest son of Dasaratha, a king of the solar race, reigning at Ayodhya. This *Rāma* is the seventh incarnation of the God *Viṣṇu*, and made his appearance in the world at the end of the *Treta* or second age. Kabir calls his presiding deity or supreme God by that name.

Ramanand: Putative *Guru* of Kabir, Ravidas, and other *Nirguna* saints.

***Ramaini*:** A type of poem. The first part of a *ramaini* consists of several couplets in *doha* style, while the concluding verse is a *chaupai* (quatrain). A *ramaini* usually has an esoteric meaning.

Ravidas: A *Nirguna* poet-saint of the 14th and 15th centuries.

***Sabad*:** Word, especially the Word of God.

***Sakhi*:** It literally means a witness. *Sant* poets like Kabir use this term for their couplets, which are otherwise also known as *dohas*.

***Sakti*:** The wife or the female energy of a deity, but especially of lord *Shiva of Hinduism*. In other words, 'Power': a generic name applied to many Indian goddesses.

***Satguru*:** 'True *Guru*', a familiar *Nirguna* designation for absolute reality (God) especially insofar as it reveals itself within the self. In Kabir it may mean God, one's inner *Guru*, or a human teacher.

***Sati*:** An ancient practice of a *Hindu* widow who is made to sacrifice herself in the funeral pyre of her deceased husband. It was mainly practised by the higher castes, and was supposed to be a voluntary act of devotion to the husband. This ancient system was in vogue in Kabir's days.

Sheikh Taki: He was a famous *Muslim Pir* or saint who was contemporary to Kabir.

***Siddha*:** One who has attained perfection. A *siddha* refers to a person who through various practices has gained powers, and attained mastery over life and death, *siddhas* are thus those who have perfected all the *Siddhis*, or supernatural powers through ascetic and other practices.

***Shiva*:** Synonyms for *Mahesvara*, the god of death and destruction in *Hindu* mythology. He is one of the three major *Hindu* deities after *Brahmā* and *Viṣṇu*. He is the great *Yogi* who practises austerities in the snows of Mount Kailash and is worshipped by members of the *Nath* sect and others who practise *Hatha Yoga*.

***Śūdra*:** Lowest of the four major caste groupings in the *Hindu* social system set out in the Laws of Manu and whose duty is to serve the other three, that is, *Brāhmaṇa*, *Kṣatriya* and *Vaiśya*.

***Vaisnava*:** Worshipper of lord *Vishnu* in *Hinduism*.

***Vedā*:** 'Divine knowledge'. The *Vedās* are the holy books which are the foundation of the *Hindu* religion. They consist of hymns written in an old form of Sanskrit and according to the most generally received opinion they were composed between 1500 and 1000 BC.

References

Behari, B. 1991. *Sufis, Mystics and Yogis of India.* Bombay: Bharatiya Vidya Bhavan.

Chandra, S. 1996. *Medieval India: Historiography, Religion and State in Medieval India.* Delhi: Har-Anand Publications.

Chopra, P. N., B. N. Puri, and M. N. Das. 1974. *A Social, Cultural & Economic History of India*, Vols. II, Medieval India. Delhi: MacMillan India Ltd.

Das, G., ed. 1991. *Couplets from Kabir.* Delhi: Motilal Banarsidass.

Karki, M. S. 2001. *Kabir: Selected Couplets from the Sakhi in Transversion.* Delhi: Motilal Banarsidass.

Krishna, N. A. 2016. 'Interweaving Divinity Through Altruistic Vision: A Study of Kabir's Poetry.' In *Bhakti Movement and Literature: Reforming a Tradition*, edited by M. Rajagopalachary and K. Damodar Rao, 107–110. New Delhi: Rawat Publications.

Mehta, J. 1990. *Advanced Study in the History of Medieval India: Medieval Indian Society and Culture*, 3rd Edition. Delhi: Sterling Publishers.

Omvedt, G. 2012. *From Buddha to Ambedkar and Beyond.* New Delhi: Orient BlackSwan.

Pandey, A. 1990. *Early Medieval India.* Allahabad: Central Book Depot.

Shekhar, G. N. 2016. 'Sant Kabir and Yogi Vemana: A Comparative Study of Their Philosophy.' In *Bhakti Movement and Literature: Reforming a Tradition*, edited by M. Rajagopalachary and K. Damodar Rao, 111–119. New Delhi: Rawat Publications.

Walker, B. 1983. *Hindu World: An Encyclopedic Survey of Hinduism*, 1st Indian Edition, Vols. 1, A–L. New Delhi: Munshiram Manoharlal Publishers.

Further Readings

Bangha, Imre. 2010. 'Kabir Reconstructed.' *Acta Orientalia Academiae Scientiarum Hungaricae* 63(3): 249–258.

Bhargava, Meena, ed. 2010. *Exploring Medieval India: Sixteenth to Eighteenth Centuries, Culture, Gender, Regional Patterns*, Vol. II. New Delhi: Orient BlackSwan.

Johnson, W. J. 2009. *A Dictionary of Hinduism*. New York: Oxford University Press, Inc.

Khilnani, Sunil. 2016. *Incarnation: India in 50 Lives*. London: Penguin Random House.

Kumar, Anil. 2015. *Madhyakaleen Bhakti Aandolan*. Lucknow: Bharat Prakashan.

Kumar, Sehdev. 1983. 'Communicating the Incommunicable.' *India International Centre Quarterly* 10(2): 206–215.

Mehta, J. L. 1990. *Advanced Study in the History of Medieval India: Medieval Indian Society and Culture*, Vol. III. New Delhi: Sterling Publishers.

Pandey, A. B. 1990. *Early Medieval India*. Allahabad: Central Book Depot.

Panjabi, Kavita, ed. 2011. *Poetics and Politics of Sufism and Bhakti in South Asia: Love, Loss and Liberation*. New Delhi: Orient BlackSwan.

Rajagopalachary, M. and K. Damodar Rao, eds. 2016. *Bhakti Movement and Literature: Reforming a Tradition*. New Delhi: Rawat Publications.

Satchidanandan, K. 1999, November–December. 'Kabir Today.' *Indian Literature* 43(6): 13–16.

Singh, Vipul. 2009. *Interpreting Medieval India: Early Medieval, Delhi Sultanate and Regions (circa 750–1550)*, Vol. 1. Delhi: Macmillan Publishers India Ltd.

Sunita. 2014. *Bharatiya Rajnitik Chintan*. New Delhi: Kaberi Books.

Tyagi, Ruchi, ed. 2014. *Prachin avam Madhyakalin Bharat ka Rajnitika Chintan: Pramukha Parampara avam Chintak*. Delhi: Delhi Viswavidyalaya, Hindi Madhyam Karyanvya Nirdeshyalaya.

18
CHAPTER

Women in *Bhakti* Tradition: A Critical Reflection

Krishna Menon

CHAPTER OUTLINE

- Introduction: Do Women Have Ideas?
- *Bhakti* Tradition in South India
- *Bhakti*—An Evaluation from a Gendered Lens
- Women *Bhakti* Poets of South India—Feminist Pioneers?
- The Respected Grandmother—Avvaiyar
- The Ghoul and Her Lord—Karaikal Ammaiyar
- Celebrating Passion—Andal
- To Hell with the Body—Akka Mahadevi
- Conclusion: Beauty, Body and *Bhakti*
- Summary
- Points for Discussion

The path of love and devotion is the easiest way to attain the Divine.

—*Nārada*

Reader's Guide

This chapter would hopefully familiarize the reader with the intellectual, artistic and religious struggles of women in medieval south India and the various challenges that they had to confront in order to express themselves. It would also familiarize the reader with women poets who are not usually mentioned in 'mainstream' canonical accounts of *Bhakti* poetry. It would also enable the reader to understand and appreciate the nascent feminist consciousness that many of these women nursed.

Introduction: Do Women Have Ideas?

Women's concerns, thoughts and words have more often than not been disregarded by history and literature. It was believed that women's lives are inextricably linked with their bodies and hence their minds would have nothing to contribute. The cruel binary between the mind and the body ensured a kind of disdain for the body and bodily activities and women came to be seen as located firmly and solely within their bodies, while men came to be seen as somehow free from their bodies and hence capable of pursuing a life of the mind. Part of the feminist project of recovering women's voices has been to unearth women's thinking and writing. Disregarded as flippant and not very serious, women's writing has only recently been seen worthy of serious engagement (Tharu and Lalita 1991).

Canonical literature and intellectual traditions have had strong gatekeepers who successfully excluded women. The fact is that women have over the centuries been keen thinkers and writers, only to be kept out of established literary and intellectual traditions through a network of social and ideological arrangements. Did women think, did they have the ability to express their emotions and their beliefs? There is enough evidence now to establish that women resisted their intellectual obliteration through heroic acts of writing or singing, more often than not surreptitiously.

Bhakti Tradition in South India

Religious devotion and faith was often an arena where women did find a voice, especially in the context of the *Bhakti* movement in India. The early *Alvars* in south India, of the 6th century—as the *Vaishnavite* men of the religion were called—were open to Buddhist and Jaina influences that had acquired deep roots in that region. From the 7th century onwards, both the *Saiva Nayanmars* and the *Vaishnava alvars* adopted an attitude of stern hostility towards Jainism and Buddhism. It was spearheaded by devotional mystics (later revered as *Hindu* saints) who extolled devotion and love to God as the chief means of spiritual perfection. The *Bhakti* movement in south India was spearheaded by the 63 *Nayanars* (*Shaivite* devotees) and the 12 *Alvars* (*Vaishnavaite* devotees), who disregarded the austerities preached by *Jainism* and *Buddhism* but instead preached personal devotion to God as a means of salvation. These saints, some of whom were also women, spoke and wrote in local languages like Tamil and Telugu and travelled widely to spread their message of love and devotion to everyone, irrespective of caste, colour and creed.

Bhakti—An Evaluation from a Gendered Lens

The philosophy and spirit of *Bhakti* challenge the rigid forms of devotion and religiosity. It has within it tremendous scope for questioning fixed notions of religion, worship and faith and ritualistic practices. This fluidity and flexibility, and indeed open endedness, made it possible even to question socially assigned roles to individuals. This is a result of *Bhakti* philosophy's attempts to question and transcend the rigid categories of caste/gender. This non-fixed nature of the *Bhakti* philosophy resulted in poetry and writing that has been characterized amongst many other things by a dialogic nature of writing and thinking, being and doing. This allowed a more colloquial and less formal employment of language that was easier for those groups that did not have access to formidable literary knowledge traditions. This made the genre of writing and music attractive to those who were otherwise on the margins of society. Thus, women and lower caste members of society were not surprisingly drawn towards the poetry and music of *Bhakti*. In fact, within the *Bhakti* tradition, the devotee has a charged and passionate relationship with the object of devotion. The devotee is understood to be ignorant and incapable of making sense of the ways of the world. Unlike the highly codified and intellectual religious and philosophical traditions so typical of *Brāhminical Hinduism*, *Bhakti* broke free and soared high.

In this tradition, therefore, it is not very surprising to see women, otherwise conspicuous by their absence in high *Hinduism*. Often this relationship is constructed along conventional heterosexual terms, where the devotee, irrespective of whether man or woman is servile and a supplicant, is dependent on the Lord's benign nature. *Bhakti* as an approach to devotion seems to have space for uncertainties and indeterminateness. Feminist epistemological studies have repeatedly argued that the arrogance of 'mainstream epistemology' emanates from its claims of finiteness and certitude and additionally discredits all other forms of knowing as irrelevant and even misplaced and misguided (Hesse-Biber 2012).

High religion and religiosity are steeped in *Gyanaas* erudition/scholarship and reason, whereas *Bhakti* comes from the word *Bhaj* which means 'to be attached or devoted to'. *Bhakti*, therefore, provides space for the 'irrational' and passionate. Women have often as per the binaries that operate in most patriarchal societies been associated with intuition and spontaneity, while men have been linked with reason. Perhaps, this is why it provided room to women and others who were out of the circle of reason and intellect. *Bhakti* as a form of devotion allows for a critique of existing power hierarchies and provides room for speech and self-articulation by non-elites and other oppressed groups—such as women and Dalit. *Bhakti* is interpreted as pure unselfish love mixed with reverence, self-denial and self-deprecations. *Bhakti* or devotion in the form of *anurag* or attachment to the Lord leads to the highest good or the attainment of God-realization.

Women *Bhakti* Poets of South India—Feminist Pioneers?

From a feminist psychoanalytical perspective, *Bhakti* poetry provided the scope for splitting of the self (Sangari 1990): The well-socialized self who is constrained by societal norms of hierarchy and order, and the other more disobedient, recalcitrant and 'straying' self that goes against the established norms. Hence, the disobedient woman who went against society's diktats is a familiar presence in the *Bhakti* tradition, immortalized by the poetry that they wrote.

Here, the focus would be on some such pioneering women from the south of Vindhyas. These women were free-spirited and creative and perhaps they found in religion and religiosity a legitimate and credible avenue for the expression of their free spiritedness. This is not to deny that the question of the relationship of women believers to God has been a vexed one and is of course a gendered one (Chakravarty 1989). Women have more often than not been excluded from rituals and worship—being allowed only the role of a bystander. In this context, *Bhakti* philosophy is a radical rupture and allowed for new voices from below a space within the fortress of religion.

The *Bhakti* saints in south India, some of whom were also women, spoke and wrote in local languages like Tamil and Telugu and travelled widely to spread their message of love and devotion to everyone, irrespective of caste, colour and creed. All these were remarkable breaks from the existing conventions about what women could or could not do. These women minstrels travelled on their own, wrote poetry—thus admitting to being thinking beings who shared their thoughts with others. This was unthinkable for women in medieval south India. Perhaps, the context of religion made it acceptable and softened the radical edges of the challenge that these women *Bhakti* poets were mounting.

The Respected Grandmother—Avvaiyar

Of the women who wrote poetry in South India—Avvaiyar from the Sangam period is very significant. Writing around the 9th century CE, she is known not only for her extraordinary poetry but also as a noble and revered saint.

The term 'Avvaiyar' means 'respected old woman' or 'Grandmother'. Avvai was an outcaste woman born of a *Brāhmaṇa* father and an outcaste mother—and by all accounts there were many Avvais—wise old women. Abandoned at birth, she was brought up by a low-caste family of traditional wandering musicians (Chakravarty 1989).

She grew up to be talented, attractive and wise. She, however, was intent on a life that did not have space within it for marriage and domesticity. There were then, as even now, few options available for such women. Religion however offered a refuge to women who did not wish to be entangled in the web of marriage, motherhood and domesticity—of being tied to one man and his command.

One of the options for her was to become a woman of religion and she channelized her musical and literary creativity into devotion to the Lord. Her body and sexuality were however encumbrances as it is for most women who seemed to be judged by their appearance and their sexuality rather than their intellect, skills and talents. Avvaiyar therefore prayed to be transformed into an old woman—wandering from land to land, sharing her wisdom. She perhaps realized that desexualizing herself would afford her legitimacy to wander and wonder, write and think and live her life on her own terms.

While her observations on marriage and the role of a wife, etc., were rather conformist, her own life was far from conformist. There is no denying that it was the adoption of *Bhakti* and of course an 'escape' into old age that helped her achieve this. Thus, she conquered new frontiers, but remained bounded on many other fronts.

The Ghoul and Her Lord—Karaikal Ammaiyar

Around 600 CE Karaikal Ammaiyar, who was born as the beautiful Punitavati, prayed to *Shiva* to transform her into a ghoulish *bhoota* who could always stand by him and worship him. She wrote poems of her longing for *Shiva*; however, her unattractive, gnarled and twisted old body repelled people. Her poetry often drew attention to her protruding teeth, sagging breasts. Her life reinforces once again that women have repeatedly had to deny or transcend their bodies in order to be taken seriously. Karaikal Ammaiyar was no exception. Like many women before and after, she had talents and urges that could not be contained within matrimony and domesticity. Not finding any legitimate outlet for these interests, she did what other women have often done, deny her womanhood and transcend her body.

Celebrating Passion—Andal

Unlike Avvaiyar who renounced her youth to avoid marriage, and Karaikal Ammaiyar who renounced her wifehood and beauty, Andal (8th CE) in her poetry talks unabashedly about her passion directed at *Viṣṇu*.

Her unabashed sexuality however was acceptable because it was directed at the Lord. Thus, Andal crossed the invisible line of sexual decorum prescribed for women by invoking passion openly; however, she was accommodated by the requirements of patriarchy and religion. One of the many legends that grew around her suggested for instance that she mysteriously disappeared into the sanctum sanctorum after a 'marriage ceremony' with her Lord *Viṣṇu* at the Srirangam Kshetra.

To Hell with the Body—Akka Mahadevi

Akka Mahadevi lived and wrote and wandered in search of *Shiva* in 12th century CE. She was a *Shiva* devotee and wrote in Kannada. Her husband tried to force himself on her. She resisted his advances and thus taught women that they need not submit without consent even to their husbands. This in itself is a powerful and radical message; Akka Mahadevi extended this logically to discuss rather unabashedly her passion and love for another man—in this case *Shiva*. She confesses to being an adulterous woman;

> Husband inside
> Lover outside
> I cannot manage them both
> This world and that other, cannot manage them both. (Jain 2011)

She is known to have roamed about without clothes in a state of poetic and devotional frenzy, paying little or no heed to the decorum and shame that a woman's body needs to be routinely subjected to. Perhaps the shield of *Bhakti* helped her do this.

> People,
> male and female,
> blush when a cloth covering their shame
> comes loose
> When the lord of lives
> lives drowned without a face
> in the world, how can you be modest?
> When all the world is the eye of the lord,
> looking everywhere, what can you
> cover and conceal?[1]

Conclusion: Beauty, Body and *Bhakti*

The four women *Bhakti* poets from south India had many things in common—desire to travel freely—both literally and metaphorically. In addition, they seemed disenchanted by the supposed charm of marital bliss and domesticity. Each of them turned this disenchantment towards a pursuit of religion and devotion to God. This allowed them a certain degree of emancipation, however, not before they resolved the vexed issue of their embodiment and sexuality.

Avvaiyar's legend is that she was a wizened old woman and thus outside the pale of sexuality and fertility. Thus, her body was of no consequence. She is immortalized in popular Tamil culture as a venerable grandmother, whose poetry is taught in schools and whose statutes dot the countryside. She did challenge the patriarchal times that she lived in, but she treaded gently not breaching too many barriers. This made her acceptance easier than some of the other women in this pantheon.

Karaikal Ammaiyar on the other hand was a beauteous woman who was compelled to deny her body in order to pursue the life that she sought. Her ghoulish appearance allowed her to write poetry, but did not win her a place within the popular Tamil imagination. She remains the scary outsider. She escaped her marriage and wandered about. Her bizarre appearance and her deliberate courting of ugliness filled people with dread. However, she is held in awe—for how could a woman willingly sacrifice her youth and beauty? But this sacrifice was of paramount importance for her to be able to live the life that she desired. Significantly, Karaikal Ammaiyar's poems unlike Avvaiyar's are neither a part of pedagogy, nor worship nor the stage.

Andal's poetry on the other hand is studied, sung at devotional gatherings and performed on the stage routinely. She is the least threatening of the four women examined here. Andal's Thiruppavai is part of *Vaishnavite* temple rituals in some parts of south India. However, very pertinently, her more erotic Nachiyar Thirumozhi is virtually forgotten for women are not considered to possess sexual agency of any kind (Chakravarty 1989).

The content of Andal's poetry is not very radical; in fact, it is often very conformist. Perhaps, this explains why her poetry finds space in school textbooks across contemporary Tamil Nadu. However, her life was incredible—mobility, poetry and wisdom gave her proximity to the powerful.

Akka Mahadevi's poetry has interestingly become an inevitable part of all feminist discussions and gender studies classrooms across India, but has not gained popular acceptance comparable to Andal's poetry. Akka Mahadevi did not project herself as a wise old grandmother, or a ghoulish woman on the margins of society or a passionate but decorous 'spouse' of the Lord, instead she was radical in her solution. She disregarded her body and thus freed herself from the social expectations associated with it. *Bhakti* traditions have over time, however, rather ironically succeeded in taming her and deifying her.

The relationship between the body and the mind, between organized religion and women and between devotion and poetry—these are some of the questions raised by the lives of these fascinating women *Bhakti* poets. Contemporary feminist writers have in some way or the other acknowledged knowingly or unknowingly the debt they owe from these foremothers.

Summary

The central theme of this chapter is an examination and appraisal of the women who wrote poetry in south India at a time when women were not expected to be engaged in literary pursuits. These were women who wrote devotional poetry and were steeped in the pursuit of religious gratification. They were also united by a restless spirit that could not be contained within the confines of everyday domesticity and traditional roles of mother and wife. They sought intellectual, literary and artistic creativity and expression and found it in the realm of religion. The journey, however, was not easy and they had to resolve the difficult questions of sexuality and their specific embodiments in a female body.

Points for Discussion

1. Discuss through the women's writing in south India a challenge to patriarchy.
2. Were female Bhakti poets feminists in their consciousness?
3. What are the elements within *Bhakti* tradition that made it possible for women and other marginalized groups to find a place?
4. Write a note on Akka Mahadevi as the forerunner of feminist movement in South India.

Endnote

1. http://www.boloji.com/index.cfm?md=Content&sd=Articles&ArticleID=10406

Glossary

***Alvars*:** The *alvars*, also spelt as *alwars* or *azhwars*, are 'those immersed in God'. They were Tamil poet-saints of south India who espoused bhakti (devotion) to the *Hindu* God *Viṣṇu* or his avatar *Krishna* in their songs of longing, ecstasy and service.

***Anurag*:** *Anurag means* love or a kind of attraction.

***Bhakti*:** Devotional worship directed to one supreme deity, usually *Viṣṇu* (especially in his incarnations as *Rāma* and Krishna) or Shiva, by whose grace salvation may be attained by all regardless of sex, caste or class. It is followed by the majority of Hindus today.

***Buddhism*:** A widespread Asian religion or philosophy, founded by Siddhartha Gautama in north-eastern India in the 5th century BC.

Canonical literature: Authoritative or standard, conforming to an accepted rule or procedure. Conforming to well-established patterns or rules.

Gender: Either of the two sexes (male and female), especially when considered with reference to social and cultural differences rather than biological ones. The term is also used more broadly to denote a range of identities that do not correspond to established ideas of male and female.

***Jainism*:** A non-theistic religion founded in India in the 6th century BC by the *Jina Vardhamana Mahavira* as a reaction against the teachings of orthodox *Brahmanism*, and still practised there. The Jain religion teaches salvation by perfection through successive lives, non-injury to living creatures and is noted for its ascetics.

***Nayanmars*:** The *Nayanmars* were a group of 63 saints (also saint poets) in the 6th–8th centuries, who were devoted to the Hindu god Shiva in Tamil Nadu.

Sangam period: Sangam period is the period of history of ancient Tamil Nadu and Kerala (known as Tamilakam) spanning from 5th century BCE to 3rd century CE. It is named after the famous Sangam academies of poets and scholars centred in the city of Madurai.

***Shiva*:** *Shiva* also known as *Mahadeva* (lit. the great God) is one of the principal deities of *Hinduism*.

Surreptitiously: In a way that attempts to avoid notice or attention; secretively.

***Vaishnavite*:** One who worships lord *Viṣṇu*. From Sanskrit *vaiṣṇava*—relating to lord *Viṣṇu*.

***Viṣṇu*:** *Viṣṇu* is one of the principal deities of *Hinduism*, and the Supreme Being or absolute truth in its *Vaishnavism* tradition. *Viṣṇu* is the 'preserver' in the *Hindu* triad (*Trimurti*) that includes *Brahmā* and *Shiva*.

References

Chakravarty, Uma. 1989. *The World of the Bhaktin in South Indian Traditions: The Body and Beyond*, pp. 18–29. New Delhi: Manushi.

Jain, Jasbir. 2011. *Indigenous Roots of Feminism: Culture, Subjectivity and Agency*. New Delhi: SAGE Publications.

Sangari, K. 1990. 'Mirabai and the Spiritual Economy of Bhakti.' *Economic and Political Weekly* 25(27): 1464–75.

Hesse-Biber, Sharlene Nagy. 2012. *Handbook of Feminist Research Theory and Praxis*. New Delhi: SAGE Publications.

Tharu, Susie, and K. Lalita, ed. 1991. *Women Writing in India: 600 BC to the Early 20th Century*. New Delhi: OUP.

19

CHAPTER

Syncretic Tradition: A Tradition of Assimilation

Rajendra Kumar Pandey

CHAPTER OUTLINE

- **Introduction**
- **Origin and Evolution of Syncretic Tradition**
- **Syncretism in *Hinduism* and *Islam***
- **Syncretism in Other Religions**
- ***Bhakti* and *Sufi* Traditions**
- ***Sufism* as a Tradition of Syncretism**
- **Conclusion**
- **Summary**
- **Points for Discussion**

Hindu–Muslim syncretism in India has deep cultural roots which has survived political and social upheavals.

—J. J. Roy Burma (1996)

Reader's Guide

The purpose of this chapter is to make the reader aware about the circumstances and trajectory of origin and evolution of syncretic tradition in India. An attempt has also been made to explain the ethos of syncretism in *Hinduism* and *Islam* and to comprehend the *Bhakti* and *Sufi* traditions of syncretism. Moreover, the chapter aims to present *Sufism* as an illustrative study of syncretism in India.

Introduction

As a tradition of assimilation, syncretism characterizes the underlying unison among the plurality of religious and cultural life of people in India. It has acted as the common philosophical thread that runs across all the faiths, convictions and beliefs in the country. Amidst the apparent diversity in intrinsic value premises and their overt functional articulation, syncretism seeks to provide such common grounds upon which the people could forge some kind of working relations, if not deep love, among themselves and live a peaceful and mutually supportive life. In a way, syncretism reorients the course of life of people in the direction of seeking ultimate truth of life in God and other godly values and activities in place of the mundane affairs of life dictated by the restrictive and, at times, parochial interpretations of religious and cultural traditions. Thus, syncretism seems to undermine the particularistic, constrictive, antagonistic and divisive portents emphasized by self-proclaimed and unscrupulous custodians of religions and cultures. In the place of those negativities, it indicates the existence of a wider and conducive milieu with loftier value systems at the higher levels of human contemplation which can accommodate all without discrimination to ensure a peaceful and fulfilling life, not only in this earthly incarnation but also in the company of God in after life.

Clearly, thus, at the heart of syncretism in India lies the cherished tradition of mysticism. Generally, mysticism is considered to be the belief that there is hidden meaning in life and that each human being can unite with God. It is a religious and cultural practice based on the conviction that knowledge of spiritual truth can be gained by praying or thinking deeply. In India, the pall bearers of mystic traditions are known as *Sufis* and *Bhaktas*. The movement heralded by these mystics brought about a new phase of renaissance in the life and thought of the Indian masses. This movement began in India at such a juncture when some people of both the prominent religions, that is, *Hinduism* and *Islam* sought to bring about an exclusivist perspective in their interpretation and following. Thus, in a way, both the *Sufi* and *Bhakti* movements were initiated as a reaction to very strong and rigid ideologies, and expressed reactions of the common people against such rigidities. Interestingly, these were not elitist reactions confined to the realm of scholars, princes or other apparent custodians of socio-religious life of people in society. They were indeed the flexible methodologies for the masses to express their innermost sentiments and to participate actively in the process of 'loving the Divine'. That way, they could not only help obliterate the hardest of inflexibilities ranging, at times, to the extent of antagonistic perspective towards the followers of other religious and cultural traditions but also widened the spectrum of tolerance and accommodation where more and more people could come and join in their pursuit of reaching nearer to God. In this chapter, an attempt has been made to critically analyse syncretism as a religious–cultural tradition of assimilation in India.

Origin and Evolution of Syncretic Tradition

Roots of syncretic tradition in India may be located in the accommodative ethos of Indian culture which provides space for all the people who come to inhabit here in the course of time. This culture which later came to be known in the name of *Hinduism* contains the element of 'anthropomorphism' which constitutes the base of eternal syncretism of *Hindu* religion and eventually of Indian society (Ahmad 1994, 36). Conceptually, anthropomorphism 'means a tendency to ascribe human qualities, attributes and any forms of exclusively human-related elements to something which is not human' (Ingvarsson 2009, 8). Anthropomorphism provides two critical inputs in the evolution of syncretic tradition in the country. First, by ascribing human qualities in everything which is not human, *Hinduism* extended the reach of loftier human virtues to almost everything existing on earth in different forms and spaces. In other words, *Hinduism* seeks to orient the human outlook towards everything in this world in a pious and generous fashion so that there does not exist any discordant or antagonistic attitude towards that. That way, *Hindus* become ardent worshippers of nature including the flora and fauna existing on the earth. It further understood everything on this earth as existing for a particular cause and therefore existence of all such things has to be taken in a positive and supplementary tone.

Deriving from the first characteristics emerges the second one which shapes the orientation of *Hinduism* towards the other people in the world. Taking the entire world as one extended family in the classical universalistic *Vedic* dictum—*vasudhaiva kutumbakam*—*Hinduism* believes in the general well-being and happiness of all and underlines that such an orientation needs to be the foundation of peace in this world. To put it differently, given *Hinduism's* penchant for seeking well-being and happiness of all, an incontrovertible argument for inculcation of syncretic tradition in India seems to get sound footing. As the *Upaniṣhadic* Rhyme exhorts:

Om, Sarvey Bhavantu Sukhinah
Sarvey Santu Niramayah
Sarvey Bhadrani Pasyantu
Ma Kashchitdukha Bhavbhavet
Om Shantih, Shantih, Shantih (*Bṛhadāraṇkya Upaniṣhad*: 1:4:14)

(May all be prosperous and happy,
May all be free from illness
May all see what is spiritually uplifting,
May no one suffer
Om Peace, Peace, Peace)

Thus, the intellectual roots of syncretic traditions in India are ancient and enmeshed in the broader worldview of *Hinduism*. Since such a worldview encompasses both living and non-living aspects of nature, and seeks to ingrain a positive and supplementary orientation towards every human being, there does not appear to be place for exclusivity, chauvinism, superiority complex and expansive tendencies in *Hinduism*. This presumably provided the perfect landscape in which the people of all faith and beliefs could seek a broader understanding on the aspects and values of life despite following different paths in their journey towards having unison with God.

Syncretism in *Hinduism* and *Islam*

Historically, India has long and cherished traditions of syncretism right from the ancient times even when religions like *Islam* and *Christianity* had not arrived in the country. The diversified and locally divergent nature of *Hinduism* had ordained such a mosaic of deities and gods within its fold that without the tradition of syncretism, many of the followers of different sects within *Hinduism* would have turned hostile to each other. Moreover, in the course of time, the advent of other indigenous religions, such as

Buddhism and *Jainism*, further complicated the socio-religious complexion of India, the best way to deal with which was none other than the tradition of syncretism. Above all, the faith system of Indian masses in different parts of the country had been so variegated that a single faith system could never be their *fait accomli*. For instance, while worship of nature and natural objects, such as rivers, mountains, trees, animals, seasons and likewise are omnipresent, there existed a lot of differences on issues like animal sacrifices, prevalence of *Tantric* or *Shaivaite* traditions and acceptance of a reigning deity for the village, area or the region. This amazing heterogeneity perplexed the minds of the seers and pioneers who sought to unify the religious affinities of the masses through means of certain common markers of reverence and identity. In this direction, the efforts of *Adi Shankaracharya* appear to be momentous given his move to establish the spiritual and cultural unity between different sections of Indian society by founding four unique seats of worship in four corners of the country. This unparalleled and colossal contribution of *Adi Shankaracharya* undoubtedly helped in bringing about some degree of syncretism in *Hinduism*.

However, due to such amorphous and accommodative nature of *Hinduism*, some people question it to be a religion in the sense *Islam* and *Christianity* are. For example, Rasheeduddin Khan avers that instead of being a closed and rigid order, *Hinduism* is a kind of umbrella system which allows the followers of all faiths and beliefs to exist and prosper in its name. Such a liberal and open-ended nature of *Hinduism* gives it the required

> flexibility and resilience and a tradition base wide enough to cover the syndrome of Indian culture. That is why sometimes the revival of *Hinduism* takes the form of revivalism of Indian culture, symbols, values, idioms and traditional pattern of living. It does not take the particular form of revival of a faith because there is no such ordained, integral and defined faith to be revived. (Khan 1987, 42)

However, instead of taking this nature of *Hinduism* as an affront to its existence as a religion, what appears more important is to cherish and nourish the values and principles enshrined in the way of life ordained by *Hinduism* and consolidate them with the similar propositions of other religions to solidify the tradition of syncretism in the country.

But the real syncretic tradition in *Hinduism* was introduced by the proponents of *Bhakti* tradition. Consolidating the tradition of 'Sants',[1] the *Bhakti* movement sought to promote eclectic faiths and loosen religious orthodoxy amongst the followers of *Hinduism*. Significantly,

> the Saints stressed the fulfilment of essential social obligations such as the need to support one's family through personal effort…Although socially involved, the Saints advocated an inner detachment from worldly ties. Seeking a true guru, keeping the company of likeminded seekers, and dedicating themselves to the incessant remembrance of God, they abandoned traditional rituals and rejected caste and religious barriers. Their creed of love embraced humanity as well as the abstract being. (Madan 1989, 134–135)

Later on, the syncretism of *Bhakti* movement proved to be the most formidable bridge between *Hinduism* and Islam by harmonizing the orthogenetic and heterogenetic elements of the distinct faith systems of the two religions. Their espousal of an uncharacteristic philosophy of life rooted in social ethics and worldly worries of the masses helped them become so attractive to the plebeians that they tended to break loosen their traditional religious bonds and embrace a faith that would address to their daily chores of life. The Sants like Kabir tried to ridicule the orthodoxies of both *Hinduism* and *Islam* in most crisp and intelligible manner. They articulated the complexities of mundane life in such a simple and touching vein that the masses flocked to their faith system effortlessly breaking loose of their rigid religious customs and traditions. Although many of such people retained their broad religious affiliation, they, nevertheless, became staunch followers of these Saints cutting across their religions. In the long run, the coming together of people of heterogeneous religious background to the fold of the Saints created a syncretic space where the exclusivity of a particular religion had become, more or less, irrelevant.

Writing about genesis of *Islamic* mysticism in India, Riaz Hassan observes,

> *Muslim* mysticism reached India almost simultaneously with the foundation of the Delhi Sultanate through the mystic orders of Chistiyya and Suhrawardiyya. In the 14th century these orders were all established in their respective zones with extensive network of *khanqahs*... there were around 2,000 *khanqahs* in Delhi and its surrounding areas. The *khanqahs*, numerous and extensive as they were, soon wove themselves into the complex cultural pattern of India and helped to remove that spirit of mistrust and isolation which honeycombed relations among the various cultural groups there. (Hassan 1987, 554)

Interestingly, the descent of *Islamic* mysticism in the form of *Sufism* tended to offer an alternative perspective of life and its relationship to God in contrast to the perspectives of more orthodox elements in *Islam* represented by the *Ulema*. Bringing out the subtle differences between the two, Madan points out that the *Ulema* stressed the realization of the true spirit of Islam through submission to 'the way' (*sharia*) God had ordained for his true followers and faith in the example and sayings of Muhammad. On the contrary, the *Sufis* evolved their own way (*tariqa*) of realizing God—through love and intermediary role of saints. Thus, while the original tradition emphasized living in faith through the material world, the *Sufi* quest was essentially spiritual. 'If knowledge strikes the heart', the *Sufis* taught, 'it is welcome: if it strikes the body it is a burden' (Madan 1989, 131). Thereby, the *Sufis* appeared to be echoing the same philosophical moorings for Islam that pervaded *Hinduism* for ages through *Upaniṣhads*. As Madan continued, the *Sufis*' quest was very similar to that of the *Upaniṣhadic* seers: the latter's *soham* ('I am He') was echoed by the former's *anal-haqq* ('I am Truth') (Ibid.).

Syncretism in Other Religions

Apart from *Hinduism* and *Islam*, the mystic and syncretic traditions are also prevalent in the other prominent religions of India like *Buddhism*, *Sikhism* and *Jainism*. Insofar as *Buddhism* is concerned, it emerged as a distinct religion in clear departure from the rituals and orthodoxy of *Hinduism*. Gradually, its spread in other parts of the world brought it in close proximity with the established norms, practices, values and customs of people of particular places. This induced the element of syncretism in it in order to make it acceptable to the masses and deep-root its preaching and teaching in the psyche of the people. Similarly, *Buddhism* has its own glorious mystic traditions both in India and abroad.[2] In India, though *Buddhism* fell out of favour of the masses by the 8th century, many of its ideas and ideals appeared to be incorporated in the broader fold of *Hinduism* so that a person remained a *Hindu* despite following the basic belief system of Buddhism.

Of all religions, *Sikhism* may arguably be reckoned as the most syncretic religion in India. Highlighting the context of such a high degree of syncretism in it, Madan writes succinctly about *Sikhism* and its founder Guru Nanak,

> Born a clean-caste Hindu, deeply influenced by the Sant tradition as well as by *Upaniṣhadic* metaphysics, and clearly aware of the teachings of *Islam* and the practice of the Nath Yogis (members

> of a Hindu sect who focus on self-perception and inner awareness), Nanak revolted against ritualism and caste rigidities, particularly the former. He also sought to combine element from the various religious traditions of India and transcend them. Worship of and submission to the will of God, honest labour, and collective sharing of the fruits of labour are believed to be the principles of his teaching. (Ibid., 135)

In fact, the holy book of Sikhs—*the Guru Granth Sahib*—consists of the couplets and creations of the people belonging to different religions. Even in their behaviour, the Sikhs share a large of number of styles, symbols, customs and ideals found in various faiths, confirming the syncretic nature of their religion.[3]

As regards *Jainism*, despite its foundation as a distinct religious order different from *Hinduism*, it remained deeply embedded in the long-held ideals and virtues of *Hinduism*. The philosophical stipulations of *Jainism* appear to be nothing more than a revisit of the loftier ideals enshrined in the *Hindu* scriptures. Hence, when it comes to the practical aspects of Jainism, there seems to be very little divergence between *Hinduism* and *Jainism*. Thus, on the whole, the traditions of mysticism and syncretism have become inalienable ingredients of socio-religious life of people in India. Given the predominance of *Hinduism* and *Islam* in the life of the masses, what has turned out to be the defining syncretic tradition is in the form of *Bhaktas* and *Sufis* who have found a number of parallels between them to secure a life of unity and peaceful coexistence for the people.

Bhakti and *Sufi* Traditions

The concrete articulation of the syncretic traditions in both *Hinduism* and Islam has been experienced through what is known as *Bhakti* and *Sufi* traditions, respectively. These traditions sought to provide a practical shape to the intellectual discourses on the syncretism and unity of man with God. Although in the course of time, the traditions of *Bhakti* and *Sufis* did not remain monotheistic and a number of varying orders emerged within them, they nevertheless represented an unconventional stream in the socio-religious life of the common people by attuning them to be receptive and accommodative to diversity and variations in society. Eventually, these two traditions came to represent Indian ethos of composite culture and shared life for followers of different religions and faith systems.

Bhakti Traditions

We have also great traditions of *Bhaktas* singing in devotion to *Krishna* or *Shiva*. The Durveshas's dance also is akin to our devotional dance. In this, everything revolves around 'Love for the Divine'. The Shaikh sits in the middle and young devotees sit around him. Then they get up and start dancing whirling and whirling about; they go round and round and it really moves the heart and spirit. It is really astounding and it is still in practice. Raslila may also be considered almost similar to this. Thus, whether it is 'Chaitanya *Bhaktas*', who do their ecstatic kirtans or the whirling Durveshes, all of them are symbolic of the essential golden thread that links together all the great religions of the world. The Christian mystics also practise identical things. This is what is said to be 'many splendoured light of the *Ātman*', what the Bible calls a 'light that lighteth every man that cometh into the world', what the *Sufis* call the *Noor-e-Ilāhī*, what the Sikhs call the *Ek Onkar*, and what the seers of the *Upaniṣhads* say: I have seen that light shining like 1,000 Suns beyond the darkness. It is that Inner Light which represents the core of the human personality and it is that Inner Light which expresses itself through both the *Sufis* and *Bhaktas*. In Kashmir, there was until recently a tradition of everybody going to the shrines for worshipping. In fact, there is a temple in Srinagar where on its upper portion there is a mosque and a *dargah* and in the lower portion, there is a temple of Kali. There is a Shah Hamadan mosque in the same building where 700 people came from Iran and practised *Sufism*. In nutshell, our mystic traditions need to be kept intact and promoted. Our intellectuals need to shoulder the responsibility in projecting our rich traditions of composite culture in the right earnest. The land of India has been the land of great saints encompassing all the three religions—*Hinduism*, *Islam* and *Sikhism*. The sayings of Baba Farid, Nizamuddin Auliya and Amir Khusro are part of our tradition. Thus,

> the *Sufi* and *Bhakti* movements blurred the differences between the two religions so much that it was very common till very recently to have a *sadguru* or a *pir* having a common following of *Hindus* and *Muslims*. And no *pir* or *sadguru* ever forced a Hindu or Muslim to give up his religion for any other. The medieval age was the period when *Sufi* and *Bhakti* thought and practice blended and coalesced at many points. (Lokhandwalla 1987, 9)

Sufism

Sufism has always been the hallmark of unity and peaceful coexistence of people in India.[4] Even in times, when the material aspirations of the people were not as astounding as they are today, spirituality and *Sufi* thought were considered by many as the only way of attaining unity and peaceful coexistence amongst different sections of society. It would probably not be an exaggeration of fact that syncretism has been the mainstay of Indian society and many other cultures and civilizations in the world sought to imbibe its one or the other facet. The basic role of *Sufism* in securing unity and peaceful coexistence between different people of the country has been through its emphasis on establishing a harmonious spiritual chord with the Almighty God by focusing on the belief that knowledge of God and of the real truth can be found through prayer and meditation, rather than through reason and the senses alone. Indeed, the unity of *Hindu* civilization itself may be argued to have found its inception in the legendary and divine efforts of *Adi Shankaracharya* to establish a spiritual and cultural affinity between different sections of people in the country. Later, this effort at bringing about a further consolidation of spiritual bonding amongst the people was heralded by the tradition of *Sufism* in which the idea of Oneness of God was emphasized with a view to create a seamless web to enable people to live a life in unity and peaceful coexistence.

Generally, *Sufism* is defined as

> a theory, doctrine, or view that considers reason to be incapable of discovering or of realising the nature of the Ultimate Truth, whatever be the nature of this ultimate truth, but at the same time believes in the certitude of some other means of arriving at it. (Dasgupta 1926, 18)

Sufism is considered to be the belief that there is hidden meaning of life and that each human being can unite with God. It is a religious practice based on the credence that knowledge of spiritual truth can be gained by praying or thinking deeply. Nevertheless, it does not necessarily mean complete renunciation of the world and the denial of significance or value of the social dimension of life. In essence, *Sufism* is a way of establishing one's intimate relationship with the Almighty in whatsoever form one finds suitable.

Sufism, thus, seeks to liberate the people from the clutches of the traditional religions in their pursuit to be in sync with God.

Sufi tradition in India was deep-rooted through the institution of *khanqahs*, a sort of socio-religious organization representing a particular strand of *Sufism*. These *khanqahs* were very broad-minded organizations where the basic thrust was on their identification with problems and issues of life of local people. As Nizami articulates,

> what mystics call *nafs-i-gira*—an intuitive intelligence that could understand, comprehend, control and direct the mind of the disciples—was needed in an abundant degree to fulfil the purpose of *khanqah* organization. Unless they identified themselves with the problems of the people, their worries, their hopes and aspirations, these *khanqahs* could not gain the confidence of the people. (Quoted in Hassan 1987, 555)

However, the trajectory of *Sufism* did not remain confined to the abstraction of *khanqahs* and gradually metamorphosed into other incarnations as well. In this regard, the analysis of J. S. Trimingham is quite illuminating (Trimingham 1971). As Hassan summarizes,

> He suggests that in its organisational aspect Sufism has passed through three stages: The *khanqah* stage, the *tariqa* stage and the *ta'ifa* stage. The *khanqah* stage, characterised by a relatively unstructured and undifferentiated religious and social life centred around the *khanqah;* the *tariqa* stage, referring to development of mystical schools and gradual systemization of mystical techniques and *Sufi* learning, leading to development of the *pir-murid* paradigm and its development of devotional saint cults; and finally, the *ta'ifa* stage, describing cult associations. (Hassan 1987, 557)

Significantly, for *Sufis*, every religion looks upon the Divine as Merciful. Drawing parallels between the essence of *Hinduism* and Islam, a renowned scholar of Indian philosophy argues that for a devout *Hindu* who is a worshipper of Shiva, the recital of the shloka 'karpoorgauramkarunaavataram' expresses his profound feeling about his Almighty which is nothing but an incarnation of love and compassion. Muslims similarly begin in the name of God by reciting *Bismillah-ir-Rehman-i-Rahim. Rahmat* means blessings, compassion and love (Singh 2007, 3). Such similarities in the outlook of the people of both the religions presumably brought a confluence of sorts as a result of which the mystic movements were started to offer a befitting reply to the orthodox elements of both the religions. Indeed, in the present scenario of India, when some people are flaring up the issues of faith and religions in a parochial and exclusivist fashion, the need of the hour seems to be the *Sufism* and *Bhakti* traditions. These movements cut across religious barriers. For instance, the *Bhakti* movement had a number of *Muslim* proponents, such as Abdul Rahim Khan-e-Khana and Malik Mohammad Jayasi. It is remarkable that when these poets were in love with the Divine, their religious and theological differences made little difference.

The *Sufis* and the *Bhaktas* had really fallen in love with the Divine, and this love binds the two socio-religious movements. In *Hinduism*, we have four main paths to the Divine. Jnana Yoga, the intellectual approach, is the way of the mind. Ibn al-Arabi and *Shankaracharya* are the great theologians of this path. *Karma Yoga* is the way of action or the way of good deeds. *Raja Yoga* is the way of *Pranayam* and inner spiritual practices. Bhakti Yoga is the way of love, where the heart overflows with love of the Divine. Maulana Jalalluddin Rumi's work deals with this aspect where there is reflection of ecstatic statements of 'Love for the Divine'. That love could be for human and for Divine, for in love there is no difference. Ultimately, it is the transcendental power and sovereign vibration of love that really brings about the meeting of hearts, which Rumi calls 'the wine of Divine intoxication'. The greatest moments in human history were the meetings of Maulana Jalaluddin Rumi and Shams Tabrez, Ramakrishna and Vivekananda, Plato and Socrates, and Hazrat Amir Khusrau and Khwaja Nizamuddin Auliya (*Ibid*).

Sufism as a Tradition of Syncretism

The outstanding *Sufis* who played a ground-breaking role in the social, cultural and religious life of the people were Khwaja Moinuddin Chisti of Rajasthan, Shaikh Fariduddin Ganj-i-Shakar of Punjab, Shaikh Bahadddin Zakariya of Punjab, Shaikh Nizamuddin Auliya of Delhi, Mir Saiyid Ali Hamedani of Kashmir, Saiyid Muhammad Gaisu Daraz of Deccan, Shaikh Latif, Shaikh Jalal Thanesri and others.[5] These *Sufis* had divided the whole of North India and some parts of South to Deccan into their Vilayats (spiritual territories). *Sufis* also preached and worked in Kashmir, Sindh, Punjab, Bihar, Bengal, Gujarat, Maharashtra, Awadh and Deccan. Through their incomparable moral standards and sweet spiritual voice, they propagated Islam in India and opened a new epoch in Indian history by bringing the cultures nearer for a better understanding of religions, culture and human values and relations (Azizuddin Hussein 2007, 296–97).

Sufis also adopted local idiom and preached message of love and universal brotherhood. Shaikh Fariduddin Ganj-i-Shakar established his *khanqah* at Ajodhan, a town in Punjab.[6] He was the first Indian *Sufi*, who had cordial relations with the *Hindu* thinkers. He wrote excellent poetry in Arabic, Persian, Punjabi and also in the local Hindavi dialect. His *ślokas* and *shabads* have been incorporated in the 'Holy *Guru Granth Sahib*' by the fifth Guru Arjan Dev. Baba Farid adopted Punjabi, and vice versa, the Sikhs adopted Persian. Baba Farid's *ślokas* and *shabads* won the hearts of people in Punjab. His Punjabi and Hindavi poetry became immortal, as even today his verses are being sung in Punjab. Significantly, Amir Khusrau, born of an Indian mother and the Turkish father, provided diffusion of two cultures, imbibing the best of both. Extremely proud of being an Indian, he was intensely devoted to *Hindavi*. He occupies a prominent position among the spiritual benefactors of mankind by his love towards the common people of India. Khusrau endeared to transform the common speech of the people into a literary language called Hindavi which he regarded as not being second to either Arabic or Persian. Khusrau brought about a synthesis of Indian and Iranian music also. 'It is not surprising, therefore, to realize that the composite culture in India originated in an environment of reconciliation, rather than refutation, cooperation, rather than confrontation, coexistence rather than mutual annihilation of the politically dominant *Islamic* strands' (Khan 1987, 36).

In the socio-religious life of Deccan, Burhanuddin Gharib Saiyid Zaninuddin Daood, Shaikh Ainuddin Saiyid Muhammad Gaisu Daraz and Shaikh Sirjuddin Junaidi played a very significant role.[7] One of the most celebrated figures in the early history of *Sufism* in Deccan was Saiyid Muhammad Gaisu Daraz, who played a monumental role in the region. *Hindus* also frequently visited him and stayed in his *khanqah* without any inhibition. He also read Sanskrit books to know the mythology of *Hindus*. Saiyid Muhammad Gaisu Daraz's father Saiyid Yusuf composed 'Manan Suhagan Nama' in Dakkani. Gaisu Daraz also wrote Mairajul Ashiqin in Dakkani which is a symbol of composite culture and social integration. The liberal attitudes of *Sufis* created a pleasant atmosphere, and their khanqahs became centres of cultural synthesis and communal harmony. Their endeavours led to the origin of a new language known as Dakkani, to take the teachings of *Sufis* nearer to the people without any inhibition.

Similarly, *Shaikh* Muhammad Baba of Shirgonda of Ahmednagar district gave his message in Marathi. With Marathi, the *Sufis* established a dialogue with and within the entire Marathi knowing community of Maharashtra. Thus, what their pursuits point out is an uncharacteristic path followed by the *Sufis* to be as closer to the natives as possible by imbibing and coexisting with their language, custom, culture, rhymes and belief systems. That way, they were able to create a long-lasting synergy between the followers of *Hinduism* and *Islam* that lie at the root of peaceful coexistence even till date.[8]

In the literary realm, some poets joined the romantic band of liberal poets of love and beauty. Such a manifestation of the eternal feminine is a radical departure from the feudal cultural system. They believed that love is not realized without beauty and one must sacrifice oneself in the fire of love. Yet, they were clearly against the sexuality and lust. Rather, they sought to transform their *Ishq-i-majazi* into the *Ishq-i-haqiqi* (Azizuddin Hussein 2007, 300). They certainly elevated the status of women from that of a figure of pleasure and dance to that of divine feminine. Among such romantic rebels of the late medieval period were Bodha, Thakur and Ghananand. Almost all of them were under the deep influence of the *Sufis*. *Ishq Nama* by Bodha and *Ishq Lata* by Ghananand are the glowing examples of this tradition. It appears that the *Sufi* influence had become a strong archetype in our cultural pattern. Rubaiyat-i-Umar Khaiyam is popularly tinted with *Sufi* thought.

A remarkable feature of Indian *Sufism* is that the *Sufis* refrained from hallow argumentation and lived a life of poverty, piety, trust, patience, resignation and love. They practised and preached these values and tried to annihilate the satanic share from human societies, and thereby they helped create a peaceful and progressive society. They shared their life with downtrodden and marginalized people in order to share their pain. They prepared them to help humanity in its progress and to hold off from the dehumanizing acts of certain people and groups. The *Sufis* had never been sectarian in their outlook or approach, because they never identified with any particular sect. All the *Sufi* poets had condemned communal hatred and religious bigotry and preached communal harmony and social integration. *Sufis* stood for cultural coexistence of different sections of the people in the country. In fact, the *Sufi* idea of cultural coexistence became the norm of mutual relations during the medieval period in India. This is a great legacy which *Sufis* have left for the succeeding generations in India. Respect for cultural diversity is perhaps the greatest contribution of *Sufis* to Indian civilization.

Through *Padmavat*, Malik Muhammad Jayasi opens the eyes of all those, who advocate separation between the followers of the two religions. He says that *viyog* of Ratan Sen for Padmavati was the same as that of Alauddin for her. It evokes emotions and feelings irrespective of caste, colour or religion. There is unity of emotion amongst all human beings. The total aim and objective of *Padmavat* is the extension of broad and liberal human values and refinement of human sentiments and feelings. During the course of his interaction, the bonds of religion, caste, sect and nationality break down automatically and there emerges a perfect being, whose heart becomes tender, liberal, permissive and powerful. Jayasi wrote thousands of verses in Awadhi, though in Persian script. His description of events smoothly goes on without any modification at the cultural and social level. Shaikh Qutban of Jaunpur wrote a book *Mirgawati*. It was an epic of love and romance in which he perfectly utilized *Hindu* mythology, astrology and many a religious symbol to weave a wonderful tale, which culminated in preaching oneness and unity of God. In retrospect, we can see that just as the basic ideas and attitudes of *Sufism* were translated from Arabic to Persian, so were they expressed in *Hindavi*, Rajasthani, Punjabi, Marathi, Sindhi and Dakkani as well. The *Sufis*, thus, promoted communal harmony with their devoted activities and attracted the caste-ridden and oppressed lower section of the Indian society to their organizational fold.[9]

Conclusion

As one of the most diverse and multi-religious societies, India has always been an enigma to find an intrinsic unity and peaceful coexistence among its people. The key concern of such inquisitiveness lies in the fact that a large number of multi-religious societies are facing numerous challenges ranging from not only their survival as a nation but also of securing habitual and spontaneous peaceful coexistence of their people. On this count, the social cohesion and mutuality of interests of different sections of Indian society present a unique example of living together irrespective of multi-religiosity underpinning their life. In the quest to find the driving force behind such unity and peaceful coexistence, a perceptive clue is provided by the long-standing syncretic traditions in Indian society. This is, however, not to argue that syncretic traditions have been the only factor that lies at the root of unity and peaceful coexistence in Indian society. As a matter of fact, there have been a host of social, economic, political and cultural motives that have been working in tandem with each for numerous centuries that led to the emergence of a composite, multicultural and multi-religious ethos of social life in the country. Subsequent improvisations, adjustments, mutual respect and, probably most unique of all, conceptualization of a transcendental life cutting across religious and cultural stereotypes, not only consolidated the roots of multicultural social setup but also led to its survival amidst various threats and challenges in time and space. Hence, what is being emphasized here is the pivotal role played by syncretic traditions, such as *Sufis*, *Bhaktas*, *Sants*, among others, in cementing unity and peaceful coexistence by making it an inalienable part and parcel of socio-religious life of common people.

In final analysis, it may be argued that the composite culture which makes India one of the best examples of multicultural and diverse societies would not have emerged without the legacy and contributions of *Sufis* and *Bhaktas*. It was the broader and selfless rendering of various forms of tributes to the Almighty by the *Sufis* and *Bhaktas* that presumably brought a confluence of the ideas and perspectives of the two devotional streams of mysticism in the country. The product of such a confluence came in the form of the composite culture which, in ultimate analysis, turned out to be the common ground for the masses to share their joy and sorrow, fairs and festivities, apart from joining each other in their personal functions and gatherings. Thus, the role of *Sufism* has been one of a connector and synthesizer to bring together the sporadic and sometimes exclusivist visions and perspectives of different sections of the society in such a way that the dreams and aspirations of the two become one.

Summary

Religious and cultural syncretism has been one of the major characteristics that has underpinned the rise and growth of composite culture in the country. Rooted in the ancient *Vedic* traditions, the religious–cultural landscape in India has never been exclusivist, with ample space existing for all the religions to get rooted and flourish. But the mainstream syncretic tradition in India has evolved with the rise of two formidable traditions in the name of *Bhakti* and *Sufi* in *Hinduism* and Islam, respectively. Rising above the confines of their respective religions, the followers of these two traditions have helped syncretism become an indelible mark of the Indian society through which both *Hindus* and *Muslims* could find a common space to interact and coexist with each other. In the contemporary times, *Sufism* has become the focal point of syncretic tradition in the country.

Points for Discussion

1. Illustrate the roots of syncretic traditions in India.
2. Examine the various strands of syncretic traditions in different religions of India.
3. Evaluate *Bhakti* and *Sufi* traditions as the traditions of syncretism.
4. Elaborate *Sufism* as the mainstay of syncretic tradition in the country.
5. How do syncretic traditions contribute to peaceful coexistence and social cohesion in India? Elucidate.

Endnotes

1. For a lucid account of the tradition of Sants in India, see, Schomer and McLeod (1987).
2. For an insightful discussion on various dimensions of Buddhist mysticism, see, Trevor (1966).
3. For a standard reference on Sikh religion, see, McLeod (1976).
4. For the most authoritative exposition of various aspects of *Sufism* in India, see, Rizvi (1982).
5. For a useful though select survey of prominent saints and shrines, see, Saiyad (1989).
6. A vivid account on the subject is given in Nizami (1955).
7. An illustrative and insightful study on role of *Sufi* saints in Deccan has been presented in Eaton (1978).
8. For a good account of *Hindu–Muslim* Syncretism, see, Roy Burman (1996).
9. Cf, Eaton (1978a).

Glossary

Assimilation: The process of adapting or adjusting to the culture of a group or nation.

***Bhakti* movement:** The theistic devotional trend in *Hinduism* emerging in the medieval period.

Chistiyya: The *Sunni Sufi* Order within the mystic *Sufi* order of *Islam* beginning at a place called *Chist* near Heart in Afghanistan.

Khanqa: A place or building designed specifically for gathering of Sufis for spiritual retreat and character reformation.

Mysticism: The belief that there is hidden meaning in life or that each human being can unite with God.

***Sufism*:** A syncretic tradition rooted in *Islam* in which people seek to experience God directly by praying and meditating.

Suhrawardiyya: A mystic *Sufi* order in *Islam* founded in Baghdad and known for the severity of its spiritual discipline.

***Ulema*:** A body of Muslim scholars recognized as having specialist knowledge of *Islamic* sacred law and theology.

***Upanişhads*:** Ancient Sanskrit texts containing some of the central philosophical concepts and ideas of *Hinduism*.

References

Ahmad, Aziz. 1994. *Studies in Islamic Culture in the Indian Sub-continent.* Oxford: Clarendon Press.

Azizuddin Hussein, S. M. 2007. 'Sufis and Communal Harmony' In *Sufism and Bhakti Movement: Eternal Relevance*, edited by Hamid Hussain, 296–7. Delhi: Manak Publications.

Dasgupta, S. N. 2003, *Hindu Mysticism* (first published in 1926). Whitefish, Montana: Kessinger Publishing Co.
Eaton, R. M. 1978. *Sufis of Bijapur, 1300–1700.* Princeton, NJ: Princeton University Press.
Eaton, R. M. 1978a. *Social Roles of Sufis in Medieval India.* Princeton, NJ: Princeton University Press.
Hassan, Riaz. 1987. 'Religion, Society, and State in Pakistan: Pirs and Politics.' *Asian Survey* 27(3), 552–65.
Ingvarsson, KjartanBor. 2009. *Anthropomorphism of Belief.* https://skemman.is/bitstream/1946/2797/1/final_fixed.pdf.
Khan, Rasheeduddin. 1987. 'Composite Culture as a New National Identity.' In *Composite Culture of India and National Integration*, pp. 62, edited by Rasheeduddin Khan. Shimla: Indian Institute of Advanced Studies.
Ling, Trevor. 1966. 'Buddhist Mysticism.' *Religious Studies* 1(2): 163–75. http://www.jstor.org/stable/20004620
Lokhandwalla, S. T. 1987. 'Indian Islam, Composite Culture and National Integration.' In *Composite Culture of India and National Integration*, pp. 107, edited by Rasheeduddin Khan. Shimla: Indian Institute of Advanced Studies.
Madan, T. N. 1989. 'Religion in India.' *Daedalus* 118(4): 134–35. http://www.jstor.org/stable/20025267
McLeod, W. H. 1976. *Guru Nanak and the Sikh Religion.* Delhi: Oxford University Press.
Nizami, K. A. 1955. *The Life and Times of ShaikhFaridud Din Ganj-i-Shukar.* Aligarh: Oriental Publications.
Rizvi, Saiyid A. A. 1982. *A History of Sufism in India*, 2 Vols. Delhi: Munshiram Manoharlal.
Roy Burman, J. J. 1996. 'Hindu-Muslim Syncretism in India.' *Economic and Political Weekly* 31(20): 1211–15.
Saiyad, A. R. 1989. 'Saints and Dargahs in the Indian Sub-Continent: A Review.' In *Muslim Shrines in India*, pp. 19, edited by C. W. Troll. Mumbai: Oxford University Press.
Schomer, Karine and W. H. McLeod, eds. 1987. *The Sants: Studies in a Devotional Tradition of India.* Delhi: Motilal Banarsidass.
Singh, Karan. 2007. 'Sufism and Bhakti Movement as Part of Great Indian Culture.' In *Sufism and Bhakti Movement: Eternal Relevance*, pp. 45, edited by Hamid Hussain. Delhi: Manak Publications.
Trimingham, J. R. 1971. *The Sufi Orders in Islam.* New York: Oxford University Press.

Further Readings

D'Souza, Leela. 2007. *Cultural History of Ancient India: Diversity, Syncretism, Synthesis.* Jaipur: Rawat Publications.
Kishor Das, N. 2003. *Culture, Religion and Philosophy: Critical Studies in Syncretism and Inter-faith Harmony.* Jaipur: Rawat Publications.
Roy Burman, J. J. 2002. *Hindu–Muslim Syncretic Shrines and Communities.* New Delhi: Mittal Publications.
Stewart, C. and Rosalind Shaw, eds. 1994. *Syncretism/Anti-Syncretism: The Politics of Religious Synthesis.* London: Psychology Press, European Association of Social Anthropologists.
Waseem, M. 2003. *On Becoming an Indian Muslim: French Essays on Aspects of Syncretism.* Oxford: Oxford University Press.

Index

absolute
  awareness, 12
  bliss, 12
  existence, 12
Abul Fazl, 194
  administration and governance method of, 198–199
  and concept of state, 195
  Badshahat, 195–198
  life sketch of, 195
  on religion, 199–201
Ain-i-Akbari (or the 'constitution of Akbar'), 170–172
Aitareya Brahmana, 118
Akka Mahadevi, 248–249
Alvars, 167
Amir Khusrau, 220
Ammaiyar, Karaikal, 247, 249
ancient civilization of India
  and western political thought, comparison between, xl
  different from other civilization, xxxiii
  limited influence of thought, reasons for, xli
  political thought, elements of, xxxvii
Andal, 248–249
Aṅuguttara Nikāya, 117, 119
āpaddhārma, 9
Āpaddhārma Anusasana Parva, 14
Āpaddhārma Parva, 133
apavarga, 8
Aranyakas, 33
Arthaśāstra (Kauṭilya), 131, 147
  and *The Discourses* (Niccolo Machiavelli), 156–157, 164
  dhārma and *daṇḍanīti*, 148–149
  main objectives, 147–148
  saptanga theory of state, 149–152
Aryan community
  division into social classes, 26
  history of, 25
  owned land with whole village, 26
āśhrama vyavastha, 43–45
āśhramadhārma, 68
Atharvavedā, 4, 35
Ātman, doctrine of, 73
atmatusti, 5
Avvaiyar (respected old woman or Grandmother), 247

Badshahat, 195
bali, 131
Bhagwadgīta, 46, 48, 63
Bhakti movement, xxxiii, xliii, 167, 205, 233, 245, 255, 258–259
Bhakti tradition
  beauty and body, 248–249
  evaluation from gendered lens, 245–246
  in south India, 245
  women poets of south India, 247
Bhāratavarṣa, 130
bhartṛpratyayalakṣaṇa, 140
Brahman/*Brāhmaṇas*/*Brahmanism*, 33–35, 39–40, 46–48
Brāhmanic (orthodox) tradition, 85–86
  and *dharmaśāstra* tradition, 40
  and *punarjanma* (life after death), 36–37
  Brahman and *Ātman* (Supreme Soul & Soul), 39
  jiva and *jagat* (creature and the universe), 39
  Karma (action), doctrine of, 36–37
  mokṣa (salvation) and its means, 39
  origin and evolution of, 34–35
  punarjanma (life after death), 38
  sanskara (observance or ordination), 37
  tyaga (sacrifice), 37–38
  varṇa and *āśhrama vyvastha*, 36
Bṛhadāraṇyaka Upaniṣhad, 70
BṛhaspatiSūtra, 76
Buddhism, xxxiv, 28, 84–85, 91–92, 245, 255
Buddhist *Saṅgha*, 27–28

Cārvāka
  epistemology of, 77–78
  ethics, 80–81
  metaphysics, 78–80
Cārvāka darśana (*lokāyata*), 76
communities of hunter-gatherers, 23
community, concept of
  changing forms and patterns of, 26–27
  historical evolution of, 23
  in prehistoric India, forms and structures, 23–24

trading, 29
types of, 22
vedic and later period, 24–26
cultural heritage of India, 33

daṇḍa, xx, 54–55, 86, 139–140, 142
function of, 59
daṇḍanīti (punishment), xxxvi, 55, 134, 138–141, 148–149
daṇḍanīti-viśārada, 139
Dasa-Rājā-Dhamma ('ten virtues of the ruler'), 126
Dhamma practice, 117
dhārma, 15–17, 132, 148–149
and *Hindu* world view, 6–7
and *patanjali*, 15
and present legal system, 6
and self, 11–12
as metaphysical truth, 4
associated with Indian culture, 5
classification of, 9–10
idea of, 5
in *Hindu* philosophy, 5
in *Ṛigvedā*, 4
in *upaniṣhads* and *Hindu* epics, 12–14
linkage with *Hinduism*, 5
meaning of, 4
sustains and maintains orders, 4
through *yajña*, *dāna*, and *tapas*, 11
vātsyāyana, 15
Dharmaśāstras, 7, 37, 53, 67–69, 107
Dharmasūtras, 7
Dīgha Nikāya, 116–117, 119–120, 123, 125
Dīn-e Ilāhī, 200

farmers' community, 21
Firoz Shah Tughlug, 186
foreigners community, 21
four noble truths (*ārya-satya*), doctrine of, 93–94

Gautam Buddha
and qualities, functions and duties of ruler, 125-126
karma theory of, 95
life sketch of, 118–120
rebelled against existing *Brāhmanical* order, 117
system of philosophy, 92–96
gemeinschaftlich relationship, 24
guṇadhārma, 68

Henotheism, 47
Hindu dhārma, 4, 9, 12
and concept of liberation, 12
duties and rights, 6
epics of, 13
sanatana dhārma, 7
Hinduism, 22, 28–29, 35, 47, 238
and individual accountability and sincerity in practice, 12
Bhakti stream of, 216
defining feature of community life, 23
Hindu Śāstras, 6

Indian community, 22
international community, 22
Islam, 164, 172, 179, 182, 199
arrival in India in late medieval era, 167
concept of universal brotherhood and equity, 187
Shari'at of, 180
Islamic tradition
and Delhi *Sultanate*, 207–208
and *Mughal* dynasty, 208–210
origin and evolution of, 205–207
revivalist tradition in, 210–213

Jaina system of philosophy
bondage and liberation philosophy, 91–92
conception of substance, 91
features of, 89
Jaina theory of knowledge, 89–90
judgment theory, 90
origin of, 88
Jainism, 84–85, 93, 256–257
sects, 88
jana, 131
jānapada, 131
Jātakas, 167
jīvanmukti, 12
karma, notion of, 69–70
Kauṭilya (also known as Chanakya or Vishnu Gupta)
ethics and politics, 155–156
foreign policy, goals of, 153–155
geopolitical analysis, 155
life sketch of, 146–147
Mandala theory or circle of states, 152–153
minister in Chandragupta Maurya kingdom, 146
on diplomacy as apparatus of war, 155
on state ideologies, 146
state, classification of functions, 152
Khaliq (or the Creator and *Khalq*), 200
khanqah, 220
Khwaja Moinuddin Chishti of Ajmer, 206, 219
king
āpaddhārma, 138
importance in state, 137–138
must recognize rights of people, 184
powers of, 138
kingship, 34, 42, 68, 72

linguistic community, 22

Mahābhārata of *Vyāsa*, 13, 42, 46, 55, 101, 105, 131–134
Mahariṣhis, 53
Manu
and kingship theory, 54–56
and organic theory of state, 56–58
establishment and preservation of *dhārma*, 59
life sketch, 53–54
social order and classification of society, 58–59
Manusmṛiti (or *Manavdharmaśāstra*), 39, 53–54, 65, 68, 148
Marx, Karl, 165
materialism (*Cārvāka*), 85
Maya, meaning of, 5
mazhar, 196

medieval age in India
- administration, features of, 167
- Akbar's contribution in, 170–172
- Asiatic mode of production, 165
- economic and social reforms in, 167–168
- economic scenario during, 169–170
- features of, xxxix
- feudal mode of production, 166
- importance in history, 164
- land policy in, 169–170
- limited influence of thoughts, reasons for, xli
- nature of state, 167
- oriental despotism, 165
- political life during, 164
- religious traditions in, 168–169

Mir Saiyid Ali Hamedani of Kashmir, 219
mokṣa, 8
mokṣadhārma, 9
Mokṣa dhārma Parva, 14, 133
Mughal era in India, emergence of syncretic culture tradition, xl
Muhammad bin Tughluq, 186
Muhammad Bin Tughluq, 186
mukti (liberation), 7
mythology, Hindu, 47, 132, 134, 260

nāstika, 85
national community, 22
Nayanaras, 167
nimmittadhārmas, 68
Nītiśāstra (Kauṭilya), 147
Nizamuddiin Auliyah of Delhi, 206
non-*Brāhmanic* or *Śhramanic* (unorthodox/heterodox) system, 85
non-existence of the soul (*Anattā-vāda*) theory, 95–96
Nyāya (the school of logic), 85

Palas, 164
Pāli Nikāyas, 97
papa (sin), concept of, 12
pastoralists, 24
Patanjali, 15
Pratiharas, 164
primitive community, 21
punya (goodness, virtue), concept of, 12
Puruṣārthas (theory of), 8, 45–46
puruṣārthas Varṇaāśhrama vyvastha, 47
Purva Mīmāṁsā or *Mīmāṁsā* (school of interpretation), 85

rājādhārma, 9, 67–68, 132
Rājādhārma Anusasana Parva, 14, 133
Rāmāyaṇa, 13, 46, 105
Rashtrakutas, 164
rāṣṭra, 131
rebirth, 69–70
religious community, 21
Ṛigvedā, 6, 10, 17, 35, 38, 42, 53, 101
Ṛigvedic
- poets, 34
- *Ṛiṣhis*, 34, 38

Ṛigvedic Purusha Sukta, xxxvi
riṣhis, 33, 53
Rita, 4
Rna, 10
Rta, 4, 10

sabhā, 131
sacred tests, role in Indian philosophy, 46
Ṣaḍdarśanasamuccaya, 76
sādharaṇadhārma, 68
Saiyid Muhammed Gaisu Daraz of Deccan, 219
salvation, *upaniṣhadic* conception of, 12
samanyadhārma, 9
Samavedā, 35
Samhitas, 33, 35
samiti, 131
sanatana dhārma, 10, 12
- and self, 7
- demand and supply conceived as *kama* and *artha*, 8
- features of, 7–8
- meaning of, 7

Sāṅkhya, 85
Śānti Parva of *Mahābhārata*, 13–14, 131
- ancient Indian state, origin and nature of, 133–136
- and *rājādhārma*, 136–138
- types of, 133

Sant Kabir Das, 225, 238
- and Ravidas, comparison between, 237
- believes in one god, 232–233
- believes in universal humanism concept, 232
- believes mankind service, 235
- criticism of caste system, 231
- earning livelihood by sweat of brow, 235
- *Hindus* to give up old practising traditions, 234
- life sketch of, 225–227
- opposed economic inequalities, 235
- path of resolution, 236–237
- property not as individual right, 235–236
- put emphasis on religious toleration, 234
- rejected ideas *sati* practice and child marriage, 231
- transcended religious differences, 233
- views on *bhakti* (or devotion), 233–234
- views on socio-religious dogmas and economic inequalities, 227–230

Sarvadarśanasaṅgraha, 76
Shaikh Ali Hajweri, 217
Shaikh Bahaduddin Zakariya of Punjab, 219
Shaikh Fariduddin Ganj-i-Shakar of Punjab, 219
Shaikh Latif, Shaikh Jalal Thanesri, 219
Shaikh Nizamuddin Auliya of Delhi, 219
Śhramanic tradition in India
- origin and evolution of, 87–88
- reformist school within *vedic* tradition, 86

represented by Jainism and Buddhism, 86
Sikhism, 256, 258
smṛitis
meaning of, 63
number of, 64
objectives of, 64
soul (*ātman*), 41
spiritual
freedom, 39
liberation, 69–70
life, 33
wisdom, 67
state
and social contract, 123–124
origin of, 120–123
students' community, 21
Sufi
heritage, 221
idea of cultural co-existence, 221
ideology, 219
masters (*Pirs*), 205–206
meaning of, 216
movement, 168, 213
saints, 205
shrines, 206
silsilahs, 216, 219
Sufism, 205–207
and *Hindu-Muslim* interaction, 222
and medieval Indian society, 219–222
as tradition of syncretism, 260–261
features of, 216–218
origin of, 216–218
Sufi Silsilahs, establishment of, 219
Sufiyah, meaning of, 216
Suhl-i-Kul, doctrine of, 200
Śukracharya (or *Asuracharya*), 101
ethics and kingship, 102–104
ideal king and his qualities, 104–107
life sketch of, 101–102
state as organic whole, 111
system of law and justice, 107–108
Śukranīti (or *Śukranītisara*) of *Śukrācārya*, 101, 131
believe in reform of laws, 109–110
king to depend on his friends on foreign policy, 104
treatise about nature and *Hindu* polity character, 110
syncretic tradition
and *Bhakti* tradition, 257–258
and Sufism, 260
in *Hinduism* and *Islam*, 254–256
in other religions, 256–257
origin and evolution of, 253–254

teachers' community, 22
theism, 47
trivarga (the group of three), 8

universal change and impermanence, doctrine of, 95
Upaniṣhadic metaphysics, 256
Upaniṣhads, 5, 8, 33–36, 38, 40, 46–47, 119, 149, 256
urban community, 22

Vaiśeṣika (the atomist school which devotes itself to the exposition of reality), 85
Vaishnava, 167
varṇadhārma, 68, 137
Varṇaāśhramadhārma, 68
varṇa vyavastha, 42–43
vātsyāyana, 15
Vedānta (or *Uttara Mīmāṁsā*), 85
Vedās, 5, 33
as an infallible source of knowledge, 85
mystic and symbolic poetry, 33
types of, 35
vedic Aryans
religion of, 33
worship of Gods, 47
Vedic Brahmanism, 96
Vedic period, 22, 28
and later communities, 24-26
Gods personalities, 47
state in, 42
Vedic republics, 118
Vedic seers, 40
Vedism, 35
village community, 22
visheshadhārma, 9
Vyāsa, (known as *Veda Vyāsa*), 132
vyavahāra, 140

Wahdatul Wujud (Unity of Being), doctrine of, 218
world (*jagat*), 41

Yājñavalkya, 73
commentaries on, 65
date of, 65
description of contents, 65–66
dialogue between *Maitreyī*, 70
life sketch, 67
pre-eminence of, 64
style and content of, 65
Yājñavalkya Brahman, 70
Yājñavalkyasmṛiti
and comparison between *Manusmṛiti*, 70–72
ethical and social virtues, 68–69
Yajurvedā, 35

Ziyauddin Barani, 186–187, 193
and theory of kingship, 180
Fatwa-i-Jahandari, 178–179
ideal polity, 181–182
life sketch, 176–177
notable works of, 176
political theory of, 184–186
qualities of, 182–184
Tarikh-i-Firuz-Shahi, 177–178

Lightning Source UK Ltd.
Milton Keynes UK
UKHW030644210720
366894UK00003B/15

9 789353 882310